LOGIC PROGRAMMING
Functions, Relations, and Equations

Doug DeGroot
Quintus Computer Systems

Gary Lindstrom
University of Utah

Prentice-Hall, Englewood Cliffs, New Jersey 07632

Library of Congress Cataloging-in-Publication Data

DeGroot, Doug.
    Logic programming, functions, relations, and
equations.

    Includes bibliographies and index.
    1. Electronic digital computers—Programming.
2. Logic, Symbolic and mathematical.   I. Lindstrom, Gary.
II. Title.
QA76.6.D435 1986   005.1   85-31176
ISBN 0-13-539958-0

Editorial/production supervision: Diana Drew
Cover design: Wanda Lubelska
Manufacturing buyer: Gordon Osbourne

Printed in the United States of America

10   9   8   7   6   5   4   3   2   1

ISBN   0-13-539958-0   025

Prentice-Hall International (UK) Limited, *London*
Prentice-Hall of Australia Pty. Limited, *Sydney*
Prentice-Hall Canada Inc., *Toronto*
Prentice-Hall Hispanoamericana, S.A., *Mexico*
Prentice-Hall of India Private Limited, *New Delhi*
Prentice-Hall of Japan, Inc., *Tokyo*
Prentice-Hall of Southeast Asia Pte. Ltd., *Singapore*
Editora Prentice-Hall do Brasil, Ltda., *Rio de Janeiro*
Whitehall Books Limited, *Wellington, New Zealand*

TABLE OF CONTENTS

PREFACE   v

Part I: Setting the Stage

On the Relationship between Logic and Functional Languages   3
    Uday S. Reddy (University of Utah)

The Unification of Functional and Logic Languages   37
    J. Darlington, A.J. Field and **H. Pull** (Imperial College)

Part II: Unification and Functional Programming

A Prological Definition of HASL, a Purely Functional Language
    with Unification-Based Conditional Binding Expressions   73
    Harvey Abramson (University of British Columbia)

QUTE: a Functional Language Based on Unification   131
    Masahiko Sato and **Takafumi Sakurai** (University of Tokyo)

FUNLOG: a Computational Model Integrating Logic
    Programming and Functional Programming   157
    P.A. Subrahmanyam (AT&T Bell Laboratories Research)
    Jia-Huai You (University of Utah)

Part III: Symmetric Combinations

LEAF: a Language which Integrates Logic, Equations and
    Functions   201
    R. Barbuti, M. Bellia and **G. Levi** (Universita' di Pisa)
    M. Martelli (CNUCE-C.N.R.)

The APPLOG Language   239
    Shimon Cohen (Schlumberger Palo Alto Research)

iii

Part IV: Programming with Equality

Equality for Prolog 279
  William A. Kornfeld (Quintus Computer Systems, Inc.)

*EQLOG: Equality, Types, and Generic Modules for Logic
     Programming* 295
  Joseph A. Goguen and **Jose Meseguer** (SRI International
  and Stanford University)

TABLOG: a New Approach to Logic Programming 365
  Yonathan Malachi and **Zohar Manna** (Stanford University)
  Richard Waldinger (SRI International)

Part V: Augmented Unification

*Constraining-Unification and the Programming Language
     Unicorn* 397
  Robert G. Bandes

*Uniform -- A Language Based upon Unification which Unfies
     (much of) Lisp, Prolog, and Act 1* 411
  Kenneth M. Kahn (Xerox PARC)

Part VI: Semantic Foundations

A Logic Programming Language Scheme 441
  Joxan Jaffar (Monash University)
  Jean-Louis Lassez and **Michael J. Maher** (University of
  Melbourne)

FRESH: A Higher-Order Language Based on Unification 469
  Gert Smolka (Cornell University)

INDEX 525

PREFACE

As has often been observed about entertainment personalities, logic programming has waited about a decade to become an overnight success. Unlike most such personalities, however, the developers of logic programming largely are conscientious in acknowledging its origins, and critically thoughtful about its need to mature in grace and power.

Logic programming shares many roots with functional programming, including an applicative nature (manipulation of values rather than assignable cells), reliance on recursion for program modularity, and provision of ample opportunities for execution parallelism. Yet these siblings have vital individual traits as well, including radically different variable treatments ("call-by-value" parameter binding vs. unification), availability of higher order program entities (in functional programming), and fundamental support for nondeterministic execution (in logic programming). Hence it was perhaps inevitable that fruitful combinations of the two language varieties would arise. For example, Robinson's and Sibert's LOGLISP was a seminal attempt in this regard that proved to be quite successful as well as instructive.

As additional language designers tried their hands at this combination, the similarities and distinctions between functional and logic programming came into sharper focus through the generalization of equational programming. By casting programs as equations, the central features of both functional programming (e.g. execution by rewriting) and logic programming (e.g. variable binding by unification) can be consolidated into one elegant model.

In this volume we attempt to illuminate both the heritage and future of logic programming, by assembling some of the most powerful, innovative, and promising ideas for its growth. The reader will find herein approaches for embedding LISP-like constructs within PROLOG, for enriching lazily-evaluated functions to deal with logical variables, for exploiting term equality, for implementing rewriting systems by narrowing, and much more. In addition, the relevant background, motivation, and theory underlying these approaches is presented. Where appropriate, we include complete system source code, so the reader may install his or her own versions of the systems described, and see them in action.

Contributions to this volume were solicited without a preconceived expositional plan. However, a satisfying breadth of scope resulted, comfortably arrangeable under six categories.

* First we have **Setting the Stage**, in which two works are offered motivating the combination of functional programming with logic programming. Uday Reddy focuses on *directionality*, an essential distinction between the two paradigms, and John Darlington, Anthony Field, and Helen Pull consider *absolute set abstraction* as a unifying vehicle.

* Under **Adding Unification to Functional Programming**, we next assemble three articles illustrating the *rapprochement* toward logic programming currently underway in many functional programming circles. Harvey Abramson presents HASL, a language founded on the notion of *unification based conditional binding*. QUTE, an *AND-parallel* language of this variety, is then presented by Masahiko Sato and Takafumi Sakurai. Finally, P. Subrahmanyam and Jia-Huai You describe FUNLOG, which is based on a notion of *semantic unification*.

* Next comes **Symmetric Combinations**, in which more egalitarian viewpoints are examined. Roberto Barbuti, Marco Bellia, Giorgio Levi, and Maurizio Martelli report their work on the conceptually comprehensive language LEAF. Shimon Cohen then follows with a description and full code for APPLOG, which embeds a LISP dialect in PROLOG.

* We then take up **Programming with Equality** and examine three quite different approaches. William Kornfeld augments PROLOG to deal with the equality relation through inclusion of appropriate assertions. In presenting EQLOG, Joseph Goguen and Jose Meseguer deal with equality through a language design particularly emphasizing rigorous semantics. Yonathan Malachi, Zohar Manna, and Richard

Waldinger close the section with a report on TABLOG, an equality–based language exploiting *deductive tableau theorem proving* as an execution method.

* The excitement surrounding unification as a basis for operational semantics leads us next to consider **Augmented Unification** as an avenue for still newer language forms. The UNICORN system of the late Robert Bandes has *constraining unification* as its centerpiece. Still more ambitiously, Kenneth Kahn uses augmented unification in UNIFORM to combine functional programming, logic programming, and *actor languages* such as SmallTalk in one coherent framework.

* We conclude the volume with two papers in which **Semantic Foundations** play a dominant role. Joxan Jaffar, Jean–Louis Lassez, and Michael Maher carefully weigh logical issues associated with hybrid languages such as those presented in earlier sections. Finally, Gert Smolka defines the FRESH language using operational semantics of the Plotkin structural variety.

Despite this diversity, we have been able to present only a representative sample, at best, of the current work in this increasingly active and significant field. Inevitably, pragmatic constraints such as space limitations, previous publication, and balance of viewpoint, as well as our personal predilections, have affected our selections. We apologize to all concerned for any omissions, inadvertent or otherwise.

We hope the reader will find this volume a lively and stimulating panorama. It has been our sincere pleasure to prepare it, and we thank all contributing authors for making it possible.

Doug DeGroot

Palo Alto, California

Gary Lindstrom

Salt Lake City, Utah

Part I:

Setting the Stage

ON THE RELATIONSHIP BETWEEN

LOGIC AND FUNCTIONAL LANGUAGES

Uday S. Reddy

Department of Computer Science
University of Utah, Salt Lake City

ABSTRACT

An essential distinction between logic and functional languages is drawn based on *input-output directionality*. Functional languages are directional in that their programs make an explicit commitment about which quantities are inputs and which are outputs. Logic programs do not make such a commitment. We show that this non-directionality makes logic languages more expressive. However, non-directionality also makes the operational behavior of logic programs hard to understand, and poses problems in developing parallel implementations of logic languages. We present a notation for introducing directionality information into logic programs, and show that directional logic programs are equivalent to first-order functional programs. Finally, we discuss how the syntax and semantics of functional languages can be extended to capture the additional expressive power of logic languages.

3

1 INTRODUCTION

Ever since logic programming in the form of Prolog has become popular, there has been an ongoing debate on the merits and demerits of logic programming as compared to functional programming. In this article, we contribute to this debate by exhibiting the objective differences between the two styles of programming while disregarding matters of taste. We assume that the reader is familiar with both of these styles of programming. For introductory expositions see [8, 21] on logic programming and [16] on functional programming.

A logic program:

```
append([], Y, Y).
append([A|X], Y, [A|Z]) :- append(X, Y, Z).
```

A functional program:

```
apnd([], Y) = Y
apnd([A|X], Y) = [A | apnd(X, Y)]
```

Example 1: Appending Lists

Example 1 shows a logic program and a corresponding functional program for appending two lists. For logic programs we use the notation of Prolog, whereas for functional programs we use notation as close as possible to that of Prolog, which is similar to the notation used in Standard ML [31], HOPE [5], SASL [46] and FEL [18, 19, 32]. One can see that the declarative content in both the programs is the same. But the computational content is different.

Logic programs are executed using *resolution*. That is, given a goal statement that contains both values and variables, such as

G1:   append([1], [2,3], L),

resolution produces all possible bindings for the variables which would make the goal statement true. Functional programs are executed using *reduction* or *term rewriting*. The equations in the program are treated as left-to-right rewrite rules. Given an expression such as

apnd([1], [2,3])

4

reduction successively rewrites it using the equations until it cannot be further rewritten. For this example, both resolution and reduction produce the same result, *viz.*, [1,2,3].

For most of this article, logic languages are those executed using resolution and functional languages are those executed using reduction. However, it is possible to design languages based upon relations which are executed using reduction, and languages based upon functions which are executed using techniques similar to resolution. An example of the former may be found in [27] and the latter will be discussed in section 7.

2 INPUT–OUTPUT DIRECTIONALITY

During reduction, the left hand side of an equation is *matched* against an expression to produce bindings for the variables in the equation. Thus, there is a transfer of information from the given expression to a use of an equation. On the other hand, during resolution, the left hand side of a clause is *unified* with a goal, potentially producing bindings for the variables in both the clause and the goal. This enables transfer of information in both directions. Stated differently, functional programs make an explicit commitment as to the inputs and outputs of a function. In contrast, logic programs make no such commitment. We examine the consequences of this difference in the rest of this section.

The goal G1 of the previous section provides inputs for the first two parameters of append and reflects an expectation that the third parameter be an output. We can thus say that G1 is in an input-output mode (in, in, out). The same resolution mechanism using the same logic program can produce bindings for goals that are in other possible modes. For example, the goal

G2:   append(L, M, [1,2,3])

is in mode (out, out, in) and can be used to produce all possible decompositions of the list [1,2,3]. The functional program for apnd given in Example 1 cannot produce the effect of such goals. For that purpose, another functional program such as that shown in example 2 is required.

```
split(Z) = split1(Z) ∪ split2(Z)
split1(Y) = {([], Y)}
split2([A|Z]) = {([A|X], Y) | (X, Y) <- split(Z)}
```

Example 2: Functional program for the mode
(out, out, in) of append.

As one might expect, this program produces a set of results for
any given list. The construct used in the equation for split2 is
called *set abstraction* [19, 46]. It may be read as "the set of all
pairs ([A|X], Y) such that (X, Y) is a member of split(Z)".
The clause (X, Y) <- split(Z), called a *generator*, is a rewrite
rule. However, unlike an equation, it denotes several possible
rewritings.

    The functional program for split contains essentially the
same declarative information as that for apnd, but makes a different commitment as to inputs and outputs.

    Thus, the first consequence of the directionality of func-
tional languages is that *a single logic program corresponds
to several functional programs which contain the same
declarative information but have different input-output
directionality.*

    Now consider another append goal:

G3:   append([P], [Q,R], [1,2,3])

The first two arguments here are non-ground, non-variable
terms (partially specified data structures). They contain input
information (length of the lists) as well as output designations
(free variables P, Q and R). Since resolution makes no distinction
between inputs and outputs, it uses the input information in
these arguments to select appropriate clauses, and also
produces bindings for the variables involved. On the other hand,
in the corresponding functional formulation, the first two arguments have to be considered to be purely output, thus using
mode (out, out, in). The effect of this goal has to be achieved by the generator

        ([P], [Q,R]) <- split([1,2,3])

which produces all possible splits of [1,2,3] and picks out the
ones that match the required pattern. There is only one such

split, viz., ([1], [2,3]). While resolution can use the input information implicit in the patterns to successfully cut down the size of the set to be examined, reduction typically generates the entire set.

Thus, the second consequence of the directionality of functional languages is that, *by not using the input information specified in the patterns, functional languages can lead to overcomputation as compared to resolution.*

Lazy evaluation can minimize the overcomputation reduction has to perform, but it cannot in general reduce it to zero. In some cases, the overcomputation may be infinite, thereby leading to nontermination. There are however contexts in which resolution overcomputes as compared to reduction, as will be seen in section 5.

Finally, consider the goal:

G4:   append([1], L, M)

which is in mode (in, out, out). Resolution produces the binding M = [1|L] and leaves L unbound. The mode of a goal for which resolution produces non-ground terms as bindings will be called an *indefinite mode.* There is no functional program that corresponds to an indefinite mode because functional programs cannot produce free variables as outputs. One may consider extending functional languages to permit non-ground terms as outputs, but then one would also have to permit non-ground terms as inputs, and function applications produce bindings for the variables in the input terms. This would require unification for parameter passing, and would destroy the directional nature of functional languages.

Therefore, the third consequence of directionality of functional languages is that *the effect of indefinite modes cannot be achieved in functional languages.*

It is often argued that suspended expressions produced as outputs during lazy evaluation achieve the same effect as indefiniteness. Though there are similarities between them, the two concepts are fundamentally different. A suspension contains all the information needed to compute its value, though its computation is as yet incomplete. On the other hand, an un-

7

bound variable produced as an output denotes a total lack of information about its value.

It should be noted that the notion of modes used here differs from other notions of modes. When the mode of a parameter is input, we insist that the corresponding argument in a goal should be a ground term. In DEC-10 Prolog [48], for instance, the argument corresponding to an input parameter is only required to be a non-variable term. In other words, only the outermost constructor of the argument should be input, the rest of it need not be. Such modes impose only a kind of partial directionality on the predicates.

3 APPLICATIONS OF NON-DIRECTIONALITY

The three consequences of directionality that we have mentioned imply additional expressive power in logic languages as compared to functional languages. While the first two imply an increase in the length of programs and in the time complexity of programs, the last one is a fundamental limitation of functional languages. There is no way to achieve the effect of indefinite modes other than by mimicking a resolution interpreter within the functional program. This is where the full power of non-directionality becomes manifest.

In logic languages, partial data structures (data structures with unbound variables in them) are treated as first-class objects, i.e., they can be input to predicates and obtained as output bindings. More importantly, the variables they contain can be bound by the application of predicates. Variables treated in this fashion have been called *logical variables* [48] and the flexibility offered by them has been noted in the literature. Warren [48] gives a logic program called serialize which uses such flexibility in an essential way. Clark and Tarnlund [6] devised a data structure called *difference lists* using logical variables upon which concatenation is a constant-time operation. Clocksin [9] shows a similar implementation of queues on which insertion is a constant-time operation. In this section, we consider a few other examples which allow us to draw general conclusions about the utility of non-directional logical variable usage.

8

Our first example is an abstraction of the *address translation* problem found in compilers and linking loaders. We are given a list whose elements are terms of two kinds: def(a) and use(a), where a is an atom. We are required to translate it into a new list so that def(a) is translated into asgn(a, n), where n is an integer address, and use(a) is translated into use(n), where n is the same integer used in asgn with a. Moreover, the atoms in the input list are to be assigned addresses starting from 1 in the same order in which their def's appear. For example, the list

[def(a), use(a), use(b), def(c), def(b)]

should be translated into

[asgn(a,1), use(1), use(3), asgn(c,2), asgn(b,3)].

A Prolog program to do this translation is shown in Example 3.

```
translate(Inlist, Outlist)
        :- map(Inlist, Outlist, Table, 1).
map([], [], _, _).
map([def(A)|Inlist], [asgn(A,N)|Outlist], Table, N)
        :- member(asgn(A,N), Table),
           map(Inlist, Outlist, Table, N+1).
map([use(A)|Inlist], [use(Addr)|Outlist], Table, N)
        :- member(asgn(A,Addr), Table),
           map(Inlist, Outlist, Table, N).

member(A, [A|X]) :- !.
member(A, [B|X]) :- member(A, X).
```

Example 3: Address Translation.

In a functional language (or an imperative language) the forward references – use's of symbols whose definitions are yet to appear – must be handled in a special way. The technique commonly used is to keep a list of all the use's of a forward referenced symbol, and then *back patch* the use's with the address after its definition appears. As backpatching involves side effects, programming it efficiently in a functional language would be rather clumsy. On the other hand, in a logic language we need make no distinction between forward references and

9

backward references. A symbol table can be built as a partial data structure with unbound addresses for forward referenced symbols, so that the variables get bound to addresses when the definitions appear. The back patching that has to be explicitly done by the programmer in a functional language is automatically achieved by resolution.

The presence of backward references involves a left-to-right data dependency with respect to the input list, whereas the presence of forward references involves a right-to-left data dependency. Functional (and imperative) languages, being strongly directional, have to align their computations in one of the two directions. This then requires a special treatment of data dependencies in the other direction. On the other hand, logic languages, being non-directional, do not have to align their computations along any data dependency. Backpatching for forward references, i.e. uses of values that are yet to be computed, is routinely done by resolution through the logical variables. *Thus, when computations involve data dependencies in opposite directions, logic programs can be expected to be more abstract than corresponding functional programs.*

The second example we consider is that of polymorphic type inference. Milner [30] presented an algorithm which can determine if a λ-calculus expression is type-correct and, if so, produce its type. The logic of the algorithm was later formalized as an inference system [10]. Example 4 shows the essential rules of this system expressed in Prolog.
Using the inference system, an expression such as $(\lambda x.x)$ (written as `lambda(x, var(x))` in the notation of our Prolog program) can be inferred to be of type τ -> τ where τ is a free variable. The types produced by the algorithm are therefore non-ground terms. Since it implements an indefinite mode of the predicate `welltyped`, Milner's algorithm explicitly incorporates the resolution mechanism. Later, Leivant [25] gave another algorithm for well-typing which has better time-complexity on a parallel machine. A closer examination shows that the two algorithms implement different resolution strategies within the same inference system. Milner's algorithm implements SLD-resolution, whereas Leivant's algorithm implements join-based resolution [34]. *Non-directionality of logic lan-*

```
welltyped(E, T) :- [] |- E:T.

A |- lambda(X, E) : (S->T)
        :- [(X:S)|A] |- E:T.
A |- var(X) : S
        :- member(X:S, A).
A |- apply(F, E) : T
        :- A |- F:(S->T), A |- E:S.
```

|-, : and -> are infix constructors denoting deducibility, the well-typing relation, and the function space respectively.

Example 4:   A type inference system in Prolog

guages allows the resolution details to be unspecified in the program, thereby leading to more transparent programs.

Thus far, we have examined the flexibility offered by non-directionality of logic programs; but this flexibility is gained at a cost. Some of the advantageous properties which (explicitly directional) functional programs possess is lost by logic programs. Before we examine these properties, we need a formalization of the concept of "directionality".

4 A THEORY OF DIRECTIONALITY

In this section, we present a simple theory of directionality within the framework of logic programs. This theory was first used in translation of logic programs into functional programs [35]. Other theories of directionality, similar in principle but different in some key aspects, have been developed independently by Bellia et al. [3], Bruynooghe [4], and Smolka [43].

Definition 1. An n-*ary mode* is an n-tuple over {in, out}. The association of an n-ary mode m with an n-ary predicate p is denoted by $p^{(m)}$.

If $\bar{x} = (x_1, \ldots, x_n)$ is an n-tuple of terms, an n-ary mode $m = (m_1, \ldots, m_n)$ can be used to split it into two parts. The *input part* (*output part*) of $\bar{x}$, denoted $\bar{x}_{in/m}$ ($\bar{x}_{out/m}$) is the tuple of x_i's whose corresponding m_i's are in (out), collected in

11

sequence. A goal $p(\bar{x})$ is said to be in mode m if the input part of $\bar{x}$ in mode m contains only ground terms. Note that a goal can be in several modes. For example, the goal $p(1, X)$ is in mode (in, out) and also (out, out), whereas the goal $p(f(1, X))$ is in mode (out).

The operational idea behind the notion of mode is that unification can be replaced by two levels of pattern matching: once for input parameters and once for output parameters. For example, if $p(1, X)$ is treated as being in mode (in, out), the input argument 1 is pattern matched against the first parameter in the clause head of p. Resolution then produces a set of values for the second parameter which are pattern matched against the output argument X, yielding a set of bindings for X. If on the other hand, $p(1, X)$ is treated as being in mode (out, out), there are no input arguments. Resolution is then used to produce all tuples for which p is true. These tuples are pattern matched against (1, X) to produce a set of bindings for X. It may be noticed that the second mode is in a sense less efficient than the first. Instead of using the ground argument 1 as an input, it suggests producing all possible values for the first argument and matching them against 1. This notion of efficiency can be formalized by defining a partial order on modes.

in $\sqsubseteq$ out, in $\sqsubseteq$ in, out $\sqsubseteq$ out

$(m_1, \ldots, m_k) \sqsubseteq (n_1, \ldots, n_k)$ iff $m_i \sqsubseteq n_i \; \forall \; i$

Every goal now has a *least* mode. The least mode of $p(1, X)$ is (in, out).

Definition 2. A mode $p^{(m)}$ is *definite* if the resolution of every goal of p in mode m, whenever it succeeds, produces only ground bindings for the variables in that goal.

Lemma 1. If a mode $p^{(m)}$ is definite and $n \sqsubseteq m$ then the mode $p^{(n)}$ is also definite.

An *atom* is of the form $p(\bar{x})$ where p is predicate and $\bar{x}$ is a tuple of terms. The elements of $\bar{x}$ are called the *parameters* of the atom. A *moded atom* is an atom with a mode, written as $p^{(m)}(\bar{x})$. Often a moded atom is also specified by annotating the parameters with in or out, e.g. reverse([A|X]:in, Y:out)

12

is the same as $reverse^{(in, out)}([A|X], Y)$.

```
reverse([], []).
reverse([A|X], Y) :- reverse(X, Z), append(Z, [A], Y).
```

Example 5: Logic program for reversing lists

Given a clause

$$p(\bar{x}) :- q_1(\bar{x}_1), \ldots, q_n(\bar{x}_n)$$

and a mode m of p, we can assign a set of modes to the right hand side atoms:

$$p^{(m)}(\bar{x}) :- q_1^{(m_1)}(\bar{x}_1), \ldots, q_n^{(m_n)}(\bar{x}_n)$$

Such an assignment is called a *clause moding*. The variables appearing in the clause can be classified into three groups:

input variables   variables appearing in the input parameters of $p^{(m)}(\bar{x})$,

output variables   variables not appearing in the input parameters of $p^{(m)}(\bar{x})$, but appearing in its output parameters, and

local variables   other variables appearing only on the right hand side of the clause.

Definition 3. A clause is *well-moded* if each output and local variable that appears on the right hand side of the clause has an output occurrence, i.e. occurs in an output parameter of some right hand side atom.

If a moding is not a well-moding, it would not be sensible. That is, there would exist an output or local variable used only in an input parameter on the right hand side; hence no binding would be established for that variable. If the mode $p^{(m)}$ is definite, all the output variables of the clause should appear on its right hand side. Then well-moding means that all the output and local variables should have output occurrences.

Example 6 shows four well-modings of the second clause of the predicate reverse (Example 5) with mode (in, out). Note that in all the well-modings the third parameter of append is output. This is necessary because the output variable Y occurs on the right hand side only in this parameter.

```
[M1] reverse([A|X]:in, Y:out) :-
        reverse(X:out, Z:out),
        append(Z:out, [A]:out, Y:out).

[M2] reverse([A|X]:in, Y:out) :-
        reverse(X:in, Z:out),
        append(Z:out, [A]:in, Y:out).

[M3] reverse([A|X]:in, Y:out) :-
        reverse(X:in, Z:out),
        append(Z:in, [A]:in, Y:out).

[M4] reverse([A|X]:in, Y:out) :-
        reverse(X:in, Z:in),
        append(Z:out, [A]:in, Y:out).
```

Example 6: Well-modings of reverse for mode (in, out).

A moding of a clause
$$p^{(m)}(\bar{x}) \; :- \; q_1^{(m_1)}(\bar{x}_1), \; \ldots, \; q_k^{(m_k)}(\bar{x}_k)$$
is said to be less than or equal to another moding
$$p^{(m)}(\bar{x}) \; :- \; q_1^{(n_1)}(\bar{x}_1), \; \ldots, \; q_k^{(n_k)}(\bar{x}_k)$$
if each m_i is less than or equal to the corresponding n_i. Just as for the modes of goals, the less the moding of a clause, the less computation is required. In Example 6 the moding M1 is the largest moding, and the modings M3 and M4 are the minimal modings. There is no least moding for this clause. However, append$^{(out, \, in, \, out)}$ used in M4 is an indefinite mode because the resolution of goals in this mode produces non-ground bindings for the first and the last parameters. The moding M3 is therefore the least well-moding with definite modes.

A moding of a clause imposes a constraint on the order in which the right hand side atoms can be resolved. If a non-input variable A occurs in an input parameter of $q_i^{(m_i)}(\bar{x}_i)$ then some atom with an output occurrence of A has to be resolved before $q_i^{(m_i)}(\bar{x}_i)$ can be resolved. A preorder[*] on the atoms that

---

[*]A preorder is a transitive relation.

satisfies this constraint is called a *dependency preorder*. In Example 6, the modings M1 and M2 do not impose any dependencies; for M3 the first atom has to precede the second; and for M4 the second atom has to precede the first.

Definition 4. A moding of a clause is *acyclic* if it has an irreflexive dependency preorder.

Acyclicity eliminates the possibility of deadlocks. Consider a well-moded clause of the form

... :- ... r(X:in, Y:out), q(Y:in, X:out) ...

and suppose that X and Y do not appear elsewhere in the clause. It is not an acyclic moding. Since the two atoms expect outputs from each other, neither can be resolved without violating modes.

The justification for the conditions of well-moding and acyclicity is provided by the following theorem from [35].

Theorem 2. Let

$$p^{(m)}(\bar{x}) :- q_1^{(m_1)}(\bar{x}_1), \ldots, q_n^{(m_n)}(\bar{x}_n)$$

be a moding of a clause such that the modes $q_i^{(m_i)}$ are definite. The moding is an acyclic well-moding if and only if every goal of p in mode m can be resolved by resolving, in some order, the goals of q_i in their respective modes m_i.

The theory of directionality presented here may be used in a compiler in two ways. Firstly, the programmer can specify the required modings of clauses and the compiler can perform "mode-checking". This involves verifying that the specified modings are acyclic well-modings, verifying that all the modes used have defining moded clauses, and verifying that all the modes are definite. Secondly, the programmer can specify the required modes of the top-level predicates and the compiler can produce modings for clauses. Since, in general, clauses do not have least modings, the compiler would be faced with a choice among the minimal modings. In practice, a combination of mode-checking and automatic moding is generally used [7, 33].

5 CONTROL SPECIFICATION THROUGH DIRECTIONALITY

We have mentioned that directionality has some advantages over non-directionality. The first of these is termination.

Let us consider the goal reverse([1,2], L) with reverse defined as in Example 5. This goal has only one solution L = [2,1], and any complete interpreter of logic should produce this binding. However, after producing this binding, should the interpreter terminate (implying that there are no more solutions) or can it continue searching forever? There is no clear answer to this question.

After one step of resolution, the above goal is rewritten to the following sequence of goals

reverse([2], Z), append(Z, [1], L).

In SLD-resolution, one of the goals is selected for the next step of resolution, and the substitution obtained in this step is applied to all the other goals. Different choices of the goal for the next step of resolution produce different termination behaviors. If the leftmost goal in the sequence is always chosen, it has the effect of using a left-to-right sequential 'and' operation. The goal reverse([2], Z) produces a single binding Z = [2] and terminates. The second goal (after substitution),

append([2], [1], L)

similarly produces a single binding L = [2,1] and terminates. If, on the other hand, the rightmost goal of the sequence is always chosen for the next step of resolution, we get the effect of a right-to-left sequential 'and' operation. The goal append(Z, [1], L) now produces an infinite set of bindings, and the interpreter goes into a loop after producing the binding L = [2,1] for the original goal.

In resolving the symmetrically opposite goal reverse(L, [2,1]), leftmost-resolution goes into a loop, whereas rightmost-resolution terminates. Therefore, the termination behavior of a logic program depends upon not only the selection function used in resolution, but also the directionality (mode) of the goal to be resolved. While termination is desirable in an or-parallel interpreter, it becomes essential in an or-sequential interpreter. (Most existing implementations of

16

logic, including all Prolog implementations, are or–sequential).
With a sequence of clauses such as

    $p(\bar{x})$:- A.
    $p(\bar{y})$:- B.

given any goal of p, an or–sequential interpreter first resolves
the goals corresponding to A, and only after their resolution terminates does it resolve the goals corresponding to B. If the
resolution of A goes into a loop, then the solutions to be obtained by resolving B would never be produced.

    Non–termination is a special case of overcomputation.
Even if all choices of the selection function produce termination,
some choices lead to more computation than the others. This
resembles the overcomputation in functional languages discussed in section 2.

    In logic languages that use *committed–choice
nondeterminism* [7, 41], of all the solutions of a goal, one solution is arbitrarily picked up and the others are discarded.
Clearly, an appropriate choice of the selection function is necessary to guarantee success of resolution. For example, given the
sequence of goals

        reverse([2], Z), append(Z, [1], L)

leftmost–resolution guarantees success, whereas rightmost-
resolution has a possibility of failure.

> *Non–directionality allows logic programs to be written
> without any specification of control information. The lack
> of control information leads to wide variations in the
> amount of computation performed for particular goals.*

    Functional programs (and moded logic programs), on the
other hand, specify the required amount of control information.
To see how, recall that different modings impose different
dependency preorders for the resolution of the right-hand side
atoms. By choosing appropriate modings for each desired mode
of the left hand side predicate, termination can be achieved. For
example, the following modings for the second clause of
reverse ensure termination of both kinds of goals involved.

17

```
reverse([A|X]:in, Y:out) :-
        reverse(X:in, Z:out),
        append(Z:in, [A]:in, Y:out).
reverse([A|X]:out, Y:in) :-
        reverse(X:out, Z:in),
        append(Z:out, [A]:out, Y:in).
```

However, directionality places more constraints on the programs than is necessary to specify the requisite amount of control information. For example, the control information implicit in the modings above can be used to resolve the goals reverse([A,B], L) and reverse(L, [A,B]). But by our definition of directionality, non-ground terms cannot be treated as inputs. How to specify control without placing extra constraints of directionality is still an open problem. While there have been some proposals for suitable notation [7, 41], they do not yet have a supporting theory.

6 FUNCTIONAL LANGUAGES

In this section we point out some characteristics of functional languages and show how they relate to logic languages. Functional languages with rewriting semantics are similar to moded logic programs as introduced in section 4. A formal translation from moded logic programs into such languages may be found in [35].

6.1 Abstraction Expressions

A construct in functional languages that is similar to (moded) Horn clauses is an *abstraction expression*. It is also sometimes called let-abstraction, following Landin [22], who showed that it was translatable to λ-calculus. In the language FEL, and in [35], it was called an equation group.

An abstraction expression is of the form

{* <expression> | <constraint>, ..., <constraint> *}

where a <constraint> may be an <equation> or a boolean valued expression. An <equation> is of the form

<term> = <expression>

where <term> is a ground or non-ground term involving only constructors (functors in Prolog). The scope of the variables

18

appearing on the left hand sides of the equations is limited to the abstraction expression. The second equation of Example 7 contains an abstraction expression.

```
rev([]) = []
rev([A|X]) = {* Y | Z = rev(X), Y = apnd(Z, [A]) *}
```

Example 7: A functional program for reversing lists.

In order to evaluate an abstraction expression, a *dependency preorder* on the constraints is found. If a constraint uses a variable X, then X should have a defining occurrence in some dependency predecessor of the constraint. The constraints are then evaluated according to the dependency preorder. If a constraint C_1 precedes C_2 in the dependency preorder, then C_1 is evaluated before C_2. If C_1 and C_2 are not related by the dependency preorder, they can be evaluated in any order or in parallel. Parallelism of this kind is called *spatial* (*horizontal*) *parallelism* [11].

In order to evaluate an equation $t = e$, the right hand side expression e is first evaluated to obtain a value v, which is pattern matched against t to obtain bindings θ for the variables occurring in t. The substitution θ is then applied to the rest of the abstraction expression.

After all the constraints are evaluated, the result expression is evaluated to produce the value of the entire abstraction expression. If the evaluation of any constraint fails or produces 'false' then the value of the abstraction expression is undefined.

The abstraction expressions allowed in most functional languages are not as general as those defined here. However, our abstraction expressions can be transformed into the more restricted ones as follows:

1. If no variable has more than one defining occurrence in the abstraction expression, then it is said to be *left-linear*. If only left-linear abstraction expressions are allowed, non-left-linear abstraction expressions can be converted into them. For every variable X that has two defining occurrences, change one of the occurrences to a new variable X' and introduce a new constraint.

19

$$\text{eq}(X,\ X').$$

2. If only equations are permitted as constraints then collect the other constraints C_1, ..., C_k and change the result expression e to

$$\text{if } C_1 \text{ and } ... \text{ and } C_k \text{ then e.}$$

(The partial conditional is undefined if the predicate is either undefined or evaluates to 'false').

Functions are defined by sets of equations of the form

    <function-name> <term> = <expression>.

If there are two equations for a function

$$f\ t_1 = e_1$$
$$f\ t_2 = e_2$$

then f is the union of the functions defined by each of the equations. The union is expected to be consistent, i.e., it should not map a value to two distinct values. The language may permit only unambiguous function equations (t_1 and t_2 not unifiable) or it may permit ambiguous definitions and assume that the union is consistent. When it is desired that f should map a value to several values, sets should be used.

6.2 Set Abstraction

Even though sets are commonplace mathematical objects, they are very hard to implement operationally. In practice, their implementation is approximated by either multisets (duplications permitted) or lists (an ordering of the elements assumed). In the following, we shall use the multiset approximation.

A set abstraction expression is of the form

    { <expression> | <constraint>, ..., <constraint> }

where a <constraint> is either an <equation>, a boolean-valued <expression> or a <generator> of the form

    <term> <- <expression>.

The right hand side of a generator should be a set-valued expression. A set value is either the empty set {}, a singleton {v}, or a union of two sets a ∪ b. An example of a set abstraction expression is shown in Example 2.

In order to evaluate a generator t <- e that occurs in a set abstraction S, the set-valued expression e is first partially evaluated until it reduces to {}, {v} or a∪b. If it reduces to {} then the generator fails. If it reduces to the singleton {v}, it is evaluated just as the equation t = v. If it reduces to the union a∪b, then the entire set abstraction S is rewritten by[*]

$$S[a/e] \cup S[b/e]$$

and both the components of the union are evaluated in parallel. The parallel evaluation is necessary to ensure that if the evaluation of one component goes into a loop, the members of the other component would still be obtained. In contrast to abstraction expressions, a set abstraction evaluates to {} when any of its constraints fails.

In order to obtain the elements of a set as they are evaluated, without waiting for the entire set to be evaluated, the following rewrite rules are used.

$$a \cup \{v\} \Rightarrow \{v\} \cup a$$
$$a \cup (\{v\} \cup b) \Rightarrow \{v\} \cup (a \cup b)$$

This operational semantics implements a lazy parallel union and is similar to or-parallelism in logic programs. The effect of sequential-or is obtained by using lists to approximate sets. The union operation is then implemented as lazy but sequential concatenation of lists.

Moded clauses of logic can be transformed into set abstraction expressions. A moded atom $q^{(m)}(\bar{x})$ corresponds to the generator

$$\bar{x}_{out/m} \; <- \; fqm(\bar{x}_{in/m})$$

where fqm is the function corresponding to the mode $q^{(m)}$. A clause

$$p^{(m)}(\bar{x}) \; :- \; A$$

then corresponds to the equation

$fpm(\bar{x}_{in/m}) = \{\bar{x}_{out/m} \mid$ generators corresponding to A}

A complete specification of the translation with proofs may be seen in [35].

---

[*]if t is an expression containing x as a subexpression, t[y/x] denotes the expression obtained by rewriting x by y in t.

6.3 Incremental Evaluation

We have mentioned that if a constraint C_1 precedes C_2 in the dependency preorder, then C_1 is evaluated before C_2. However, by using incremental evaluation, C_1 and C_2 can be overlapped. It is done as follows:

1. C_1 is partially evaluated to produce partial bindings θ for the defined variables in terms of new variables.
2. The partial bindings are then substituted in C_2, and C_1 is rewritten by new constraints C_1' for the new variables.
3. $C_2\theta$ is now partially evaluated as C_1' is evaluated to produce the next level of partial bindings.

Complete evaluation:

```
{* X | Y = apnd([1,2],[3]), X = apnd(Y,[4]) *}
⇒ {* X | X = apnd([1,2,3],[4]) *}
⇒ [1,2,3,4]
```

Incremental evaluation:

```
{* X | Y = apnd([1,2],[3]), X = apnd(Y,[4]) *}
⇒ {* X | Y1 = apnd([2],[3]), X = apnd([1|Y1],[4]) *}
⇒ {* [1|X1] | Y2 = apnd([],[3]),
                X1 = apnd([2|Y2],[4]) *}
⇒ {* [1,2|X2] | X2 = apnd([3],[4]) *}
⇒ {* [1,2,3|X3] | X3 = apnd([],[4]) *}
⇒ [1,2,3,4]
```

Example 8:   Incremental evaluation.

Example 8 shows the reduction of an expression with two constraints under complete and incremental evaluations. Without incremental evaluation, the first constraint is evaluated completely to produce the binding $Y = [1,2,3]$, and this binding is substituted in the second constraint. On the other hand, with incremental evaluation, the first constraint is first evaluated partially to produce the binding $Y = [1|Y1]$, where Y1 is a new variable. The constraint itself gets rewritten to

22

$$Y1 = apnd([2], [3]).$$

The partial binding of Y is now available to the second constraint and both the constraints are evaluated in parallel. As the second constraint produces the binding $X = [1|X1]$, the first constraint produces $Y1 = [2|Y2]$. Thus, the first constraint, the producer of bindings for Y, and the second constraint, the consumer of the bindings, can proceed in parallel, despite the dependency between them. This form of parallelism, that is similar to pipelining, is called *temporal* (*vertical*) *parallelism*.

Incremental evaluation may be *eager* or *lazy*. Under eager evaluation, the consumer waits for the producer to produce bindings. Under lazy evaluation, the producer also waits for the consumer to get ready to consume the bindings. The advantage of lazy evaluation is that bindings for variables which are not used elsewhere need never be produced. This also provides a means of obtaining finite portions of infinite data structures.

Incremental evaluation is also useful in resolution of logic programs. However, the early efforts to use *incremental resolution* [2, 15, 47] disregarded the non-directional nature of logic programs. Some of the more recent efforts [41] have implemented incremental resolution without imposing directionality. Given a conjunction of two goals A_1 and A_2 that share variables, incremental resolution requires that we resolve the goals in parallel, incrementally producing partial bindings for the variables. *However, since there is no producer-consumer relationship between the goals, either of them can produce a binding for a shared variable which has to be immediately made available to the other goal.* Hence, the implementation must ensure mutual exclusion of access to the shared variables.

Lazy evaluation, as in functional programs, is not immediately available in logic programs. In contrast to an equation in an abstraction expression, a goal cannot be merely viewed as a producer of bindings. Successful resolution of a goal involves demonstrating the existence of a binding for each variable in it. This demonstration is required independent of whether there is a consumer for the bindings [45].

However, there is a notion of laziness in resolution which is useful for achieving the termination effects discussed in section 5. If the resolution of one of the goals in the conjunction

A_1, A_2 fails, continuing the resolution of the other goal is useless. The entire conjunction may fail immediately. We have shown in section 5 that the rightmost-resolution of the goal statement

$$\text{reverse}([2], Z), \text{append}(Z, [1], L)$$

does not terminate. But, under lazy rightmost-resolution, the second goal would eventually produce the partial binding $Z = [A1, A2 \mid Z1]$. The first goal fails with this binding of Z. So, the entire goal statement fails immediately. *Thus, while lazy evaluation of functional programs leads to early success instead of looping, lazy resolution leads to early failure instead of looping.* Fair resolution strategies [24, 49], including BF-resolution, exhibit this kind of lazy behavior and are strongly complete with respect to finite failure.

7 FUNCTIONAL LANGUAGES WITH RESOLUTION SEMANTICS

As it became clear that logic languages have more expressive power than functional languages, efforts were made to capture the additional expressive power within the framework of functional languages. In this section, we shall briefly survey such efforts. We shall discuss three classes of functional languages, named **N**, **F**, and **R**, which use resolution or a similar mechanism as their operational semantics. Each of them has the expressive power of logic languages.

7.1 Narrowing of Non-Ground Expressions

It appears at first sight that functional languages should be as expressive as logic languages simply because every predicate is a function, and all logic programs can be trivially rewritten as functional programs (Example 9). The flaw in this argument is that functional programs are executed by reduction, which is not as general as resolution. There is however an operational mechanism called *narrowing* under which functional programs behave like logic programs. Narrowing was originally introduced for theorem proving in equational theories [13, 23, 42], and was subsequently used as the operational semantics of functional and equational languages in [14, 26].

24

First let us make a distinction between expressions and terms. *Expressions* can contain function applications whereas *terms* contain only constructor applications. Both expressions and terms may be ground or non-ground. Intuitively, expressions are programs and terms are values. The reduction of a ground expression, unless it fails, yields a ground term. This is how functional programs are conventionally executed. We denote the reduction relation by $\rightarrow$.

A non-ground expression is a partially specified program. It can sometimes reduce to a non-ground term, e.g.

$$rev([A,B]) \rightarrow [B,A].$$

But, in general, a non-ground expression may not completely reduce to a term, e.g.,

$$rev([A|X]) \rightarrow apnd(rev(X), [A]).$$

The latter expression cannot be further reduced because X, the argument for rev, does not have enough information to match the formal parameters in the two equations of rev.

We may ask the question "for what values of X does the program produce a value?". To answer such a question, narrowing can be used. It makes an assumption about the value of X and proceeds to reduce the expression under that assumption. Such assumptions are represented by a substitution θ for the variables in the original expression. Narrowing is a ternary relation denoted as

$$e \xrightarrow{\theta} d$$

We say e can be narrowed to d using the *narrowing substitution* θ. The triples that belong to the narrowing relation are a subset of those satisfying $e\theta \rightarrow d$. Narrowing is a generalization of reduction in that if $e \rightarrow d$ is a reduction, then $e \xrightarrow{id} d$, where id is the identity substitution, is a narrowing. Moreover, whenever there exists a substitution T such that $eT \rightarrow t$ there exists a narrowing $e \xrightarrow{\theta} d$ and a substitution θ' such that

$$T = \theta \; \theta'$$

$$t = d \; \theta'$$

A "complete" narrowing interpreter should produce enough narrowings to cover any reduction of the form $eT \rightarrow t$.

Narrowing is implemented by replacing matching in reduction by unification. The substitutions produced by unification for the variables in the input expression are collected and output as the narrowing substitution. For example, the expression rev(X) is narrowed as follows:

rev(X) $\xrightarrow{X=[]}$ [ ]

rev(X) $\xrightarrow{X=[A1|X1]}$ apnd(rev(X1), [A1]) $\xrightarrow{X1=[]}$ [A1]

rev(X) $\xrightarrow{X=[A1|X1]}$ apnd(rev(X1), [A1])

$\qquad \xrightarrow{X1=[A2|X2]}$ apnd(apnd(rev(X2), [A2]), [A1])

$\qquad \xrightarrow{X2=[]}$ [A2,A1]

. . .

We shall call any functional language with narrowing as its operational semantics, an **N**-language. Narrowing may be seen as a restricted version of general paramodulation that is used for equational reasoning. It is obtained by placing two restrictions on paramodulation. Firstly, a source term e is unified against only left hand sides of equations. Secondly, only non-variable subterms of the given expression are unified against left hand sides.

append([ ], Y, Y) = true
append([A|X], Y, [A|Z]) = append(X, Y, Z)

reverse([ ], [ ]) = true
reverse([A|X], Y) =
        and(reverse(X, Z), append(Z, [A], Y))

Example 9:   Logic programs in an **N**-language.

Resolution of logic programs can now be seen as a special case of narrowing. All predicates are partial boolean-valued functions, i.e., they map all inputs to either "undefined" (often treated as false) or true. A goal statement is a non-ground boolean expression which can only narrow to true. Each narrowing of a goal statement

$$g \xrightarrow{\theta} \text{true}$$

produces a resolvent θ.

Just as with reduction, narrowing may be eager or lazy. Furthermore, narrowing can be failure-lazy (like fair resolution) to make it complete with respect to finite failure. When an expression f(e1, e2), where f is a strict primitive function, has to

26

be narrowed, both e1 and e2 are narrowed in parallel with the substitutions produced in each narrowing being immediately made available to the other. This failure-laziness is required even if the narrowing is eager. Finally, as in resolution, the searching of narrowings has to be done breadth-first to achieve completeness.

At the time of this writing, we do not know of any existing implementations of a general narrowing interpreter for programming purposes. The language FGL+LV presented in [26] restricts each function to have a single defining equation so that any expression has at most one narrowing. EQLOG [14] uses narrowing with equational languages (which are more general than functional languages). TABLOG [28] uses a deductive-tableau that achieves the same effect as narrowing. More recent work on **N**-languages includes [12, 17, 36, 37, 40, 44].

Note that we have only extended the operational semantics of functional languages without modifying their syntax. So, functions cannot introduce fresh variables in their outputs. All the variables that appear in the outputs are either those which appear in the inputs or those introduced in bindings of input variables.

7.2 Non-Ground Outputs

In order to allow functions to introduce fresh variables in their outputs, we may trivially extend functional languages to have non-ground expressions. A function such as

$$f(X) = [X|Y]$$

would then be valid. Narrowing can be the operational semantics. But, the mathematical semantics of such a language is not clear. Is f a mathematical function? What does it map a given value of X to?

To arrive at a mathematically consistent language that deals with free variables, we can use set abstraction. An expression e with a free variable X is not meaningful in itself. But, the set expression $\{e\}$ is meaningful. Given a generator for X, it yields a set value. (It is thus similar to a function that yields a value when applied to a value). We shall call set abstraction expressions with free variables *free sets*. A functional language with free sets will be called an **F**-language. We have mentioned in section 2 that the mode append$^{(in,out,out)}$ is indefinite and so does not correspond to a functional program. However, in an F-language, there exists a functional program corresponding this mode (Example 10).

```
ap(nil) = {(Y,Y)}
ap([A|X]) = {(Y,[A|Z]) | (Y,Z) <- ap(X)}
```

Example 10: Function corresponding to mode append$^{(in,out,out)}$.

Reduction of expressions in an F-language incorporates narrowing. In order to reduce a free set {e} the non-ground expression e is narrowed. If the possible narrowings of e are

$$e \xrightarrow{\theta_1} t_1, \ldots, e \xrightarrow{\theta_k} t_k$$

then the free set {e} is said to reduce to the following union of free sets*

$$\{e\} \rightarrow \{t_1 \mid \theta_1^{-1}\} \cup \ldots \cup \{t_k \mid \theta_k^{-1}\}$$

For example, the reduction of {rev(X)} yields the infinite union

$$\{[\ ]|[\ ]=X\} \cup \{[A1]|[A1]=X\} \cup \{[A2,A1]|[A1,A2]=X\} \ldots$$

Note that each member of the union is a free set with X free and so yields a set given a generator for X.

Free set expressions were first used in a functional language in [35] but narrowing was not used as the operational semantics. John Darlington is responsible for the idea of using free sets to achieve the effect of logical variables in functional programs.

7.3 Resolution as Operational Semantics

Functional programs can be translated into logic programs and resolution used as their operational semantics. We call a functional language treated in this fashion an R-language.

Functional languages allow hierarchical expressions with nested function applications. For example, the expression apnd(rev([1]), [A]) has the application rev([1]) nested in-

---

*A substitution θ is treated as a set of equations. θ^{-1} then contains all the equations of θ with their left and right hand sides interchanged.

side the outer application. In order to use resolution as the operational semantics the nested function applications have to be first eliminated. This can be done using abstraction expressions. We call an expression *elementary* if it is either a term or a function applied to a term. A simple or set abstraction expression is *elementary*, if the result expression is a term and each constraint contains only elementary expressions. All expressions can be translated into elementary abstraction expressions. (This can be done by a compiler, so that the source language supports nested function applications). For example, the expression apnd(rev([1]), [A]) can be translated into

$$\{* \; Y \; | \; Y = apnd(Z, [A]), Z = rev([1]) \; *\}$$

Each equation in the abstraction may be treated as a goal as follows: "=" is a binary predicate (it should be distinguished from syntactic equality), the first argument is a term, and the second argument is an elementary application expression. We now treat all functions as constructors with the knowledge that they always appear as the outermost constructors of the second arguments of "=". The other types of constraints (generators and boolean constraints) may be similarly treated as goals.

To resolve equality goals, the function equations have to be rewritten as Horn clauses with equality atoms as their heads. An equation with a simple abstraction expression

$$f(t) = \{* \; u \; | \; C_1, \; ..., \; C_k \; *\}$$

is translated into

$$u = f(t) \; :- \; C_1, \; ..., \; C_k$$

Example 11 shows functional programs translated to Horn clauses.

```
Y = apnd([], Y).
[A|Z] = apnd([A|X], Y)  :-  Z = apnd(X, Y).

([], Y) <- split(Y).
([A|X], Y) <- split([A|Z])  :-  (X, Y) <- split(Z).

[] = rev([]).
Y = rev([A|X]) :- Z = rev(X), Y = apnd(Z, [A]).
```

Example 11: Function definitions as clauses.

29

In order to evaluate the expression append(rev([1]), [A])
we only need to resolve its constraints in the elementary
abstraction form

$$Y = \text{apnd}(Z, [A]), \quad Z = \text{rev}([1])$$
$$\xrightarrow{Z=[1|Z1]} Y = \text{apnd}([1|Z1], [A]), \quad Z1 = \text{rev}([])$$
$$\xrightarrow{Y=[1|Y1]} Y1 = \text{apnd}(Z1, [A]), \quad Z1 = \text{rev}([])$$
$$\xrightarrow{Z1=[]} Y1 = \text{apnd}([], [A])$$
$$\xrightarrow{Y1=[A]} \text{true.}$$

The binding produced for Y, *viz.*, [1,A], is the value of the expression.

Resolution semantics now subsumes reduction. However,
in addition to evaluating expressions, resolution can be used
resolve a variety of other goals with logical variables. For example, the goal

$$[1|T] = \text{apnd}(\text{rev}(X), [A])$$

can be resolved as follows.

$$[1|T] = \text{apnd}(Z,[A]), \quad Z = \text{rev}(X) \xrightarrow{T=[A],\ X=[1],\ Z=[1]} \text{true}$$

An **R**-language was originally presented as a part of a very
general logic language based on natural deduction [15]. The
functional sublanguage of LEAF [1] presented in this volume is
also an **R**-language. The reader can see that article for more
details about R-languages.

7.4 Conclusion

We have not dealt with languages such as LOGLISP [38],
QLOG [20], POPLOG [29], PARLOG [7], Qute(83) [39] and
FUNLOG [45]. These languages combine a conventional functional language with reduction semantics and a conventional
logic language with resolution semantics, and provide an interface between the two. They should be distinguished from the
language classes **N**, **F** and **R**, which provide both functional and
logic programming within a single operational framework.

While an **F**-language is an extension of an **N**-language,
these languages differ from **R**-languages in the use of directionality. Recall that, while the absence of directionality makes
logic languages more expressive than functional languages, it
also prevents adequate control information to be specified in a
program. **N**- and **F**-languages attempt to achieve non-

directionality without losing the benefits of directionality. On the other hand **R**-languages eliminate directionality completely and thereby lose control information.

For example, consider the goal

E1:   append([P], T, [1,2,3]).

In an **N**-language, the goal itself can be narrowed using a definition of append (Example 9). Alternatively, one of the expressions

E2:   [1,2,3] = apnd([P], T)

E3:   ([P], T) <- split([1,2,3])

can be narrowed using a directional incarnation of append. All of them yield the same bindings P = 1 and T = [2,3]. But, they perform different amounts of computation. E1 has only one possible narrowing. E2 requires the subexpression apnd([P], T) to be narrowed independent of the required result, and so has infinite number of narrowings with bindings T = [], T = [A1], T = [A1,A2] etc. If the narrowing is eager this leads to nontermination. The generator E3 computes all possible splits of [1,2,3].

On the other hand, in an **R**-language, both E2 and E3 perform the same amount of computation as E1. The programs for append, apnd and split are semantically and computationally equivalent. Thus, functions in an **R**-language merely serve as syntactic sugar. They make no contribution to directionality.

The use of directionality in **N**- and **F**- languages sets up a dependency preorder on a set of constraints. By using an appropriate moded version of a predicate the programmer can control the order in which the constraints are evaluated. This is especially useful for parallel implementations as the input-output annotations in parallel logic languages [7, 41] are required for exactly the same purpose.

ACKNOWLEDGEMENTS

Thanks are due to J.-L. Lassez and Lee Naish for comments on the draft of this paper.

This research was supported by a grant from IBM Corporation.

REFERENCES

1. Barbutti, R., Bellia, M., Levi, G., Martelli, M. LEAF: A language which integrates logic, equations and functions. In *Logic Programming: Functions, Relations and Equations*, DeGroot, D., Lindstrom, G., Eds., Prentice-Hall, 1985.

2. Bellia, M., Degano, P., Levi, G., Dameri, E., Martelli, M. *Lecture Notes in Comp. Sci.* Volume 137: Applicative communicating processes in first order logic. In *International Symposium on Programming*, Dezani-Ciancaglini, M., Montanari, M., Eds., Springer-Verlag, 1982, pp. 1-14.

3. Bellia, M., Levi, G., Martelli, M. On compiling Prolog programs on demand driven architectures. Proceedings of Logic Programming Workshop, Albufeira, Portugal, 1983.

4. Bruynooghe, M. Adding redundancy to obtain more reliable and more readable Prolog programs. Proc. First Intl. Logic Programming Conf., 1982, pp. 129-133.

5. Burstall, R. M. , MacQueen, D. B., Sanella, D. T. HOPE: an experimental applicative language. ACM LISP Conference, 1980, pp. 136-143.

6. Clark, K. L., Gregory, S. A first-order theory of data and programs. Information Processing, 1977, pp. 939-944.

7. Clark, K.L., Gregory, S. PARLOG: A Parallel Logic Programming Language. Research Report DOC 83/5, Imperial College of Science and Technology, London, May, 1983.

8. Clocksin, W. F., Mellish, C. S.. *Programming in Prolog*. Springer-Verlag, 1981.

9. Clocksin, W. F. "Real-time functional queue operations using the logical variable". *Inf. Proc. Lett. 17* (Nov. 1983), 173-175.

10. Damas, L. and Milner, R. Principal type-schemes for functional programs. ACM Symp. Principles of Prog. Lang., 1982, pp. 207-212.

11. Davis, A. L., Keller, R. M. "Data flow program graphs". *IEEE Computer 15*, 2 (Feb. 1982), 26–41.

12. Dershowitz, N., Plaisted, D. A. Logic programming cum applicative programming. Symposium on Logic Programming, IEEE, Boston, 1985.

13. Fay, M. First-order unification in an equational theory. Fourth Workshop on Automated Deduction, Austin, Texas, 1979, pp. 161–167.

14. Goguen, J. A., Meseguer, J. Equality, types, modules and generics for logic programming. Proc. 2nd Int. Logic Prog. Conf., Uppsala, 1984, pp. 115–125.

15. Hansson, A., Haridi, S., Tarnlund, S-A. Properties of a logic programming language. In *Logic Programming*, Clark, K. L., Tarnlund, S-A., Eds., Academic Press, 1982, pp. 267–280.

16. Henderson, P.. *Functional Programming: Application and Implementation*. PHI, 1980.

17. Jayaraman, B. An equational language and its evaluator. Manuscript, University of North Carolina at Chapel Hill, 1985.

18. Keller, R. M. FEL (Function Equation Language) Programmer's Guide. AMPS Technical Memorandum 7, University of Utah, April, 1982.

19. Kim, J. FEL + Set Abstraction = Database Query Language. Master Th., University of Utah, 1983.

20. Komorowski, H. J. QLOG – The programming environment for PROLOG in LISP. In *Logic Programming*, Clark, K. L., Tarnlund, S.-A., Eds., Prentice-Hall, 1982, pp. 315–323.

21. Kowalski, R. A.. *Logic for Problem Solving*. North-Holland, 1979.

22. Landin, P. "The next 700 programming languages". *Comm. ACM 9*, 3 (March 1966).

23. Lankford, D. S. Canonical Inference. ATP-32, Univ. Texas at Austin, 1975.

24. Lassez, J.-L., Maher, M. J. "Closures and fairness in the semantics of programming logic". *Theoretical Computer Science* (May 1984), 167-184.

25. Leivant, D. Polymorphic type inference. ACM Symp. Principles of Prog. Lang., Jan., 1983, pp. 88-98.

26. Lindstrom, G. Functional programming and the logical variable. ACM Symp. Principles of Prog. Lang., 1985.

27. MacLennan, B. J. Introduction to relational programming. Conf. Functional Prog. Lang. and Comp. Arch., ACM, 1981, pp. 213-220.

28. Malachi, Y., Manna, Z., Waldinger, R. TABLOG: the deductive-tableau programming language. ACM Symp. LISP and Functional Prog., 1984, pp. 323-330.

29. Mellish, C., Hardy, S. Integrating PROLOG in the POPLOG environment. In *Implementations of PROLOG*, Campbell, J. A., Ed., Ellis Horwood, 1984.

30. Milner, R. "A theory of type polymorphism in programming". *J. Computer and System Sciences 17* (1978), 348-375.

31. Milner, R. A proposal for Standard ML. ACM Symp. LISP and Functional Prog., 1984, pp. 184-197.

32. Mishra, P. Data Types in Applicative Languages: Abstraction and Inference. University of Utah, 1983.

33. Naish, L. Automating control for logic prorams. 83/6, University of Melbourne, Australia, 1984. (to appear) *J. Logic Programming*.

34. Pollard, G. H. *Parallel Execution of Horn Clause Programs*. Ph.D. Th., Imperial College, London, 1981.

35. Reddy, U. S. Transformation of logic programs into functional programs. Intern. Symp. Logic Prog., IEEE, 1984, pp. 187-197.

36. Reddy, U. S. Narrowing as the operational semantics of functional languages. Logic Programming Symposium, IEEE, Boston, 1985.

37. Reti, P., Kirchner, C., Kirchner, H., Lescanne, P. Narrower, a new algorithm for unification and its application to logic programming. First Intl. Conf. Rewriting Techniques and Applications, Dijon, France, 1985.

38. Robinson, J. A., Sibert, E. E. LOGLISP: motivation, design and implementation. In *Logic Programming*, Clark, K. L., Tarnlund, S.-A., Eds., Academic Press, 1982, pp. 299–314.

39. Sato, M., Sakurai, T. Qute: a Prolog/Lisp type language for logic programming. Eighth Intern. Joint Conf. Artificial Intelligence, 1983.

40. Sato, M., Sakurai, T. Qute: a functional language based on unification. Intl. Conf. Fifth Generation Computer Systems, ICOT, 1984, pp. 157–165.

41. Shapiro, E. Y. A Subset of Concurrent Prolog and Its Interpreter. TR-003, ICOT- Institute of New Generation Computer Technology, January, 1983.

42. Slagle, J. R. "Automated theorem-proving for theories with simplifiers, commutativity and associativity". *J. ACM 21*, 4 (1974), 622–642.

43. Smolka, G. Making the control and data flow of logic programs more explicit. ACM Symp. LISP and Functional Prog., 1984, pp. 311–322.

44. Smolka, G., Panangaden, P. A higher-order applicative language based on unification and generic quantification. In *Logic Programming: Functions, Relations and Equations*, DeGroot, D., Lindstrom, G., Eds., Prentice-Hall, 1985.

45. Subrahmanyam, P. A., You, J.-H. FUNLOG = functions + logic: a computational model integrating functional and logical programming. Intern. Symp. Logic Prog., IEEE, 1984, pp. 144–153.

46. Turner, D.A. SASL Language Manual. St. Andrews University, 1976.

47. van Emden, M. H., de Lucena Filho, G. J. Predicate logic as a language for parallel programming. In *Logic Programming*, Clark, K. L., Tarnlund, S-A., Eds., Academic Press, 1982, pp. 189–198.

48. Warren, D., Pereira, L. M., Pereira, F. "Prolog – the language and its implementation compared with Lisp". *SIGPLAN Notices 12*, 8 (1977).

49. Wolfram, D. A., Maher, M. J., Lassez, J-L. A unified treatment of resolution strategies for logic programs. Second Intern. Logic Prog. Conf., Uppsala, 1984.

THE UNIFICATION

OF FUNCTIONAL AND

LOGIC LANGUAGES

J. Darlington, A.J. Field, H. Pull

Department of Computing
Imperial College of Science and Technology
London SW7 2BZ

ABSTRACT

Certain aspects of logic programs give them greater expressive power than functional programs. In particular, the presence of logical variables enables relations to be used in arbitrary modes and allows components of data structure templates to be bound by unification. However, functional programs can in turn be more expressive than logic programs because of their cleaner syntax, which is devoid of output variables, and because of their higher-order capabilities. The run time behaviour of functional programs is much simpler to control than that of logic programs, particularly in a parallel execution context. Techniques, such as graph reduction and data flow, have been evolved for the parallel evaluation of functional languages taking advantage of their simplicity of execution, and it would be advantageous if these techniques could also be used to support languages with the extra expressive capability of logic. This paper discusses the differences between the two styles and proposes an extended functional language (HOPE with unification) which provides all of the expressive power of logic programs whilst retaining most of the underlying functional simplicity. This is achieved by the introduction of absolute set abstraction which allows logical variables to be introduced within set expressions on the right hand sides of function-defining equations.

We propose a technique for compiling certain types of functions defined implicitly within set expressions into explicit functions. This effectively involves synthesising function inverses using the processes of symbolic unification and program transformation. When this can be achieved, logical variables can be eliminated altogether and replaced by function composition.

1 INTRODUCTION

In recent years there has been growing interest in the, so called, declarative languages. These languages represent a radical departure from the concepts prevalent in conventional languages in widespread use today such as Pascal or Ada. Such conventional or imperative languages are intimately tied to the von Neumann model of computation, whereas the origin of the declarative languages lies in mathematical formalisms developed separately from the construction of computing machinery. The mathematical well-foundedness of the declarative languages conveys certain intrinsic benefits, e.g. greater expressive power, possibility of formal manipulation and ease of parallel evaluation, which make it possible that the next generation of computing systems will be based on these languages.

Within the declarative languages, at the moment, there are two main schools: **functional** languages trace their origins to the lambda calculus and recursion equation systems, [3, 11] whereas **logic programming** languages are based on a procedural interpretation of the First Order Predicate Calculus [12]. Although both styles of language share most of the benefits that accrue from their basic declarative nature, there are important fundamental and stylistic differences between them, and each school has its enthusiastic advocates. In this paper we examine the differences between these languages and propose a route to a unified language which seems to have all the benefits of both camps. We assume the reader has a basic familiarity with the

38

concepts of functional and logic languages as outlined in [7] and [13].

In section 2 below we examine the origin of the differences between logic and functional languages and look at some of the consequences of these differences. In section 3 we propose a method of reconciling these differences by extending functional languages to give them capabilities presently only found in logic languages and present some examples of programs in such an extended functional language. In section 4 we present techniques for transforming or compiling such an extended functional language to a conventional one in order to retain as much as possible of the simplicity of implementation of functional languages, particularly in a parallel execution context. Section 5 outlines a trial implementation of such an extended functional language and section 6 compares our ideas to related work in logic and functional languages.

2   COMPARISON OF FUNCTIONAL AND LOGIC LANGUAGES

2.1   Introduction to Functional and Logic Languages

A program in a modern functional language (the examples given in this paper are written in a version of HOPE [1]) consists of a set of equations defining functions. For example, the following is a program which calculates the length of a list of elements of arbitrary type:

dec length : list alpha -> num ;

--- length(nil) <= 0 ;
--- length(x::l) <= 1 + length(l) ;

Points to note are that HOPE is a polymorphically typed language so the first line of the above program giving the type for length involves a type variable alpha, and that :: is an infix form for the list constructor function. Executing a functional language program involves **reducing** an expression using the equations as left to right rewrite rules until it contains no defined functions, only constants or constructor functions.

For example, to calculate the length of the list [1,2,3] one would evaluate the expression length([1,2,3]), which would involve the following rewrites:

```
length([1,2,3])
        ->    1 + length([2,3])
        ->    1 + (1 + length([3]))
        ->    1 + (1 + (1 + length([])))
        ->    1 + ( 1 + (1 + 0))
        ->    3
```

All mature functional languages are **higher order,** that is functions are first class objects and can be passed as parameters and returned as values. For example, the following functions are found to be very useful

```
dec map : list alpha x  (alpha -> beta)
          -> list beta ;

--- map(nil,f)  <= nil ;
--- map(x::l,f) <= f(x)::map(l,f) ;
```

Such 'iterators' provide generic functions that enable one to avoid the use of many explicit recursions as in

```
dec double : list num -> list num ;
--- double(l) <= map(l,times2) ;

dec times2 : num      -> num ;
--- times2(n) <= 2*n ;
```

So double([1,2,3]) evaluates to [2,4,6].

Logic programs, as exemplified in an impure form by Prolog, [6], are untyped and consist of sets of **clauses** defining relations. Thus the length program above in Prolog would be

```
        length(nil,0)     <-
        length(x::l,n+1) <- length(l,n)
```

In contrast with the reduction process used by functional languages, logic languages use **resolution**. To execute a logic program one submits a **goal statement** involving variables, and the system attempts to discover all values of the variables that make the statement true. For example, to compute the length of [1,2,3] one submits the goal statement length([1,2,3], n), which succeeds in just one way (with n bound to 3).

2.2 Differences between Functional and Logic Languages

(i) Typing

Prolog and other logic programming languages are currently all untyped whereas most modern functional languages, such as HOPE, and ML [17], are strongly typed and allow polymorphism. (It is our experience with HOPE that the existence of a strong but flexible type checking regime greatly enhances programmer productivity.)

(ii) Higher order

Logic programming languages are first order languages, again in contrast to most functional languages. We also feel that the ability to write higher order functions increases the expressive power of the language, enabling many related algorithms to be realised as specific instances of one generic function, resulting in shorter programs and improved readability.

(iii) Functional versus relational notation

Output from each function in a functional program is defined implicitly by construction on the right hand side(s) of the equation(s) defining the function. The equivalent definition in a logic language would require each output component to be named explicitly within clause heads; extra variables must also be introduced within the clause body to represent what in the functional program would be simply function composition. For example, the program to reverse a list in HOPE is:

```
dec reverse : list alpha -> list alpha ;

--- reverse(nil) <= nil ;
--- reverse(x::l) <= append(reverse(l),[x]) ;

dec append  : list alpha x
                 list alpha -> list alpha ;

--- append(nil,l)    <= l ;
--- append(x::l1,l2) <= x::append(l1,l2) ;
```

whereas in Prolog it is rendered thus:

```
reverse(nil,nil) <-
reverse(x::l,lr) <- reverse(l,lr1) and
                  append(lr1,[x],lr)

append(nil,l,l)  <-
append(x::l1,l2,x::l3) <- append(l1,l2,l3)
```

Note how the second clause of the reverse relation in the Prolog program necessitates the introduction of an extra variable, lr1. (As it is well known that inventing sensible names for variables is one of the hardest tasks in programming, this clearly presents a serious impediment to programmer productivity!)

(iv) Multi-mode use of relations

Relational notation and resolution give logic languages a very elegant and powerful capability not found in the functional languages. Because a logic program makes no commitment as to which variables in a relation are to be considered as inputs and which variables are to be considered as outputs, a relation once defined can be used in several modes. For example, the append relation defined above can be used in a 'functional' way to join two lists together by means of a goal statement such as

```
append([1,2],[3,4],l)
```

which will bind l to [1,2,3,4]. But it can also be
used 'backwards' to split a given list by means of a
goal statement such as

```
append(l1,l2,[1,2,3,4])
```

which will produce values for l1 and l2 that when
appended together give [1,2,3,4], viz.

```
        []. [1,2,3,4]
    and [1],   [2,3,4]
    and [1,2],  [3,4]
    and [1,2,3],  [4]
    and [1,2,3,4], [].
```

In contrast, functional programs are committed as to
what they regard as inputs and what they regard as
outputs. Consequently, the append function cannot be
used to split a list as above; a separate function
would have to be defined. Thus logic programs are, on
this count, more expressive than functional programs in
that one logic program can represent many functional
ones.

(v)   Non ground outputs

Another capability found in logic programming but not
in functional programming is that results produced need
not be totally ground, i.e. they may involve variables.
For example given the length relation defined earlier a
goal statement of the form

```
length(l,2)
```

will produce a binding for l of the form u1::(u2::nil)
where u1 and u2 are variables. Such a data structure
is a skeleton for all lists of length 2. Data
structures involving such, so called, **logical variables**
are first class objects in logic languages and lead to
many succinct and elegant specifications as in the
following program

```
front(n,1,11) <- length(11,n) and append(11,12,1)
```

Frontof is true if the third argument is of length n and appears as an initial segment of the second argument e.g.

```
front(2,[1,2,3,4],11)
```

binds 11 to [1,2].

If this is executed as a Prolog program, i.e. using depth first backtracking and left to right selection of goals in a conjunction. length(11,2) is first evaluated binding 11 to u1::(u2::nil) which is then passed on to the second conjunct which is executed as

```
append(u1::(u2::nil), 12, [1,2,3,4])
```

causing u1 and u2 to be bound to 1 and 2 respectively. [5], [19] and [24] all give examples where this ability to imbed logical variables in data structures enables one to write programs that are more abstract and efficient than would be possible otherwise.

Functional languages are restricted in that only constants and constructor functions can appear in the output so in this sense they are less powerful than logic languages.

(vi)   Determinism

Functional languages are deterministic i.e. the forms one can write are syntactically restricted so that they denote proper many to one functions. Only one output value will be computed for any input value. Furthermore certain Church-Rosser and safeness properties can be shown to hold for functional languages so no searching is necessary when evaluating a functional language program. As long as the leftmost outermost reducible subexpression is amongst those rewritten at each step the answer is guaranteed to be reached if it exists.

In contrast, logic programming languages are inherently nondeterministic and any query may give rise to several solutions. Furthermore, evaluating a logic program involves a search process since at any point in the evaluation there may be several different ways of attempting to prove a subpart of the goal, not all, or any, of which may succeed. Although there exist **complete** search strategies for Horn clause logic programs e.g. breadth first search, Prolog implements an incomplete strategy, because depth first backtracking may choose to explore one nonterminating part of the search space before exploring a terminating part. Thus Prolog may fail to find solutions when such solutions exist according to the denotational reading of the program. This has the important consequence that a Prolog programmer must be aware of the operational behaviour of the interpreter executing his program, an idea somewhat at variance with the aims of declarative programming. Furthermore, even if a complete search strategy is employed, different choices as to what parts of the search space to explore next can have vastly different consequences with regard to the amount of computation that has to be performed to find a solution.

2.3 Origin of the Differences

If one looks for the main reason for the differences between functional and logic languages, it seems to lie in the difference between the calling mechanisms employed by the two languages. Functional languages employ **pattern matching**, while logic languages employ **unification**. As unification subsumes pattern matching this gives logic languages capabilities not possessed by functional languages.

In unification both the goal and the head of the clause being resolved against are allowed to contain variables, and a successful unification produces two separate substitutions: an **input substitution** mapping variables in the clause head to terms, and an **output substitution** mapping variables in the goal to terms. For example, matching the goal length(m, 2)

to the head of the clause

        length(x::l, n+1) <- length(l,n)

produces the input substitution n->1 and the output
substitution m->(x::l).
    It is the existence of the output substitution that
gives logic languages their extra power. In functional
languages the expression being reduced cannot contain
variables, being composed only of defined functions,
constructor functions and constants and therefore no
output substitution is involved in the pattern
matching. Indeed, functional languages do not involve
the notion of 'variables' at all - their use of
identifiers being simply as bound symbols.   For
example, matching the expression

        length(1::nil)

against the equation

        length(x::l) <=   1+length(l)

produces the input substitution x->1, l->nil.
    Although the ability to use a relation in several
modes conveys extra expressive power, the picture is
complicated operationally as different uses of the same
relation can have vastly different computational
consequences. Consider the simple definition for
reverse

        reverse(x::l,lr) <- reverse(l,lr1) **and**
                            append(lr1,[x],lr)
        reverse(nil,nil) <-

    When interpreted as a Prolog program, i.e. with a
sequential left to right depth-first backtracking
search strategy, such a definition works perfectly when
used with ground values in the first argument e.g.
reverse([1,2],l). However, if one attempts to use it
in the other mode e.g. reverse(l,[1,2]) the computation

never terminates. This is due to the fact that the
goal generated is

    reverse(l,lr1) **and** append(lr1,[x],[1,2])

Prolog selects the first conjunct for further expansion
and, with the clauses ordered the way they are, this
results in a further call with an identical first
conjunct. The computation thus never terminates and
no answer is found even though one is logically implied
by the axioms. Thus, in a sequential context, a
programmer must be conscious of the operational
behaviour of each mode of use for a given relation.
    This use of the logical variable is also at the
core of the problems encountered when attempting to
develop parallel interpretation schemes for logic
programs. Although a full and-or breadth first
parallel search strategy is complete, the existence of
a logical variable shared between otherwise independent
conjuncts means that computational effort is needed to
ensure that instantiations are applied consistently to
the shared variable. Furthermore, different modes can
imply vastly different computational effort. For
example, for the goal

    reverse(l,lr1) **and**   append(lr1, [x],[1,2])

much work is saved by postponing exploration of the
first conjunct until the second conjunct (which is
deterministic) has produced the value [1] for lr1.
    When one considers that one generic definition is
being used to represent several quite separate
algorithms or operational interpretations by being used
in different modes, it is perhaps too much to expect
all of these uses to be efficient algorithms in both
the sequential and parallel context. Generally a
programmer, without employing any extra annotations,
can only be expected to write his program so as to be
operationally efficient when used in one mode, and the
fact that other modes are at least achievable, without
extra programming effort, should be regarded as a
bonus. Our view is, therefore, that the power this
multimode facility provides should be used to write
specifications, i.e. declarative statements of WHAT the

program should compute, as succinctly and economically as possible, but that we should not expect such specifications to be executed efficiently in all cases without extra work, of an analytical or transformational nature, being done.

The conclusion we draw from this analysis is that each language style has something to offer the other and that a route to an improved language could be found by either camp importing features from the other. In the following section we show how a functional language can be simply extended to provide all the 'missing' capability, and explore the use of this language.

3   AN EXTENDED FUNCTIONAL LANGUAGE

We base our extension on the **set abstraction** construct currently found in many functional languages. For example, one can define a function to remove all odd numbers from a given set of numbers thus:

```
dec removeodd : set num  ->  set num ;
--- removeodd(S) <= {n | n in S and even(n)} ;

dec even : num  ->  truval ;
--- even(0)   <= true ;
--- even(1)   <= false ;
--- even(n+2) <= even(n) ;
```

The definition of removeodd uses the notation of relative set abstraction borrowed from mathematics. Operationally this sets up an iteration through the set S, including in the result set all those members that satisfy the predicate even. Thus one has to base all such set abstractions on pre-defined sets, so this construct, although very useful, represents no more than special syntax for a form of higher order iterator already definable in functional languages.

Our proposal involves removing the requirement to base every abstraction on a predefined set and moving to **absolute set abstraction,** where the members of the set are defined implicitly by a set of **conditions.** In our case the conditions will be **equations** involving functional expressions.   For example, given append

48

defined normally, e.g.

```
    dec append : list alpha x list alpha -> list alpha ;
    --- append(nil,l)    <= l ;
    --- append(x::11,12) <= x::append(11,12) ;
```

one can use it in a multimode manner, say in the
definition of the function split that returns all ways
of decomposing a given list, i.e.

```
    dec split : list alpha
               -> set(list alpha x list alpha) ;
    --- split(l) <= {11,12 | append(11,12) = l} ;
```

Several things should be noted. The 11 and 12 in the
above definition act as **logical variables.** We adopt
the convention that any symbol not a function or
constant or input variable is to be regarded as a
logical variable whose scope extends to the enclosing
set brackets. Note also that split is a set-valued
function. This is our way of introducing the nondeterminism associated with unification. Any 'function'
that in a logic context would be a nondeterministic
relation becomes a set valued function.
  The declarative meaning of a definition such as the
above is simply the set of all instantiations for the
logical variables that make the associated conditions
true. For example, split([1,2]) rewrites to

```
    {11,12 | append(11,12) = [1,2]}
```

which according to our declarative reading should be
equivalent to

```
    {([],[1,2]),([1],[2]),([1,2],[])} .
```

  Operationally such expressions can be evaluated by
unifying the equations forming the conditions against
the equations of the program. Thus in

```
    {11,12 | append(11,12) = [1,2]}
```

the defining equation

        append(l1,l2) = [1,2]

unifies against the second equation of the program
(with variables renamed)

        append(x::ll1,ll2) <= x::append(ll1,ll2)

with the substitutions

        Output substitution   Input substitution
            l1 -> 1::ll1   x -> 1
            l2 -> ll2   append(ll1,ll2) -> [2]

Note the last substitution: this is not strictly a
legitimate substitution but means that the other
substitutions unify the two equations for any values of
ll1 and ll2 such that append(ll1,ll2) = [2]. In
general we allow a subexpression whose outermost call
involves a defined function to match any term and set
up a further condition to attempt to justify this
assumption. This is the analogue of a recursive call.
        The above substitutions allow us to refine our set
expression to:

        {1::ll1,ll2 | append(ll1,ll2) = [2]}

        There is another unification for append(l1,l2) =
[1,2]. This is with the equation

        append(nil,l) = l

with the substitutions

        Input substitution   Output substitution
            l -> [1,2]   l1 -> nil
                                             l2 -> [1,2]

This gives an alternative elaboration, viz.

        {(nil, [1,2])}

without any qualifying condition.
        These two different elaborations constitute
independent contributions to the final result set and

are to be unioned together; this constitutes the exact
analogue of or-parallelism in logic programming. Thus
we have

    split([1,2]) => {nil,[1,2]} U
                    {1::l11,l12 | append(l11,l12) = [2]}

The second component can be further elaborated until we
obtain the final solution containing no unresolved
conditions

    {[],[1,2]} U {[1],[2]} U {[1,2],[]}

Any set component with a condition that is demonstrably
false denotes the empty set. Any set component with a
residual condition that cannot be elaborated further
represents an uncompleted proof in logic terms and does
not constitute part of the answer.
    A set may be defined using more than one condition.
For example the logic program for front defined earlier
can be exactly mimicked in our extended functional
language thus,

    dec front : num x list alpha -> set(list alpha) ;
    --- front(n,l) <= {l1 | length(l1) = n and
                           append(l1,l2) = l} ;

where length and append are defined normally, viz.

    dec length : list alpha -> num ;
    --- length(nil) <= 0 ;
    --- length(x::l) <= 1 + length(l) ;

    dec append : list alpha x list alpha -> list alpha ;
    --- append(nil,l)   <= l ;
    --- append(x::l1,l2) <= x::append(l1,l2) ;

Thus evaluation of front(2,[1,2,3]) reduces to

    {l1 | length(l1) = 2 and append(l1,l2) = [1,2,3]}

There are several choices of how to proceed. If we
choose to unify the first condition, this will only
unify with the second equation for length as 0 will not

51

match 2. The substitutions for the successful unification are

Input Substitution	Output Substitution
length(l) -> 1 (as 2=1+1)	l1 -> x::l

These enable us to reduce the above to

    {x::l | length(l) = 1 **and** append(x::l,l2) = [1,2,3]}

Again there are several ways to proceed. Choosing the second condition, this only unifies with the second equation for append with the substitutions

Input Substitution	Output Substitution
x -> 1	x -> 1
end(l1,l2) -> [2,3]	l -> l1
	l2 -> l2

Giving

    {1::l1 | length(l1) = 1 **and** append(l1,l2) = [2,3]}

A further two similar unifications produces

    {1::(2::l1) | length(l1) = 0 **and**
                  append(l1,l2) = [3]}

Now the first condition only unifies with the first equation for length, setting l1=nil and append(nil,l2)=[3] matches only with the first equation for append, setting l2=[3]. Thus, our solution is

    {[1,2]}

This is, of course, a singleton set - a consequence of the fact that front is a deterministic function. We propose allowing the programmer to indicate when this is the case in the type declaration and use special syntax for the definition thus:

    dec front : num x list alpha -> list alpha ;
    --- front(n,l) <= l1 **st** length(l1) = n
                        and append(l1,l2) = 1;

52

where **st** is read "such that".

3.1 Evaluation Strategy

As we saw in the above example, there are generally
several alternative ways of proceeding corresponding to
the various choices of what conditions(s) to elaborate
next and what equation(s) with which to match them. The
situation is totally analogous to logic programming.
Always choosing the leftmost condition and using the
first equation it matches from the list of equations
corresponds directly to Prolog's depth first evaluation
strategy. Parallel breadth first evaluation stategies
seem more appealing, but we still have all the problems
associated with parallel evaluation of logic programs
such as the treatment of shared (logical) variables in
and-parallel evaluation. We will return to this
problem in section 4 below.
   We can allow conditions to be more complex than
the simple equations previously treated. For example,
nested functional expressions are natural as in

> **dec** revstring : list alpha x list alpha
>   -> set(list alpha) ;
> --- revstrings(11,12) <=
>   {1 | append(11,append(reverse(1),112)) = 11 **and**
>   append(121,append(1,122)) = 12} ;
>
> **dec** reverse : list alpha -> list alpha ;
> --- reverse(nil) <= nil ;
> --- reverse(x::1) <= append(reverse(1), [x]) ;

Revstrings computes the set of all the sublists of one
list that appear in reverse order somewhere in the
other list. Such nested functional equations can be
executed using the above mechanisms, the leftmost
outermost function being the one with which the match
is performed. In a parallel context any nested
subexpression not containing any logical variables
could be a candidate for reduction in the normal
functional manner.
   Our approach extends smoothly to 'database' style

applications. For example, the familiar family
relationship example can be rendered thus

```
    dec father,mother : name -> name ;
    --- father(Heather) <= John ;
    --- mother(Heather) <= Kate ;

    dec parents,grandparents : name -> set name ;
    --- parents(n)        <= {father(n)} U {mother(n)} ;
    --- grandparents(n) <= parents(parents(n)) ;
```

As a notational convenience we have overloaded
functional application in the last equation by writing
parents(parents(x)) to stand for

$$\bigcup_{p \,\in\, parents(x)} parents(p)$$

All styles of data base querying available to logic
programmers are available in our extended functional
notation. For example. given the above program we can
define

```
    dec children : name -> set name ;
    --- children(n) <= {y | parents(y) ∋ n} ;
```

Note the use of (set membership) in the last
equation. This again is simply a notational
convenience. Given the function member, defined
normally, the above could be written using equalities
as

```
    --- children(n) <= {y | member(n,parents(y)) = true}
```

We can also augment the rules used to unify equations
to cope with these cases. A simple evaluation is

```
    children(John)
            => {y | parents(y) ∋ John}
    match   => {y | {father(y)} U {mother(y)} ∋ John}
    simplify => {y | father(y) = John} U
               {y | mother(y) = John}
    match   => {Heather} U {y | mother(y) = John}
```

3.2 Imbedded Logical Variables

In section 2.2(v) we highlighted the extra power
gained by the logic languages' ability to generate non
ground output and pass around data structures
containing logical variables.   Exactly the same
capability can be provided by our extended functional
language.   The first thing to note is that a data
structure containing logical variables is actually a
very succinct way of denoting the set of all data
structures with the logical variables consistently
instantiated. i.e. the list skeleton

    u::(v::nil)

denotes the infinite set of all two element lists e.g.

    {u::(v::nil) | u,v   U}

where U is the universe of discourse, i.e. the set of
all elements of the correct type.
    Given this reading we can be precise as to what it
means to apply a function to a structure containing
logical variables.

    f(u::(v::nil))

means

    {f(u::(v::nil)) | u,v   U}

Given that f is defined by normal functional
equations, we may be able to match f(u::(v::nil)) in
several ways to the left hand sides of the equations
for f,   thereby generating different output
substitutions.   To allow this to happen consistently,
we alter our interpretation of function application to
structures involving logical variables to

    {l' | f(u::(v::nil)) = l'}

and the picture is exactly as before and our unification process will automatically take care of any
possible matches.

55

Thus if we have

```
dec f,g : list num -> list num ;
--- f(nil)  <= nil ;
--- f(1::l) <= 2::f(l) ;
--- f(2::l) <= 3::f(l) ;

--- g(nil)  <= nil ;
--- g(1::l) <= 4::f(l) ;
```

and we evaluate

    append(f(l1), g(l1)) **where** l1 == u::(v::nil)

then this is interpreted as

    {l | append(f(u::(v::nil)), g(u::(v::nil))) = l}

which reduces to

    {[2,2,4,4]}

With this reading of imbedded logical variables we can support the whole apparatus of logic, but we know exactly the places where unification may be needed. Any function call not appearing in an equality condition in an implicit set expression can be performed using simple pattern matching and reduction. In section 4 below we will see that many of the uses of the logical variable, even in set expressions, can be eliminated by transformation.

3.3   Higher Order Capabilities

As noted earlier functional languages are normally higher order. Thus all objects, including functions, have full rights and can be passed as parameters and returned as values. If we apply this doctrine to our extended functional language we would expect logical variables to be able to bind objects of function type, and unification to produce function values for them. This immediately takes us into the realm of higher order unification, which is known to be undecidable above second order. However, we can still use the higher order apparatus to write succinct specifications, a subset of which will be efficiently executable. thus giving ourselves a capability beyond that of standard logic programming.

For example, given the family relationship example from section 4 we can write queries of the form

    f   st f(Heather) = John

where f is a function valued logical variable. We can certainly match such logical variables against named functions. Matching with the equation father(Heather) = John gives us the solution f->father.

The unification process becomes more troublesome if we do not have a named function to match with directly, but need to develop a function definition for the logical variable. However, some of these cases seem tractable, as in the following example

```
dec map : list alpha x (alpha -> beta)
            -> list beta ;
-- map(nil,f)  <= nil ;
-- map(x::l,f) <= f(x)::map(l,f) ;
```

Map takes a list and a function and returns the list formed by applying the function to every element of the input list.

Given map we can write

```
dec isto : list alpha x list beta
              -> set (alpha -> beta) ;
--- isto(l1,l2) <= {f | map(l1,f) = l2} ;
```

where isto defines the set of all functions that map one list onto another. For any given pair of lists this set may be empty (e.g. isto([1,1],[2,3]) or infinite, as any valid function can be extended on domain elements not in the input list. We can however produce finite specifications of these functions as in

```
isto([1,2], [2,4])
    => {f | map([1,2],f) = [2,4])}
```

The defining equation only matches the second equation for map, with the following substitutions resulting

Input substitution	Output substitution
x -> 1	f -> f
l -> [2]	
f(1) -> 2	
map([2],f) -> [4]	

enabling us to rewrite the above as

   {f | f(1) = 2 **and** map([2],f) = 4}

Two further matches with the equations for f get us

   {f | f(1) = 2 **and** f(2) = 4}

which is a precise description of the set of functions defined.

The area of unification of high order objects requires more investigation. We need to delineate the form of expressions that are executable and those that can only be treated as specifications. We envisage an interpreter that accepts such specifications syntactically and attempts to execute them, but stops if called upon to do any matching involving function valued logic variables that is beyond its capabilities. In this case the programmer would be required to modify or transform his or her specification into a form that is directly executable.

4   COMPILATION AND TRANSFORMATION OF EXTENDED FUNCTIONAL LANGUAGES

The incorporation of unification and nondeterminism certainly increases the expressive power of a functional language. However, as we saw in section 2, it brings with it problems of implementation efficiency. These largely concern the management of the search space of possible evaluations and co-ordinating updates to shared logical variables. In this section we will argue that some of the expressive power these language features provide should be reserved for use at the **specification** level and not be directly supported at run time. We will present techniques for **compiling** or **transforming** such specifications into programs which are of a purely functional nature, i.e. which have no run time support for unification and logical variables.

If we examine one of the capabilities available in an extended functional language, i.e. that of using a single function in several modes, we can see that we can often improve its run-time behaviour by transformation. Normal functions have only one mode of use. Ground terms are passed in as input values and ground terms are returned as the values. Relations in a logic language and functions used in implicit definitions (i.e. as equational conditions in set expressions) in our extended functional language may have several modes of use. Thus a single function definition may support many different modes of use. However, as we have observed, modes of use other than the normal mode may require unification for execution and introduce inefficiencies if these modes are supported at run time. However, if one restricts oneself initially to considering only variables which are either inputs which are totally ground or output variables, each mode of use corresponds to the 'normal' execution of a particular function. Our compilation technique is based on the idea of analysing the mode of use of functions used in implicit definitions and transforming the original function definition into one whose normal mode of use is the one required to produce (functionally) values for the output variables within the set expression. That is, we explicitly synthesise the appropriate function inverses. Our implicit definitions then reduce to compositions of these synthesised functions which can then be executed more efficiently using only pattern matching and deterministic computation. Such a transformation eliminates the use of logical variables. reducing the whole program back to a 'normal' functional program. The analysis of the mode of use and selection of a particular mode for the component functions corresponds to a commitment to a particular evaluation strategy. A half way house would be to synthesise direct functions for all modes of use employed for a particular function and leave the discrimination of which mode to employ until run time.

As an example, let us take the program for front introduced previously

```
dec append : list alpha x list alpha -> list alpha ;
--- append(nil,l) <= l ;
--- append(x::l1,l2) <= x::append(l1,l2) ;

dec length : list alpha -> num ;
--- length(nil)  <= 0 ;
--- length(x::l) <= 1 + length(l) ;

dec front : num x list alpha ->  list alpha ;
--- front(n,l) <= l1   st  length(l1) = n and
                             append(l1,l2) = l ;
```

Any execution of front involves length and append being used in several nonstandard modes. One evaluation strategy is to concentrate on the second condition first and produce all splits of the input list l, and then select the one of the required length. This corresponds to using append in the mode append(out,out)in and length in the mode length(in)in. The latter mode for length represents its use as a filter on a set of possible values.

Another evaluation strategy is to explore the length condition first producing a skeleton list of the appropriate length. This corresponds to the mode length(out)in. We will return to consider this mode later. Returning to append being used in the mode append(out,out)in we can see that this use corresponds to the normal use of a function, app* say, with definition

```
dec app* : list alpha
            ->  set(list alpha x list alpha) ;
--- app*(nil)  <= {nil,nil} ;
--- app*(x::l) <= {x::l1,l2 | l1,l2 in app*(l)} U
                   {nil,x::l} ;
```

Denotationally, app* is equivalent to the split function defined earlier, but operationally it is expressed using relative set abstraction and can therefore be executed using the normal functional apparatus.

Similarly there is a function leng* corresponding to the mode length(in)in viz.

```
dec leng* : list alpha  x  num  -> truval ;
--- leng*(nil,0)     <= true ;
--- leng*(x::1,0)    <= false ;
--- leng*(nil,n+1)   <= false ;
--- leng*(x::1,n+1)  <= leng*(1,n) ;
```

Given these two functions, front can be rendered

```
--- front(n.1) <= 11 st (11,12) in app*(1) and
                       leng*(11,n) ;
```

which can be run using normal functional apparatus. There is still some flexibility of behaviour possible with this definition, e.g. lazy evaluation gives efficient execution. however, as we shall see below, further transformation does even better.

The crucial question is, of course. where do the definitions of app* and leng* come from? They are derived from their definitions by a compilation/transformation process that mimics their execution using unification at a symbolic level using the unfold/fold transformation methodology outlined in [2].

For example, taking the definition of app*, this is

```
dec app* : list alpha
           -> set(list alpha x list alpha) ;
--- app*(1) <= {11,12 | append(11,12) = 1} ;
```

Instantiating this definition with 1 set to nil we get

```
app*(nil) <= {11,12 | append(11,12) = nil}
```

The condition only matches the first equation for append giving

```
app*(nil) <= {nil,nil}
```

Returning to the definition of app* and reinstantiating l to x::l we get

    app*(x::l) <= {l1,l2 | append(l1,l2) = x::l}

This time the condition matches both equations for
append. Unioning the results of the two matches
together gives

    app*(x::l) <= {nil,x::l} U
                  {x::l1,l2 | append(l1,l2) = l}

In the second component append is again being used in
the mode append(out,out)in. i.e. it is a recursive call
to app*. Formally this is just a fold with the
definition of app* giving

    app*(x::l) <= {nil,x::l} U
                  {x::l1,l2 | l1,l2 **in** app*(l)}

The derivation of leng* is equally straightforward.
Its definition is

    dec leng* : list alpha x num -> truval ;
    --- leng*(l,n) <= length(l) = n ;

and the derivation proceeds:

    leng*(nil,0)   <= length(nil) = 0
                                        Instantiation
                        <= 0 = 0
                                        Unfolding
                        <= true ;
                                            law
            leng*(x::l,0) <= length(x::l) = 0
                                        Instantiation
                        <= 1+length(l) = 0
                                        Unfolding
                        <= false ;
                                            law
          leng*(nil,n+1) <= length(nil) = n+1
                                        Instantiation
                        <= 0 = n+1
                                        Unfolding
                        <= false ;

62

$$\text{leng}^*(x::l, n+1) \quad \Leftarrow \quad \text{length}(x::l) = n+1$$

Instantiation

$$\Leftarrow \quad 1+\text{length}(l) = n+1$$

Unfolding

$$\Leftarrow \quad \text{length}(l) = n$$

law

$$\Leftarrow \quad \text{leng}^*(l,n) \;;$$

Folding

As mentioned earlier for this example. though not in general, we can do better. Returning to our new definition of front

    --- front(n.l) <= l1 **st** l1,l2 **in** app*(l) **and**
                           leng*(l1,n) ;

the transformation can be continued to produce a single recursive definition for front. Briefly

    front(0,nil)   <= l1   **st**   l1,l2 **in** app*(nil) **and**
                                 leng*(l1,0)

Instantiating

                     <= nil **st** leng*(nil,nil)

Unfolding

                     <= nil

Unfolding

Similarly

    front(0,x::l)   <= nil

    front(n+1,x::l) <= l1   **st** l1,l2 **in** app*(x::l) **and**
                                 leng*(l1,n+1)

Instantiating

                     <= nil   **st** leng*(nil,n+1)
                               or
                        x::l1 **st** l1,l2 **in** app*(l) **and**
                                 leng*(x::l1,n+1)

Unfolding

                     <= nil   **st** false
                               or
                        x::l **st** l1,l2 **in** app*(l) **and**
                                 leng*(l1,n)

Unfolding

<pre><code>   <= x::l1 st l1,l2 in app*(l) and
                        leng*(l1,n)
                                        Simplifying
              <= x::front(n,l)
                                        Folding
</code></pre>

Simplifying our definition for front is finally

<pre><code>   front(0,l)   <= nil ;
    front(n+1,x::l) <= x::front(n,l) ;
</code></pre>

Returning briefly to the mode length(out)in; if we repeat the transformation process we can derive a definition for a function, leng** say,

<pre><code>   dec leng**:num -> list alpha
    --- leng**(0)   <= nil;
    --- leng**(n+1) <= u::leng**(n);
</code></pre>

where the u in the last equation is a logical variable, a consequence of the fact that the main equation for length

<pre><code>   ---length(x::l) <= 1+length(l)
</code></pre>

has an input paramater, x, that appears on the left hand side but not on the right, so that when it is inverted x appears free. Thus leng** produces a skeleton, a data structure containing logical variables. We cannot make such a structure an input to a 'pure' function so we cannot use the mode append(in,out)in. However if we transform the partial definition

<pre><code>   --- front(n,l) <= l1 st app(leng**(n), l2) = l;
</code></pre>

we arrive at a definition for front identical to the one derived above using different modings.

This result should not really surprise us. As the top level call, first, is a function, the overall input-output behaviour will be the same whatever internal modings are used, and this will be achievable by a completely functional program. The fact that the same functional program is reached via two different routes is an indication that this program is, in some sense, the optimal one.

With the treatment of imbedded logical variables outlined in section 3.2 all uses of the logical variable are treated uniformly and are amenable to this transformation technique. For example the, rather unlikely, program

```
dec h : list alpha -> set num ;
dec g : list alpha -> num ;
--- g(nil)  <= 0 ;
--- g(x::l) <= 1 ;
--- h(l) <= {n | app(l,l2) = l1 and g(l1) = n} ;
```

transforms simply to

```
--- h(nil)  <= {0} U {1} ;
--- h(x::l) <= {1} ;
```

It should now be clear that the full power of the logical variable cannot always be achieved within a language employing reduction as its operational semantics. Programs such as difference list append from [5] allow variables to be introduced into a data structure and later bound by unification. Because this binding is performed at a time which cannot be determined statically i.e. at compile time, our techniques of symbolic unification will not yield a function which can be evaluated solely by reduction. In such cases, we must provide run-time support for unification. Since we can detect at compile time where unification is required, we propose that this be achieved by compiling the unification as an explicit call to a procedure which performs restricted (one-way) unification. This is exactly the way in which unification is supported in PARLOG implementations [4] (one-way unification is a primitive operation in the PARLOG kernel language). No implementation of such a compiler yet exists.

5   IMPLEMENTATIONS

Trial implementations of the ideas presented here have commenced.   The HOPE in HOPE interpreter, [18], has been extended to support the extended set abstraction facility and is working although experiments with varying execution strategies and higher order capabilities are continuing. Many of the examples contained in this paper have been executed.

The interpreter operates on the abstract structure of the program, represented as a HOPE data structure. For extended set expressions a basic breadth first search strategy is employed, but with some run time mode analysis to attempt to improve performance by intelligent selection of what condition to resolve next.

6   RELATED WORK

The growing interest in declarative languages has led to several studies of the relationships between the functional and logical styles of programming, and to a number of attempts to integrate features from both sides.

One approach to providing both language features to the programmer has been to introduce separate functional and logical programming facilities and to provide an interface between the two.   Such is the case with languages such as FUNLOG [22], LOGLISP [21] and ·POPLOG [16].

The provision of both langauges features within a single unified framework has been approached from both the logic and functional programming angles.

Lambda PROLOG [15] permits functions to be defined by conditional equalities and allows expressions to occur both within equation bodies and within clause heads.   Function-defining equations are then converted to rules. and expressions are replaced by a condition and an auxiliary logical variable in the obvious way. Thus lambda PROLOG supports functions purely within a framework of logic programming.   Resolution remains the operational semantics of the language.

Narrowing, as described by Fay [8] and Hullot,

[10], and later by Goguen and Meseguer [9] and Reddy
[19], involves replacing pattern matching in functional
languages by unification. Logic programs can then be
expressed as functions which map their inputs to either
undefined or true. A goal succeeds with resolvant θ if
the goal statement is mapped to true under the
substitution(s) in θ. Lindstrom [14] describes an
extended functional language (FGL+LV) which allows
expressions within formal parameter lists and which
allows information to pass in both directions through a
formal parameter variable. A restricted form of
narrowing is used as the operational semantics of the
language. Goguen and Meseguer [9] use narrowing as a
means of implementing equality within EQLOG which is a
combined functional/logic language. A formal
semantics of narrowing has been presented by Reddy in
[20].

Reddy [19], categorises our proposed language as an
'F-Language' since our ideas are based upon the ideas
of **free sets** (sets in which logical variables may be
introduced).

7   FUTURE WORK

We hope that we have indicated that functional
languages can be extended to provide capabilities
previously found exclusively in logic programming
languages, and that this extension can be done without
damaging the fundamental properties of the languages
that make them attractive to both programmers and
implementors.

Much work still needs to be done. In particular we
intend to investigate the use of higher order functions
in an attempt to more accurately delineate the
executable forms. More investigation is also needed
into evaluation strategies and how thoroughly compile
time mode analysis and transformation can remove the
need to support unification and logical variables at
run time.

REFERENCES

1. Burstall, R.M., D.B MacQueen, and D.T. Sannella. "HOPE: An Experimental Applicative Language", Proc. 1980 LISP Conference, Stanford, California pp 136-143.

2. Burstall, R.M. and J. Darlington. "A Transformation System for Developing Recursive Programs", JACM 24, 1, pp 44-67, 1977.

3. Church, A. "The Calculi of Lambda Conversion", Princeton University Press. Princeton. N.J. (1941).

4. Clark, K. and S. Gregory. "Notes on the Implementation of PARLOG", Internal Report DoC 84/16, Department of Computing, Imperial College, 1984. (To appear in Journal of Logic Programming.)

5. Clark, K., and S.A. Tarnlund. "A First Order Theory of Data and Programs", Proc. IFIP 77, North Holland, pp 939-944.

6. Colmerauer, A. "Les Systemes-Q ou un Formalisme pour Analyser et Synthetiser des Phrases sur Ordinateur. Publication Interne No. 43, Dept. d'Informatique, Universite de Montreal.

7. Darlington, J. "Functional Programming", in 'Distributed Computing', ed. by Chambers, F.B., Duce, D.A. and Jones. G.P., APIC Studies in Data Processing No. 20, Academic Press, 1984.

8. Fay, M. "First Order Unification in an Equational Theory", Proc. 4th Workshop on Automated Deduction, Austin, Texas, February 1979, pp 161-167.

9. Goguen, J.A., and J. Meseguer. "Equality, types, modules and generics for logic programming". Proc. 2nd Int. Logic Prog. Conf., Uppsala, 1984, pp 115-125.

10. Hullot, J.-M. "Canonical Forms and Unification", Proc. 5th Conference on Automated Deduction, Lecture Notes in Computer Science, Volume 87, Springer-Verlag, 1980, pp 318-334.

11. Kleene, S.C. "General Recursive Functions of Natural Numbers", Mathematical Annals, 112, pp 727-742 (1936).

12. Kowalski, R.A. "Logic as a Programming Language", Proc. IFIP Congress 1974, North Holland Publishing Co., 1974.

13. Kowalski, R.A. "Logic for Problem Solving", North Holland Publishing Co., 1979.

14. Lindstrom, G. "Functional programming and the logical variable". ACM Symp. Principles of Prog. Lang., 1985.

15. McCabe, F.G. "Lambda PROLOG". Internal Report, Department of Computing, Imperial College, (in preparation).

16. Mellish, C., and S.Hardy. "Integrating PROLOG in the POPLOG environment In Campbell, J. A., Ed., "Implementations of PROLOG", Ellis Horwood, 1984.

17. Milner, R., "The Standard ML Core Language", University of Edinburgh Internal Report.

18. Pull, H. "A HOPE in HOPE Interpreter", BSc. Undergraduate Thesis, Dept. Computing, Imperial College, 1984.

19. Reddy, U.S. "On The Relationship Between Logic and Functional Languages", this volume.

20. Reddy, U.S. "Narrowing as the Operational Semantics of Functional Languages", Research Report, Dept. of Computer Science, University of Utah, Utah, 1985.

21. Robinson, J.A., E.E. Sibert. "LOGLISP: motivation, design and implementation". In Clark, K. L., Tarnlund. S.-A., Eds., "Logic Programming", Academic Press, 1982, pp 299-314.

22. Subrahmanyam, P.A., and J.-H. You. "FUNLOG = functions + logic: a computational model integrating

functional and logical programming". Intern. Symp.
Logic Prog., IEEE, 1984, pp 144-153.

23. Turner, D. "Recursion Equations as a Programming
Language", Functional Programming and its Applications
- and Advanced Course, ed. by J. Darlington, P.
Henderson and D.A. Turner, Cambridge University Press,
1982.

24. Warren, D., L.M. Pereira, and F. Pereira. "Prolog -
the Language and its Implementations Compared With
LISP", SIGPLAN Notices 12, 8 (1977).

Part II:

Unification and Functional Programming

A PROLOGICAL DEFINITION OF HASL:

A PURELY FUNCTIONAL LANGUAGE WITH

UNIFICATION-BASED

CONDITIONAL BINDING EXPRESSIONS*

Harvey Abramson

Department of Computer Science
University of British Columbia
Vancouver, British Columbia
Canada V6T 1W5

ABSTRACT

We present a definition in Prolog of a new purely functional (applicative) language HASL (*HA*rvey's *S*tatic *L*anguage). HASL is a descendant of Turner's SASL but, among other features, introduces a one-way unification based conditional binding expression, one-way in the sense that of the two expressions being unified, only one may contain variables. This one-way unification based conditional binding construct is used to structure the design of the compilation of HASL clausal definitions to combinators which may then be reduced. The specification of HASL and its reduction machine is entirely in Prolog, thus providing an executable specification -

---

*This is a substantially revised version of the paper "A Prological Definition of HASL a Purely Functional Language with Unification Based Conditional Binding Expressions" by Harvey ABRAMSON appearing in New Generation Computing, Vol. 2 No. 1, pp. 3-35, 1984 © OHMSHA, LTD. 1984.

implementation - of the language. Since HASL programs may be considered a syntactic sugaring of combinator code, we adapt techniques derived from compiling practice to specify the language and its reduction machine. The definition is divided into four parts. The first part defines the lexical structure of the language by means of a simple Definite Clause Grammar which relates character strings to "token" strings. The second part defines the syntactic structure of the language by means of a more complex Definite Clause Grammar and relates token strings to a parse tree. The third part is semantic in nature and translates the parse tree definitions and expressions to a variable-free string of combinators and global names. The fourth part of the definition consists of a set of Prolog predicates which specify how strings of combinators and global names are reduced to "values", i.e., integers, truth values, characters, lists, functions, fail, and has an operational flavour: one can think of this fourth part as the definition of a normal order reduction machine.

1 INTRODUCTION

In this paper we shall present the logical definition and implementation of the purely functional language HASL (*HA*rvey's *S*tatic *L*anguage).

Our primary motivation in defining HASL was the desire to incorporate an explicit operator for a limited kind of unification within the setting of functional programming languages, and thus outside the traditional setting of theorem proving and logic programming where unification was born. Introducing full unification into the setting of functional programming languages presents a number of serious problems, one of which is the extension of functional programming language semantics to include something akin to the logical variable. (See our comments in the final section.) We have taken a somewhat smaller step, and incorporated in HASL what we have called "one-way unification" in Abramson [1]. The limitation of one-way unification is such that in:

$$A \ \{- \ B$$

where {- is the *left crossbow symbol* and is used to denote the unification operator, only *A* may contain variables to be instantiated. (There is also, for convenience, a *right crossbow symbol* used in: B -} A .) This operator is embedded in the *unification based conditional binding* expression

$$A \; \{\text{-}\; B => C \; ; D$$

which means: unify B with A and if the unification succeeds, the value of the expression is the value of C, with any of the variables of A occurring in C replaced by the bindings established by the unification; otherwise, if the unification fails, the value of the expression is the value of D, completely unaffected by any bindings involved in the failed unification attempt.

A somewhat similar limited form of unification (though called "pattern matching") had been implicitly used earlier in other functional languages such as Turner's SASL, but only in the language's parameter binding mechanism to "unpack" structures. For example,

$$hd \; (a : x) = a$$

takes a list (":" is SASL's infix *cons*) and splits it into a head and a tail. Failure of unification can be utilized only for selection of another clausal definition in the course of function application; if there is no following clausal definition, failure of unification is hidden as a fatal error in function application.

Our unification-based conditional binding expressions may be thought of as a way of permitting the definition of anonymous functions in a setting where named functions are specified by clausal definitions. Indeed, the unification-based conditional binding expression is used below to structure HASL's compilation of clausal definitions to combinators. The expression

$$(a : x) \; \{\text{-}\; y => a \; ; \textit{fail}$$

where *fail* is the single member of a failure domain (i.e., {*fail*}), is an anonymous function. A clausal definition of the form:

$$hd \; (a : x) = a$$

is treated as

$$hd \ y = (a : x) \ \{\text{-} \ y => a \ ; fail$$

during the compilation of HASL to combinators.

The language HASL - like SASL before it - may be thought of as a syntactically sweetened version of a combinatory logic with two primitive operations: function application and cons-ing. HASL differs from SASL in a number of details (including the unification-based conditional binding expressions) which permit a somewhat cleaner and simpler reduction machine. (See the end of Section 2 and the remarks at the end of Section 6 about these topics. It should also be noted that the limited kind of unification we use has some applications in the compilation of code for subsumption checks and demodulation in theorem provers Wos et al [29], and is also used in Clark and Gregory [7]'s Parlog.)

A secondary motivation in defining HASL was to apply logic programming to the definition of a full scale, experimental language. Earlier work (referenced below) had established that programming languages could be specified logically, but for the most part, these applications of logic to language definition were to toy languages. There are, of course, many ways of formally defining programming languages, and many translator writing systems for implementing languages. One attractive feature of logic programming, however, is that a specification can be read procedurally as well as declaratively. If, in general, logic programming's motto is "The specification is the program", in terms of language definition the motto is "The definition is the language processor". Logic programming thus provides the possibility of rigorously defining languages and, at the same time, implementing them. Language experimentation drops out of the class of "thought experiments" and into the laboratory.

The specification of HASL is in Prolog, an *approximation* to logic programming using the Horn clause subset of first order logic. Although we do not present a purely logical definition of HASL, we feel that the departures from Horn clause logic in the definition presented below (clause order sensitivity; the use of the cut for control; negation as failure; and extension of HASL's database of globally defined functions) are not significant enough to mar the formality of the definition or its comprehensibility. The definition can be used as a specification of HASL, as an interpretive implementation of HASL, and as a guide to a more efficient implementation of HASL in some systems programming language.

The specification in the sections which follow may be regarded as steps in the refinement of the definition of a relation

$$hasl\,(Expression\,,\,Value\,)$$

which relates a HASL *Expression* to its reduced *Value* (if it exists). As remarked above, HASL may be thought of as a syntactically sweet version of a combinatory logic. We may therefore refine the definition of the relation *hasl* by techniques derived from compiling practice: HASL expressions are lexically analyzed to a list of tokens; these tokens are syntactically analyzed and a parse tree is produced; the parse tree is traversed and semantically analyzed to produce a combinator expression; the latter is finally reduced to produce a value:

```
hasl (Expression ,Value ) :-
    lexical (Expression ,Tokens ),
    syntactic ( Tokens ,Tree ),
    semantic ( Tree ,Combinators ),
    Combinators =>>HeadNormal ,
    HeadNormal >>>Value.
```

The reduction from *Combinators* to *Value* is broken up into two steps. In the first step, reduction rules defining the relation "=>>" are applied to the top-level combinator expression. If this sequence of reductions terminates, the second step makes any further necessary reductions and also has the side effect of printing the HASL value. The relation ">>>" makes non-trivial reductions when the value of a HASL expression is, for example, a list of HASL values: in that case, the relation "=>>" has only reduced the head of the final *Value* . See Section 7 and Appendix IV for details.

To specify the lexical and syntactic relations we make use of one kind of logic grammar, the Definite Clause Grammar or DCG. Definite Clause Grammars may be thought of as a generalization of context-free grammars: the non-terminal symbols may have arguments attached to them, and these arguments may be logical variables which are instantiated during parsing. Definite Clause Grammar rules are compiled into Prolog clauses which include "hidden" arguments which represent the string to be parsed as a difference list. Terminal symbols are represented as lists or strings. In the following, for example, we define the non-terminals *digits*, *lords* and *word*. Assuming suitable definitions of *digit* and *letter*, these definitions state that *digits* consists of a *digit* followed by more *digits* or that *digits* is empty, symbolized by the empty list []; that *lords* consists of a *letter* or *digit* followed by more *lords* or that *lords* is empty; and that a *word* consists of a *letter* followed by *lords*. The arguments in the rules for *digits* collect the various *digit*s which have been recognized into a list which is eventually converted to an integer constant (not shown here: see Appendix I). Similarly, the arguments in the definitions of *lords* and *word* collect *digit*s and *letter*s for later conversion to atoms.

```
digits([D|Ds]) --> digit(D) , digits(Ds).
digits([])     --> [].

lords([L|Ls]) --> ( letter(L) ; digit(L) ) , lords(Ls).
lords([])     --> [].

word([L|Ls]) --> letter(L) , lords(Ls).
```

The logic grammar notation is a great convenience, obviously, in defining languages: one specifies the syntax and various constraints on the syntax and one automatically obtains a parser for the language which has been defined! Logic grammars were first introduced in Colmerauer [8]'s definition of the class of metamorphosis grammars. One application of metamorphosis grammars was to the writing of a compiler for a simple programming language. Definite Clause Grammars, a special case of metamorphosis grammars were introduced in Pereira and Warren [19] and also shown to be effective in "compiling", i.e., translating a subset of natural language into first order logic. Metamorphosis grammars (M-grammars) have been used to describe several languages, namely ASPLE,

Prolog, and a substantial subset of Algol-68 Moss [14] and [15]; see also Moss [16] for the use of Prolog and grammars as tools in language definition. Although neither M-grammars nor DCGs were mentioned in Warren [27], that paper is of interest in the use of Prolog as a compiler writing tool. The use of DCGs and Prolog for the implementation of SASL (Turner [24], [25], and [26]) a purely applicative language, was reported in Abramson [2]. Other classes of logic grammars have subsequently been introduced by Abramson [4], [5] and Dahl and Abramson [10].

In section 2 we shall informally and briefly describe HASL. Section 3 contains a description of the general definition strategy: HASL expressions are compiled to variable-free strings of combinators, global names, and uses of the two primitive operations of function application (--->) and pair construction (:). Following this are sections devoted to: the DCG for lexical analysis; the DCG and associated predicates which perform syntactic analysis and parse tree formation; the translation to combinators; and the HASL reduction machine. A final section suggests some further work which may be pursued.

2 HASL - INFORMALLY AND BRIEFLY

HASL is descended from Turner's SASL (see Turner [24], [25], and [26]) and obviously owes much to it. We have chosen to name this language HASL not to suggest presumptuously that what we present is totally original, but that there are enough departures from SASL to warrant a new designation. At the source level HASL resembles SASL except that (see below): all clauses defining a function must have the same arity; unification-based conditional binding expressions may be used in HASL expressions; and *fail* is a HASL data object. The differences between the two languages lead to a simpler reduction machine than Turner's original machine. The credit for introducing the notion of a combinator reduction machine, of course, goes to Turner.

A HASL program is an expression such as:

[1,2,3] ++ [4,5,6]

with value:

[1,2,3,4,5,6]

or an expression with a list of equational definitions qualifying the expression:

```
f x where
  x= hd y,
  hd (a:x) = a,
  y = 3:y,
  f 0 = 1,
  f x = x * f(x-1)
```

with value 6.

We note in this list of definitions that:

1. A function such as *f* may be defined by a list of clauses. The order of the clauses is important: in applying *f* to an argument the first clause will be "tried", then the second, etc.

2. In the definition of *hd* the argument must be a constructed pair, specified by *(a:x)* where ":" is the HASL pair constructor. Structure specifications may involve arbitrary list structures of identifiers and constants.

3. HASL makes use of normal order evaluation which is "lazy" (Henderson and Morris [11]) so that infinite lists such as *y* may be defined, and elements of such lists may be accessed, as in *hd y,* without running into difficulties.

A list may be written as:

[1,2,3]

which is syntactic sugaring for:

1: 2: 3: []

where [] denotes the empty list, and the notation 'string' is a sugaring for the list of character denotations:

%s: %t: %r: %i: %n: %g: []

There are functions such as *number, logical, char* and *function* which may be used to check the types of HASL data objects. The following HASL expressions all reduce to the value *true:*

```
number 12 = true
logical 5 = false
char %% = true
function hd = true
```

Functions may be added to HASL's global environment as follows:

```
def
string [] = true,
string (a:x) = char a & string x,
string x = false,
cons a b = a:b
;
```

Each clause defining a HASL function *f* must have the same number of arguments or arity. Thus above, each clause in the definition of *string* has arity one. In the second clause for *string* however, a single structured argument is designated. Although HASL functions may be written as if they had several arguments, such as *cons* above, HASL functions are all considered to have in fact single arguments. The single argument is a HASL data object which may be a character, a truth value, an integer, fail, a list of HASL objects, or a function of HASL objects to HASL objects. The value of such a function may be any HASL object - including a function. Thus the value of:

```
cons %a
```

is the HASL function which puts *%a* in front of lists. The reader is reminded that the order of clauses in a definition is important.

The HASL object *fail* is the result of, for example, applying *hd* to an atom or indeed to anything which is not a non-empty list:

```
hd 5 = fail
```

The object *fail* is not a SASL object and is one of our departures from that language.

Another departure, as mentioned in Section 1, is in the introduction of the restricted unification-based conditional binding constructs "{-" and "-}" of Abramson [1]. Consider:

formals {- exp1 => exp2 ; exp3

The meaning of this expression is that if *exp1* can be unified with the list of *formals*, then the value of this expression is the value of *exp2* qualified by the bindings induced by the match; otherwise, it is the unqualified value of *exp3*. This may be expressed somewhat inefficiently using the HASL conditional expression *(a -> b ; c)*:

```
(fail = f exp1  where f formals = exp2) ->
exp3 ;
(f exp1 where f formals = exp2)
```

Thus the unification expression may be regarded as the definition and application of an anonymous function.

The unification expression is in fact the basis of the compilation of HASL clausal definitions into a single function. If *member* is defined by the following clauses:

```
def
member a [] = false,
member a (a:x) = true,
member a (b:x) = member a x
;
```

then the HASL specification and interpreter treats this as:

```
member x1 x2 =
  a [] {- x1 x2 => false;
  (a (a:x) {- x1 x2 => true;
   (a (b:x) {- x1 x2 => member a x;
    fail))
```

Here we use nesting of unification-based conditional binding expressions to model selection of the appropriate clause in an application of *member*. If the arguments $x1$ and $x2$ unify with *a* and [], respectively, the value of the application is *false*; if not, then unification is attempted with *a* and $(a:x)$, respectively, etc. Parentheses have been used to make explicit the nesting of the unification-based conditional binding expressions: they are not strictly necessary since

$$a \{\text{-} b \Longrightarrow c; d \{\text{-} e \Longrightarrow f; g$$

is parsed as:

$$a \{\text{-} b \Longrightarrow c; (d \{\text{-} e \Longrightarrow f ; g)$$

The other unification operator "-}" is defined in terms of "{-":

$$b \text{ -}\} a \Longrightarrow c ; d$$

is a convenience and is equivalent to:

$$a \{\text{-} b \Longrightarrow c ; d$$

3 THE TOP LEVEL OF THE HASL SPECIFICATION

We use Edinburgh C-Prolog Pereira [18] as our metalanguage.

A HASL expression denotes a value. We may express this by the notation:

hasl(Expression,Value).

This relation requires some refinement, however. The expression is written as a sequence of characters, including spaces, carriage returns, etc., and the characters must be grouped into a sequence of meaningful HASL "tokens". These tokens must then be grouped into meaningful syntactic units determined by the syntax of HASL expressions. These two relations, the lexical and syntactic, are expressed by means of two DCGs: one DCG defines the relation between a sequence of characters and a sequence of HASL tokens; a second DCG defines the relation between a sequence of HASL tokens and a representation of the syntactic structure of a HASL expression as a tree.

Further, the expression of the relation between the tree and the value denoted by the original sequence of characters requires refinement. The tree represents the abstract syntax of the HASL expression. A semantic relation holds between this tree and a sequence of combinators, global names, function application operators (--->) and pair construction operators (:). This relation therefore defines a translation from a syntactically sweet string of symbols (HASL) to a mathematically equivalent - but rather unreadable - sequence of symbols suitable for mechanical evaluation or reduction. The reduction relation ($=>>$) specifies how such a sequence of symbols is related to another sequence of symbols which is the head normal form of the first. A final relation ($>>>$) between head normal form and HASL values (normal form) completes the specification of the relation *hasl:*

> *hasl* (*Expression* , *Value*) :–
>   *lexical* (*Expression* , *Tokens*),
>   *syntactic* (*Tokens* , *Tree*),
>   *semantic* (*Tree* , *Combinators*),
>   *Combinators* $=>>HeadNormal$,
>   *HeadNormal* $>>>Value.$

The lexical relation is specified in terms of the relation *lexemes* (see next section):

> *lexical* (*Expression* , *Tokens*) :–
>   *lexemes* (*Tokens* , *Expression* , []).

and the syntactic relation is specified in terms of the relation *hasl_program* (see Section 5):

> *syntactic* (*Tokens* , *Tree*) :–
>   *hasl_program* (*Tree* , *Tokens* , []).

The two relations *lexemes* and *hasl_program* are defined below by definite clause grammars.

4 THE LEXICAL SPECIFICATION OF HASL

This relation requires little comment. A sequence of characters such as

"def fac 0 = 1, fac x = x * fac(x-1);"

is grouped into the following string of tokens:

[def,id(fac),constant(num(0)),op(3,cEQ),constant(num(1)),
  comma,id(fac),id(x),op(3,cEQ),id(x),op(5,cMULT),id(fac),
  lparen,id(x),op(4,cSUB),constant(num(1)),
  rparen,semicolon]

Identifiers, such as *fac,* are represented as in *id(fac);* constants, such as 0, are represented as in *constant(num(0)).* Some reserved words and punctuation marks are represented by atoms such as *def* and *comma.*

A sequence of definite clause rules such as:

tIDENT(id(Id)) --> [id(Id)].

defines the symbols which are to be the terminals for syntactic analysis and also their representation in the parse tree.

The lexical specification also contains the declaration of the operators for function application (--->), pair construction (:), reduction to head normal form (=>>), and reduction to normal form (>>>).

The complete Prolog specification of HASL is at the end of this paper following the References.

5 THE SYNTACTIC SPECIFICATION OF HASL

As mentioned above, the *syntactic* relation is between token strings and parse trees which represent the abstract syntax of HASL expressions.

The leaves of a parse tree may be identifiers such as *id(fac),* constants such as *logical(true), num(123), char(C)* or *fail,* or they may be the names of certain known HASL combinators such as *cADD* for addition, *cMATCH* used in unification, etc. These names follow the convention of a lower case *c* followed by some other letters (usually upper case), digits or underline characters.

There are several kinds of branch nodes. A branch may be labeled by the HASL function application arrow (--->) or by the HASL pair construction colon (:). The arrow associates to the left, the colon to the right. Thus the linear parse tree representation of *a+1* is:

cADD ---> id(a) ---> num(1)

and that for *hd 'abc'* is:

cHD ---> %a : %b : %c : []

Another kind of branch node is labeled with the functor *where* and has one subtree which is an expression and another which is the subtree for a list of definitions qualifying the expression:

where(Exp,Defs)

Global definitions are subtrees of a tree where the root is labeled with the functor *global:*

global(Defs)

For each definition there is a branch node labeled with the functor *def* and with three subtrees: the name of the identifier being defined; the arity associated with the name being defined; and the expression or list of clauses to be associated with the name. For a name with arity 0 such as in:

def b = a + 1;

the definition node looks like:

def(id(b),0,cADD--->id(a)--->num(1))

When a function is being defined, the arity is at least one, and the third argument is a list of clauses, each of the form:

func(Fseq,Exp)

where *Fseq* is a list of arguments of length *arity* for the function being defined and *Exp* is the expression associated with that clause. Thus, the definition of *member* in Section 2 is represented in a parse tree as:

```
def(id(member),2,
  [func([id(a)|flist(id(b):id(x))],id(member)--->id(a)--->id(x)),
   func([id(a)|flist(id(a):id(x))],logical(true))|
   func([id(a)|const(nil)],logical(false))])
```

The functor *flist* is used to label a branch of a tree in which a list structured argument to a function is specified. The context sensitive restriction that each clause defining a function have the same arity is specified by the predicate *mergedef* which merges separate clauses for a function into one node of the above description. (See the next two sections for further discussion of this restriction.)

One other point to note is that a list of definitions of arity 0 such as

$$[x,y,z] = x$$

is represented as a list of definition nodes:

```
[def(id(x),0,cHD--->id(x)),
 def(id(y),0,cHD--->(cTL--->id(x)))|
 def(id(z),0,cTL--->(cTL--->id(x)))]
```

This is specified by the predicate *expandef*.

The last remaining kind of branch node is that for a unification-based conditional binding expression.

```
(a:x){-y=>x;fail
y-}(a:x)=>x;fail
```

would both be represented as:

```
unify(flist(id(a):id(x)),id(y),id(x),fail)
```

The DCG specifying the syntax of HASL is fairly straightforward. There is some slight intricacy in the specification of the grammar rules for expressions involving the HASL operators: operator precedence techniques are used to build the appropriate subtrees.

The function symbols beginning with a lower case *t* are the terminals for this grammar and specify HASL tokens as defined by the lexical DCG.

6 THE SEMANTIC SPECIFICATION OF HASL

The *semantic* relation is one which holds between parse trees, as specified in the previous section, and certain strings of combinators, constants, global names, and the primitive HASL operations of function application ("--->") and pair construction (":"). These strings may in fact be regarded as modified parse trees in which the *global, where, def, func, flist* and *unify* nodes have been eliminated and replaced by variable-free subtrees. The elimination of these nodes depends on a discovery of the logician Schoenfinkel: that variables, although convenient, are not necessary.

Schoenfinkel's discovery that variables can be dispensed with relies on a sort of cancellation related to extensionality. If in HASL we defined:

successor x = plus 1 x
plus a b = a + b

then we could say that

successor = plus 1

for both sides, when applied to the same argument, are always equal.

Schoenfinkel related a variable, an expression which may contain that variable, and an expression from which that variable had been abstracted (removed), with the aid of the following combinators:

cS x y z = x z (y z)
cK x y = x
cI x = x

(Our convention is that a lower case *c* followed by an identifier, usually in upper case - designates a combinator.)

The specification of the abstraction or removal of a variable is given by the predicate *abstr0:*

```
abstr0(V,X--->Y,cS--->AX--->AY) :- ! ,
    abstr0(V,X,AX) ,
    abstr0(V,Y,AY).
abstr0(V,V,cI) :- !.
abstr0(V,X,cK--->X).
```

Here, V is a variable to be abstracted (removed), X is an
expression, and the third argument of *abstr0* is the expression
with the given variable removed. So in the following:

```
abstr0(id(x),plus--->num(1)--->id(x),X).
```

we obtain:

$$X = cS--->(cS--->(cK--->plus)--->(cK--->num(1)))--->cI$$

with no variables, and with only the constants *plus* and
num(1), the combinators and --->.

When the resulting expression is applied to actual arguments, these combinators, speaking anthropomorphically, place
the actual arguments in the right places so that the evaluated
result is the same as would be given (by extensionality) by
evaluating the original expression with variables and by making the appropriate substitutions of actual arguments for variables. The advantage of not using variables, of course, is that
an environment is not necessary and that no substitution
algorithm is necessary.

It is clear that this abstraction specification *(abstr0)*,
albeit elegant, leads to expressions much longer than the original. It is possible, however, to control the size of the resulting
expression by introducing combinators which are "optimizing"
in the sense that if a variable which is being abstracted is not
used in the original expression, then the resulting expression
will not have any redundancies. Some of these optimizing
combinators introduced by Curry are described in Curry and
Feys [9] and Burge [6]; a more effective set was introduced by
Turner who also extended the notion of abstraction of variables to a context in which there was a primitive operation of
pair construction in addition to the primitive operation of
function application Turner [25].

The predicate for abstraction from a single expression in the specification of HASL's semantics is based on Turner's technique: *abstract* specifies how a list of variables is to be removed; *abstr* specifies how a single variable is removed; and *combine* specifies the optimizations which control the size of the resulting expressions. The last clause of *abstract* introduces an application of a strict list uncurrying combinator which splits a structure into its components, and is an aspect of HASL's (restricted) unification. When a formal argument on the left hand side of a clausal definition is being "opened up", the combinator cU_s, being strict, generates the value *fail* if the actual argument does not have the appropriate list structure. Since constants may be HASL arguments, the abstraction predicate must specify what the resulting expression ought to be: removing a constant from an expression E means that when the resulting expression is applied to an actual argument, that argument must match exactly the removed constant, and so the parse tree is modified from E to:

cMATCH ---> X ---> E

where X is the constant being abstracted. One of the clauses of *abstract* is also involved in the treatment of repeated formal arguments: see (1) below.

We may now examine the *semantic* relation in detail. The *semantic* relation specifies a traversal of the parse tree which results in a new tree from which all identifiers except global identifiers have been removed. For a subtree of the form $X : Y$ or $X ---> Y,$ the resulting tree is specified by:

semantic(X:Y,Sx:Sy) :- semantic(X,Sx),semantic(Y,Sy).
semantic(X--->Y,Sx--->Sy) :- semantic(X,Sx),semantic(Y,Sy).

Related to a subtree of the form *where(Exp,Defs)* is a subtree *Combinators* specified by:

semantic(where(Exp,Defs),Combinators) :-
abstract_locals(where(Exp,Defs),Combinators).

The predicate *abstract_locals* reforms the *where* node into an *Abstraction* from which all local variables have been removed.

abstract_locals(where(Exp,Defs),Abstraction) :-
    semantic(Exp,SExp),
    comp_defs(Defs,Ids,Abs),
    abstract_equations(SExp,Ids,Abs,Abstraction).

In *abstract_locals*, after semantic processing of *Exp*, *comp_defs* takes the list of definitions *Defs* and produces a list of defined identifiers (*Ids*) and a list of defining expressions from which all argument variables have been removed (*Abs*). These two lists represent a set of equations in which the only non-global variables are the ones in the list *Ids*. *abstract_equations* reduces this set of equations to a single combinator expression by means of an algorithm of Hudak and Kranz [12]. *abstract_equations* eliminates equations one at a time, abstracting one of the identifiers in *Ids* out of each of the equations and forming a new set of equations smaller by one than the original equation set. The process stops when all variables in *Ids* have been removed, leaving a single combinator expression free of local variables. In the process, applications of HASL's fixed point combinator, cY, are introduced. The reduction rule for cY is defined by:

$$cY \text{-->} X =>> Res :- X \text{-->} (cY \text{-->} X) =>> Res.$$

This is read as: $cY\text{-->}X$ reduces to *Res* if $X\text{-->}(cY\text{-->}X)$ reduces to *Res*. A predicate *optimize* simplifies the combinator code by making some obvious, trivial reductions. (See Hudak and Krantz [12] for a fuller description of their algorithm for abstracting local variables from a set of mutually recursive equations, and for a discussion of the problem which can cause Turner's to generate an expression whose reduction may not terminate. They also provide a lengthier discussion of optimizations possible in a combinator setting.)

The predicate *comp_defs* builds the list of identifiers and abstractions by compiling each definition in *Def* using the predicate *comp_def*. A definition of arity 0 is left unchanged by the first clause of *comp_def*. As was mentioned in Section 2, the clauses defining a function are compiled as if one large unification expression had been specified. This compilation is specified by the predicate *comp_func*. The variables which are

91

introduced by *comp_func* are of the form *id(1),id(2)*, etc., (these are not HASL variables) and must later be abstracted from *Code0* which is returned by *comp_func* to yield the *Code* tree for a definition:

```
comp_def(def(Name,0,Def),def(Name,0,Def)) :- !.
  comp_def(def(Name,Arity,Funcs),def(Name,Arity,Code)) :-
  Arity > 0,
  comp_func(Funcs,Arity,Code0),
  generate_seq(Arity,Ids),
  abstract(Ids,Code0,Code).
```

The predicate *generate_seq* specifies a relation between *Arity* and the list of introduced identifiers *Ids* which later gets removed!

A function is compiled clause by clause in reverse order. The last clause of any function is compiled by *comp_func* to:

cCONDF ---> Abs ---> fail

where *Abs* is variable-free. *cCONDF* is a combinator defined as follows:

```
cCONDF ---> X ---> Y =>> Res :-
  X =>> Rx, !,
  cond_fail(Rx,Y,Res).
```

and is read: *cCONDF--->X--->Y* reduces to *Res* if *X* reduces to *Rx* and if *Rx* is not *fail* as determined by *cond_fail;* otherwise, *cond_fail* specifies that the value of *Res* is the value of the reduction of *Y*.

Remaining clauses defining a function are compiled by *comp1_func* to:

cCONDF ---> Abs ---> Sofar

where *Abs* is the compiled clause and *Sofar* is the code for the clauses already compiled.

A clause is compiled by the predicate *comp_clause:*

```
comp_clause(func(Fseq,Exp),Arity,Abs) :-
   note_repeats(Fseq,MarkedFseq),
   semantic(Exp,Sexp),
   abstract(MarkedFseq,Sexp,Aps),
   generate_applies(Aps,Arity,Abs).
```

In the definition of *comp_clause* note that:

1. The predicate *note_repeats* relates a list of formals, *Fseq,* to a marked list of formals *MarkedFseq,* where the second, third, etc., occurrences of a formal identifier *id(x)* have been replaced by *match(id(x))*. When *id(x)* is eventually abstracted from the right-hand side of a clause, this insures - by unification - that each occurrence of *id(x)* is matched to the same value. In the definition of *member* for example,

    member a (a:x) = true

    both occurrences of *a* must be bound to the same value. The *abstract* predicate treats repeated occurrences of an identifier in the way it treats constants.

2. *Exp* is related by the *semantic* relation to *Sexp*.

3. The marked formal sequence is abstracted from *Sexp* to yield *Aps*.

4. The identifiers *id(1)*, *id(2)*, etc., are introduced.

The interested reader may follow on his own the specification of the *semantic* relation for subtrees labeled by the functor *unify* and for trees rooted at the functor *global*. It only needs to be said that a global definition such as:

    def suc x = 1 + x;

results in the following clause being added to HASL's database:

global(suc,cC1--->cCONDF--->(cADD--->num(1))--->fail).

Global names in any HASL expression are replaced at reduction time by their value as specified by the second component of *global*.

Some comments are due about the way we have compiled clauses into a function. In SASL, Turner allowed different clauses defining a function to have different arities. For example:

f 0 b = c
f 1 = d
f x y z = e

Thus, when an application of *f* is encountered in a SASL expression, it is impossible to know in advance, i.e., at compile time, how much of the SASL expression to the right of *f* would actually be used by *f*. To cope with this, Turner introduced what he called a combinator "TRY, with rather peculiar reduction rules" Turner [26]. We had earlier implemented SASL in Prolog, and the specification of TRY in logic caused an enormous amount of trouble: it seemed to require at reduction time a stack to hold everything to the right of *f* in a SASL expression (ie, either to the end of the SASL expression, or to the first right parenthesis). The TRY combinator itself seemed to come in two arities: one of arity 3 for stacking everything to the right to be passed to each clause to be tried; and one of arity 2 to attempt clauses in order to find the applicable one. No other combinator seemed to require this explicit stack, but at reduction time the stack had to be passed as part of the state of the reduction to each combinator rule in case some clausally defined function were invoked. The presence of the stack in the logical specification seemed too operational and too distasteful, and there seemed no way to write the SASL reduction rules completely without it. This may have been simply a result of our confusion, or more profoundly a case where Wittgenstein's dictum held: *Was sich ueberhaupt sagen laesst, laesst sich klar sagen; und wovon man nicht reden kann, darueber muss man schweigen.* (This can loosely be translated as: *Whatever can be said, can be said clearly; and we should keep quiet about everything else.* See Wittgenstein [28]) At any rate, HASL was born partly as a result of the hassle of trying to understand and simplify the SASL reduction machine.

The cCONDF combinator was introduced to deal with a kind of conditional expression which arises often in dealing with unification-based conditional binding expressions and in applying clausally defined functions: we could simply use the cCOND combinator, but the resulting code would be longer. Either way is simpler and clearer than using the TRY combinator! It should finally be noted that the restriction that all clauses defining a function have the same arity, a suggestion made by Turner as possible future work and which makes use of the cCONDF combinator feasible for compiling functions, imposes no loss of generality on what can be expressed in HASL: the sole interesting example in Turner [26] which makes use of different arities can be expressed without utilizing clauses of different arities.

7 THE SPECIFICATION OF HASL REDUCTION

The specification of the HASL reduction relation consists mainly of a set of rules as to how the HASL combinators are reduced. The combinator cS, for example, introduced in the previous section, is reduced as follows:

$$cS \longrightarrow X \longrightarrow Y \longrightarrow Z \Longrightarrow\!> Res :-$$
$$X \longrightarrow Z \longrightarrow (Y \longrightarrow Z) \Longrightarrow\!> Res.$$

Here, "$\Longrightarrow\!>$" is the infix reduction operator. The above specification is read:

$$cS \longrightarrow X \longrightarrow Y \longrightarrow Z$$

reduces to *Res* if

$$X \longrightarrow Z \longrightarrow (Y \longrightarrow Z)$$

reduces to *Res*.

Associated with each combinator is an *arity;* for example:

$$arity(cS,3)$$

which indicates the number of arguments necessary for the reduction to take place. An expression such as

$$cS \longrightarrow X \longrightarrow Y$$

cannot be further reduced as it is already in head normal form. The reduction rules are listed in order of increasing arity; at the end of each group of rules for a given arity, there is a rule such as:

$$C \dashrightarrow X \dashrightarrow Y =>> C \dashrightarrow X \dashrightarrow Y :- \\ arity(C,D) \; , \; D >= 3 \; , \; !.$$

which would specify that $cS \dashrightarrow X \dashrightarrow Y$ is already in head normal form.

The general reduction rule is to reduce the leftmost node of the combinator tree (the leftmost redex); if that node has not been reached, none of the combinator reduction rules apply. To handle the case of moving to the leftmost redex, the following (last but one) reduction rule applies:

$$X \dashrightarrow Y \dashrightarrow Z =>> Res :- \\ X \dashrightarrow Y =>> Rxy, \\ not \; same(X \dashrightarrow Y, Rxy), \\ Rxy \dashrightarrow Z =>> Res.$$

The reduction rules are recursively applied to try and reduce $X \dashrightarrow Y$ to head normal form; if $X \dashrightarrow Y$ is not in head normal form, then Rxy is the head normal form for $X \dashrightarrow Y$ and $Rxy \dashrightarrow Z$ is reduced to Res.

The last reduction rule $X =>> X$ specifies that X is already in head normal form.

Some combinators, such as the combinator $cCONDF$, defined in the last section, recursively call on the reduction machine. So does the combinator $cMATCH$ which specifies unification:

$$cMATCH \dashrightarrow X \dashrightarrow Y \dashrightarrow Z =>> Res :- \\ X =>> Redx, !, \\ Z =>> Redz, !, \\ eqnormal(Redx, Redz, Y, fail, Req), \\ Req =>> Res.$$

X and Z are reduced to Redx and Redz, respectively, and if they have the same normal form, Y is unified with Req and is reduced to Res; otherwise, *fail* is unified with Req and a trivial reduction reduces the entire match to *fail*. The binding of arguments to HASL formal variables - another part of HASL's restricted unification - is accomplished at the reduction stage by the combinators simply placing the actual arguments in their proper places for evaluation!

HASL numbers, truth values, and characters are tagged by the functors *num*, *logical* and *char*. (Lists are tagged by *:*). Various parts of the reduction machine use these functors for type checking. For example, the addition component of the "arithmetic unit" specifies that addition is strict:

add(num(X),num(Y),num(Z)) :- Z is X + Y, !.
add(X,Y,fail).

HASL type checking functions, such as *number*, are defined globally and apply type checking combinators such as:

cNUMBER ---> X =>> Res :- type_check(num(X),Res).

The predicate *type_check* is specified by:

type_check(Form,logical(true)) :- Form, !.
type_check(Form,logical(false).

The reduction from head normal form to normal form is specified by the relation $>>>$. A number of predicates are defined to print out the value of a HASL expression in an appropriate format, and these are the last predicates specified in Appendix IV.

8 SUMMARY AND FUTURE DIRECTIONS

We have presented the definition of the functional language HASL. The unification-based conditional binding expressions which it incorporates arose out of the following considerations. The unification phenomenon is best known to most people in the setting of theorem proving and logic programming. It is, however, possible to present unification as the result of a mathematical theory of substitutions in a language of applicative expressions, and indeed, that is what Robinson has done in the chapter "Unification" in his book "Logic: Form and Function" Robinson [20]. Since unification may be thought of as a substitution mechanism, it is natural to consider using it as a parameter passing mechanism in applicative programming languages. In full unification, variables may occur in either of the applicative expressions being unified. In the HASL functional setting, however, we have restricted the occurrence of variables to only one of the expressions, the one which contains the formal parameters. This one-way unification is used implicitly during function application, and explicitly, in the unification-based conditional binding expressions. These latter are, in fact, a kind of anonymous function definition. The unification-based conditional binding expressions, moreover, have been used to structure the design of the HASL compiler: clauses defining a function are gathered together into a single conditional binding expression. (One way unification has been similarly used in Clark and Gregory [7] to define the "standard form" of Parlog clauses. Representation in "standard form" is a stage in the compilation of Parlog clauses.) The unification-based conditional binding expressions constitute a simple and straightforward extension of functional programming.

It is possible to think of incorporating full unification in a functional language and Lindstrom [13] reports progress in this direction: he has been able to introduce "an upward compatible logical variable extension to a graph reduction language". There are problems in such an undertaking, however, because it means information flow becomes bidirectional between formal and actual parameter evaluation, possibly requiring delicate suspensions of function applications until arguments have been instantiated "enough" for evaluation. Lindstrom reports as strengths of his effort to incorporate unification: the incorporation of the logical variable into a graph reduction language; global, but not local, determinism in the resulting computation model; and an approach to its implementation on a distributed reduction architecture. Weaknesses reported are: some loss of purity in the functional model; strictness with respect to unification failure (compare our conditional one-way unification which can make use of failure of unification for control of evaluation); and an inability to return, as Prolog does, results involving unbound variables.

One aspect of HASL's unification may be extended to provide a more sophisticated structure specification mechanism. In

HASL when we write:

$$(a:x) \{- \; Y => a \; ; \; 'not \; a \; list \;'$$

the head of Y is returned if it is a list, or else the string *'not a list '* is returned. Whether Y is a list or not is determined by unification with $(a:x)$; if it is a list, unification also deconstructs Y and yields a as its its head and x as its tail. This is the only kind of structural specification or typing possible in HASL.

HASL's pair structuring may be considered as an instance of a more general structure specification mechanism in which context free grammars specify data types (see Abramson [5]). HASL's pair construction mechanism could be specified by the following grammar:

empty:pair ::= []
list: pair ::= hd:hasl_object, ":", tl:hasl_object

In this notation, *empty* and *list* name the two productions for *pair*, and *hd* and *tl* name the *hasl_object*s (predefined) which are constituents of a *pair* which is a *list*. From this grammatical specification we can derive predicates *is_empty* and *is_list* which when applied to an empty list and a non-empty list, respectively, return the value *true*, and *false* otherwise. Similarly, we could also derive functions *hd* and *tl* which, when applied to a *pair* which is a *list* return the appropriate *hasl_object*s. From this specification a pair construction function could also be derived. Unification could be used for analysis and construction of *list*s of *hasl_object*s, and we could consider the combinator reduction rules for *cHD*, *cTL* and *:* as being derived from this grammar.

From other context free grammars new analysis and construction functions, as well as new combinator reduction rules could be derived for manipulating new data types. Expressions using these new data types could occur as formal parameters (in either named functions or in conditional binding expressions) and unification could then be used to ensure that actual parameters were appropriately structured. Some type checking could be done on HASL programs at compile time.

99

This approach of using context free grammars for type specification has been incorporated in the design of a typed functional programming language *Kaviar* (which, however, is not implemented by HASL's combinator reduction technique: see Syrotiuk [23]). An earlier language which makes implicit use of this sort of grammatical unification is Mosses' DSL, a part of his Semantics Implementation System Mosses [17].

Having defined HASL in Prolog, we may consider HASL as a step towards providing a functional sublanguage for Prolog. Currently, HASL is a functional language implemented in Prolog and we cannot as yet (at least, not easily and cleanly) call on HASL for functional evaluation from within Prolog, nor can we call on Prolog for logical deduction from within HASL. A number of researchers have been attracted by the idea of a computing system composed of a deduction machine, such as Prolog, and a reduction machine, such as HASL. A model of such a system is provided by LOGLISP Robinson and Siebert [21] and [22] in which LOGIC is the deduction machine and LISP is the reduction machine. In the case of LOGLISP, however, it took quite a lot of work to define a suitable reduction mechanism for LISP: the notion of reduction of LISP expressions is fairly complex and is *not* identical to the customary evaluation of LISP expressions. A number of fairly tricky reductions, for example, had to be introduced in LOGLISP in order to reduce some of LISP's "special" forms, and there are even some LISP forms which are irreducible. (See the cited references for details.) We suggest that since HASL is defined in terms of a notion of reduction *ab initio,* it is simpler and perhaps cleaner mathematically to consider a deduction-reduction machine with HASL as the reduction component.

A few other interesting observations suggest avenues for further exploration. The HASL reduction machine, for example, has some notion of partial evaluation. If one defines

def f cond a b = cond -> a ; b

then *f true* is the function which when applied to two arguments selects the first one. In terms of combinators, the reduction of *f true* is:

$$cC \text{---} > (cB1 \text{---} > (cB1 \text{---} > cC1) \text{---} > cCONDF \text{---} >$$
$$cCOND \text{---} > logical(true)) \text{---} > fail$$

Another observation is that the abstraction of variables from an expression is a relation between a variable, an expression, and another expression without that variable. The abstraction may be run "backwards" and a variable may be put into a variable-free combinator expression to get something more readable. For example, in:

$$abstr0(id(x),E,$$
$$cS \text{---} > (cS \text{---} > (cK \text{---} > plus) \text{---} > (cK \text{---} > num(1))) \text{---} > cI).$$

we have:

$$E = plus \text{---} > num(1) \text{---} > id(x).$$

HASL abstraction is more complicated than this, but in principle one may think of *decompiling* variable-free expressions.

One might consider combining these two observations to get a notion for a debugging method for applicative languages: a partially evaluated expression may have some variables put back into it, and then one might try using the lexical and syntactic DCGs as generators rather than as recognizers to produce a readable HASL expression.

It may not be entirely frivolous to think in fact of generating programs which compute a given value. The reduction relation may be run backward to derive combinator strings which could be translated into HASL expressions. Of course there are infinitely many such expressions and most of them are trivial and/or uninteresting. Could one place constraints on the searching of the space of HASL expressions which compute a given value to produce interesting expressions?

As a final comment, we would like to state that pragmatically Prolog is a fine tool for designing and testing experimental languages. One tends not to carry out language experiments other than on paper - or in one's head - if implementation requires extensive coding in a low level language. But - the HASL interpreter described here, implemented in CProlog to run on a VAX 780 under Berkeley UNIX, is *slow*. A Prolog compiler which optimizes tail recursion is an absolute necessity.

ACKNOWLEDGEMENTS

This work was supported by the Natural Science and Engineering Research Council of Canada. I would like to thank Richard Currie for many useful suggestions.

REFERENCES

1. Abramson, H. Unification-based Conditional Binding Constructs. Proceedings First International Logic Programming Conference, Marseille. (1982).

2. Abramson, H. A Prolog Implementation of SASL. Logic Programming Newsletter 4, Winter 1982/1983.

3. Abramson, H. "A Prological Definition of HASL, a Purely Functional Language with Unification Based Conditional Binding Expressions." *New Generation Computing 2* (1984), 3-35.

4. Abramson, H. Definite Clause Translation Grammars. Proceedings 1984 International Symposium on Logic Programming, Feb. 6-9, 1984, (1984), 233-241.

5. Abramson, H., Definite Clause Translation Grammars and the Logical Specification of Data Types as Context Free Grammars. Proceedings International Conference on Fifth Generation Computer Systems - Tokyo. (1984), 678-685.

6. Burge, W.H. *Recursive Programming Techniques.* Addison-Wesley, 1975.

7. Clark, K., and S. Gregory. Parlog: Parallel Programming in Logic, Research Report DOC 84/4, Department of Computing, Imperial College, 1984.

8. Colmerauer, A. Metamorphosis Grammars. In *Natural Language Communication with Computers: Lecture Notes in Computer Science 63,* Springer, 1978.

9. Curry, H.B., and R. Feys. *Combinatory Logic Volume I.* North-Holland Publishing Company, 1958.

10. Dahl, V., and H. Abramson. Gapping Grammars. Proceedings Second International Logic Programming Conference, Uppsalla, Sweden, 1984.

11. Henderson, P., and J.H. Morris. A lazy evaluator. Conference Record of the 3rd ACM Symposium on Principles of Programming Languages, pp. 95-103, 1976.

12. Hudak, P., and D. Krantz. A Combinator-based Compiler for a Functional Language. Proceedings - Symposium on Principles of Programming Languages, pp. 122-132, 1983.

13. Lindstrom, G. Functional Programming and the Logical Variable. Proceedings 12th ACM Symposium on Principles of Programming Languages, New Orleans, Jan. 14-16, 1985.

14. Moss, C.D.S. A Formal Description of ASPLE Using Predicate Logic. DOC 80/18, Imperial College, London, 1980.

15. Moss, C.D.S. *The Formal Description of Programming Languages using Predicate Logic.* Ph.D. Th., Imperial College, 1981.

16. Moss, C.D.S. How to Define a Language Using Prolog. Conference Record of the 1982 ACM Symposium on Lisp and Functional Programming, Tittsburgh, Pennsylvania, pp. 67-73, 1982.

17. Mosses, P. *SIS - Semantics Implementation System: Reference Manual and User Guide,* DAIMI MD-30, Computer Science Department, Aarhus University, Denmark, 1979.

18. Pereira, F.C.N. (editor). C-Prolog User's Manual. University of Edinburgh, Department of Architecture, 1982.

19. Pereira, F.C.N., and D.H.D. Warren. "Definite Clause Grammars for Language Analysis." *Artificial Intelligence 13,* (1980) 231-278.

20. Robinson, J.A. *Logic: Form and Function.* North-Holland and Edinburgh University Press, 1979.

21. Robinson, J.A., and E.E. Siebert. LOGLISP - an alternative to Prolog. School of Computer and Information Science, Syracuse University, 1980.

22. Robinson, J.A., and E.E. Siebert. Logic Programming in LISP. School of Computer and Information Science, Syracuse University, 1980.

23. Syrotiuk, V. *A Functional Programming Language with Context Free Grammars as Data Types.* M.Sc. Th., Dept. of Computer Science, University of British Columbia, 1984.

24. Turner, D.A. SASL Language Manual. Department of Computational Science, University of St. Andrews, 1976, revised 1979.

25. Turner, D.A. A new implementation technique for applicative languages, *Software - Practice and Experience 9* (1979) 31-49.

26. Turner, D.A. *Aspects of the Implementation of Programming Languages: The Compilation of an Applicative Language to Combinatory Logic.* Ph.D. Th., Oxford, 1981.

27. Warren, D.H.D. Logic programming and compiler writing. DAI Research Report 44, University of Edinburgh, 1977.

28. Wittgenstein, L. *Tractatus Logico-Philosphicus.* Routledge and Kegan Paul, 1922.

29. Wos, L., et al. *Automated Reasoning.* Prentice-Hall, 1984.

APPENDIX I LEXICAL RULES

% Operator declarations

% reduction to normal form:
:- op(603,yfx,'>>>').
% reduction to head normal form:
:- op(603,yfx,'=>>>').
% function application:
:- op(602,yfx,'--->').
% pair construction:
:- op(601,xfy,':').

reserved(true,constant(logical(true))).
reserved(false,constant(logical(false))).
reserved(fail,constant(fail)).
reserved(def,def).
reserved(where,where).

lexemes(X)   --> space , lexemes(X).
lexemes([X|Y]) --> lexeme(X) , lexemes(Y).
lexemes([])   --> [].

lexeme(Token) -->
  word(W) , ! ,
  { name(X,W) , (reserved(X,Token) ; id(X) = Token) }.
lexeme(constant(Con)) --> constant(Con) , !.
lexeme(Punct)   --> punctuation(Punct) , !.
lexeme(op(Pr,Comb))   --> op(Pr,Comb) , !.

space --> " " , !.
% an ascii magic number for carriage return:
space --> [10], !.

num(num(N)) --> number(Number) , ! ,
  { name(N,Number) }.

number([D|Ds]) --> digit(D) , digits(Ds).

```
% ascii magic numbers for 0-9:
digit(D) --> [D] , { D>47, D<58 }.

digits([D|Ds]) --> digit(D) , digits(Ds).
digits([])     --> [].

word([L|Ls]) --> letter(L) , lords(Ls).

% magic numbers for ascii: a-z, A-Z:
letter(L) --> [L] , { (L>96,L<123 ; L>64,L<90) }.

lords([L|Ls]) --> ( letter(L) ; digit(L) ) , lords(Ls).
lords([])     --> [].

% in op(N,O) N designates the binding power
% of the operator O.
op(0,cAPPEND) --> "++" , !.
op(0,cCONS)   --> ":" , !.
op(1,cOR)     --> "|" , !.
op(2,cAND)    --> "&" , !.
op(3,cLSE)    --> "<=" , !.
op(3,cGRE)    --> ">=" , !.
op(3,cNEQ)    --> "\=" , !.
op(3,cEQ)     --> "=" , !.
op(3,cGR)     --> ">" , !.
op(3,cLS)     --> "<" , !.
op(4,cADD)    --> "+" , !.
op(4,cSUB)    --> "-" , !.
op(5,cMULT)   --> "*" , !.
op(5,cDIV)    --> "/" , !.
op(6,cB)      --> "." , !.

hasl_string(C:Cs) --> stringchar(C) , hasl_string(Cs).
hasl_string(nil) --> [].

hasl_char(C) --> "%" , stringchar(C) , !.
```

```
stringchar(char(A))    --> [C] ,
    { C =\= 39 , name(A,[C]) } , !.
stringchar(char(''''))  --> ''''''  , !.

string(S) --> ''''  , hasl_string(S) , '''' ,!.

constant(N)    --> num(N) , !.
constant(C)    --> hasl_char(C) , !.
constant(S)    --> string(S) , !.
constant(nil)  --> ''[]'' , !.

punctuation(tilde)          --> ''~'' , !.
punctuation(comma)          --> '','' , !.
punctuation(lparen)         --> ''('' , !.
punctuation(rparen)         --> '')'' , !.
punctuation(condarrow)      --> ''->'' , !.
punctuation(rightcrossbow) --> ''-}'', !.
punctuation(leftcrossbow)  --> ''{-'', !.
punctuation(lbrack)         --> ''['', !.
punctuation(rbrack)         --> '']'', !.
punctuation(unifyarrow)     --> ''=>'', !.
punctuation(semicolon)      --> '';'' , !.
```

The following predicates constitute the interface
between lexical and syntactic analysis. Predicates
with names starting with 't', eg, tCOLON, are the
terminals in syntactic analysis.

```
tCOLON          --> [op(0,cCONS)].
tPLUSPLUS       --> [op(0,cAPPEND)].
tCOMMA          --> [comma].
tLBRACK         --> [lbrack].
tRBRACK         --> [rbrack].
tLPAREN         --> [lparen].
tRPAREN         --> [rparen].
tUNIFYARROW     --> [unifyarrow].
tLEFTCROSSBOW  --> [leftcrossbow].
tRIGHTCROSSBOW --> [rightcrossbow].
tCONDARROW      --> [condarrow].
tEQUAL          --> [op(3,cEQ)].
tSEMICOLON      --> [semicolon].
```

```
tWHERE        --> [where].
tDEF          --> [def].
tNOT          --> [tilde].
tNEGATE       --> [op(4,cSUB)].
tPLUS         --> [op(4,cADD)].
tIDENT(id(Id)) --> [id(Id)].
tCONSTANT(C)   --> [constant(C)].
tOP(Pr,Comb)  --> [op(Pr,Comb)].
```

APPENDIX II SYNTACTIC RULES

```
hasl_program(H) ---> def(H).
hasl_program(H) ---> expression(H).


def(global(Ds)) -->
  tDEF , defs(Ds) , tSEMICOLON.
.sp

definition(def(Id,Arity,func(Fseq,Exp))) -->
  tIDENT(Id) , fseq(Fseq) , ! ,
  tEQUAL , expression(Exp) ,
  { seq_length(Fseq,Arity) }.

definition(Def) -->
  formal(Formal) , ! , tEQUAL , expression(Exp) ,
  { expandef(def(Formal,0,Exp),Def) }.

defs(Ds) --> definition(D) , ! ,
  { append_def(D,[],Deflist) } ,
  defs1(Deflist,Ds).

defs1(D,Ds) --> tCOMMA , definition(Def) , ! ,
  { mergedef(D,Def,Dm) } , defs1(Dm,Ds).
defs1(D,D) --> [].

fseq(Fseq) --> formal(Formal) , ! , fseq1(Formal,Fseq).

fseq1(F1,[F1|F]) --> formal(F2) , ! , fseq1(F2,F).
fseq1(F,F) --> [].
```

```
formal(Id) --> tIDENT(Id) , !.
formal(const(C)) --> tCONSTANT(C) , !.
formal(flist(Flist)) -->
  tLBRACK , flist(Flist) , ! , tRBRACK.
formal(flist(Flist)) -->
  tLPAREN , fprimary(Flist) , ! , tRPAREN.

flist(F1:F2) --> fprimary(F1) , ! , flist1(F2).
flist(const(nil)) --> [].

flist1(F) --> tCOMMA , flist(F).
flist1(const(nil)) --> [].

fprimary(F) --> formal(F1) , ! , fprimary1(F1,F).

fprimary1(F1,F1:F) -->
  tCOLON , formal(F2) , ! , fprimary1(F2,F).
fprimary1(F,F) --> [].

expression(E) --> unification(E1) , ! , expression(E1,E).

expression(E1,where(E1,Ds)) --> tWHERE , defs(Ds).
expression(E,E) --> [].

unification(unify(Fseq,E1,E2,E3)) -->
  fseq(Fseq) , tLEFTCROSSBOW ,
  expression(E1) , tUNIFYARROW ,
  expression(E2) , tSEMICOLON , expression(E3).

unification(U) --> condexp(U).

condexp(E) --> exp1(E1,0) , ! , condexp1(E1,E).

condexp1(E1,cCOND ---> E1 ---> E2 ---> E3) -->
  tCONDARROW , expression(E2) , ! ,
  tSEMICOLON , condexp(E3).
condexp1(E1,unify(Fseq,E1,E2,E3)) -->
  tRIGHTCROSSBOW , fseq(Fseq) , tUNIFYARROW ,
  expression(E2) , tSEMICOLON , expression(E3).
condexp1(E,E) --> [].
```

exp1(E,P) --> tPLUS , exp1(E1,6) , ! , exp2(E1,E,P).
exp1(E,P) --> tNEGATE , exp1(E1,6) , ! ,
  exp2(cNEGATE ---> E1,E,P).
exp1(E,P) --> tNOT , exp1(E1,3) , ! ,
  exp2(cNOT ---> E1,E,P).
exp1(E,P) --> comb(E1) , ! , exp2(E1,E,P).

% since : or cons is a primitive in HASL:
exp2(E1,E,0) --> tCOLON , exp1(E2,0) , ! ,
  exp2(E1 : E2,E,1).

% since ++ or append
% is the only other zero level operator:
exp2(E1,E,0) --> tPLUSPLUS , exp1(E2,0) , ! ,
  exp2(cAPPEND ---> E1 ---> E2,E,1).

% : and ++ are right associative;
% all others are left associative:
exp2(E1,E,P) --> tOP(Q,Op) , { P < Q } , ! ,
  exp1(E2,Q) ,
  exp2(Op ---> E1 ---> E2,E,P).

exp2(E,E,P) --> [].

comb(C) --> primary(P) , ! , comb1(P,C).

comb1(P1,C) --> primary(P) , ! , comb1(P1 ---> P,C).
comb1(C,C) --> [].

primary(L) --> tLBRACK , explist(L) , ! , tRBRACK.
primary(I) --> tIDENT(I) , !.
primary(C) --> tCONSTANT(C) , !.
primary(E) --> tLPAREN , expression(E) , ! , tRPAREN.

explist(E1 : E2) --> expression(E1) , ! , explist1(E2).
explist(nil) --> [].
explist1(E) --> tCOMMA , explist(E).
explist1(nil) --> [].

```
%  The following predicates are used
%  to check that each clause
%  defining a function has the same arity,
%  and to merge all definitions made at the
%  same time into a single list of definitions.

mergedef(Deflist,Def,Defmerge) :-
  flat(Def,FlatDef) ,
  merge(Deflist,FlatDef,Defmerge).

merge(Deflist,[Def|Defs],Defmerge) :-
  merge(Deflist,Def,Deflist1) ,
  merge(Deflist1,Defs,Defmerge).

merge([def(id(X),0,D)|Deflist],
      def(id(X),0,D1),
      [def(id(X),0,D)|Deflist]) :-
  write(X) ,
  write(' is a constant already defined: ') ,
  write(D) , nl ,
  write('definition ignored: ') ,
   write(D1) , nl.
merge([def(id(X),N,D)|Deflist],
      def(id(X),N,D1),
      [def(id(X),N,[D1|D])|Deflist]) :- !.
merge([def(id(X),N,D)|Deflist],
      def(id(X),M,D1),
      [def(id(X),N,D)|Deflist]) :-
  write('wrong number of arguments in definition of:') ,
  write(def(id(X),M,D1)) ,
  write('should be ') , write(N) , nl.
merge([def(id(Y),M,Dy)|Deflist],
      def(id(X),N,D),
      [def(id(Y),M,Dy)|Deflist]) :-
  defined(X,Deflist,Dx) , ! ,
  write(X) ,
  write(' already defined: ') ,
  write(Dx) , nl ,
  write(def(id(X),N,D)) ,
  write(' ignored.') , nl.
```

```
merge(Deflist,
    Def,
    [Def|Deflist]).

defined(Y,[def(id(Y),_,Dy)|_],Dy).
defined(Y,[def(id(X),_,_)|Deflist],Dy) :-
  defined(Y,Deflist,Dy).

seq_length([F|G],N) :- ! ,
  seq_length(G,M) ,
  N is 1 + M.
seq_length(F,1).


append_def(def(A,B,C),Z,[def(A,B,C) |Z]) :- !.
append_def([X|Y],Z,[X|W]) :-
  append_def(Y,Z,W).

flat(def(X,Y,Z),def(X,Y,Z)).
flat([def(X,Y,Z)|Defs],[def(X,Y,Z)|FDefs]) :-
  flat(Defs,FDefs) , !.
flat([DefHd|DefTl],Flat) :-
  flat(DefHd,FlatHd) ,
  flat(DefTl,FlatTl) ,
  append_def(FlatHd,FlatTl,Flat).

expandef(Defs,Def) :-
  expand(Defs,Def1) ,
  flat(Def1,Def).

expand(def(flist(X:const(nil)),0,Exp),Defx) :-
  expand(def(X,0,Exp),Defx).
expand(def(flist(X:Y),0,Exp),[Defx|Defy]) :-
  expand(def(X,0,cHD ---> Exp),Defx) ,
  expand(def(flist(Y),0,cTL ---> Exp),Defy).
expand(def(flist(X),0,Exp),def(X,0,Exp)).
expand(def(F,0,Exp),def(F,0,Exp)).
```

APPENDIX III SEMANTIC RULES

```
semantic(X:Y,Sx:Sy) :-
  semantic(X,Sx)  ,
  semantic(Y,Sy).
semantic(X--->Y,Sx--->Sy ) :-
  semantic(X,Sx) ,
  semantic(Y,Sy).
semantic(where(Exp,Defs),Combinators) :-
  abstract_locals(where(Exp,Defs),Combinators).
semantic(unify(Fseq,E1,E2,E3),cCONDF--->Exp--->Se3) :-
  semantic(E1,Se1) ,
  semantic(E2,Se2) ,
  semantic(E3,Se3) ,
  translate_unification(Fseq,Se1,Se2,Exp).
semantic(global(Defs),global) :-
  installdefs(Defs).
semantic(X,X).


abstract(nil,Abs,Abs).
abstract(flist(Flist),Exp,Abs) :-
  abstract(Flist,Exp,Abs).
abstract([X|Y],E,Abs) :-
  abstract(Y,E,Abs1) ,
  abstract(X,Abs1,Abs).
abstract(id(X),E,Abs) :-
  abstr(id(X),E,Abs).
abstract(const(X),E,cMATCH ---> X ---> E).
abstract(match(X),E,cMATCH ---> X ---> E).
abstract((X : Y),E,cU_s ---> Abs) :-
  abstract(Y,E,Abs1) ,
  abstract(X,Abs1,Abs).


abstr(V,X ---> Y,Abs) :-
  abstr(V,X,AX) ,
  abstr(V,Y,AY) ,
  combine(--->,AX,AY,Abs) , !.
abstr(V,(X : Y),Abs) :-
  abstr(V,X,AX) ,
```

```
      abstr(V,Y,AY) ,
      combine(:,AX,AY,Abs) , !.
   abstr(id(X),id(X),cI) :- !.
   abstr(V,X,cK ---> X).

_ combine(--->,cK ---> X,cK ---> Y,
     cK ---> (X ---> Y)).
   combine(--->,cK ---> X,cI,X).
   combine(--->,cK ---> (X1 ---> X2),Y,
     cB1 ---> X1 ---> X2 ---> Y).
   combine(--->,cK ---> X,Y,cB ---> X ---> Y).
   combine(--->,cB ---> X1 ---> X2,cK ---> Y,
     cK ---> Y,cC1 ---> X1 ---> X2 ---> Y).
   combine(--->,X,cK ---> Y,cC ---> X ---> Y).
   combine(--->,cB ---> X1 ---> X2,Y,
     cS1 ---> X1 ---> X2 ---> Y).
   combine(--->,X,Y,cS ---> X ---> Y).
   combine(:,cK ---> X,cK ---> Y,cK ---> (X : Y)).
   combine(:,cK ---> X,Y,cB_p ---> X ---> Y).
   combine(:,X,cK ---> Y,cC_p ---> X ---> Y).
   combine(:,X,Y,cS_p ---> X ---> Y).

   generate_seq(1,id(1)) :- !.
   generate_seq(N,Y) :-
     N1 is N - 1 ,
     gen_seq(N1,id(N),Y).

   gen_seq(1,X,[id(1)|X]) :- !.
   gen_seq(N,X,Y) :-
     N1 is N - 1 ,
     gen_seq(N1,[id(N)|X],Y).

   generate_applies(X,N,Y) :-
     generate_seq(N,Seq) ,
     gen_applies(X,Seq,Y).

   gen_applies(X,[Hd|Tl],Y) :- ! ,
     gen_applies(X ---> Hd,Tl,Y).

   gen_applies(X,S,X ---> S).
```

```
restructure(X ---> (Y ---> Z),W) :- restruct(X,Y ---> Z,W).
restructure(X ---> Y,X ---> Y).

restruct(X,Y ---> Z,A ---> Z ) :- restruct(X,Y,A).
restruct(X,Y,X ---> Y).

comp_clause(func(Fseq,Exp),Arity,Abs) :-
  note_repeats(Fseq,MarkedFseq) ,
  semantic(Exp,Sexp) ,
  abstract(MarkedFseq,Sexp,Aps) ,
  generate_applies(Aps,Arity,Abs).

comp_func([func(Fseq,Exp)|Funcs],Arity,Code) :-
  comp_clause(func(Fseq,Exp),Arity,Abs) ,
  comp1_func(Funcs,Arity,cCONDF--->Abs--->fail,Code).
comp_func(func(Fseq,Exp),Arity,cCONDF--->Abs--->fail) :-
  comp_clause(func(Fseq,Exp),Arity,Abs).

comp1_func([func(Fseq,Exp)|Funcs],Arity,Sofar,Code) :-
  comp_clause(func(Fseq,Exp),Arity,Abs) ,
  comp1_func(Funcs,Arity,cCONDF--->Abs--->Sofar,Code).
comp1_func(func(Fseq,Exp),
        Arity,
        Sofar,
        cCONDF--->Abs--->Sofar) :-
  comp_clause(func(Fseq,Exp),Arity,Abs).

comp_def(def(Name,0,Exp),def(Name,0,SExp)) :- !,
  semantic(Exp,SExp).
comp_def(def(Name,Arity,Funcs),def(Name,Arity,Code)) :-
  Arity > 0 , ! ,
  comp_func(Funcs,Arity,Code0) ,
  generate_seq(Arity,Ids) ,
  abstract(Ids,Code0,Code).

comp_defs([Def|Defs],Ids,Abs) :-
  comp_def(Def,def(id(Id),Arity,Abs1)) ,
  comp_defs1(Defs,[id(Id)],[Abs1],Ids,Abs).
```

```
comp_defs1([],Ids,Abs,Ids,Abs).
comp_defs1([Def|Defs],IdsIn,AbsIn,Ids,Abs) :-
  comp_def(Def,def(id(Id),Arity,Abs1)) ,
  comp_defs1(Defs,[id(Id)|IdsIn],[Abs1|AbsIn],Ids,Abs).

abstract_locals(where(Exp,Defs),Abstraction) :-
  semantic(Exp,SExp),
  comp_defs(Defs,Ids,Abs) ,
  abstract_equations(SExp,Ids,Abs,Abstraction).

abstract_equations(Exp,[id(Id)|Ids],[Exp1|Exps],Abstraction) :-
  abstr(id(Id),Exp1,Exp1prime),
  optimize(cY ---> Exp1prime,Y),
  abstr_list(id(Id),Exps,Y,Expsprime),
  abstr(id(Id),Exp,Exprime),
  abstract_equations(Exprime--->Y,
               Ids,Expsprime,Abstraction).
abstract_equations(Abstraction,[],[],Abstraction).

abstr_list(id(Id),[Exp|Exps],Y,[Exprime ---> Y|YExps]) :- !,
  abstr(id(Id),Exp,Exprime),
  abstr_list(id(Id),Exps,Y,YExps).
abstr_list(id(Id),[],Y,[]).

optimize(cY--->(cK--->X),OptX) :- !, optimize(X,OptX).
optimize(cS---> cK,cK--->cI) :- !.
optimize(cS---> (cK--->cI),cI) :- !.
optimize(cS---> (cK---> (cK--->X)),
       cK---> (cK--->OptX)) :- !,
  optimize(X,OptX).
optimize(cS---> (cK---> X)---> cI,OptX) :- !,
  optimize(X,OptX).
optimize(cS---> (cK---> X)---> (cK--->Y),
       cK---> (OptX--->OptY)) :- !,
  optimize(X,OptX),
  optimize(Y,OptY).
optimize(cS---> F---> G---> X,
       OptF---> OptX---> (OptG--->OptX)) :- !,
  optimize(F,OptF),
  optimize(G,OptG),
  optimize(X,OptX).
```

```prolog
optimize(cI--->X,OptX) :- !,
  optimize(X,OptX).
optimize(cK--->X--->Y,OptX) :- !,
  optimize(X,OptX).
optimize(X--->Y,OptX--->OptY) :- !,
  optimize(X,OptX),
  optimize(Y,OptY).
optimize(X:Y,OptX:OptY) :- !,
  optimize(X,OptX),
  optimize(Y,OptY).
optimize(X,X).

translate_unification(Fseq,E1,E2,Exp) :-
  note_repeats(Fseq,MarkedFseq) ,
  abstract(MarkedFseq,E2,Abs) ,
  restructure(Abs ---> E1,Exp).

installdefs(Defs) :-
  comp_defs(Defs,Ids,Abs) ,
  install(Ids,Abs).

install([id(Id)|Ids],[Def|Defs]) :-
  global(Id,DefId) , ! ,
  write(Id) , write(' already globally defined.') ,
  write(' New definition ignored.') , nl ,
  install(Ids,Defs).
install([id(Id)|Ids],[Def|Defs]) :-
  assertz(global(Id,Def)) ,
  install(Ids,Defs).
install([],[]).

member(Id,[Id|_]).
member(Id,[_|Ids]) :- member(Id,Ids).

note_repeats(Fseq,Marked) :-
  mark_repeats(Fseq,[],_,Marked).

mark_repeats(id(Id),In,In,match(id(Id))) :-
  member(Id,In) , !.
mark_repeats(id(Id),In,[Id|In],id(Id)).
```

mark_repeats(flist(Flist),In,Out,flist(Marked)) :-
  mark_repeats(Flist,In,Out,Marked).
mark_repeats(Hd:Tl,In,Out,MarkedHd:MarkedTl) :-
  mark_repeats(Hd,In,In1,MarkedHd) ,
  mark_repeats(Tl,In1,Out,MarkedTl).
mark_repeats([Hd|Tl],In,Out,[MarkedHd|MarkedTl]) :-
  mark_repeats(Hd,In,In1,MarkedHd) ,
  mark_repeats(Tl,In1,Out,MarkedTl).
mark_repeats([],In,In,[]).
mark_repeats(const(C),In,In,const(C)).

APPENDIX IV REDUCTION RULES

id(X) ---> id(Y) =>> Res :-
  global(X,DefX) ,
  global(Y,DefY) ,
  DefX ---> DefY =>> Res.

id(X) =>> Def :-
  global(X,Def) , !.

id(X) =>> _ :-
  nl ,
  write('not defined: ') ,
  write(X) , nl , abort.

cI ---> X =>> Res :-
  X =>> Res.

cY ---> X =>> Res :-
  X ---> (cY ---> X) =>> Res.

cHD ---> (X : Y) =>> Res :- ! ,
  X =>> Res.

cHD ---> X =>> Res :-
  X =>> (Hd : Tl) , ! ,
  Hd =>> Res.

cTL ---> (X : Y) =>> Res :- ! ,
  Y =>> Res.

```
cTL ---> X =>> Res :-
  X =>> (Hd : Tl) , ! ,
  Tl =>> Res.

cCHAR ---> X =>> Res :-
  type_check(char(X),Res).

cFAILURE ---> X =>> Res :-
  type_check(failure(X),Res).

cLOGICAL ---> X =>> Res :-
  type_check(logical(X),Res).

cFUNCTION ---> X =>> Res :-
  type_check(function(X),Res).

cNUMBER ---> X =>> Res :-
  type_check(num(X),Res).

cNOT ---> X =>> Res :-
  X =>> Rx , ! ,
  choose(Rx,logical(false),logical(true),Res).

cNEGATE ---> X =>> Res :-
  arith(sub,num(0),X,Res).

num(X) ---> Y =>> num(X).

logical(X) ---> Y =>> logical(X).

char(X) ---> Y =>> char(X).

nil ---> X =>> nil.

C ---> X =>> C ---> X :-
  arity(C,D) ,
  D >= 2 , !.

id(X) ---> Y =>> Res :-
  global(X,Def) , ! ,
  Def ---> Y =>> Res.
```

```
id(X) ---> Y =>> Res :-
  nl ,
  write('not defined: ') ,
  write(X) , nl , abort.


Y ---> id(X) =>> Res :-
  global(X,Def) , ! ,
  Y ---> Def =>> Res.

Y ---> id(X) =>> Res :-
  nl ,
  write('not defined: ') ,
  write(X) , nl , Y ---> fail =>> Res.

(X : Y) ---> num(1) =>> Res :- ! ,
  X =>> Res.

(X : Y) ---> num(Z) =>> Res :- ! ,
  Z > 1 ,
  Z1 is Z - 1 ,
  Y ---> num(Z1) =>> Res.

(X : Y) ---> Z =>> Res :-
  Z =>> num(Num) , ! ,
  X : Y ---> num(Num) =>> Res.

cK ---> X ---> Y =>> Res :-
  X =>> Res.

cU_s ---> X ---> (Y : Z) =>> Res :- ! ,
  X ---> Y ---> Z =>> Res.
cU_s ---> X ---> Y =>> Res :-
  Y =>> (Hd : Tl) , ! ,
  X ---> Hd ---> Tl =>> Res.
cU_s ---> X ---> Y =>> fail.

cAND ---> X ---> Y =>> Res :-
  X =>> Rx , ! ,
  choose(Rx,Y,logical(false),Res).
```

```
cOR ---> X ---> Y =>> Res :-
  X =>> Rx , ! ,
  choose(Rx,logical(true),Y,Res).

cEQ ---> X ---> Y =>> logical(Res) :-
  X =>> Rx , ! ,
  Y =>> Ry , ! ,
  eqnormal(Rx,Ry,true,false,Res).

cNEQ ---> X ---> Y =>> logical(Res) :-
  X =>> Rx , ! ,
  Y =>> Ry , ! ,
  eqnormal(Rx,Ry,false,true,Res).

cAPPEND ---> nil ---> Z =>> Z :- !.
cAPPEND ---> (X : Y) ---> Z =>> (X : Res) :- ! ,
  cAPPEND ---> Y ---> Z =>> Res.
cAPPEND ---> X ---> Y =>> Res :-
  X =>> Resx , ! ,
  not same(X,Resx) ,
  cAPPEND ---> Resx ---> Y =>> Res.

cLSE ---> X ---> Y =>> Res :-
  cNOT ---> (cGR ---> X ---> Y) =>> Res , !.

cGRE ---> X ---> Y =>> Res :-
  cNOT ---> (cLS ---> X ---> Y) =>> Res , !.

cLS ---> X ---> Y =>> Res :-
  arith(ls,X,Y,Res) , !.

cGR ---> X ---> Y =>> Res :-
  arith(gr,X,Y,Res) , !.

cADD ---> X ---> Y =>> Res :-
  arith(add,X,Y,Res) , !.

cSUB ---> X ---> Y =>> Res :-
  arith(sub,X,Y,Res) , !.
```

```
cMULT ---> X ---> Y =>> Res :-
  arith(mult,X,Y,Res) , !.

cDIV ---> X ---> Y =>> Res :-
  arith(div,X,Y,Res) , !.

cCONDF ---> X ---> Y =>> Res :-
  X =>> Rx , ! ,
  cond_fail(Rx,Y,Res).

C ---> X ---> Y =>> C ---> X ---> Y :-
  arity(C,D) ,
  D >= 3 , !.

cCOND ---> X ---> Y ---> Z =>> Res :-
  X =>> Resx , ! ,
  choose(Resx,Y,Z,Res).

cMATCH ---> nil ---> Y ---> Z =>> Res :-
  match(nil,Z,Y,Res).
cMATCH ---> num(X) ---> Y ---> Z =>> Res :-
  match(num(X),Z,Y,Res).
cMATCH ---> char(X) ---> Y ---> Z =>> Res :-
  match(char(X),Z,Y,Res).
cMATCH ---> logical(X) ---> Y ---> Z =>> Res :-
  match(logical(X),Z,Y,Res).
cMATCH ---> X ---> Y ---> Z =>> Res :-
  X =>> Redx , ! ,
  Z =>> Redz , ! ,
  eqnormal(Redx,Redz,Y,fail,Req) , ! ,
  Req =>> Res.

cS_p ---> X ---> Y ---> Z =>> Res :-
  (X ---> Z) : (Y ---> Z) =>> Res.

cB_p ---> X ---> Y ---> Z =>> Res :-
  X : (Y ---> Z) =>> Res.

cC_p ---> X ---> Y ---> Z =>> Res :-
  X ---> Z : Y =>> Res.
```

cS ---> X ---> Y ---> Z =>> Res :-
  X ---> Z ---> (Y ---> Z) =>> Res.

cB ---> X ---> Y ---> Z =>> Res :-
  X ---> (Y ---> Z) =>> Res.

cC ---> X ---> Y ---> Z =>> Res :-
  X ---> Z ---> Y =>> Res.

C ---> X ---> Y ---> Z =>> C ---> X ---> Y ---> Z :-
  arity(C,D) ,
  D >= 4 , !.

cS1 ---> W ---> X ---> Y ---> Z =>> Res :-
  W ---> (X ---> Z) ---> (Y ---> Z) =>> Res.

cB1 ---> W ---> X ---> Y ---> Z =>> Res :-
  W ---> X ---> (Y ---> Z) =>> Res.

cC1 ---> W ---> X ---> Y ---> Z =>> Res :-
  W ---> (X ---> Z) ---> Y =>> Res.

X ---> Y ---> Z =>> Res :-
  X ---> Y =>> Rxy ,
  not same(X ---> Y,Rxy) , ! ,
  Rxy ---> Z =>> Res.

X =>> X.

% The following predicates are used by various combinators
% and constitute a "lower level" of the reduction machine,
% a sort of microcode

same(X,X).

choose(logical(true),Y,Z,Res) :-
  Y =>> Res , !.
choose(logical(false),Y,Z,Res) :-
  Z =>> Res , !.
choose(X,Y,Z,fail).

```
match(X,Y,Z,Res) :-
  Y =>> Ry , ! ,
  eqnormal(X,Ry,Z,fail,R) , ! ,
  R =>> Res , !.

eqnormal(X,Y,T,F,T) :-
  equals(X,Y) , !.
eqnormal(X,Y,T,F,F).

equals(num(X),num(X)).
equals(char(X),char(X)).
equals(logical(X),logical(X)).
equals(nil,nil).
equals((A : B),(X : Y)) :-
  A =>> Reda ,
  X =>> Redx ,
  equals(Reda,Redx) , ! ,
  equals(B,Y).

is_failure((X ---> Y)) :-
  is_failure(X).
is_failure(fail).

is_function((X ---> Y)) :- is_function(X).
is_function(X) :- arity(X,_).
```

% The clauses defining arity are used to check whether an
% expression may not already be in head normal form

```
arity(cI,1).
arity(cY,1).
arity(cV,1).
arity(cHD,1).
arity(cTL,1).
arity(cNOT,1).
arity(cFUNCTION,1).
arity(cCHAR,1).
arity(cLOGICAL,1).
arity(cNUMBER,1).
arity(cFAILURE,1).
arity(cK,2).
```

```
arity(cU,2).
arity(cU_s,2).
arity(cEQ,2).
arity(cNEQ,2).
arity(cAND,2).
arity(cOR,2).
arity(cAPPEND,2).
arity(cCONDF,2).
arity(cSUB,2).
arity(cADD,2).
arity(cMULT,2).
arity(cDIV,2).
arity(cGRE,2).
arity(cLSE,2).
arity(cLS,2).
arity(cGR,2).
arity(cS,3).
arity(cC,3).
arity(cB,3).
arity(cS_p,3).
arity(cCOND,3).
arity(cMATCH,3).
arity(cB_p,3).
arity(cC_p,3).
arity(cS,3).
arity(cS1,4).
arity(cB1,4).
arity(cC1,4).


type_check(Form,logical(true)) :- Form , !.
type_check(Form,logical(false)).

char(X) :- X =>> char(_).

logical(X) :- X =>> logical(_).

num(X) :- X =>> num(_).

failure(X) :- X =>> Rx , ! , is_failure(Rx).
```

% "list" is a pre-defined HASL function
list(X) :- id(list) ---> X =>> logical(true).

function(X) :- X =>> Rx , ! , is_function(Rx).

add(num(X),num(Y),num(Z)) :- Z is X + Y , !.
add(X,Y,fail).

sub(num(X),num(Y),num(Z)) :- Z is X - Y , !.
sub(X,Y,fail).

mult(num(X),num(Y),num(Z)) :- Z is X * Y , !.
mult(X,Y,fail).

div(num(X),num(Y),num(Z)) :- Z is X / Y , !.
div(X,Y,fail).

eq(X,Y) :- X =:= Y.

gr(num(X),num(Y),logical(true)) :- X > Y , !.
gr(num(X),num(Y),logical(false)) :- !.
gr(X,Y,fail).

ls(num(X),num(Y),logical(true)) :- X < Y , !.
ls(num(X),num(Y),logical(false)) :- !.
ls(X,Y,fail).

cond_fail(X,Y,X) :- not is_failure(X) , !.
cond_fail(_,Y,Ry) :- Y =>> Ry.

arith(Operation,X,Y,Res) :-
  X =>> Rx ,
  Y =>> Ry ,
  arithop(Operation,Rx,Ry,Res).

arithop(add,X,Y,Z) :-
  add(X,Y,Z).
arithop(sub,X,Y,Z) :-
  sub(X,Y,Z).
arithop(mult,X,Y,Z) :-
  mult(X,Y,Z).

```
arithop(div,X,Y,Z) :-
  div(X,Y,Z).
arithop(ls,X,Y,Z) :-
  ls(X,Y,Z).
arithop(gr,X,Y,Z) :-
  gr(X,Y,Z).
```

% reduce to normal form

```
num(X) >>> num(X) :-  !.
```

```
char(X) >>> char(X) :-  !.
```

```
logical(X) >>> logical(X) :- !.
```

```
X >>> fail :- is_failure(X), !.
```

```
nil >>> nil :- !.
```

```
Hd : Tl >>> Nhd : Ntl :-
  Hd =>> Redhd , ! ,
  Redhd >>> Nhd ,
  Tl =>> Redtl ,
  Redtl >>> Ntl.
```

```
X >>> X.
```

%predicates for output of HASL values

```
is_string(nil) :- !.
is_string(char(_):Y) :- is_string(Y).
```

```
is_list(nil) :- !.
is_list(_:Y) :- is_list(Y).
```

```
write_hasl(X) :-
  is_string(X), !,
  write('''),
  write_string(X),
  write(''').
```

```
write_hasl(X:Y) :-
  is_list(X:Y),
  write('['),
  write_list(X:Y),
  write_hasl(']').
write_hasl(nil) :-
  write('[]').
write_hasl(num(X)) :-
  write(X).
write_hasl(logical(X)) :-
  write(X).
write_hasl(char(X)) :-
  write('%'),
  write(X).
write_hasl(fail) :-
  write(fail).
write_hasl(X) :-
  write(X).

write_string(nil) :- !.
write_string(char(X):Y) :- write(X), write_string(Y).

write_list(nil) :- !.
write_list(X:nil) :- !, write_hasl(X).
write_list(X:Y) :- write_hasl(X), write(','), write_list(Y).

show(Source) :- hasl(Source,Value) , ! ,
    Value >>> Nvalue , nl , write_hasl(Nvalue).
```

QUTE:

A FUNCTIONAL LANGUAGE

BASED ON UNIFICATION

Masahiko Sato and Takafumi Sakurai

Department of Information Science
Faculty of Science, University of Tokyo

ABSTRACT

A new programming language called Qute is introduced. Qute is a functional programming language which permits parallel evaluation. While most functional programming languages use pattern matching as the basic variable-value binding mechanism, Qute uses unification as its binding mechanism. Since unification is bidirectional, as opposed to pattern matching which is unidirectional, Qute becomes a more powerful functional programming language than most existing functional languages. This approach enables the natural *unification* of logic programming languages and functional programming languages. In Qute it is possible to write a program which is very much like one written in a conventional logic programming language, say, Prolog. At the same time, it is possible to write a Qute program which looks like an ML (a particular functional language) program. Qute programs can be evaluated in parallel (and-parallelism) with the same result obtained irrespective of the particular order of evaluation. This is guaranteed by the Church-Rosser property enjoyed by the evaluation algorithm. A completely formal semantics of Qute is given in this paper.

1 INTRODUCTION

In this paper we introduce a new programming language called Qute and define its semantics formally. The name Qute may be confusing to some readers, since we have already described previous versions of Qute in [9]. The new Qute, which we describe in this paper, is rather different from the previous ones although it inherits many things from them. In spite of this, we have decided to also call the new language Qute.

Qute is a functional programming language which permits parallel evaluation. While most functional languages use pattern matching as their basic variable-value binding mechanism, Qute uses unification as its binding mechanism. Since unification is bidirectional, as opposed to pattern matching which is unidirectional, Qute becomes a more powerful functional language than most existing functional languages.

This approach enables the natural *unification* of logic programming languages and functional languages. In Qute it is possible to write a program which is very much like one written in conventional logic programming language, say, Prolog ([6]). At the same time, it is possible to write a Qute program which looks like an ML program ([4]).

In the design of Qute we tried to minimize the number of basic concepts, so that the language is easy to learn and specify. These concepts were selected from logical considerations, and as a result some of them were inherited from Concurrent Prolog ([11], [12]) and ML. In particular, we imported the concepts of 'parallel and' and 'sequential and' from Concurrent Prolog. Furthermore, Qute has 'if-then-else' as one of the basic programming constructs. Though the construct also is selected from the logical consideration, it acts as synchronization mechanism in 'parallel and'.

A Qute program can be evaluated in parallel (and-parallelism only) and the same result is obtained irrespective of the particular order of evaluation. This is guaranteed by the Church-Rosser property enjoyed by the evaluation algorithm. Although it is possible to orthogonally add nondeterministic features to Qute, this point is not discussed in this paper.

Qute is a programming language that evaluates an expression under a certain environment. The evaluation process can be considered as a reduction process of the given expression, and the evaluation stops when the expression has been reduced to a *normal expression* for which no more reduction is possible. Through the process of evaluation the given environment is also changed to another environment by unification. Therefore the result of an evaluation can be considered as a pair of a normal expression and an environment. We explain these points in the following order. In 2 we define the syntax of Qute, and in 3 we define the fundamental concepts of unification and environment. In 4 we explain the semantics of Qute informally and in 5 we give some examples. In 6 we give a completely formal semantics of Qute.

A translator of a Qute program into a Prolog program has been implemented under TOPS-20 on a DEC 2060. The translator is written in DEC-10 Prolog.

2 SYNTAX OF QUTE

2.1 Symbolic Expressions

We define the domain of symbolic expressions (*sexps*, for short) which is used to define the semantics of Qute. Namely, later in this paper we give the formal semantics of Qute by interpreting Qute programs in the domain of sexps. Symbolic expressions are constructed by the following clauses:

1. $*$ (*nil*) is a sexp.
2.   If s and t are sexps then $[s \cdot t]$ is a sexp.
3.   If s and t are sexps then $(s \cdot t)$ is a sexp.

All the sexps are constructed only by the iterated applications of the above three clauses, and sexps constructed differently are distinct.

We introduce dot notation and list notation as notations for sexps. (We use the symbol '$\equiv$' as an informal equality symbol and reserve the symbol '$=$' as the formal equality sign used in the programming language Qute.)

$$[. \, x] \equiv x$$
$$[x_1, \cdots, x_n \cdot x_{n+1}] \equiv [x_1 \cdot [x_2, \cdots, x_n \cdot x_{n+1}]] \ (n \geq 1)$$
$$[x_1, \cdots, x_n] \equiv [x_1, \cdots, x_n \cdot *] \ (n \geq 0)$$

2.2 Symbols and Variables

Although it is possible to define the concept of an expression as a string of characters defined by a certain set of grammatical rules, we will define the concept of an expression as a certain sexp. We take this approach only because the formal semantics of Qute which we explain in section 6 can be conveniently given for an expression represented as a sexp. We

133

first define two auxiliary concepts of a symbol and a variable.

A sexp of the form $(*.t)$ is called a *symbol*. Symbols are used to represent basic data objects, and for this paper, we assume that the domain of integers and the domain of strings of ASCII characters are represented by two disjoint sets of symbols. (How they are actually represented is not important.) We use usual decimal notation for integers, and a string of characters will be represented by enclosing it between a pair of '""' signs. Thus, for example,

> "apple"

is a symbol which represents a word of length 5. We also choose a certain symbol (which is neither an integer nor a string) and call it *unit*. We use the notation '()' to denote the unit. From now on we will consider only those symbols which are either a unit, an integer or a string.

A sexp of the form ("var" . s) where s is a string, is called a *pure variable*. We define a *variable* by the following inductive clauses.

(i)   A pure variable is a variable.

(ii)   If x is a variable then ("free" . x) is a variable.

For a string " $\cdots$ " we use $\cdots$ to denote the pure variable ("var" . " $\cdots$ "). Thus, for example,

> X

denotes the pure variable ("var" . "X").

A sexp of the form ("gvar" . s) where s is a string, is called a *global variable*. We use a similar convention to denote global variables. In order to avoid notational ambiguity, we reserve strings whose lengths are at least 2 and which begin with a lower case character for global variables. Thus 'foo' is a global variable, while 'x' is a pure variable. (Global variables are of less significance. The reason we need them is explained in section 2.5.)

In the following we call both variables and global variables simply variables and we use x, y, z etc. to denote variables.

2.3 Expressions

We define an *expression* by the following inductive definition.

(E1) A variable is an expression.

(E2) A symbol is an expression.

(E3) * is an expression.

If a, b, c are all expressions then the following are also expressions:

(E4) $[a . b]$

(E5) ("and" . $(a . b)$)

(E6) ("lambda" . $(a . b)$)

(E7) ("seqand" . $(a . b)$)

(E8) ("if" . $(a . (b . c))$)

(E9) ("not" . a)

(E10)("apply" . $(a . b)$)

(E11)("equal" . $(a . b)$)

We use a, b, c, d etc. to denote expressions. We call an expression defined by (E6) a *function*, (E7) a *sequential-and*, (E8) an *if-then-else*, (E9) a *negation*, (E10) an *application*, and (E11) a *unification*.

2.4 Abbreviations for Expressions

We introduce the following abbreviations for expressions:

(a) for a
$\#x$ for ("free" . x)
$\#^0 x$ for x
$\#^{n+1}x$ for ("free" . $\#^n x$) $(n \geq 0)$
a, b for ("and" . $(a . b)$)
a, b, c for $a, (b, c)$ etc.
$\lambda a.b$ for ("lambda" . $(a . b)$)
$a; b$ for ("seqand" . $(a . b)$)
$a; b; c$ for $a; (b; c)$ etc.
if a **then** b **else** c for ("if" . $(a . (b . c))$)
$\neg a$ for ("not" . a)
$a b$ for ("apply" . $(a . b)$)
$a b c$ for $(a b) c$ etc.
$<a>$ for $(\lambda().a)()$
$a = b$ for ("equal" . $(a . b)$)
fail for $0 = 1$

135

2.5 Free Variables

For an expression a, we define the set $FV(a)$ of *free variables in* a. $FV(a)$ is defined by $FV_0(a)$ where $FV_n(a)$ $(n \geq 0)$ is defined as follows:

$a \equiv \#^k x$ where x is a pure variable $\Rightarrow$

$$FV_n(a) \equiv \begin{cases} \phi & \text{if } k < n \\ \{\#^{k-n} x\} & \text{if } k \geq n \end{cases}$$

a is a global variable $\Rightarrow FV_n(a) \equiv \{a\}$
a is a symbol $\Rightarrow FV_n(a) \equiv \phi$
$FV_n(*) \equiv \phi$
$FV_n([a . b]) \equiv FV_n(a) \cup FV_n(b)$
$FV_n(a, b) \equiv FV_n(a) \cup FV_n(b)$
$FV_n(\lambda a . b) \equiv FV_{n+1}(a) \cup FV_{n+1}(b)$
$FV_n(a; b) \equiv FV_n(a) \cup FV_n(b)$
$FV_n(\text{if } a \text{ then } b \text{ else } c) \equiv FV_{n+1}(a) \cup FV_{n+1}(b) \cup FV_n(c)$
$FV_n(\neg a) \equiv FV_n(a)$
$FV_n(a \ b) \equiv FV_n(a) \cup FV_n(b)$
$FV_n(a = b) \equiv FV_n(a) \cup FV_n(b)$

This definition means that pure variables appearing in a function or an if/then-part of an if-then-else are 'localized', but the effect can be canceled by #s preceding the variables. (Global variables are introduced to avoid writing many #s.) When $\lambda a . b$ is given, we call the free variables of the function its *non-local variables* and the other variables *local variables*. When **if** a **then** b **else** c is given, we call the free variables of **if** a **then** () **else** () non-local variables of the if-part, the free variables of **if** () **then** b **else** () non-local variables of the then-part, and the other variables of **if** a **then** b **else** () local variables of the if/then-part of the if-then-else. (How the non-local variables of an if-then-else are used is explained in section 4.2.)

Example

Consider the expressions:

$a \equiv$ **if** $\#x = *$ **then** $\#y$ **else** b
$b \equiv$ **if** $\#x = [X1.X2]$ **then** c **else fail**
$c \equiv (\lambda u . foo(u, \#X1, \#\#y))(\#z, X2)$

Then we have:

$FV(a)$
$\equiv FV_1(\#x = *) \cup FV_1(\#y) \cup FV(b)$
$\equiv \{x\} \cup \{y\} \cup FV_1(\#x = [X1.X2]) \cup FV_1(c) \cup FV(0 = 1)$
$\equiv \{x\} \cup \{y\} \cup \{x\} \cup FV_2(u) \cup FV_2(foo(u, \#X1, \#\#y)) \cup FV_1((\#z, X2)) \cup \phi$

$$\equiv \{x\} \cup \{y\} \cup \{x\} \cup \phi \cup \{foo,y\} \cup \{z\} \cup \phi$$
$$\equiv \{x,y,z,foo\}$$

and:

> x is a non-local variable of the if-part of *a*
> y is a non-local variable of the then-part of *a*
> x is a non-local variable of the if-part of *b*
> foo, y, and z are non-local variables of the then-part of *b*
> X1 and X2 are local variables of the if/then part of *b*

□

3 UNIFICATION AND ENVIRONMENTS

As we explained in the introduction, unification plays a fundamental role in our programming language Qute. Because unification enjoys a kind of Church-Rosser property, Qute is a functional language which permits parallel evaluation. Martelli and Montanari [8] introduced a nondeterministic unification algorithm and proved the Church-Rosser theorem for the algorithm. Lassez and Maher [7] utilized the Church-Rosser property for unification, and proved the equivalence of various resolution strategies elegantly. Jaffar [5] considered the unification problem for the domain over regular infinite trees and proved the Church-Rosser theorem for his algorithm.

Our unification algorithm, which we are about to explain, constitutes a conceptual simplification of the algorithms by Martelli and Montanari [8] and by Jaffar [5].

3.1 Unification

We first define a *pattern* by the following inductive definition:

(P1) A variable is a pattern.

(P2) A symbol is a pattern.

(P3) * is a pattern.

(P4) If p, q are patterns then $[p \cdot q]$ is a pattern.

(P5) If p, q are patterns then p, q is a pattern.

(P6) If a, b are expressions then $\lambda a.b$ is a pattern.

We use p, q, r to denote patterns. Note that patterns can be classified into 6 mutually disjoint *categories* (P1 - P6).

We define an *equation* as follows. There are two types of equations: *marked* and *unmarked*. An *unmarked equation* is a finite, nonempty set of patterns. An unmarked equation is *simple* if

137

all of its members are variables. For a simple unmarked equation A, the singleton set $\{A\}$ is called a *mark*. A finite set such that (i) its members are patterns or marks and (ii) it contains at least one mark is called a *marked equation*. We use A, B, C to denote equations. Informally an unmarked equation means that all the members of the equation should be equated. The meaning of a marked equation is explained in section 6.2.

Consider two distinct patterns which are not variables. They are defined to be *incompatible* if: (i) they are two distinct symbols, (ii) they are two different functions or (iii) they belong to different *categories*. An equation is said to be *inconsistent* if it contains two patterns which are incompatible.

A finite (possibly empty) set of equations is called a *system of equations* or simply a *system*. A system is said to be *inconsistent* if it contains an inconsistent equation; otherwise it is said to be *consistent*. We use Γ, Δ, Π etc. to denote systems. For a system Γ we define a relation $\to_\Gamma$ on Γ as follows. Let A and B be equations in Γ. Then $A \to_\Gamma B$ if and only if there exists a pattern p and a variable x such that (i) $p \in A$, (ii) $x \in B$, (iii) p belongs to the category (P4) or (P5) and (iv) $x \in FV(p)$. A system Γ is said to *contain a loop* if there exist a sequence of equations $A_1, \cdots, A_n$ $(n \geq 2)$ in Γ such that

$$A_1 \to_\Gamma A_2 \to_\Gamma \cdots \to_\Gamma A_n$$

and $A_1 \equiv A_n$; otherwise Γ is said to be *loop free*.

We now define a binary relation $\Gamma < \Delta$ between systems by the following three clauses.

(1) If A, B are members of Γ and A, B have a variable in common then $\Gamma < (\Gamma - \{A\} - \{B\}) \cup \{A \cup B\}$.

(2) If $\{[p \cdot q], [p' \cdot q']\} \subseteq A \in \Gamma$ then $\Gamma < \Gamma \cup \{\{p, p'\}, \{q, q'\}\}$.

(3) If $\{(p, q), (p', q')\} \subseteq A \in \Gamma$ then $\Gamma < \Gamma \cup \{\{p, p'\}, \{q, q'\}\}$.

If $\Gamma < \Delta$ and $\Gamma \not\equiv \Delta$ we say that Γ *reduces* to Δ. In this case Γ is said to be *reducible*; otherwise Γ is said to be *irreducible*. We let $\leq$ be the reflexive and transitive closure of the relation $<$. We then have the following theorems.

Theorem 1.

If $\Gamma \leq \Delta_1$ and $\Gamma \leq \Delta_2$ then $\Delta_1 \leq \Pi$ and $\Delta_2 \leq \Pi$ for some Π.

Theorem 2.

There is no infinite sequence of systems Δ_i $(i \geq 0)$ such that Δ_i reduces to Δ_{i+1} for all i.

Theorem 3.

For any system Γ *there uniquely exists an irreducible* Δ *such that* $\Gamma \leq \Delta$.

We will denote the Δ in Theorem 3 by Γ^* and we will call it the *solution* of Γ.

Theorem 1 states that the reduction process (or unification process) has the Church-Rosser property and Theorem 2 states that the reduction process always terminates. Theorem 3 is just a consequence of Theorems 1 and 2. We do not prove these theorems here, since they can be proved similarly as [8].

3.2 Environments

By the results of the previous subsection, the unification process of the given system Γ ends up with the unique solution Γ^*. We then have one of the following three mutually disjoint conditions.

(i) Γ^* is inconsistent.

(ii) Γ^* is consistent and contains a loop.

(iii) Γ^* is consistent and is loop free.

Condition (i) means the failure of unification. Condition (ii) corresponds to the failure by the occur-check of the usual unification algorithm, so that in this case the solution must be regarded as unacceptable if we were to solve the equation in the *finite* sexps. (This also means that it is possible to separate the occur-check from the unification process.) On the other hand the same solution becomes acceptable if we interpret it in the domain of *regular infinite* sexps. In this paper we take the latter position, and consider that condition (ii) gives an acceptable solution. (The following text remains valid and is even simpler if we consider (ii) as unacceptable.)

We therefore define an *environment* as a consistent, irreducible system. So, for any system Γ, Γ^* becomes an environment if and only if it is consistent. We use E, F, G to denote environments. An environment E is said to be *suspended* if E contains an equation A such that (i) it contains two distinct marks or (ii) it contains a mark and a non-variable pattern.

The value of a pattern is determined relative to an environment. For instance, if $E \equiv \{\{x, y, 1\}, \{z, 2\}\}$ then the value of $[x, y, z]$ is $[1, 1, 2]$. In general, the *value of* a pattern p *in* the environment E, which we will denote by p_E, is defined as follows.

(i)   If p is a variable and there exists no equation in E which contains p then $p_E \equiv p$.

(ii)   If p is a variable and there exists an equation A in E which contains p then:

    (ii.i)   if A is simple then $p_E \equiv p$,

    (ii.ii) else if there is a loop containing A then $p_E \equiv p$,

    (ii.iii) else $p_E \equiv q_E$ where q is a non-variable pattern in A.

(iii)   If p is a symbol then $p_E \equiv p$.

(iv) $*_E \equiv *$.

(v) $[p \cdot q]_E \equiv [p_E \cdot q_E]$.

(vi) $(p, q)_E \equiv (p_E, q_E)$.

(vii) $(\lambda a \cdot b)_E \equiv \lambda a \cdot b$.

If x is a variable and satisfies (i) or (ii.i), we say that x is an undefined variable in E.

4 SEMANTICS OF QUTE

Here, we explain the semantics of Qute informally.

4.1 Evaluable Subexpressions

For an expression a, we define the set Σa of all the *evaluable subexpressions* of a as follows.

If p is $*$, a symbol, a variable or a function then $\Sigma p \equiv \phi$

$\Sigma[a \cdot b] \equiv \Sigma a \cup \Sigma b$

$\Sigma(a, b) \equiv \Sigma a \cup \Sigma b$

$$\Sigma(a;b) \equiv \begin{cases} \Sigma a & \text{if } \Sigma a \not\equiv \phi \\ \Sigma b & \text{if } \Sigma a \equiv \phi \text{ and } \Sigma b \not\equiv \phi \\ \{a;b\} & \text{if } \Sigma a \equiv \Sigma b \equiv \phi \end{cases}$$

$\Sigma(\text{if } a \text{ then } b \text{ else } c) \equiv \{\text{if } a \text{ then } b \text{ else } c\}$

$\Sigma \neg a \equiv \{\neg a\}$

$$\Sigma(a\ b) \equiv \begin{cases} \{a\ b\} & \text{if } \Sigma a \equiv \Sigma b \equiv \phi \\ \Sigma a \cup \Sigma b & \text{otherwise} \end{cases}$$

$$\Sigma(a = b) \equiv \begin{cases} \{a = b\} & \text{if } \Sigma a \equiv \Sigma b \equiv \phi \\ \Sigma a \cup \Sigma b & \text{otherwise} \end{cases}$$

It is easy to check that for any expression a, $\Sigma a \equiv \phi$ if and only if a is a pattern. If $b \in \Sigma a$, we say that b is an *evaluable subexpression* of a.

Example

$$x = 1, f(g(x), y = h(x)), (z = [u, v]; k(z))$$

The evaluable subexpressions of this expression are

$$x = 1, g(x), h(x) \text{ and } z = [u, v]$$

☐

4.2 Semantics

The evaluation of an expression proceeds by selecting an evaluable subexpression nondeterministically and by reducing it following the rules which we explain in the following. If the reduced evaluable subexpression has evaluable subexpressions, they also are candidates for selection. If the reduction of an evaluable subexpression of a given expression fails, then the evaluation of the whole expression fails. The evaluation of an expression terminates when:

(i)   there are no more evaluable subexpressions, i.e. the expression is reduced to a pattern. (In this case, we say that the evaluation succeeds.)

(ii) the reduction of an evaluable subexpression fails.

(iii) every evaluable subexpression is suspended. (The condition of suspension is explained in the following.)

Although evaluable subexpressions may be selected nondeterministically, the result of the evaluation is unique so long as it terminates due to the Church-Rosser property.

Qute evaluates an expression relative to an environment, and the environment is changed as the evaluation proceeds.

As is evident from the definition of an evaluable subexpression, unification, sequential-and, application, if-then-else, and negation are all candidates for an evaluable subexpression. We explain when they become evaluable subexpressions and how they are reduced.

We say that *b* is a *renamed expression* of *a* (or, *a* is *renamed to b*) if *b* is obtained from *a* by substituting a new global variable for each free pure variable in *a* and removing one # from each non-global variable in *a* which is free and non-pure. (This operation is formally defined as ↓ in section 6.1.)

Example

$$X = Y, (\lambda Z. \text{foo}(\#X, Z, \#\#W))Y, \#X = Z$$

is renamed to

$X' = Y', (\lambda Z. foo(X', Z, \#W))Y', X = Z'$

where X', Y', and Z' are new global variables. $\square$

In the following examples, we use $\triangleright$ to represent one step of reduction.

1. unification

$a = b$ becomes an evaluable subexpression after a and b are reduced to patterns p and q. If E is an environment at that time, p and q are unified under E, i.e. $F \equiv (E \cup \{\{p,q\}\})^*$ is computed. If F is inconsistent, the reduction of $p = q$ fails. Otherwise, $p = q$ is reduced to p and further reductions proceed under F. The environment is changed only by unification.

Example

$z = [x . y], x = 1, y = 2$ in E_0
$\triangleright z, x = 1, y = 2$ in E_1
$\triangleright z, x, y = 2$ in E_2
$\triangleright z, x, y$ in E_3

where

$E_0 \equiv \phi$
$E_1 \equiv \{\{z, [x . y]\}\}$
$E_2 \equiv \{\{z, [x . y]\}, \{x, 1\}\}$
$E_3 \equiv \{\{z, [x . y]\}, \{x, 1\}, \{y, 2\}\}$

The value of z, x, y in E_3 is $[1 . 2]$, 1, 2.

Although this example shows only one possible order of reduction ($z = [x . y]$, $x = 1$, and $y = 2$ are evaluable subexpressions), the result is the same irrespective of the order of the reduction. This holds because of the Church-Rosser property of the unification algorithm. $\square$

2. sequential-and

In reducing $a; b$, a is reduced to a pattern p first and then b is reduced. If b is reduced to a pattern q, $p; q$ becomes an evaluable subexpression and is reduced to q.

Example

$z = [x . y]; x = 1; y = 2$ in E_0
$\triangleright z; x = 1; y = 2$ in E_1
$\triangleright z; x; y = 2$ in E_2
$\triangleright z; x; y$ in E_3
$\triangleright z; y$ in E_3
$\triangleright y$ in E_3

where E_0, E_1, E_2 and E_3 are the same as those of the previous

142

example.

Note that in this example the order of reductions is unique. (See the definition of evaluable subexpressions.) □

Logically, sequential-and can be defined as a function which takes p,q as an argument and returns q, that is, there is no problem in evaluating a and b of $a;b$ in parallel. It is necessary to give the order to the reductions only to control the side effects (e.g. read, write, $\cdots$).

3. application

$a\,b$ becomes an evaluable subexpression after a and b are reduced to patterns p and q. This means application is computed by call-by-value. If the value of p is $\lambda a\,.b$, a,b is renamed to a',b' to avoid collision of names. $p\,q$ is reduced to $a'=q;b'$, i.e. the formal parameter a' is bound to the actual parameter q by $a'=q$ and then the body b' is reduced.

Example

> cons(1,2)   in F_0
> ▷ $(x',y') = (1,2);$ $[x'.y']$ in F_0
> ▷ $(x',y');$ $[x'.y']$ in F_1
> ▷ $[x'.y']$ in F_1

where

> x' and y' are new global variables
> $F_0 \equiv \{\{cons, \lambda x,y\,.[x.y]\}\}$
> $F_1 \equiv F_0 \cup \{\{(x',y'), (1,2)\}, \{x', 1\}, \{y', 2\}\}$

The value of $[x'.y']$ in F_1 is $[1.2]$. □

4. If-then-else

Roughly speaking, **if** a **then** b **else** c is reduced to b if the evaluation of a succeeds and to c if the evaluation of a fails. This, however, is a problematic definition. We point out the problem by an example. Consider the evaluation of the expression:

(**if** $\#x = 0$ **then** 0 **else** 1), x = 1

In the empty environment. Both **if** $\#x = 0$ **then** 0 **else** 1 and x = 1 are evaluable subexpressions. If **if** $\#x = 0$ **then** 0 **else** 1 is reduced first, the evaluation of the if-part succeeds, and the environment is changed to $\{\{x, 0\}\}$. Then the reduction of x = 1 fails and the evaluation of the whole expression fails. If x = 1 is reduced first, **if** $\#x = 0$ **then** 0 **else** 1 is reduced under the environment $\{\{x, 1\}\}$. Therefore the evaluation of the if-part fails, and **if** $\#x = 0$ **then** 0 **else** 1 is reduced to 1. This contradicts the

Church-Rosser property which we are going to establish. Reconsider the former case. Intuitively, the if-part of **if** #x = 0 **then** 0 **else** 1 means x *is* 0, and we reduce it to know whether it holds or not. However, since x is an undefined variable at that time, the value of x may become 0, 1, or some other value later. That is, it is too early to decide whether x is not 0 or not. (The condition that x is not 0 cannot be explained in the environment.) Therefore the decision should be suspended until x is instantiated enough to decide whether x is 0 or not, i.e., in this case until x = 1 is reduced.

In general, **if** a **then** b **else** c is reduced as follows. Let E be an environment, V be the set of non-local variables of the if-part, FVL be the list of free variables in $\{x_E \mid x \in V\}$, and a', b' be the renamed expression of a, b. a' is evaluated under E. The following cases exist:

(1) The evaluation of a' succeeds: Let F be the environment after the evaluation.

   (1.1) FVL is not instantiated: This case means that the evaluation of a' will succeed whatever instantiation may be done on FVL. Therefore **if** a **then** b **else** c is immediately reduced to b' and further reductions proceed under F.

   (1.2) FVL is instantiated: In this case, there is a possibility that the reduction of other evaluable subexpressions may cause an instantiation of FVL which is incompatible with the current instantiation. Therefore the reduction of **if** a **then** b **else** c is suspended and further reductions proceed under E. (The environment is not changed.)

(2) The evaluation of a' fails: The evaluation will fail whatever instantiation may be done on FVL. Therefore **if** a **then** b **else** c is immediately reduced to c and further reductions proceed under E. (The environment is not changed.)

(3) The evaluation of a' is suspended: The reduction of **if** a **then** b **else** c is suspended and will be tried again later.

5. negation

Negation can be defined by if-then-else, that is,

   ¬a ≡ **if** a' **then** **fail** **else** ()

where a' is obtained from a by adding one # to the free, non-global variables of a. We include negation as a primitive

144

construct only for convenience.

5 EXAMPLES

In this section, we give some examples to show the expressiveness of Qute.

We use the abbreviation $a\ b \Leftarrow c$ for $a = \lambda b.c$ when a is a global variable. The evaluation of such an expression binds the function $\lambda b.c$ to the global variable a, and has the side effect of preserving the binding after the evaluation.

First, we give an easy example: quick sort.

Example 1

```
qsort X ⇐ qsort1(X, R, []); R.
qsort1(L, R, RO) ⇐
        if #L = [X . LO] then
                partition(LO, X, Lls, Lgt),
                qsort1(Lls, #R, [X . R1]), qsort1(Lgt, R1, #RO)
        else
                R = RO.
partition(L, X, Lls, Lgt) ⇐
        if #L = [XO . LO] then
                if less(#XO, ##X) then
                        ##Lls = [#XO . Lls1];
                        partition(#LO, ##X, Lls1, ##Lgt)
                else
                        #Lgt = [XO . Lgt1];
                        partition(LO, #X, #Lls, Lgt1)
        else
                Lls = Lgt = [].
```

The meaning of this program should be clear if regarded simply as a pure Prolog program. (However, see also Example 3.) □

In the following two examples, the sieve of Eratosthenes is implemented by a stream programming technique, but Example 2 is an ML-style program and Example 3 a Concurrent-Prolog-style program.

Example 2

```
primes() ⇐ outstream(sift(integers 2)).
integers n ⇐ (n, (λ (). integers(#n+1))).
sift (p, s) ⇐ (p, (λ (). sift(filter(#p, #s())))).
filter(p, (n, s)) ⇐
        if mod(#n, #p) = 0 then
                filter(#p, #s())
```

145

$$(n, (\lambda(). \text{ filter}(\#p, \#s())))).$$
outstream (n, s) $\Leftarrow$ write n; outstream(s()).

In this example, a stream is represented by a pair of an integer (which is the first element of the stream) and a function (which produces the tail of the stream when an argument () is supplied). Note that a function is a normal expression and can be passed as an argument of a function without causing a funarg problem (see [1]). □

Example 3

```
primes() ⇐ integers(2, s), sift(s, t), outstream t.
integers(n, [n . s]) ⇐ integers(n+1, s).
sift(s, t) ⇐
    if #s = [p . s1] then
        #t = [p . t1]; filter(p, s1, r), sift(r, t1)
    else
        fail.
filter(p, s, r) ⇐
    if #s = [n . s1] then
        if mod(#n, ##p) = 0 then
            filter(##p, #s1, ##r)
        else
            #r = [n . r1]; filter(#p, s1, r1)
    else
        fail.
outstream s ⇐
    if #s = [n . s1] then
        write n; outstream s1
    else
        ().
```

This is an example of parallel-and evaluation and the synchronization mechanism. In this example, a stream is represented by a list whose tail is undefined, that is, an incomplete data structure.

integers(2,s), sift(s,t), outstream t

In the definition of primes and

filter(p,s1,r), sift(r,t1)

in that of sift are evaluated in parallel, and the evaluation of the if-part (e.g. #s = [p . s1], #s = [n . s1]) succeeds and the then-part is evaluated only if the non-local variables of the if-part (e.g. s) are not instantiated by the evaluation of the if-part; otherwise, just before the variables are instantiated the evaluation of the if-then-else suspends and waits until they are instantiated through the evaluation of some other expression.

In Example 1, the then-part of the definition of qsort1 can be evaluated in parallel. In that case, the if-parts in the definitions of partition and qsort1 control the reduction of evaluable subexpressions similarly.

Therefore the if-part of the if-then-else works as the synchronization mechanism, which is similar to that of Parlog [3] and that of Concurrent Prolog in a sense. Though our first motivation was not to invent such a synchronization mechanism but to find the natural semantics, we obtained both as a result.

(Note: The formal semantics of Qute does not necessarily imply fair evaluation. For example, consider the evaluation of primes(). It is first reduced to three evaluable subexpressions integers(2,s), sift(s,t) and outstream t. An implementation which continues to reduce integers(2,s) and never reduce the other two evaluable subexpressions is a correct implementation. An actual implementation of Qute provides fair evaluation and tries to reduce all the three evaluable subexpressions little-by-little.) □

Example 4 is a program which produces a hamming sequence, that is, an ordered sequence of natural numbers of the form $2^i 3^j 5^k$.

Example 4

```
hamming() ⇐ ham S, outstream S.
ham S ⇐
    S = [1 . ST];
    smul(S, 2, S2), smul(S, 3, S3), smul(S, 5, S5),
    select(S2, S3, S5, ST).
smul(S, N, MS) ⇐
    if #S = [X . ST] then
        #MS = [#N×X . MST];
        smul(ST, #N, MST)
    else
        fail.
select(S2, S3, S5, S) ⇐
    if #S2 = [M2 . S2T], #S3 = [M3 . S3T],
        #S5 = [M5 . S5T] then
        #S = [Min = min(M2, M3, M5) . ST];
        select(news(Min, M2, S2T),
               news(Min, M3, S3T),
               news(Min, M5, S5T),
               ST)
```

```
            else
                fail.
    min(X, Y, Z) ⇐ min2(min2(X, Y), Z).
    min2(X, Y) ⇐
        if less(#X, #Y) then #X
        else Y.
    news(Min, M, S) ⇐
        if less(#Min, #M) then [#M . #S]
        else S.
    outstream S ⇐
        if #S = [X . S1] then
                write X; outstream S1
        else
                ().
```

The technique used in this program is the same as that of Example 3. □

The last example is a fixed point combinator due to Carolyn Talcott [13].

Example 5

```
    Rec = λ f. (λ g. (λ x. ##f(#g #g)x))
                (λ g. (λ x. ##f(#g #g)x));
    Append = λ App . (λ (x, y). (
        if #x = [] then #y
        else if #x = [x . X] then [x . ##App(X, #y)]
        else fail
    ));
    (Rec Append)([1, 2], [3, 4]).
```

Rec is a fixed point combinator, that is, it satisfies

$$(\text{Rec } F)X \equiv F(\text{Rec } F)X$$

for any patterns F and X. This equation is proved as follows. Let G be

$$\lambda g. \lambda x. F(\#g\ \#g)x,$$

then

$$(\text{Rec } F) \equiv \lambda x. F(G\ G)x$$
$$(G\ G) \equiv \lambda x. F(G\ G)x$$

by some steps of reduction. (To be strict, if F has free variables, it is necessary to add extra #s to the free variables of F in the above functions.) Therefore,

$$(\text{Rec } F)X \equiv F(G\ G)X \equiv F(\text{Rec } F)X.$$

The essential difference from the Curry's Y-combinator (see [2]) is that this works even in the case of normal order reduction, that is, call-by-value evaluation. Note that the evaluation does not terminate if we use the Y-combinator as below:

$$Y = \lambda\, f.\, (\lambda\, x.\, \#f(x\ x))$$
$$(\lambda\, x.\, \#f(x\ x));$$
$$\text{Append} = \cdots;$$
$$(Y\ \text{Append})([1, 2], [3, 4])$$

□

6 FORMAL SEMANTICS

Here, we present a completely formal semantics of Qute. First we give some definitions and then define the semantics.

6.1 Definitions

An element of the free monoid $\{0, 1\}^*$ is called a *path*. We use σ, τ etc. to denote paths. The *empty path* (i.e., empty word) is denoted by Λ. For a path σ and sexps s, u, we define $s_\sigma[u\,]$ as follows:

$$s_\Lambda[u\,] \equiv u$$
$$(s \,.\, t)_{0\sigma}[u\,] \equiv (s_\sigma[u\,] \,.\, t)$$
$$[s \,.\, t]_{0\sigma}[u\,] \equiv [s_\sigma[u\,] \,.\, t\,]$$
$$(s \,.\, t)_{1\sigma}[u\,] \equiv (s \,.\, t_\sigma[u\,])$$
$$[s \,.\, t]_{1\sigma}[u\,] \equiv [s \,.\, t_\sigma[u\,]]$$

Informally, $s_\sigma[u\,]$ means the result of substituting u for the sub-sexp of s which can be reached from the root of s by following the path σ. (Here, the character 0 (1) in the path σ means to take the left (right, resp.) subtree.)

We sometimes regard a path σ as a sexp by the following identification:

Λ is identified with *
0σ is identified with $[0 \,.\, \sigma]$
1σ is identified with $[1 \,.\, \sigma]$

A sexp of the form $(\text{"gvar"} \,.\, (s \,.\, \sigma))$ where s is a string and σ is a path, is also called a *global variable*. For a variable $x \equiv (\text{"var"} \,.\, s)$ and a path σ, x_σ denotes the global variable $(\text{"gvar"} \,.\, (s \,.\, \sigma))$.

For an expression a and a path σ, we define an expression $a{\downarrow}\sigma$ by $a{\downarrow}_0\sigma$ where $a{\downarrow}_n\sigma$ ($n{\geq}0$) is defined as follows:

149

$a \equiv \#^k x$ where x is a pure variable $\Rightarrow$

$$a\downarrow_n \sigma \equiv \begin{cases} a & \text{if } k < n \\ x_\sigma & \text{if } k = n \\ \#^{k-1}x & \text{if } k > n \end{cases}$$

a is a global variable $\Rightarrow a\downarrow_n \sigma \equiv a$

a is a symbol $\Rightarrow a\downarrow_n \sigma \equiv a$

$*\downarrow_n \sigma \equiv *$

$[a . b]\downarrow_n \sigma \equiv [a\downarrow_n \sigma . b\downarrow_n \sigma]$

$(a, b)\downarrow_n \sigma \equiv (a\downarrow_n \sigma), (b\downarrow_n \sigma)$

$(\lambda a . b)\downarrow_n \sigma \equiv \lambda(a\downarrow_{n+1}\sigma).(b\downarrow_{n+1}\sigma)$

$(a; b)\downarrow_n \sigma \equiv (a\downarrow_n \sigma); (b\downarrow_n \sigma)$

(**if** a **then** b **else** c)$\downarrow_n \sigma \equiv$ (**if** $a\downarrow_{n+1}\sigma$ **then** $b\downarrow_{n+1}\sigma$ **else** $c\downarrow_n \sigma$)

$(\neg a)\downarrow_n \sigma \equiv \neg (a\downarrow_n \sigma)$

$(a\ b)\downarrow_n \sigma \equiv (a\downarrow_n \sigma)\ (b\downarrow_n \sigma)$

$(a = b)\downarrow_n \sigma \equiv (a\downarrow_n \sigma) = (b\downarrow_n \sigma)$

$\downarrow$ is used in reducing application. (See the rule in section 6.2.) $\downarrow$ is a formal definition of the renaming of an expression which we explained in section 4.2.

Example

$((\lambda x.x = \#y)y)\downarrow_{10} \equiv (\lambda x.x = y_{10})y_{10}$

(**if** $\#x = [u.v]$ **then** foo($\#x,\#y,v$) **else** y)$\downarrow_{11}$
$\equiv$ (**if** $x_{11} = [u.v]$ **then** foo(x_{11},y_{11},v) **else** y_{11})

$\square$

We redefine Σa as a set of paths so that the occurrence of a subexpression can be indicated explicitly.

If p is $*$, a symbol, a variable or a function then $\Sigma p \equiv \phi$

$\Sigma[a . b] \equiv 0\Sigma a \cup 1\Sigma b$

$\Sigma(a,b) \equiv 10\Sigma a \cup 11\Sigma b$

$$\Sigma(a;b) \equiv \begin{cases} 10\Sigma a & \text{if } \Sigma a \neq \phi \\ 11\Sigma b & \text{if } \Sigma a \equiv \phi \text{ and } \Sigma b \neq \phi \\ \{\Lambda\} & \text{if } \Sigma a \equiv \Sigma b \equiv \phi \end{cases}$$

$\Sigma(\textbf{if } a \textbf{ then } b \textbf{ else} c) \equiv \{\Lambda\}$

$\Sigma \neg a \equiv \{\Lambda\}$

$$\Sigma(a\ b) \equiv \begin{cases} \{\Lambda\} & \text{if } \Sigma a \equiv \Sigma b \equiv \phi \\ 10\Sigma a \cup 11\Sigma b & \text{otherwise} \end{cases}$$

$$\Sigma(a = b) \equiv \begin{cases} \{\Lambda\} & \text{if } \Sigma a \equiv \Sigma b \equiv \phi \\ 10\Sigma a \cup 11\Sigma b & \text{otherwise} \end{cases}$$

150

It is again easy to check that for any expression a, $\Sigma a \equiv \phi$ if and only if a is a pattern. We call an expression a *redex* if $\Sigma a \equiv \{\Lambda\}$.

Henceforth, we use the notation $a_\sigma[b]$ only when $\sigma \in \Sigma a$. Furthermore, we use the notation $a_\sigma(b)$ to denote an expression a such that $a_\sigma[b] \equiv a$. In this case we say that b is an *evaluable subexpression* of a. We note that an evaluable subexpression is a redex.

6.2 Semantics

We call a pair consisting of an environment E and an expression a a *form* and use the notation $E \llbracket a \rrbracket$ for it. Moreover we include $\perp$ and ! (which we call *fail* and *suspension*, respectively) as forms. We use e, f, g etc. to denote forms.

We now define a binary relation $\triangleright$ on forms, which represents the reduction step of forms. Actually we define the relation $\triangleright_\sigma$ for each path σ. Then the relation $\triangleright$ is defined as $\triangleright_\Lambda$. In the following, $\geq_\sigma$ denotes the reflexive, transitive closure of $\triangleright_\sigma$.

We call a form e *normal* if $e \triangleright f$ holds for no f.

In the following rules, it can be seen that environments are changed only by unification, and the rules of subexpression show how such change of environments affects the evaluation of other subexpressions.

For an environment E and an expression a, we define the environment $E(a)$ as follows. First we let V be the collection of all the free variables appearing either in a or in some equations in E, and we put $F \equiv (E \cup \{\{x\} \mid x \in V\})^*$. Then we define $E(a)$ by:

$$E(a) \equiv (F - \{A \mid A \text{ is simple and } A \in F\}) \cup$$
$$\{\{A\} \cup A \mid A \text{ is simple and } A \in F\}$$

This kind of environment is used in the rules of if-then-else and negation so that the marked equations detect suspension. (Recall the definition of the suspended environment in section 3.2.) However, unlike the informal explanation in section 4, the state of suspension cannot be recovered. Therefore, for example, in evaluating (if $\#x = 0$ then 0 else 1), $x = 1$ in the empty environment,

$$\phi \llbracket (\text{if } \#x = 0 \text{ then } 0 \text{ else } 1), x = 1 \rrbracket$$
$$\triangleright_\Lambda \{\{x,1\}\} \llbracket (\text{if } \#x = 0 \text{ then } 0 \text{ else } 1), x \rrbracket$$
$$\triangleright_\Lambda \{\{x,1\}\} \llbracket 1, x \rrbracket$$

is the only possible order of the reduction. The rules of suspension appearing in 2, 3, 4, 7 and 8 below show when and how the

151

suspension of a subexpression causes the suspension of the whole expression.

1. subexpression

$$E \llbracket a \rrbracket \triangleright_{\tau\sigma} F \llbracket b \rrbracket \Rightarrow E \llbracket c_\sigma(a) \rrbracket \triangleright_\tau F \llbracket c_\sigma[b] \rrbracket$$
$$E \llbracket a \rrbracket \triangleright_{\tau\sigma} \perp \Rightarrow E \llbracket c_\sigma(a) \rrbracket \triangleright_\tau \perp$$

2. list

$$E \llbracket a \rrbracket \triangleright_{\sigma 0} ! \Rightarrow E \llbracket [a . q] \rrbracket \triangleright_\sigma !$$
$$E \llbracket b \rrbracket \triangleright_{\sigma 1} ! \Rightarrow E \llbracket [p . b] \rrbracket \triangleright_\sigma !$$
$$E \llbracket a \rrbracket \triangleright_{\sigma 0} !, \; E \llbracket b \rrbracket \triangleright_{\sigma 1} ! \Rightarrow E \llbracket [a . b] \rrbracket \triangleright_\sigma !$$

3. and

$$E \llbracket a \rrbracket \triangleright_{\sigma 10} ! \Rightarrow E \llbracket a, q \rrbracket \triangleright_\sigma !$$
$$E \llbracket b \rrbracket \triangleright_{\sigma 11} ! \Rightarrow E \llbracket p, b \rrbracket \triangleright_\sigma !$$
$$E \llbracket a \rrbracket \triangleright_{\sigma 10} !, \; E \llbracket b \rrbracket \triangleright_{\sigma 11} ! \Rightarrow E \llbracket a, b \rrbracket \triangleright_\sigma !$$

4. sequential-and

$$E \llbracket p; q \rrbracket \triangleright_\sigma E \llbracket q \rrbracket$$
$$E \llbracket a \rrbracket \triangleright_{\sigma 10} ! \Rightarrow E \llbracket a; b \rrbracket \triangleright_\sigma !$$
$$E \llbracket b \rrbracket \triangleright_{\sigma 11} ! \Rightarrow E \llbracket p; b \rrbracket \triangleright_\sigma !$$

5. if-then-else

$$E(\langle a \rangle) \llbracket \langle a \rangle \rrbracket \geq_\sigma F \llbracket p \rrbracket \Rightarrow$$
$$E \llbracket \text{if } a \text{ then } b \text{ else } c \rrbracket \triangleright_\sigma$$
$$\begin{cases} F \llbracket \langle b \rangle \rrbracket & \text{if } F \text{ is not suspended} \\ ! & \text{if } F \text{ is suspended} \end{cases}$$
$$E(\langle a \rangle) \llbracket \langle a \rangle \rrbracket \geq_\sigma \perp \Rightarrow$$
$$E \llbracket \text{if } a \text{ then } b \text{ else } c \rrbracket \triangleright_\sigma E \llbracket c \rrbracket$$
$$E(\langle a \rangle) \llbracket \langle a \rangle \rrbracket \geq_\sigma ! \Rightarrow$$
$$E \llbracket \text{if } a \text{ then } b \text{ else } c \rrbracket \triangleright_\sigma !$$

6. negation

$$E(a) \llbracket a \rrbracket \geq_\sigma F \llbracket p \rrbracket \Rightarrow$$
$$E \llbracket \neg a \rrbracket \triangleright_\sigma \begin{cases} \perp & \text{If } F \text{ is not suspended} \\ ! & \text{if } F \text{ is suspended} \end{cases}$$
$$E(a) \llbracket a \rrbracket \geq_\sigma \perp \Rightarrow E \llbracket \neg a \rrbracket \triangleright_\sigma E \llbracket () \rrbracket$$
$$E(a) \llbracket a \rrbracket \geq_\sigma ! \Rightarrow E \llbracket \neg a \rrbracket \triangleright_\sigma !$$

7. application

$$E \llbracket p q \rrbracket \triangleright_\sigma \begin{cases} E \llbracket a \downarrow \sigma = q; b \downarrow \sigma \rrbracket & \text{If } p_E \equiv (\lambda a . b) \\ ! & \text{if } p_E \text{ is a variable} \\ \perp & \text{otherwise} \end{cases}$$

152

$$E[\![\,a\,]\!]\ \triangleright_{\sigma}10\,! \;\Rightarrow\; E[\![\,a\ q\,]\!]\ \triangleright_{\sigma}\,!$$
$$E[\![\,b\,]\!]\ \triangleright_{\sigma}11\,! \;\Rightarrow\; E[\![\,p\ b\,]\!]\ \triangleright_{\sigma}\,!$$
$$E[\![\,a\,]\!]\ \triangleright_{\sigma}10\,!,\ E[\![\,b\,]\!]\ \triangleright_{\sigma}11\,! \;\Rightarrow\; E[\![\,a\ b\,]\!]\ \triangleright_{\sigma}\,!$$

8. unification

$$E[\![\,p=q\,]\!]\ \triangleright_{\sigma} \begin{cases} \perp & \text{if } F \text{ is inconsistent} \\ F[\![\,p\,]\!] & \text{otherwise} \end{cases}$$

$$\text{where } F \equiv (E \cup \{\{p,q\}\})^{\bullet}$$
$$E[\![\,a\,]\!]\ \triangleright_{\sigma}10\,! \;\Rightarrow\; E[\![\,a=q\,]\!]\ \triangleright_{\sigma}\,!$$
$$E[\![\,b\,]\!]\ \triangleright_{\sigma}11\,! \;\Rightarrow\; E[\![\,p=b\,]\!]\ \triangleright_{\sigma}\,!$$
$$E[\![\,a\,]\!]\ \triangleright_{\sigma}10\,!,\ E[\![\,b\,]\!]\ \triangleright_{\sigma}11\,! \;\Rightarrow\; E[\![\,a=b\,]\!]\ \triangleright_{\sigma}\,!$$

We now have the following theorems which capture basic properties of reduction processes.

Theorem 4.

If $e \geq f_1$ and $e \geq f_2$ then $f_1 \geq g$ and $f_2 \geq g$ for some g.

Theorem 5.

If $e \geq f_1$ and $e \geq f_2$ and f_1 and f_2 are both normal then $f_1 \equiv f_2$.

The meanings of these theorems should be clear. We wish to supply proofs of these theorems in a future publication.

7 Conclusions

We have introduced a functional language Qute which is based on unification. In particular, we have shown that processes running in parallel can communicate with each other through shared variables (that is, the variables common to these processes), and that we can synchronize the processes by the if-then-else construct. Our approach is logically more sound compared to, for example, that of Concurrent Prolog which achieves synchronization by read-only variables. The reason for this claim is that Qute enjoys the Church-Rosser property which is essential to make it a functional language, while in Concurrent Prolog the results of an evaluation may change depending on the particular evaluation strategy.

We have also shown that, by virtue of unification, Qute can handle incomplete data structures just as in usual logic programming languages. We can, for instance, represent potentially infinite sequence of integers as a list ending with a logical variable.

We have introduced functions to Qute as first class citizens of the language which can be passed as arguments to other functions or can be returned as the values of expressions.

153

We believe that these features have made Qute a simple but powerful functional programming language.

Acknowledgements

We would like to thank Dr. Doug DeGroot, who read the orignial manuscript very carefully and gave helpful comments and suggestions.

REFERENCES

1. Allen, J.R. *Anatomy of Lisp.* McGraw-Hill, 1978.

2. Barendregt, H.P. *The Lambda Calculus.* North-Holland, 1981.

3. Clark, K. and S. Gregory. PARLOG: Parallel Programming in Logic. Research Report DOC 84/4, Imperial College, 1984.

4. Gordon, M., R. Milner, and C. Wadsworth. *Edinburgh LCF, Lecture Notes in Computer Science 78.* Springer-Verlag, 1979.

5. Jaffar, J. "Efficient Unification over Infinite Terms". *New Generation Computing 2,* **3** (1984), 207-219.

6. Kowalski, R.A. *Logic for Problem Solving.* North-Holland, 1979.

7. Lassez, J-L. and M.J. Maher. *The Semantics of Logic Programs.* Oxford University Press, 1985. in preparation

8. Martelli, A. and U. Montanari. "An Efficient Unification Algorithm". *ACM Transaction on Programming Language and System 4* (1982), 258-282.

9. Sato, M. and T. Sakurai. Qute: A Prolog/Lisp type language for logic programming. In *Proceedings of the Eighth International Joint Conference on Artificial Intelligence*, 1983, pp. 507-513.

10. Sato, M. and T. Sakurai. Qute: A Functional Language Based on Unification. In *Proceedings of International Conference on Fifth Genaration Computer Systems*, 1984, pp. 157-165.

11. Shapiro, E.Y. A Subset of Concurrent Prolog and Its Interpreter. ICOT Technical Report, TR-003, 1983.

12. Shapiro, E.Y. and A. Takeuchi. "Object Oriented Programming in Concurrent Prolog". *New Generation Computing 1,* **1** (1983), 25-48.

13. Talcott, C. personal communication, 1984.

FUNLOG: A COMPUTATIONAL MODEL

INTEGRATING LOGIC PROGRAMMING

AND FUNCTIONAL PROGRAMMING

P.A. Subrahmanyam[**] and **Jia-Huai You**

Department of Computer Science
University of Utah
Salt Lake City, Utah 84112

ABSTRACT

Funlog involves a computational model which integrates functional programming and logic programming. This model is described, along with evaluation strategies to support the execution of programs based upon it. A lazy reduction mechanism, *pattern-driven reduction*, is developed for the underlying functional model and cleanly and naturally achieves *reduction-by-need*. The notion of *semantic unification* is discussed. Semantic unification can be viewed as a restricted form of *E-unification*. Semantic unification serves as a basis for achieving the desired integration of functions and logic, and can be used to replace the conventional unification procedure in logic programming systems. The resulting model supports computations with infinite data structures while avoiding the introduction of complicated control issues at the user level. In addition, it provides the programmer the flexibility of choosing between a backtracking free computation framework and a conventional logic computation framework, i.e., a nondeterministic one involving backtracking. The use of this facility is illustrated via examples. The model can be extended to include the notion of equality when complete E-unification algorithms are used.

---

*This is a substantially revised version of two previously published papers appearing in *Proceedings of the IEEE 1984 International Conference on Logic Programming,* pp. 144–53, © IEEE, 1984, and *Proceedings of the Eleventh Principles of Programming Languages Conference,* 1984, pp. 228–34, © ACM, 1984.

[**]Current Address: AT&T Bell Laboratories Research.

1 INTRODUCTION

Functional programming and logic programming have attracted several researchers in recent years, both approaches being prime candidates as basic programming paradigms in concurrent computer architectures. Although each of these paradigms has its advantages, each also has its shortcomings when compared to the other.

The basic formalization of functional programming languages, as compared to logic programming languages (e.g., Prolog) lacks knowledge-based inferencing abilities to cope with computations involving search. In addition, there are several well-known problems for which functional solutions are either very complex or somewhat inscrutable [3]. In contrast, the solutions to several of these problems expressed in Prolog are relatively elegant. This is mainly because Prolog can save intermediate computational results for subsequent use by sibling computations (cf. [34]).

Current Prolog systems, however, lack (1) the concept of "evaluation" of "function invocations", leading to the logic base sometimes being not transparent, and (2) a means to describe terminating computations on conceptually infinite data structures. The "clean" control of program execution is another challenging problem in the Prolog context -- one which is significantly alleviated when using a functional style.

The advantages of being able to compute with infinite data structures have been cogently argued by several researchers e.g., [14, 20]. There are certain inherent difficulties that arise in Prolog when attempting to terminate computations on infinite data structures. By "computing with infinite data structures", we mean that the program can manipulate as a whole data objects that are conceptually infinite, even though the user may, in any given computation, only wish to obtain a finite portion of the potentially infinite objects. This ability provides a programming style in which one can separate the data processing aspect from possibly complex boundary conditions, thus enabling elegant solutions to certain classes of problems.

In this paper, Funlog, a computational model that integrates functional and logic programming models, is described. First, an underlying functional model is characterized whose reduction mechanism is "lazy" in the sense of [11, 14]. The notion of semantic unification is then discussed. Semantic unification allows executable functions to be used in Horn clauses and to be "reduced by need", i.e. the underlying resolution is based upon semantic unification. The resulting computation model can be viewed as a restricted version of first-order logic with equality. If the full flavor of first-order logic with equality is desired, E-unification algorithms can be used. The problem of unification in the presence of an equational theory is called E-unification. An equational theory is defined by a set of equations. We show by means of examples that our approach accommodates computations with infinite data structures, and that such "infinite" computations can be gracefully terminated without explicit control specifications by the user. We argue that this approach also alleviates the degree of control difficulties typically encountered in Prolog programs for solving certain classes of problems. This is achieved (1) by providing the ability to write program segments where the underlying computing mechanism is function reduction without any backtracking; and (2) by explicitly embodying the concept of "evaluation" (of function invocations) in Funlog programs.

The paper is organized as follows. Section 2 introduces a functional programming model whose reduction mechanism is based on *pattern-driven lazy reduction*. Section 3 then discusses a combined model supporting both functions and logic. Parallel execution strategies are discussed in Section 4. Related work is discussed in Section 5.

In what follows, we will use Edinburgh DEC-10 Prolog notation. We will sometimes use ^ (up arrow) for the list constructor *cons*, for example, writing [A|X] as A^X for convenience. The reader should think of this and other constructors as merely symbols without pre-defined meanings. We assume that the reader is familiar with logic programming in general.

2 THE UNDERLYING FUNCTIONAL MODEL

The functional model described here consists of a set of function definitions where each function is defined by a set of equations. We will assume the existence of a set of pre-defined primitives, e.g., some primitive boolean functions and arithmetic operations.[*] Furthermore, if a variable appears in the right-hand side of an equation it must appear in the left-hand side of that equation. We will henceforth denote the set of function definitions by EQN. Base constructors (e.g., 0, [ ], Ø, etc.) and constructors (e.g., successor, cons, push, etc.) can be freely invented by the user. The left-hand side of an equation can have more than one set of parameters (see Example 2 below). The following examples serve to illustrate the syntax of functional declarations.

Our first example deals with data type Queue which has been widely used as an example in the literature related to algebraic specifications. A queue is a first-in-first-out storage structure. The operations on the queue shown below are self-explanatory. The function *add* is used as a constructor, and is used to "build up" queues.

Example 1. *Data type Queue*

```
is_empty(newq) = true
is_empty(add(Item, Queue)) = false
remove(add(Item, Queue))
        = if is_empty(Queue) then newq
          else add(Item, remove(Queue))
front(add(Item, Queue))
        = if is_empty(Queue) then Item
          else front(Queue)
```

The function if_then_else can be defined as:

```
if_then_else(true, X, Y) = X
if_then_else(false, X, Y) = Y □
```

---

[*]This assumption is merely for convenience, since such a set of primitives can in fact be defined equationally.

Example 2. *A Curried version of the function map*

    map(F)([]) = []
    map(F)(A^L) = F(A)^map(F)(L)

The syntax of this example resembles the Curried version of function definitions. This example illustrates that the result of a computation can be a function; we will call such functions *resulting functions*. As a consequence, the function variable F can be instantiated by a resulting function. A function call like

    map (map(plus1)) ([[1,2], [3,4]])

is valid, and can be reduced to [[2,3], [4,5]] where the function plus1 is defined as plus1(N) = N+1, and map(plus1) is a resulting function. □

2.1 Reduction of Function Terms

A set of equations can be viewed as a term rewriting system, where each equation serves as a rewrite rule, if such a term rewriting system has the confluence property. Intuitively, the confluence property says that if a term A can be reduced to either of two terms B or C by two distinct reduction sequences, then there must exist a term D such that both B and C can be reduced to D. The problem of determining whether a term rewriting system has the confluence property is unsolvable in the general case. Sufficient conditions have, however, been worked out that enable one to test a given term rewriting system for this property; see, for example, [15, 26, 30]. Furthermore, the Knuth–Bendix completion procedure [21] can be used to make a term rewriting system complete in some cases. For the convenience of our exposition, we will assume that EQN represents a confluent term rewriting system. This essentially implies that the equations in EQN can be viewed as rewrite rules.

The reduction of a function term $f(s_1,...,s_n)$ can be viewed as the process of finding a substitution σ for the left-hand side $f(t_1,...,t_n)$ of an equation such that $\sigma(f(t_1,...,t_n)) = f(s_1,...,s_n)$. The "result" of the reduction (the "reduced version" of $f(s_1,...,s_n)$) is obtained by applying σ to the right-hand side of the equation. Such a one way unification is called *biased unification* in this paper -- biased because the substitution σ is applied only to the left-hand side of the equation $f(t_1,...,t_n)$, but not to the term $f(s_1,...,s_n)$. The corresponding reduction procedure is called *One_Step_Reduction*.

In trying to unify two terms, say, $f(t_1,...,t_n)$ and $f(s_1,...,s_n)$, suppose there are subterms t_i and s_i that are not unifiable in the conventional sense. In such a case, if s_i (or t_i) is reducible and a reduced version of it is unifiable with t_i (respectively s_i), then we say that $f(t_1,...,t_n)$ and $f(s_1,...,s_n)$ are *semantically* unifiable. The corresponding process is called *semantic unification*. In the general case, both subterms s_i and t_i can be reduced, but certain restrictions must be imposed. This will be discussed in Section 3.1. By combining semantic unification with biased unification we obtain the notion of *biased semantic unification*. In this case, only the subterms in $f(s_1,...,s_n)$ are considered for reduction. We can now formally give the definition for reducibility of a function term.

Definition 1. *Reducibility of Function Terms*
Let $f(s_1,...,s_n)$ be a function term to be reduced. Let $g_1,...,g_p$, where $p \geq 0$, be function calls contained in $f(s_1,...,s_n)$. The function term $f(s_1,...,s_n)$ is *reducible* if there exists a function term $f(s'_1,...,s'_n)$ obtained from $f(s_1,...,s_n)$ by performing zero or more reductions for each of $g_1,...,g_p$, an equation whose left-hand side is $f(t_1,...,t_n)$ and a substitution σ such that $\sigma(f(t_1,...,t_n))$ = $f(s'_1,...,s'_n)$. $\square$

A lazy evaluation effect is achieved by requiring that a biased unification algorithm perform "reduction-by-need", that is, perform only those reductions that are necessary in order to make two terms semantically unifiable. For example, the reduction of a function term if_then_else($f(a)$, $g(b)$, $h(c)$) will cause $f(a)$ to be matched against the boolean constant true or false, which will in turn demand the reduction of $f(a)$. Notice that neither $g(b)$ nor $h(c)$ is reduced during this reduction step, because they are both matched to a variable, respectively. Consider the following example of summing the infinite sequence 2,4,8,16,....

Example 3.

$$g(N) = N\char94 g(2*N)$$
$$sum(A\char94 L) = A + sum(L)$$

The process of reducing the function term $sum(g(4))$ demands that $sum(g(4))$ be unified with $sum(A\char94 L)$. This in turn demands that $g(4)$ be unified with $A\char94 L$. The biased semantic unification algorithm yields the unifier $\{A=4, L=g(2*4)\}$, and the procedure One_Step_Reduction returns $4+sum(g(2*4))$. Note that the value of the expression $2*4$ is not yet demanded in the current reduction. □

The above example serves to provide some intuition about the notions of pattern-driven reduction and reduction-by-need. When the terms $A\char94 L$ and $g(4)$ were matched, $g(4)$ was reduced once to yield $4\char94 g(2*4)$; this was then matched with $A\char94 L$, resulting in A bound to 4 and L to $g(2*4)$. If we try to match, say, $A\char94 B\char94 L$ with $g(4)$, then $g(4)$ will be reduced twice and become $4\char94 2*4\char94 g(2*2*4)$. Thus, such reductions of function terms are in fact driven by *patterns*. The actual number of reductions carried out is based on the *need* to match a pattern. Notice that by adopting an equational model the notion of lazy evaluation extends to any algebraic data type in a very natural way without increasing language complexity.

2.2 A Biased Semantic Unification Algorithm

We now provide a biased semantic unification algorithm which is described in Figure 1 and uses the procedure One_Step_Reduction detailed in Figure 2. As illustrated in Example 2, functions can have more than one set of parameters. For clarity of our exposition, however, we will write function terms with only one set of parameters.

Note that in the algorithm of Figure 1, we assume that the subterms appearing in the left-hand side of an equation cannot contain common variables.[*] As a result, the equations in the set I will not be interrelated, thus eliminating the necessity of processing equations that are interrelated by common variables.

---

[*]It is possible to relax this condition although this increases the complexity of the resulting algorithm.

A Biased Semantic Unification Algorithm

Input: The left-hand side of an equation $f(t_1,...,t_n)$, a function
term $f(s_1,...,s_n)$ and EQN.

Output: A failure report or a substitution
$$\sigma = \{x_1 = m_1, \; x_2 = m_2,...,x_p = m_p\},$$
where x_i are distinct variables and m_i are terms.

begin

  $I <- \{t_1 = s_1, \; ...,t_n = s_n\};$

  $Q <- \emptyset;$

  repeat until $I = \emptyset$

    remove an equation $t_i = s_i$ from I;

      case 1. t_i is identical to s_i

          do nothing

      case 2. t_i is a variable

          add $t_i = s_i$ to Q

      case 3. t_i is a compound term or a constant and
          s_i is a compound term

          let $t_i = g(t'_1,...,t'_p)$ and $s_i = g'(s'_1,...,s'_q)$
          where $p \geq 0$ and $q > 0$, and t_i is a constant if $p=0$;

        subcase a. $g = g'$ and $p = q$

            add $t'_i = s'_i$ for all i in 1..p   to I

        subcase b. $g \neq g'$ or $p \neq q$ and

            One_Step_Reduction(s_i) $\neq$ "irreducible"

            add $t_i =$ One_Step_Reduction(s_i) to I

      case 4. none of the above applies

          stop with failure

  end repeat;

  output Q;

end.

    Figure 1:   A biased semantic unification algorithm.

Procedure One_Step_Reduction(f(s$_1$,...,s$_n$));
begin
  S <- all the equations of the form
      f(t$_1$,...,t$_n$) = RHS in EQN;
  repeat until a success is reported or S=∅
    remove an equation of the form f(t$_1$,...,t$_n$) = RHS from S;
    apply the biased semantic unification algorithm
    with input terms f(t$_1$,...,t$_n$) and f(s$_1$,...,s$_n$);
    if the algorithm returns a substitution σ
        then report a success
  end repeat
  if a success has been reported
      then
      return σ(RHS)
        where σ is the substitution returned
        by the biased semantic unification
        algorithm
    else return "irreducible"
end.

Figure 2: The procedure One_Step_Reduction.

Note also that we use the phrase *compound term* to refer to those terms that are built up from variables and function symbols (including constant functions). In implementing the procedure One_Step_Reduction, if the set S contains more than one equation, the order of choosing equations needs to be specified. We assume that equations are chosen in the order in which they appear in the program.

Biased semantic unification fails to terminate only in some unusual situations. To show this, we first need a definition.

Definition 2. A function f is said to be *cyclic* if there is a defined function h which appears as the outermost functor infinitely many times in some reduction sequence of the function

165

f. □

The following functions are examples of simple cyclic functions:

$$h(N) = h(N+1)$$
$$f(N) = g(N+1)$$
$$g(N) = f(N+1).$$

Lemma 1. The biased unification algorithm terminates if there are no cyclic functions defined in EQN. □

The proof of this lemma can be found in [36] and is omitted here.

The condition in Lemma 1 can be further relaxed by dividing EQN into two subsets of the equations, EQN_1 and EQN_2, where EQN_1 represents a canonical (confluent *and* terminating) term rewriting system, and EQN_2 consists of the set of equations EQN – EQN_1, that is, the rest of equations in EQN. We then require only that EQN_2 contain no cyclic functions.

2.3 An Interpreter for Function Reductions

An interpreter for function reductions is presented in Figure 3. The top level driving process is called Reduce. It is not difficult to see that if the interpreter terminates for a given input term M and returns an output term N, then none of the subterms in N (including N itself) is reducible. N is usually called the *normal form* of M. An illustration of the reduction process is given in Example 4.

Example 4. *Computing any finite portion of an infinite sequence whose elements are pairs of consecutive integers and their squares, both increased by 1.*

```
pairs(N) = [N, N*N]^pairs(N+1)
first_N_pairs(N)
        = truncate(N, map(map(plus1))(pairs(1)))
plus1(N) = N+1
truncate(0, L) = []
truncate(N, A^L) = A^truncate(N-1, L)
```

166

```
Reduce(term)
    begin
        if term is a constant or a variable or
                none of its subterms (including itself) is reducible
            then return term;
        let term be f(t₁,...,tₙ)
        if One_Step_Reduction(term) returns "irreducible"
            then return f(Reduce(t₁),...,Reduce(tₙ))
        else return Reduce(One_Step_Reduction(term))
    end.
```

Figure 3: An interpreter for function reductions.

The function map is defined in Example 2. Note that we have used $[N,N*N]$ (which is the Prolog list representation) to represent $N\char94 N*N$ for clarity. The sequence of reductions in interpreting the function term first_N_pairs(2) is shown in Figure 4.

3 A COMBINED COMPUTATIONAL MODEL FOR FUNCTIONS AND LOGIC

In this section we describe a computation model that combines functions and logic. We first generalize the notion of biased semantic unification to semantic unification, and then discuss general unification in the presence of an equational theory. The semantic foundations of Funlog are also discussed.

3.1 A General Semantic Unification Algorithm

The process of unifying two terms can be viewed as one of solving simultaneous equations [25]. For example, the problem of unifying $f(s_1,...,s_n)$ with $f(t_1,...,t_n)$ is equivalent to solving the set of equations $\{s_1=t_1,\ s_2=t_2,\ ...,\ s_n=t_n\}$. A solution of these equations, if one exists, is of the form $\{x_1=p_1,\ x_2=p_2,\ ...,\ x_m=p_m\}$ where the x_i are variables and the p_i are terms.

```
first_N_pairs(2)
|
v
truncate(2, map(map(plus1))(pairs(1)))
|
v
truncate(2, map(map(plus1))([1, 1*1] ^ pairs(1+1)))
|
v
truncate(2, map(plus1)([1, 1*1])
|            ^ map(map(plus1))(pairs(1+1)))
v
map(plus1)([1,1*1])
|       ^ truncate(2-1, map(map(plus1))(pairs(1+1)))
v
[plus1(1), plus1(1*1)]
|       ^ truncate(1, map(map(plus1))(pairs(1+1)))
v
......
|
v
[2,2]^map(plus1)([2, 4])
|       ^ truncate(0, map(map(plus1))(pairs(1+1+1)))
v
......
|
v
[2,2]^[3,5]^[]
```

Figure 4: A sample reduction sequence for Example 4.

In conventional unification, an equation $g(t_1,...,t_p) = g'(s_1,...s_q)$ is not solvable if g and g' are not identical or if $p \neq q$, since g and g' are both treated as constructors. In contrast, semantic unification allows either g or g' or both (or any function symbol in the equation) to be functions that are defined in EQN. Two terms are semantically unifiable if there exist semantically equivalent forms (obtained by reduction(s) on any reducible term in the equation) which are unifiable. An algorithm reflecting this idea is given in Figure 5.[*]

The facility of using reduction to simulate *equality* of function terms has limited power: certain restrictions must be imposed in order not to lose completeness. One such restriction is that the function terms involved in the two input terms must be *ground*. (We call that a term $f(t_1,...,t_n)$ is a function term if f is defined in EQN.) However, this is quite adequate for the programming features we advocate in this paper. Recall that our initial goal was to combine functional programming and logic programming. Functional programming in this context does not completely subsume the facility of "reasoning about equations". For example, consider the two terms $p(f(X))$ and $p(g(Y))$, and an equation $f(a) = g(b)$. Although there exists a substitution $\sigma = \{x = a\}$ such that $\sigma(p(f(x)))$ is equivalent to $p(g(b))$ (since $f(a)$ can reduce to $g(b)$ after the substitution), which is unifiable with $p(g(Y))$ with Y bound to b, the notion of semantic unification cannot handle such situations. A more powerful computational mechanism is needed; for example, the narrowing method described in [23]. We will come back to this point a little later in Section 3.2.

The termination of the semantic unification algorithm is obviously dependent on the characteristics of the user defined functions. Since we are dealing with term rewriting systems that may not have the termination property, certain restrictions need to be imposed in order for the algorithm to terminate. Recall that we assume that EQN represents a confluent term rewriting system, and that in general EQN can be divided into two subsets of equations EQN_1 and EQN_2, where EQN_1 is a canonical (confluence *and* terminating) term rewriting system

---

[*]We ignore the so called occur checks [6].

169

A Semantic Unification Algorithm

Input: Two terms $p(s_1,...,s_n)$ and $p(t_1,...,t_n)$, and EQN.

Output: A failure report or a set of equations

$$\sigma = \{x_1 = m_1, x_2 = m_2, ..., x_p = m_p\}$$

where x_i are variables and m_i are terms.

begin

$I <- \{t_1 = s_1, ...,t_n = s_n\};$

Repeatedly attempt any of the following transformations, if no transformation applies, stop with success.

1. Eliminate any equations of the form $x = x$.

2. If x and y are distinct variables, $x = y$ is in I and x has other occurrences in I, then replace these occurrences of x by occurrences of y.

3. Replace $t = x$ by $x = t$ if x is a variable and t is not.

4. If x is a variable and t_1 and t_2 are not, replace $x=t_1$ and $x=t_2$ by $x=t_1$ and $t_1=t_2$.

5. If an equation is of the form $g(t'_1,...,t'_p) = g'(s'_1,...,s'_q)$

    case a. g is a constructor, and $g = g'$,

        replace the equation by $\{t'_1=s'_1,...,t'_p = s'_q\}$;

    case b. both terms $g(t'_1,...,t'_p)$ and $g'(s'_1,...,s'_q)$ have subterms that are reducible,

        replace the equation by

        $\text{Reduce}(g(t'_1,...,t'_p)) = \text{Reduce}(g'(s'_1,...,s'_q))$;

    case c. $g(t'_1,...,t'_p)$ is reducible but $g'(s'_1,...,s'_q)$ is not,

        replace the equation by

        $g'(s'_1,...,s'_q) = \text{One\_Step\_Reduction}(g(t'_1,...,t'_p))$;

    case d. $g'(s'_1,...,s'_q)$ is reducible but $g(t'_1,...,t'_p)$ is not,

        replace the equation by

        $g(t'_1,...,t'_p) = \text{One\_Step\_Reduction}(g'(s'_1,...,s'_q))$;

    case e. none of the above applies, stop with failure.

end.

Figure 5: A semantic unification algorithm.

and EQN$_2$ is confluent, but may or may not be terminating. The condition for termination of the semantic unification algorithm is as follows:

1. EQN$_2$ should not contain any cyclic functions. This restriction is the same as in the case of biased semantic unification.
2. When an equation in the set I of the algorithm is of the form $g(t'_1,...,t'_p) = g'(s'_1,...,s'_q)$ and both g and g' are defined in EQN, then both reduction sequences must terminate.

The confluence property tells us that two terms are equal if and only if there exist reduction sequences that lead them to a common term. This implies that we should try every possible search path in order to prove that the two given terms are equal whenever they are indeed equal. It is obvious that this search space can grow very fast. Furthermore, the confluence property cannot guarantee the decidability of proving two terms equal. It is therefore necessary to make a tradeoff between the power and execution efficiency of the constructs one chooses to incorporate in a language. In practice, when a user debugs his or her program, a warning should be issued if there exists a function that is defined in EQN$_2$. Under the two conditions described above, the termination of the semantic unification algorithm can be proved in a manner similar to Lemma 1. Termination plus the confluence property for EQN guarantees that the algorithm will eventually produce a unifier for two given terms A and B if and only if A and B are unifiable and the ground term condition on A and B is observed. All the examples given in this paper fall into this class of computations. The semantic unification algorithm can be implemented using the method of solving sets of *multiequations* given in [25].

Examples of general semantic unification:
The function terms

```
front(add(c, add(a, remove(add(b, newq)))))
front(remove(add(a, add(b, newq))))
```

are semantically unifiable given the assumption that the equations of Example 2 are contained in EQN. This is because both terms can be reduced to the atom a. As another example, assume that we have the following equations

```
filter(P, []) = []
filter(P, A^L) = if P(A) then A^filter(P, L)
                 else filter(P, L)
```

Applying the semantic unification algorithm to the following two terms

```
p(X, filter(odd, [2,5,9]))
p(bad, First^Rest),
```

we get the unifier

$$\sigma = \{X=bad, First=5, Rest=filter(odd, [9])\}.$$

The function term `filter(odd, [9])` is the result of reducing `filter(odd, [2,5,9])` twice. The reductions were driven by the pattern `First^Rest`. This assumes that the function odd is either defined in EQN or is a primitive.

3.2 Complete Unification Algorithms

The notion of semantic unification discussed above is a special case of general unification in the presence of an equational theory. Such a form of general unification is called E-unification, and the corresponding unifiers are called E-unifiers. An equational theory, denoted by $=_E$, can be described by a set of equations. In E-unification, a substitution σ is an E-unifier of two terms A and B, iff $\sigma(A) =_E \sigma(B)$. The most general unifier is now no longer necessarily unique. We are typically interested in complete unification algorithms. Informally, given two terms A and B, a complete unification algorithm with respect to an equational theory produces a set of unifiers Σ of A and B, which is a subset of the set of all unifiers of A and B, such that for every unifier σ of A and B there is a unifier θ in Σ which is either more general than σ or at least as general as σ. If the set contains all of the "unrelated" most general unifiers and no others then the corresponding algorithm is said to be *minimal and complete*. A minimal and complete set of unifiers may not be finite for some equational theories (see, for example,

[9, 16, 32] for rigorous expositions). The reason it is important to have all of the most general unifiers in a theorem prover is that unless all of them have been tried, the theorem prover cannot declare a statement to be false. This is analogous to the situation in Prolog wherein a failure cannot be reported unless one has tried every possible search path (by means of backtracking).

It is not difficult to prove that under the conditions (1) that the function terms involved in the two given unifiable terms are ground terms, and (2) that the equations in EQN are confluent, the most general unifier is unique (up to the equivalence $=_E$), and that the semantic unification algorithm indeed produces this unifier if the termination of the algorithm is guaranteed. Although the programming paradigm combining functions and logic as advocated in this paper is supported by this computational model, semantic unification does not provide a general capability for reasoning about equations. Consider, for example, the function append defined by equations:

$$append([\,], L) = L$$
$$append(A^\wedge L1, L2) = A^\wedge append(L1, L2).$$

The question "what is X such that the equation $append(a^\wedge X, c^\wedge d^\wedge[\,]) = append(a^\wedge b^\wedge c^\wedge[\,], d^\wedge[\,])$ holds" cannot be solved by the semantic unification algorithm. To solve this equation, a complete unification algorithm for the theory generated by the above two equations is needed. In [12], a complete unification algorithm based on narrowing [10, 17] is used under the condition that the underlying theory can be described by a canonical term rewriting system. It has been shown in [37] that the narrowing method also yields a complete unification algorithm for some subclasses of confluent, but not necessarily terminating term rewriting systems. Two problems are associated with Fay's algorithm. First, the algorithm, while complete, does not in general produce a *minimal* and complete set of unifiers. The practical impact of this is that a theorem prover can waste time (duplicate effort) by considering unifiers that are not the most general. The second problem relates to termination: Fay's algorithm does not always terminate, even for those equational theories which have finite minimal and com–

plete sets of unifiers.[*] A sufficient termination condition has been given in [17] for a subclass of theories that admit a canonical term rewriting system. The most important goal for an E-unification algorithm is to produce minimal and complete sets of unifiers, and when such a set is finite, the algorithm terminates.[*] We now elaborate on the role that E-unification plays in the semantics of Funlog.

3.3 Semantic Foundations

A Funlog program generally consists of a set of equations and a set of Horn clauses. A Horn clause is of the form

$$A :- B_1, B_2, ..., B_n.$$

where a predicate B_i in the clause body can be of the form M $=_E$ N where M and N are terms. An equation A $=_E$ B in a goal will invoke E-unification (or semantic unification). A term can involve function symbols defined by some equations. The operational semantics for Funlog as a whole is the resolution procedure based on E-unification, or the semantic unification algorithm if its limitations on expressiveness are acceptable. (In the interpreter design described later, only the semantic unification algorithm is discussed.) Let P be a program and A' be a predicate. A' is *provable* in P iff there exists a clause

$$A :- B_1, B_2, ..., B_n.$$

and a substitution σ, such that $\sigma(A') =_E \sigma(A)$ and $\sigma(B_1)$, $\sigma(B_2)$, ..., and $\sigma(B_n)$ are all provable. In the case that n = 0, A' is provable in P iff $\sigma(A') =_E \sigma(A)$. The actual proof is carried out by a resolution procedure based on complete E-unification algorithms.

The meaning of a Funlog program can be described as follows. The set of equations in EQN defines the finest con-

---

[*] In those cases where the unification problem is not decidable but is semi-decidable, or the minimal and complete set of unifiers is not finite, we cannot fault the algorithm. Bear in mind that even Prolog implements only a semi-decision procedure.

[*] However, there exist equational theories that do not have a minimal and complete set of unifiers for some unifiable terms [9].

gruence relation $=_E$ over the Herbrand universe H. $=_E$ can be viewed as being obtained by using substitutions and by replacing equals by equals. Let P denote a Funlog program and A′ a predicate. The denotation of A′ is a set of tuples defined by:

$$\{[t_1, t_2, ..., t_n] \mid (P \text{ implies } A'(t'_1, t'_2, ..., t'_n)) \, \& $$
$$t_1 =_E t'_1 \, \& \, t_2 =_E t'_2 \, \& \, ... \, \& \, t_n =_E t'_n\}.$$

The coincidence of derivability and logical implication is a direct result of Plotkin's work [28]. This assumes that the unification algorithm for the theory defined in P is complete.

3.4 A Funlog Interpreter

The Funlog interpreter we have designed is best conceptualized as consisting of two cooperating processes. One is called the *driving process* and the other the *answer-collector process*. The driving process invokes the modified resolution procedure which is based on semantic unification. The process answer-collector does "back substitutions" (analogous to standard Prolog): it invokes the procedure Reduce to reduce the function terms that provide bindings for the variables that relate to the ultimate answers. In the case that a function term is not reducible because of its being "blocked" by some uninstantiated variables, further bindings can reactivate its reduction. Note that function reductions can be directly supported by the answer-collector process: a goal statement like ?- X = f(a) will cause f(a) to be reduced by the answer-collector. Notice also that as long as only ground terms are allowed for reduction, the user can write conditional rewrite rules, like

$$f(t_1,...,t_m) = g(s_1,...,s_n) \text{ :- } P_0, \, ..., \, P_k.,$$

where $P_0, ..., P_k$ are Prolog predicates. The applicability of a conditional rewrite rule depends on the evaluation of the predicates in the body. This provides a way for the user to use Prolog predicates as conditions for reduction. As another programming feature, the user can write goals like

?- A^B = filter(odd, [2,5,7,9]).

To prove the equality, the interpreter directly invokes the semantic unification, which reduces the term filter(odd,

175

[2,5,7,9]) until two sides become unifiable.

Example 5. *Evaluating a polynomial of order n at a series of x values in a given range. (Such evaluations are used in plotting curves.)*

A polynomial of order n is represented by a list of n coefficients. For example, $2*x^2 + 4*x - 5$ is represented by the list [-5, 4, 2]. The parameters used in the clauses defining curve_in_range and range are briefly explained below:

Start: the starting point for the plot on the X-axis.

End: the end point for the plot on the X-axis.

Inc: the intervals on the X-axis at which the curve is to be plotted.

Coeffs: coefficients of a polynomial.

Y_value: the values on Y-axis, i.e., the points defining the plot.

Current: the current x value being used for plotting.

```
poly(X, An^L) = X*poly(X, L) + An
poly(X, []) = 0
curve(X, Inc, L) = poly(X, L) ^ curve(X+Inc,Inc,L)

curve_in_range(Start, End, Inc, Coeffs, Y_values)
      :- range(Start, End, Inc,
                curve(Start, Inc, Coeffs), Y_values).
range(Current, End, Inc, L, []) :- Current > End.
range(Current, End, Inc, A^L1, A^L2)
      :- range(Current+Inc, End, Inc, L1, L2).
```

In defining the function *curve,* one does not have to worry about boundary conditions, that is, the engineering of how the function terminates. This makes it easier to program and yields improved flexibility.

Several steps in the execution of the goal

```
?- curve_in_range(-10, 10, 1, [2,5], L)
```

are shown in Figure 6. We assume that the default control strategies are those used in Edinburgh DEC-10 Prolog. The substitutions, denoted by sub$_i$, are used to show the bindings of interest. Please note the convention of renaming variables by attaching "primes" or "subscripts" to them.

Driving Process   **Answer-collector**

?- curve_in_range(-10, 10, 1, [2,5], L)

|

| sub1 = {L = Y_values}   / created and waits for the

| binding of Y_values /

V

?- range(-10, 10, 1, curve(-10, 1, [2,5]), Y_values)

|

| sub2 = {A = poly(-10, [2,5])   / demands reduction of

| L1 = curve(-9, 1, [2,5])   poly(-10, [2,5])

| Y_values = A^L2}   and waits for the

V   binding of L2 /

?- range(-9, 10, 1, curve(-9, 1, [2,5]), L2)

|

| sub3 = {A' = poly(-9, [2,5])   / demands reduction of

| L1' = curve(-8, 1, [2,5]) poly(-9, [2,5])

| L2 = A'^L2'}   and waits for the

V   binding of L2' /

?- range(-8, 10, 1, curve(-8, 1, [2,5]), L2')

....

Figure 6:   A sample execution of Example 5.

Finally, we will have L bound to a list of twenty-one integers. Note that it was the second process that actually demanded complete reductions for unexpanded function calls of *poly*. □

3.5 The Composition of Funlog Programs

In general, the composition of Funlog program is largely dependent on the user's intuitions about the problem to be solved and his or her preference of the way he or she wants to solve it. Typically, it is appropriate to write function definitions for those program segments that are best thought of as one way computations that involve no backtracking, and Prolog clauses for the remaining program segments. Funlog then provides a natural environment for such an interweaving of logic and functions. In addition, it also provides the ability of using *already existing* (large) functional and logic programs. A large programming task may thus be partitioned into segments that involve coding the functional and logic components separately, and subsequently integrated.

We believe that the utility of such features are manifest primarily in large pieces of software. However, the following small scenario may help illustrate some of this flavor. Suppose that given a list of integers, we want to build up an ordered binary tree and then perform some other operations on it. Assume further that we prefer to define the function insert as follows:

```
insert(A, empty) = tree(empty, A, empty)
insert(A, tree(L, B, R))
    = if A = B then tree(L, B, R)
      else if A < B then tree(insert(A, L), B, R)
      else tree(L, B, insert(A, R))
```

and then write a Funlog clause for building up the tree using the function insert as follows:

```
build_up(empty, Tr, Tr).
build_up(A^L, Tr, NewTr)
        :- build_up(L, insert(A, Tr), NewTr).
```

where NewTr serves simply to hold the resulting tree for further operations. Suppose next that we want to perform the following operation on the tree. The nodes of the tree are to be visited by inorder traversal and scaled as follows: 1 is to be

178

subtracted from the first node visited, 2 subtracted from the second node visited, 3 from the third, and so on. This has been argued by Berztiss [3] to be a difficult problem from the point of view of functional programming. There is, therefore, good reason to program this in Prolog. One such Prolog solution is given by Wise in [34]. He claims that the reason for the difficulties with functional programming languages in solving this problem is due to their inability to save intermediate results for sister computations. Equipped with this solution for *scale*, we can then write the program *solve* which builds an ordered tree, and then scales it, as follows:

```
solve(L, Tr) :- build_up(L, empty, Tr1),
                scale(Tr1, Tr).
```

where L is the given list, and scale performs the desired scaling.

4 PARALLEL EXECUTION STRATEGIES

As a result of the rapid decline in hardware costs and the need for modeling distributed computations, parallel programming and models for parallel execution of programs have been an active research area in recent years. Among others, functional programming (represented by data flow languages, e.g., [1, 7, 8]) and logic programming (e.g., [5, 24, 31, 35]) have emerged as two promising formalizations for parallel processing. In this section we will argue that our functional model is amenable to data flow processing, and that the parallel execution model for Funlog can be viewed as an embedding of a data flow model into a parallel execution model for logic programs.

The purpose of the example presented below is twofold: (1) it serves as a further demonstration of the power of the proposed computational model; (2) it illustrates how Horn clauses involving executable functions can be executed in a data flow model.

Example 6. *Finding the First N Lucky Numbers.*
A well-known number-theoretic computation involves the computation of lucky numbers [29], which proceeds as follows:

179

from the list of numbers 1,2,3,4,... we remove every second number, leaving the list 1,3,5,7,9,.... Since 3 is the first number (except for 1) that has not been used in "sifting", we remove every third number from the remaining numbers, obtaining 1,3,7,9,13,15,19,21,.... Every seventh number is next removed, leaving 1,3,7,9,13,15,21,.... and so on. The numbers that are never removed from the list are the lucky numbers.

The difficulty with computational frameworks that do not support computations with infinite data structures is that it may require complex number-theoretic calculations to estimate *a priori* how many integers should be produced in order to get the first N lucky numbers. One can, of course, use a liberal range of integers to search for the first N lucky numbers -- in which case some of the computations will be redundant.

A program that computes the first N lucky numbers without any redundant computations is given below (where the clauses are numbered for later reference):

(1) gen(N) = N^gen(N+2)
(2) sift(M^L, N) = M^sift(sieve(L, M, N), N+1)
(3) sieve(A^L, M, N) = if M=N then sieve(L, M, 1)
                        else A^sieve(L, M, N+1)

(4) truncate(0, Infinite, []).
(5) truncate(N, A^Infinite, A^Finite)
        :- truncate(N-1, Infinite, Finite).
(6) first_N_lucky_numbers(N, L)
        :- truncate(N, 1^sift(gen(3), 3), L).

The function *gen* is used to generate all odd numbers (since no even number can be a lucky number). The function *sift* incrementally outputs the first number M in the current list as a lucky number, calls on the function *sieve* to remove every Mth number in the list, and then starts the same process again on the remaining list. The variable N is used to count the position of each number in the list in order to determine whether the number should be removed or not. □

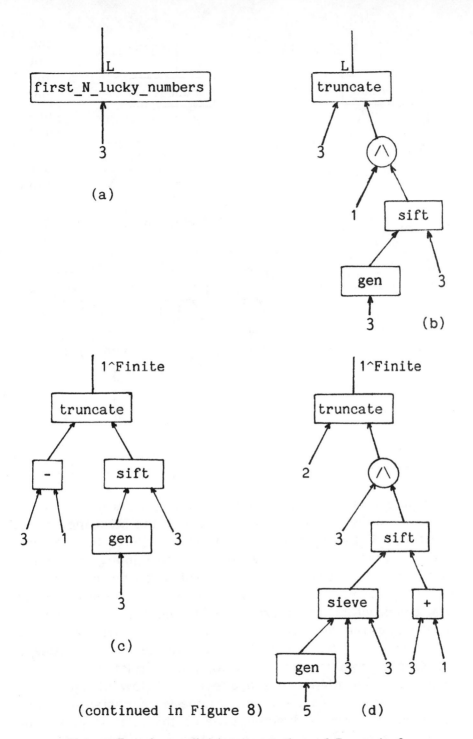

(a)

(b)

(c)

(d)

(continued in Figure 8)

Figure 7: A parallel interpretation of Example 6.

181

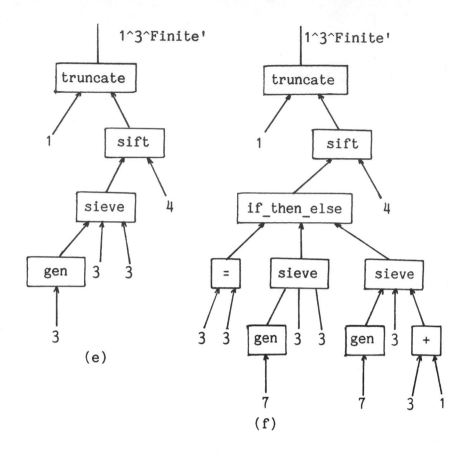

Figure 8: Continuation of Figure 7.

Figure 7 and Figure 8 show some snapshots in the execution of a parallel interpreter, resulting from the invocation of the goal `first_N_lucky_numbers(3,L)`. In the figure, the computation is represented as a dynamically changing graph, where each of the functions and relations (which can be thought of as *computing agents*) is represented by a square node in the graph; data constructors are represented by circles, while "tokens" travel along the arcs which connect nodes. Arcs emanating from function nodes are directed, and represent input streams and output streams. Arcs emanating from relation nodes are undirected, indicating that the direction of flow of data is not pre-determined. In case a function node is connected to a relation node, the arc is directed towards the relation node. This reflects the fact that the corresponding parameter in the rela-

182

tion is used in "input mode" (for the use of "modes" see, e.g., [27] or [4]). The execution can be either "eager" or "lazy" although in the figures only lazy evaluation is illustrated. Figure 7b represents the goal truncate(3,1^sift(gen(3),3),L), which resolves with the clause (6), resulting in the goal in Figure 7c where the first lucky number becomes available. The attempt to semantically unify this goal with the clause (6) demands the reduction of the function term sift(gen(3),3), which in turn demands the reduction of gen(3). This results in Figure 7d, where the semantic unification succeeds. The next goal is shown in Figure 8e, where the second lucky number becomes available after a resolution step. The computation continues in Figure 8f. In an eager evaluation mode, all the function and relation nodes can be made to produce partial results whenever possible. This can increase the degree of parallelism at the expense of performing some computations that may be redundant. An unpredictable increase of space may also occur. A combination of eager and lazy evaluation can be used if buffering is provided; this permits each process to produce one or more partial results before they are demanded. Additional parallelism can be achieved in the following ways: (1) The subterms involved in the reductions of a function term can be reduced in parallel; (2) In the execution of biased semantic unification, the applicability of the various defining equations can be tested in parallel. The parallel evaluation model sketched here is actually a variant of the Kahn–MacQueen parallel interpreter [18]. In our model, computing agents consist of functions and relations, and both eager and lazy evaluations, as well as possibly a combination of the two.

5 RELATED WORK AND DISCUSSION

We have described Funlog, a computational model which integrates functional programming and logic programming. The underlying function model is characterized by a term rewriting system with the confluence property. The reduction mechanism is based on pattern-driven lazy reduction. By embedding pattern-driven reduction into the conventional unification algorithm, we obtain the notion of semantic unification, which provides the key mechanism for combining functional programming and logic programming. This enhances logic based computational frameworks by adding the ability to gracefully terminate computations on infinite data structures, and extends the functional computational frameworks by providing a knowledge-based inferencing ability. Furthermore, the current model can be extended to include logic programming with equality (for certain equational theories) if we use E-unification algorithm(s) to replace the semantic unification algorithm. This then provides the ability to reason about equations.

Several languages based upon first-order predicate logic support computations on infinite data structures and provide a notion of functions. FPL [2] is an extension of a functional language, and enjoys a first-order logic axiomatic flavor. However, the language only defines (deterministic) functions. A demand-driven lazy evaluation rule is provided in the language described in [13] and provides the ability to terminate computations on infinite data structures. This language is based on natural deduction and provides a functional notation. Its semantics, however, is not quite clear and it is also not evident how a full notion of equality can be provided. Kornfeld's work [22] demonstrates the practical benefits of incorporating equality into Prolog. Kahn's work on Uniform [19], and Parlog [5] are also relevant. Recently, Goguen and Meseguer have extended the work in a more general setting [12]. Their work, however, does not account for the case when the underlying equations cannot be described by a canonical term rewriting system. We have treated this in some restricted cases, and have demonstrated by examples the practical use of combining nonterminating term rewriting systems and logic programming.

ACKNOWLEDGMENTS

We would like to acknowledge helpful feedback on an early version of this paper from Prof. Robert Keller. We also highly appreciate Prof. Gary Lindstrom's detailed comments on earlier drafts of this paper.

We are grateful to Doug DeGroot for his interest in our

project. The version of the interpreter included here was developed in IBM Prolog by his group at Yorktown Heights.

The research done by Jia-Huai You was supported by ONR under contract N00014-83-k-0317.

APPENDIX
```
/* A  Simple F U N L O G  Interpreter */

/* Definitions of operators, operator types and */
/* associated priorities */

op(':',rl,101).
op(else,rl,80).
op(then,rl,70).
op(if,prefix,90).
op(in,lr,70).
op(let,prefix,90).
op('=..',rl,100).
op('==',rl,100).
op('>',rl,100).
op('=>',rl,59).
op('+',lr,60).
op('-',lr,60).
op('@',lr,100).
op('/',lr,100).
op('+',prefix,120).
op('-',prefix,120).
op('?',suffix,4).

/* "<-" corresponds to ":-" in DEC-10 Prolog */
/* "/" is the cut symbol */
```

```
/* "&" corresponds to "," in DEC-10 Prolog, and */
/* denotes an ANDing of goals */
/* "*" is a "don't care" variable */


<- delax(X = X).
    /* retract any existing definition of "=" */


solve(G) <- solve(G,G).
    /* double goals in order to provide "or" */


solve(true,*) <- /.
solve(P,*) <- built-in(P) & / & eval_args(P,P1) & P1.
    /* Prolog built-in predicates get proved in */
    /* Prolog itself with arguments evaluated */


solve(/,G) <-  / & solve(G,*). /* provide "cut" */


solve(X & Y,G)  <- / & solve(X,G) & solve(Y,G).
    /* conjunctive goals */
solve(X | Y,G)  <- / & (solve(X,G) | solve(Y,G)).
    /* disjunctive goals */
solve(P,*) <-
    cfind(P,(H <- B)) & unify(P,H) & solve(B,P).
        /* find a candidate clause H <- B */
        /* where H matches P, and resolve */


/* built-in predicates */
built-in(find(*,*,*)).
built-in(diff(*,*,*)).
built-in(prod(*,*,*)).
built-in(quot(*,*,*)).
built-in(sum(*,*,*)).
built-in(rem(*,*,*)).
```

```
built-in(eq(*,*)).
built-in(gt(*,*)).
built-in(ge(*,*)).
built-in(le(*,*)).
built-in(lt(*,*)).
built-in(ne(*,*)).
built-in(atom(*)).
built-in(cons(*,*)).
built-in(int(*)).
built-in(skel(*)).
built-in(var(*)).
built-in(write(*)).
built-in(ax(*,*)).
built-in(delax(*)).
built-in(op(*,*,*)).
built-in(ancestor(*)).
built-in(fail).
built-in(delax(*)).
built-in(op(*,*,*)).
built-in(* ^= *).

eval_args(gt(X,Y),gt(X1,Y1)) <-
    not(var(X)) & not(var(Y)) & X => X1 & Y => Y1 & /.
/* "=>" is the Reduce procedure; other */
/* built-in predicates can be defined similarly*/


eval_args(X,X).

cfind(P,(L <- R)) <-
    functor(P,F,N) & functor(L,F,N) &
    ax(L,C) & form(C,L,R).
/* get the functor and arity for P and the form */
/* a template for P; get the clause C whose head */
```

187

```
/* matches L; and get the head L and body B from C */

form(L <- R,L,R) <- /.
form(L,L,true).
functor(T,F,N) <- var(T) & length(Args,N) &
                  cons(F.Args,T) & /.

functor(T,F,N) <- cons(F.Args,T) &
                  length(Args,N) & /.

/* semantic unification */
unify(X,X) <- /.
unify(T,S) <-
    functor(T,F,N) & functor(S,F,N) &
    gt(N,0) & T =.. F.Ts & S =.. F.Ss & / &
    unify_list(Ts,Ss) & / .
/* succeed if T and S are already unifiable */

/* otherwise, try and reduce either the first or */
/* second argument and try again */
unify(T,S) <- one_step_reducible(S,S1) & / &
              unify(T,S1).
unify(S,T) <- one_step_reducible(S,S1) & / &
              unify(T,S1).

/* special treatment for primitives */
unify(T,S) <- primitive(S) & reducible(S,R) &
              S ^= R & / & unify(T,R).
    /* "^=" is "same as \==" in DEC-10 Prolog */

unify(S,T) <- primitive(S) & / &
              reducible(S,R) & S ^= R & unify(T,R).
```

```
unify_list(Ts,Ss) <- apply(Ts,Ss,unify).


/* apply R to every element of a list */
apply(nil,nil,R) <- /.
apply(A.X,B.Y,R) <- R:(A.B.nil) & apply(X,Y,R).


R:Ts <- X =.. R.Ts & X.
    /* evaluates function application */
X =.. Y <- cons(Y,X).
  /* defines the operator "=.." which is not */
  /* built-in in IBM Prolog using "cons" which is */
  /* a built-in  operator in IBM Prolog. */


one_step_reducible(S,S1) <- find(S,Eqn,B) & B &
                            reducible(S,Eqn,S1) & /.
    /* find an (conditional) equation Eqn */
    /* prove the conditions B */
    /* S is reduced to S1 by the equation */


/* note that a conditional equation is actually a */
/* Prolog clause with the head as an equation, as */
/* of the form A = B <- C1, C2, ..., CN. */


find(S,(L = R),B) <-
    functor(S,F,N) & functor(L,F,N) &
    ax((L = R),C ) & form(C,L = R,B).
        /* similar to cfind, but the clause */
        /* found is a (conditional) equation */


reducible(S,(L=R),R) <- sunify(L,S).
        /* defined later for primitives */
/* note that the substitutions for the variables */
/* in R are automatically done as a result of */
```

```
/* variable sharing in the clause */


/* biased semantic unification */
/* only ground terms are reduced */
/* the mode is */
/* sunify(in:lhs_term, in:function_term) */
sunify(X,Y) <- nonground(Y) & / & fail.
sunify(X,X) <- /.
sunify(T,S) <- primitive(S) & / & reducible(S,R) &
               S ^= R & sunify(T,R) .
sunify(T,S) <- functor(T,F,N) & functor(S,F,N) &
               gt(N,0) & T =.. F.Ts & S =.. F.Ss &
               / & sunify_list(Ts,Ss) & /.
sunify(T,S) <- one_step_reducible(S,S1) &
               sunify(T,S1) & /.
sunify_list(Ts,Ss) <- apply(Ts,Ss,sunify).


nonground(X) <- var(X) & /.
nonground(X) <- X =.. F.Ts & either(Ts,nonground).
either(X.L,R) <- R:(X.nil) & /.
either(X.L,R) <- either(L,R).


/* the interpreter for function reductions */
red(T) <- T=>R & write(R).


T => R <- primitive(T) & reducible(T,R) & /.
T => R <- one_step_reducible(T,T1) &
          T ^= T1 & T1 => R & /.
T => R <- T =.. F.Ts & reduce_list(Ts,Rs) &
          R =.. F.Rs & /.
T => T.
reduce_list(X,Y) <-  apply(X,Y,=>).
```

```
/* define primitive functions */
primitive(X1 == X2).
primitive(let X1 in X2).
primitive(X1 > X2).
primitive(X1 + X2).
primitive(X1 - X2).
primitive(X1 @ X2).    /* multiplication */
primitive(X1 / X2).
primitive(+X).
primitive(-X).
primitive(X) <- int(X).


/* reduce primitives */
reducible(X,X) <- (atom(X) | int(X)) & /.
reducible(let (X = F) in G,H) <-
        not(var(F)) & sunify(X,F) & G => H & /.

reducible(X == X,true) <- /.
reducible(X1 == X2,true) <- X1 => R & X2 => R & /.

reducible(X1 == X2,false) <- X1 ^= X2 & /.

reducible(X1 > X2,true) <-
        X1 => R1 & X2 => R2 &
        int(R1) & int(R2) & gt(R1,R2) & /.

reducible(X1 > X2,false) <-
        int(X1) & int(X2) & /.
reducible(X1 + X2,R) <-
        / & X1 => A & X2 => B &
        int(A) & int(B) & sum(A,B,R).

reducible(X1 - X2,R) <-
```

```
        / & X1 => A & X2 => B &
        int(A) & int(B) & diff(A,B,R).

reducible(X1 @ X2, R) <-
        / & X1 => A & X2 => B &
        int(A) & int(B) & prod(A,B,R).

reducible(X1 / X2, R)<-
        / & X1 => A &  X2 => B &
        int(A) & int(B) & quot(A,B,R).

reducible(+X,R) <- / & reducible(X,R).
reducible(-X,R) <- / & reducible(0-X,R).

/*---------Examples of Funlog programs---------- */

if false then X else Y = Y.
if true then X else Y = X.

if true then X = X.

app(nil,X) = X.
app(A.X,Y) = A.app(X,Y).

inorder(tr(0,N,0)) = N.nil.
inorder(tr(L,N,R)) = app(inorder(L),N.inorder(R)).

ints = ints(0).
ints(X) = X.ints(1 + X).

select(N,L) = if (N == 0) then nil
              else hd(L).select(N - 1,tl(L)).
hd(X.L) = X.
```

```
tl(X.L) = L.


exp(X,0) = 1.
exp(X,Y) = if (Y > 0) then exp(X,Y-1) @ X.


mod(X,Y) = X - Y @ (X/Y).


/* an example of a conditional equation /*
fact(0) = 1.
fact(N) = N @ fact(N-1) <- N > 0.


primes = filter(ints(2)).
filter(P.L) = P.filter(delete(P,L)).
delete(P,X.L) = if (mod(X,P) == 0) then delete(P,L)
                else X.delete(P,L).
sort(nil) = nil.
sort(A.X) =
    app(sort(X1),A.sort(X2)) <- par(A,X,X1,X2).
        /* another conditional equation */
par(A,nil,nil,nil).
par(A,B.L1,B.L2,L3) <- gt(A,B) & par(A,L1,L2,L3).
par(A,B.L1,L2,B.L3) <- le(A,B) & par(A,L1,L2,L3).


qsort(nil) = nil.
qsort(A.X) =  let (X1.X2.nil = partition(X,A)) in
                app(qsort(X1),A.qsort(X2)).
/* notice the use of "let ... in" syntax */


partition(nil,A) = nil.nil.nil.
partition(B.X,A) =
    let (X1.X2.nil = partition(X,A)) in
    (if (A > B) then  (B.X1).X2.nil
      else X1.(B.X2).nil).
```

```
/* a Prolog program remains as it is */
nrev(nil,nil).
nrev(X.L1,L3) <- nrev(L1,L2) & append(L2,X.nil,L3).

/* Example 5 in the paper */
poly(X,An.L) = X @ poly(X,L) + An.
poly(X,nil) = 0.
curve(X,Inc,L) = poly(X,L).curve(X+Inc,Inc,L).

curve_in_range(S,E,I,C,Ys) <-
        range(S,E,I,curve(S,I,C),Ys).
range(C,E,I,L,nil) <- gt(C,E).
range(C,E,I,A.L1,A.L2) <- range(C+I,E,I,L1,L2).
```

REFERENCES

1. Ackerman, W.B. "Data flow languages". *Computer 15,* 2 (February 1982), 15–25.

2. Bellia, M., P. Degano, and G. Levi. The call by name semantics of a clause language with functions. In *Logic Programming,* K.L. Clark and S.-A. Tarnlund, Eds., Academic Press, 1982, pp. 281–298.

3. Berztiss, A., and B. Thatte. Specification and implementation of abstract data types. In *Advances in Computers, Volume 22,* Marshall C. Yovits, Ed., Academic Press, 1983, pp. 296–350.

4. Clark, K.L., and S. Gregory. A relational language for parallel programming. Functional programming and computer architecture, October, 1981, pp. 171–179.

5. Clark, K.L., and S. Gregory. Parlog: a parallel logic programming language. Doc 83/5, Dept. of Computing, Imperial College of Science and Technology, University of London, 180 Queen's Gate London SW7 2BZ, March, 1983.

6. Colmerauer, A. Prolog and infinite trees. In *Logic* Programming, K. L. Clark and S.-A. Tarnlund, Eds., Academic Press, 1982, pp. 231–252.

7. Davis, A.L., and R.M. Keller. "Data Flow Graphs". *Computer 15,* 2 (February 1982), 26–41.

8. Dennis, J.B. First Version of a Data Flow Procedure Language. In *Lecture Notes in Computer Science, Volume 19,* G. Goos and J. Hartmanis, Eds., Springer-Verlag, New York, 1974, pp. 362–376.

9. Fages, F., and G. Huet. Complete sets of unifiers and matchers in equational theories. Proceedings, 5th Conference on Trees, Algebra and Programming, 1983, pp. 205–220.

10. Fay, M.J. First-order unification in an equational theory. Master Th., Department of Information Science, University of California at Santa Cruz,June 1978.

11. Friedman, D.P., and D.S. Wise. CONS should not evaluate its arguments. In *Automata, Languages and Programming*, S. Michaelson and R. Milner, Eds., Edinburgh University Press, Edinburgh, 1976.

12. Goguen, J., and J. Meseguer. Equality, types, modules and generics for logic programming. Proc. Second International Logic Programming Conference, Uppsala, July, 1984.

13. Hansson, A., S. Haridi, and S.-A. Tarnlund. Properties of a logic programming language. In *Logic Programming*, K.L. Clark and S.-A Tarnlund, Eds., Academic Press, New York, 1982, pp. 267-280.

14. Henderson, Peter. *Functional programming: Application and Implementation*. Prentice-Hall, 1980.

15. Huet, G. Confluent reduction. Proc. 18th IEEE Symposium on Foundations of Computer Science, 1977.

16. Huet, G., and D.C. Oppen. Equations and rewrite rules: a survey. In *Formal Language Theory: Perspectives and Open problems*, R.V. Book, Ed., Academic Press, 1980, pp. 349-405.

17. Hullot, J.M. Canonical forms and unification. Proc. 5th Conference on Automated Deduction, 1980, pp. 318-334.

18. Kahn, G., and D.B. MacQueen. Coroutines and networks of parallel processes. Information Processing 77, 1977, pp. 993-998.

19. Kahn, K.M. Uniform -- a language based upon unification which unifies (much of) List, Prolog, and Act 1. Proc. of the Workshop on Logic Programming for Intelligent Systems, 1981. Also appears in this volume.

20. Keller, R.M. Semantics and applications of function graphs. UUCS-8-112, University of Utah, Dept. of Computer Science, October, 1980.

21. Knuth, D., and P. Bendix. Simple word problems in universal algebras. In *Computational Problems in Abstract Algebra*, J. Leech, Ed., Pergamon Press, 1970, pp. 163-279.

22. Kornfeld, Bill. Equality for Prolog. Proc. 8th International Joint Conference on Artificial Intelligence, Karlsruhe, West Germany, August, 1983. Also appears in this volume..

23. Lankford, D.S. Canonical inference. ATP-32, Department of Mathematics and Computer Science, University of Texas at Austin, December, 1975.

24. Lindstrom, G., and P. Panangaden. Stream-based execution of logic programs. Proc. of the International Symposium on Logic Programming, Atlantic City, New Jersey, February, 1984, pp. 168-176.

25. Martelli, A., and U. Montanari. "An efficient unification algorithm". *ACM Transaction on Programming Languages and Systems 4*, 2 (April 1982), 258-282.

26. O'Donnell, M. Computing in systems described by equations. In *Lecture Notes in Computer Science, Volume 58*, Springer-Verlag, New York, 1977.

27. Pereira, L.M., F.C.N. Pereira, and D.H.D. Warren. *User's Guide to DECsystem-10 Prolog.* University of Edinburgh, 1978.

28. Plotkin, G. Building-in equational theories. In *Machine Intelligence 7*,
Edinburgh University Press, 1972, pp. 73-90.

29. Reingold, E.M., J. Nievergelt, and N. Deo. *Combinatorial Algorithms: Theory and Practice.* Prentice-Hall, 1977.

30. Rosen, B.K. "Tree-manipulation systems and Church-Rosser Theorems". *JACM 20*, 1 (1973).

31. Shapiro, E.Y. A subset of concurrent Prolog and its interpreter. TR-003, ICOT- Institute of New Generation Computer Technology, January, 1983.

32. Siekmann, J., and P. Szabo. Universal unification and a classification of equational theories. Proc. 6th Workshop on Automatic Deduction, New York, June, 1982, pp. 369–389.

33. Subrahmanyam, P.A., and J.-H. You. Conceptual basis and evaluation strategies for integrating functional and logic programming. Proc. of International Symposium on Logic Programming, Atlantic City, New Jersey, February, 1984, pp. 144–153.

34. Wise, M.J. "Epilog = Prolog + data flow: arguments for combining Prolog with a data driven mechanism". *SIGPLAN Notices Notices 17*, 12 (December 1982), 80–86.

35. Wise, M.J. A parallel Prolog: the construction of a data driven model. Conference on LISP and Functional Programming Languages, 1982.

36. You, J.-H. A note on the termination properties of a semantic unification algorithm. An unpublished note.

37. You, J.-H., and P.A. Subrahmanyam. A class of term rewriting systems and unification. unpublished manuscript.

Part III:

Symmetric Combinations

LEAF: A LANGUAGE WHICH INTEGRATES LOGIC, EQUATIONS AND FUNCTIONS

R. Barbuti, M. Bellia, G. Levi,

Dipartimento di Informatica, Universita' di Pisa.
Corso Italia 40, I56100 Pisa.

M. Martelli

CNUCE-C.N.R.
Via S. Maria 36, I56100 Pisa.

ABSTRACT

The paper describes a language which integrates a declarative language, consisting of Horn clauses and equational theories with constructors, and a first order functional language. Both language components will eventually be directly supported by a hardware machine. The declarative component permits the definition of both relations and functions, possibly dealing with infinite data structures. A formal semantics, coping with the novel language features, is given in the standard style (operational, model-theoretic and fixpoint). The functional (procedural) component is essentially the functional (deterministic) sublanguage of the declarative one. It has a lazy evaluation based parallel interpreter and allows efficient programming of system software, tools and algorithms. The technique for integrating these two language components is based on using the procedural component as the metalanguage of the declarative component, thus allowing procedural programs to act on meta-objects such as declarative theories and (possibly infinite) sets of solutions of declarative programs. Examples are given of tools for the declarative component and of integrated procedural-declarative applications.

1 INTRODUCTION

Recent progress in hardware technology makes it feasible and appealing to build high level machines that provide a Prolog-like machine language oriented towards knowledge representation and inference [32]. Indeed, logic programming languages [25] are suitable for writing intelligent programs because of their highly declarative style, their goal directed computational strategy and their ability to cope with relations.

A fully declarative language, however, does not seem to be adequate as a machine language. In fact, both at the system and at the application levels there exist software components which are intrinsically procedural. Defining them declaratively would, on the one hand, be unnatural, and, on the other hand, make them less efficient. Examples of typical procedural components are operating systems and programming tools. Another example can be found in most existing Prolog implementations, where some primitive data types (typically numbers) are procedurally defined. Most "intelligent" applications can be naturally decomposed into two parts: a set of declarative programs which produce information through inferences on the knowledge base, and a set of algorithms which process such information in a rather standard way.

One solution for the problem of expressing algorithms in logic in a natural way is to super-impose a control language [26]. We claim that this goal can be better achieved by integrating a logic programming language with a functional language oriented towards system implementation. Such an integration will allow easy combination of declarative knowledge and procedural knowledge. The integration of logic programming with functional programming is currently being pursued by several projects. The aim of such efforts is the definition of a powerful programming language which, on the one hand, is adequate for the needs of intelligent applications, and on the other hand, can efficiently be executed by special-purpose machines.

2 LOGIC AND FUNCTIONAL LANGUAGES

A variety of approaches can be followed to obtain the integration of logic and functional languages. The first approach (LOGLISP [34] and POPLOG [30]) is to combine a logic language with an existing powerful functional language, such as LISP or POP-2, by means of a suitable interface.

The main advantages of this approach are the availability of excellent programming environments and the possibility of exploiting existing programming expertise. On the other hand, fairly complex mechanisms have to be defined to interface the two language components.

Our alternative approach [3,7] is to design a new functional language which has a (mathematical and operational) semantics compatible with the logic language semantics, yet can easily and efficiently be implemented.

Semantic compatibility requires the two languages to operate on the same data (Herbrand terms) and to share both the basic control mechanism (rewriting) and the basic parameter passing and parameter return mechanism (matching or unification). Moreover, the functional language must have a minimal Herbrand model semantics [14]. This design decision should make the integration conceptually simpler and could be supported by a single architectural model.

Many other recent language proposals [19,24,36] address the problem of logic and functional programming integration essentially by extending Horn clause logic with functional equations. The resulting functional sublanguage, however, still behaves as a logic programming language. For example, functions have logical variables and can be inverted. Moreover, the operational semantics is based on proving existentially quantified equalities, and can lead to non-deterministic results. Such an extension is very useful to improve the expressive power of the logic programming (declarative) language.

Our language, LEAF (Logic, Equations And Functions), provides such features in the declarative component by integrating Horn clause logic with equational theories with constructors. However, we think that the functional (procedural) component should be much simpler. Namely, it should be deterministic, and it should be based only on parameter passing by pattern matching instead of unification (i.e. no logical variables are permitted).

Our procedural component [4,5,7] is obtained by putting some constraints on the declarative component. These constraints are :

i)   mode declarations [11,12,13,38] which have widely been used to provide control information in logic programs, and, in our case guarantee the absence of logical variables.

ii) syntactic conditions which guarantee determinacy.

The resulting procedural component is essentially a language based on deterministic graph rewritings. It subsumes tree rewriting systems originally developed for algebraic data type specifications [10,18,27]. Tree rewriting systems have been given a minimal Herbrand model semantics [28] and can be viewed as equational theories with constructors, but without logical variables. By analogy, graph rewriting systems can be viewed as an algorithmic (without logical variables) version of Horn clauses.

In our view the distinguishing features of the logic component with respect to the procedural one are logical variables and search-based computation. In LEAF, the procedural component has no logical variables and does not require any search, while in the declarative component all the variables are logical and the computation is based on searching.

In other logic programming languages (e.g. the and-parallel component of PARLOG [13] and Concurrent Prolog [35]) logical and non-logical variables can occur in the same clause and "committed choice" non-determinism is adopted. This solution provides powerful programming constructs to control program execution. However, a declarative semantics is very hard to define for such languages.

Let us finally mention another promising approach which starts with a clean functional language and extends it with typical logic programming features such as logical variables, searching and set operations [8]. Other proposals in this direction can be found in [1,29].

3 THE LANGUAGE

As already mentioned, LEAF consists of a declarative and a procedural component. The main features of the declarative component are:

-   the combination of Horn clause logic (relations) and equational theories with constructors (functions);

-   the absence of separate proof method (such as semantic unification [36] or narrowing [17,21,22]) for dealing with functions;

-   a computational model based on networks of processes and a demand driven strategy;

-   a new inference rule which corresponds to a call-by-name semantics and allows us to handle infinite data structures;

a model theoretic (and equivalent fixpoint) semantics which copes with the above new features.

The combination of relations and functions in a single logic programming language has been proposed by several authors [19,20,24,36]. A comprehensive set of motivations can be found in [24].

The language in [20] and FUNLOG [36] share several features with LEAF, such as the demand driven strategy and infinite data structures. However, in FUNLOG the integration is based on an incomplete extension of the unification algorithm (as is the case for the language in [24]), and a formal semantics is not given. The language in [20] suggests an inference rule suitable for dealing with infinite objects, even if the model theoretic semantics is not given. The language is a superset of Horn clause logic with equality and its implementation is based on natural deduction techniques.

Finally, in EQLOG [19] functions are handled by narrowing, which provides a complete implementation of equality. This approach forces the set of equations to be confluent and terminating. EQLOG defines a call-by-value semantics and does not allow infinite data structures. Of all the above mentioned languages, EQLOG is the only language which was given a formal semantics definition.

The procedural component of LEAF essentially has all the features of the declarative component, the major differences being:

- relations are replaced by tuple-valued functions;
- the inference rule only allows pattern matching (on parameters) instead of unification (on logical variables);
- as a consequence of the above features, the language is deterministic.

LEAF has several other interesting features that will not be described in this paper. Let us mention:

- types, polymorphisms and modules which are present in algebraic specification languages, in last-generation imperative programming languages, and which have recently been proposed for logic programming languages [2,19,33];
- constructs oriented toward concurrency control, which are typical of systems programming languages and allow one to describe, both procedurally and declaratively, low-level synchronization problems [16].

In the next section we will formally define the declarative component. Section 5 will consider the procedural component LCA (Logic for Communicating Agents) which is extensively described elsewhere [4,5,7], and will not be formally defined here. Rather we will focus on those language features which are relevant to machine architecture, on the one hand, and to the integration with the declarative component, on the other hand.

4 THE DECLARATIVE COMPONENT

4.1 Syntax

The language alphabet is $A = \{C, D, V, F, R\}$, where:
   C is a set of constant symbols,
   D is a set of data constructor symbols,
   V is a set of variable symbols,
   F is a set of function symbols, and
   R is a set of predicate symbols.

A *data term* is:

i)   a constant symbol,

ii)   a variable symbol, or

iii)   a data constructor application $d(t_1, \ldots, t_n)$ where d in D and $t_1, \ldots, t_n$ are data terms.

A *term* is:

i)   a data term,

ii)   a data constructor application $d(t_1, \ldots, t_n)$ where d in D and $t_1, \ldots, t_n$ are terms, or

iii)   a function symbol application $f(t_1, \ldots, t_n)$ where f in F and $t_1, \ldots, t_n$ are terms.

An *atom* is:

i)   a functional atom $f(t_1, \ldots, t_n) = t$ where f is a function symbol and $t_1, \ldots, t_n$ are terms, and t (the *right part* of the atom) is a term, or

206

ii)   a relational atom $p(t_1, \ldots, t_n)$ where p is a predicate symbol and $t_1, \ldots, t_n$ are terms.

A *header* is:

i)   a relational header $p(t_1, \ldots, t_n)$ where p is a predicate symbol and $t_1, \ldots, t_n$ are data terms, or

ii)   a functional header $f(t_1, \ldots, t_n) = t$ where f is a function symbol, $t_1, \ldots, t_n$ are data terms, t is a term and each variable occurring in t is *functionally derived* in the corresponding clause.

A variable x is *functionally derived* in a clause

$$c: \quad f(t_1, \ldots, t_n) = t <-- B_1, \ldots, B_k$$

if:

i) x occurs in one of the t_i's, or

ii) x occurs in an atom B_j of the form $\tau_j = x$ where all the variables in τ_j are functionally derived in c.

A *clause* is:

i)   the *empty clause* $\square$,

ii)   a *unit clause* $A <--$ where A is a header, or

iii)   a *definite clause* $A <--B_1, \ldots, B_n$ $(n \geq 1)$ where A is a header and the *body* $B_1, \ldots, B_n$ is a collection of atoms.

A *program* is a set of clauses $c_1, \ldots, c_n$ such that, for each pair of functional headers $f'(t'_1, \ldots, t'_n) = t'$ and $f''(t''_1, \ldots, t''_m) = t''$ $f'(t'_1, \ldots, t'_n)$ and $f''(t''_1, \ldots, t''_m)$ are not unifiable (superposition free).

A *goal clause* G is a formula of the form

$$<-- B_1, \ldots, B_n \quad (n \geq 1)$$

where $B_1, \ldots, B_n$ are atoms.

The set of all variables occurring in G is denoted by Var(G).

Consider the following example:

207

1.1 N(0) < −−
1.2 N(S(x)) < −− N(x)

2.1 +(0,x)=x < −− N(x)
2.2 +(S(x),y) = S(+(x,y)) < −− N(y)

3.1 nat(x) = CONS(x,nat(S(x))) < −−

4.1 odd(CONS(x,CONS(y,z))) = CONS(x,odd(z)) < −−

5.1 sqrlist() = CONS(0,sqrlist1(0,odd(nat(S(0))))) < −−

6.1 sqrlist1(x,CONS(y,z)) =
            CONS(+(x,y),sqrlist1(+(x,y),z)) < −−

7.1 Hyp(x,y,z) < −− sqrlist() = w,sqr(z,w) = +(sqr(x,w),sqr(y,w))

8.1 sqr(0,CONS(x,y)) = x < −−
8.2 sqr(S(x),CONS(y,z)) = sqr(x,z) < −−

The example defines the following functions and relations:

N   is the relation which defines the set of natural numbers;

+   is the standard plus operation on naturals (the conditions in the equations guarantee that the function is defined only if the second argument is a natural);

nat   is the function which defines the infinite, increasing sequence of naturals starting from the argument value;

odd   is the function which, when provided with an infinite sequence of elements, returns the subsequence of its elements with odd indices;

sqrlist
        is the function which computes the infinite increasing sequence of all the squares of natural numbers. The square of n is obtained as the sum of the first n odd numbers;

Hyp   is the relation which defines the set of triples $\{<x,y,z>\}$ such that $z^2 = x^2+y^2$. The three squares are computed by sharing the infinite sequence of squares.

Note that our language is a Horn clause logic with equality. The subset of a program consisting of unit clauses with functional headers is

208

an equational theory with constructors (because of the separation between function and data constructor symbols). Definite clauses with functional headers (e.g. clauses 2.1 and 2.2 in the example) can be viewed as conditional equations. The non-superposition and the functionally derivability properties on functional headers guarantee that function symbols denote functions. However, as will be shown in section 4.4 (unification of functional atoms), equations define first-class relations.

4.2 The Canonical Form of LEAF

Both the interpretation of a goal clause as a network of processes and the underlying formal semantics are based on a *canonical form* of LEAF.

A *canonical program* is a set of *canonical clauses*.

A *canonical clause* is:

i)   the empty clause,

ii)   any unit clause, or

iii)   a definite clause $A < -- B_1, \ldots, B_n$ where $A, B_1, \ldots, B_n$ are canonical atoms.

A *canonical atom* is:

i)   a functional atom $f(t_1, \ldots, t_n) = t$ where f is a function symbol and $t, t_1, \ldots, t_n$ are data terms, or

ii)   a relational atom $p(t_1, \ldots, t_n)$ where p is a predicate symbol and $t_1, \ldots, t_n$ are data terms.

Note that, in the canonical form, data terms are required wherever (possibly functional) terms were used in the definitions of atoms and functional headers. In other words, the canonical form does not allow function composition, which is replaced by conjunctions of atoms. The canonical form makes explicit those relations between inputs and outputs which are implicit in function compositions.

Each clause of a LEAF program is reduced to the canonical form by the following transformation:

Clause transformation to canonical form

Let c be a clause

$$c: A < -- B_1, \ldots, B_k$$

i)   if A is a functional header $f(t_1, \ldots, t_n) = t$, c' is the *expansion of clause c with respect to t*, otherwise c' = c;

ii)   for each atom in the body of c' of the form $p(t_1, \ldots, t_n)$ or $f(t_1, \ldots, t_{n-1}) = t_n$ (where p is a predicate symbol and f a function symbol), c" is the expansion of c' with respect to $t_1, \ldots, t_n$.
Repeat step ii) on c" until the clause does not contain nested function applications.

The *expansion of a clause c with respect to a term t* replaces the outermost function application in t with a new variable and adds to the clause body the corresponding functional atom. Namely, given a clause c and a term t occurring in c, the expansion of c with respect to t results in a clause c' obtained as follows:

i)   if t is a data term, c' = c;

ii)   if t has the form $f(t_1, \ldots, t_n)$ (where f is a function symbol), c' is obtained from c by replacing t by a new variable symbol v, and adding the atom $t = v$ in the clause body;

iii)   if t has the form $d(t_1, \ldots, t_n)$ (where d is a data constructor symbol), c' is the expansion of c with respect to $t_1, \ldots, t_n$.

A further step is useful to eliminate variants, i.e. atoms of the form $f(t_1, \ldots, t_n) = v_1$ and $f(t_1, \ldots, t_n) = v_2$ (where v_1 and v_2 are different variable symbols). Variants are possibly generated by the transformation to canonical form.

Variant elimination

Given a clause c with two variants $t = v_1$ and $t = v_2$, we can obtain a clause c' equivalent to c by eliminating the atom $t = v_1$ and replacing v_2 for all the occurrences of v_1.
The elimination proceeds as long as variants are present.

Let us give an example of the transformation by using the clause 6.1. The transformation to canonical form produces the following clause:

6.1c sqrlist1(x,CONS(y,z)) = CONS(v_1, v_2) < --
$\qquad$ +(x,y) = v_1,sqrlist1(v_3,z) = v_2,+(x,y) = v_3

The elimination of variants produces:

6.1e sqrlist1(x,CONS(y,z)) = CONS(v_1,v_2) < --
  +(x,y) = v_1, sqrlist1(v_1,z) = v_2

Different problems arise when transforming a goal clause to canonical form. Given a goal G, the transformation is performed as in step ii) above, thus obtaining a new goal clause G'. Given two variants $t = v_1$ and $t = v_2$ in G', the variant elimination applies in the following cases:

i) v_1 and v_2 are not in Var(G); or

ii) v_1 belongs to Var(G) and v_2 does not. In this case the eliminated atom is necessarily $t = v_2$.

Note that no elimination occurs involving variables of G. The set of global outputs of G' (Global(G')) is exactly Var(G). As will be pointed out later, the variables in Global(G') are the only variables whose values are produced as the result of the computation. Values of the variables introduced during either the transformation or the computation (local variables) are not shown as results.

4.3 Process Interpretation

A goal clause can be interpreted as a network of processes, and a computation as an evolution of that network. Analogous interpretations can be found in [5,13,15,20].

In the process interpretation of **LEAF** (in canonical form) each atom corresponds to a process and variables can be viewed as channels connecting different processes. Both one-way and two-way channels can be present in the network. A one-way channel corresponds to a variable appearing in the right part of a functional atom. The direction of the channel is from the functional atom (producer) to any other atom using the corresponding variable (consumer). Other variables are modeled by two-way channels. The global outputs of the goal are modeled by open channels emerging from the network of processes.

As an example let us consider the following goal (not in canonical form):

< -- Hyp(x,S(S(S(0))),S(S(S(S(S(0)))))),+(+(S(x),S(0)),x) = z

Its canonical form is:

$$< -- \text{Hyp}(x,S(S(S(0))),S(S(S(S(S(0)))))),+(v_1,x) = z,+(S(x),S(0)) = v_1$$

and its representation is given in Figure 1.

In the graph representation the processes are nodes, two-way channels are edges, one-way channels are arcs (directed edges), square nodes are data constructor applications and data structures are labeled arcs.

A computation step is achieved by rewriting, i.e. by replacing a process with the network of processes representing the body of the clause used in the rewriting.

As an example, the rewriting of the above goal with clause 7.1 (considered in canonical form) yields the goal in Figure 2.

It is worth noting that networks can be cyclic and multiple consumers are allowed. Multiple producers (represented by arc joins) define conditions on the values computed by functional atoms forcing values produced by different processes to be unifiable.

The language in [20] does not allow multiple producers. On the other hand, all its edges are directed since a producer-consumer interpretation is also given to relational atoms.

4.4 Inference Rules and Computation Strategy

In the following we will assume that clauses and goals are in canonical form.

The basic inference rule is resolution. Given a goal clause

$$G: < -- A_1, \ldots, A_n$$

and a clause

$$A < -- B_1, \ldots, B_m$$

if A_i and A are unifiable, with most general unifier λ, then the new goal

$$G': < -- [A_1, \ldots, A_{i-1}, B_1, \ldots, B_m, A_{i+1}, \ldots, A_n]_\lambda$$

is derived, where $[\beta]_\lambda$ is the result of the application of the substitution λ to the conjunction of atoms β.

212

Note that in applying resolution to functional atoms, equality is viewed as a predicate symbol.

Resolution affects the set of globals of a goal clause. Let V be the set of all the variables v_i such that λ contains the substitution $\bar{v}_i = t_i$, where $\bar{v}_i \in$ Global(G) and t_i contains v_i; then

$$\text{Global(G')} = \text{Global(G)} \bigcup V.$$

A new inference rule (*atom elimination*) is needed to provide a proof theoretic characterization of call-by-name derivations, corresponding to lazy evaluations and demand driven computations. In the network interpretation of a goal, a process such that its outputs:

- are not global outputs, or

- are not input to other processes, or

- are not constrained by any arc join with a data structure containing either constants or outputs of other processes

should be deleted. This can only be the case for processes corresponding to functional atoms, since relational atoms have no directed output channels.

Atom elimination inference rule is defined as follows.

Consider a goal

$$G: <-- A_1, \ldots, A_n$$

where A_i is $f(t_1, \ldots, t_m) = t$. If t does not contain any constant symbols and for each variable v_i in t, v_i does not belong to Global(G) and does not occur in the formulas $A_1 \ldots, A_{i-1}, A_{i+1} \ldots, A_n$, then the new goal

$$G': <-- A_1, \ldots, A_{i-1}, A_{i+1} \ldots, A_n$$

can be derived.

Atom elimination, similar to the termination rule defined in [20], allows one to define non-strict functions (and relations). That is, a function (or relation) can be defined even if applied to some undefined arguments, possibly computed by non-terminating processes, including, as a special case, functions (generators) producing infinite data structures.

The computation strategy of LEAF consists of:

213

1) A computation rule, that is a rule to select in the current network processes to be "evaluated".
   The computation rule is the selection of any process in the *set of outermost processes* which contains:
   - all the relational atoms,
   - the functional atoms which produce a variable in Global(G), and
   - the functional atoms whose outputs are not consumed by any other atom.

2) An inference rule to be applied to the selected process in the current network.
   The inference rule is: apply first atom elimination, if possible, otherwise apply resolution.

3) A search rule to handle non-determinism in the application of resolution.
   The rule is only assumed to be fair.

4) A (demand-driven) control mechanism for the application of the resolution inference rule.
   According to this mechanism, a process P is suspended if its rewriting forces values to be produced on some input channel x and there exist other processes $P_1, \ldots, P_n$ possibly producing on x. P, if suspended, activates any of the P_i's. P is resumed when some other process produces a data structure approximation on x. Cycles of suspended processes must be recognised and the rewriting of a process in the cycle is forced.

The following algorithm gives a precise definition of the demand-driven control mechanism.
Consider a network G, a process A in G and a clause

   c: $B <-- B_1, \ldots, B_m$.

i)   if A and B are not unifiable, the algorithm returns failure, otherwise

ii) let λ be the most general unifier of A and B.
     If
     a)   no input channel of A is bound by λ to a non-variable term, or
     b)   an input channel x of A is bound by λ to a non-variable term, and all the processes in G which produce on x are marked (i.e. A is in a cycle of suspended processes),
     then apply resolution to G with respect to process A with a clause c thus obtaining the network G'.

214

Otherwise, *A* is suspended and marked.

Let *D* be any process producing on *x*. *D* is now selected to be "evaluated" in the current network. If the evaluation fails, the algorithm returns failure. Otherwise, the evaluation returns a new network *G'* which has possibly some data structure approximation on the input channel *x* of process *A*.

The algorithm continues at step i).

As an example of computation, let us consider the following set of clauses (in canonical form):

1.1 $nat(x) = CONS(x,y) < -- nat(S(x)) = y$

2.1 $select(0,CONS(y,z)) = y < --$
2.2 $select(S(x),CONS(y,z)) = w < -- select(x,z) = w$

and the following goal clause:

(1) $< -- select(S(0),nat(0)) = select(y,nat(0))$.

The canonical form of (1) is

(2) $< -- select(S(0),w) = z, select(y,w) = z, nat(0) = w$

where y is the only global output.

The corresponding network of processes is represented in Figure 3.

The outermost atoms are (a) and (b). Let us select (a) which can be rewritten with 2.2. The unification of (a) with the header of 2.2 causes the suspension of (a) and the "evaluation" of (c). Atom (c) can be rewritten with 1.1, resulting in the new goal

(3) $< -- select(S(0),CONS(0,w_1)) = z, select(y,CONS(0,w_1)) = z,$
$\qquad nat(S(0)) = w_1$

represented in Figure 4.

The evaluation of (a) is resumed, leading to the goal

(4) $< -- select(0,w_1) = z, select(y,CONS(0,w_1)) = z, nat(S(0)) = w_1$

represented in Figure 5. The outermost atoms still are (a) and (b). Let us select (a) which can be rewritten with 2.1. The unification of (a) with the header of 2.1 causes the suspension of (a) and the evaluation of (c). The rewriting of (c) with 1.1 results in the new goal

$$(5) \quad < -- \; select(0,CONS(S(0),w_2)) = z,$$
$$select(y,CONS(0,CONS(S(0),w_2))) = z, \; nat(S(S(0))) = w_2$$

represented in Figure 6.

The evaluation of (a) is resumed, leading to the goal

$$(6) \quad < -- \; select(y,CONS(0,CONS(S(0),w_2))) = S(0), \; nat(S(S(0))) = w_2$$

represented in Figure 7.

The only outermost atom is now (b). (b) can be rewritten with 2.2 only. The unification produces the binding $y = S(y_1)$ and the rewriting results in the goal

$$(7) \quad < -- \; select(y_1,CONS(S(0),w_2)) = S(0), \; nat(S(S(0))) = w_2$$

represented in Figure 8.

The only outermost atom is still (b) and the next rewriting with 2.1 results in the binding $y_1 = 0$ and the new goal

$$(8) \quad < -- \; nat(S(S(0))) = w_2$$

represented in Figure 9.

Note that, in rewriting the atom (b) of the goal (7), a backtrack point is set for the possible choice of 2.2.

The empty clause is obtained by applying the atom elimination rule to the goal (8).

The evaluation of the goal (2) results in the binding $y = S(S(0))$; if other values for y are demanded, the computation is resumed causing a backtracking to the goal (7). In this case the computation proceeds indefinitely.

The example shows some interesting features of LEAF, namely:

Functional atoms allow us to define a partial ordering on the atoms of a goal. This partial ordering corresponds to an external (outermost) evaluation rule (or demand driven strategy).

Atom elimination rule allows the termination of computations on functional atoms which are not necessary and could possibly be non-terminating. As a consequence, non-strict functions and infinite data structures are supported.

The basic inference rule for functional atoms is standard resolution. Therefore a functional equality behaves as a relation. For example, a refutation of a functional equality $f(t_1, \ldots, t_n) = t$ can produce values for variables in $f(t_1, \ldots, t_n)$.

The functional notation is more natural than the relational one when functions are involved. Moreover, the relational notation would not allow one to define an explicit partial ordering. The partial ordering allows to define a rewriting process which we assert to be as efficient as those based on special purpose inference systems (semantic unification, narrowing). Finally no finite termination property is required as is the case for narrowing, which would rule out functions producing infinite data structures.

The output channel of a functional atom (because of elimination of variants) may have several consumers. Any approximation of the output channel value is shared by all the consumers.

Let us finally note that the refutation of a goal (or sub-goal) corresponding to the evaluation of a closed (purely functional) expression does not require any searching (i.e. it is deterministic). This case corresponds to Kahn-McQueen networks, where all the channels are directed and no multiple producers are allowed [23].

4.5 Semantics

Since LEAF has a call-by-name semantics, the set of constant symbols C must be extended to contain a distinct symbol ω, which stands for undefined and models data components which do not need to be evaluated.

Interpretations are defined on the Herbrand Universe H, which, in the case of LEAF, is defined as follows:

i)   all the constant symbols in C (including ω) belong to H;

ii)   for each data constructor symbol d of arity n in D, H contains all the terms $d(t_1, \ldots, t_n)$ such that $t_1, \ldots, t_n$ are in H and at least one of the t_i's is different from ω.

Note that H does not contain fully undefined terms (apart from ω). Fully undefined terms, i.e. terms whose only constant symbols are ω, are all identical to ω. Thus, our notion of partial data structure is different from the standard notion in lazy evaluation methods since our partial data structures contain useful information only if at least one component is not undefined (i.e. our data constructors cannot be lazy in all their arguments).

H is partially ordered by the reflexive relation $\leq$ defined as follows:

i)   for each term $t \in$ H, $\omega \leq t$;

ii)   for each n-adic data constructor symbol d,

$$d(t_1, \ldots, t_n) \leq d(t'_1, \ldots, t'_n)$$

Iff $t_1 \leq t'_1 \ldots, t_n \leq t'_n$.

The partial ordering relation reflects the intuitive notion of value approximation.

Interpretations are defined on the Herbrand Base B, defined as follows:

i)   for each n-adic function symbol f, all the atoms $f(t_1, \ldots, t_n) = t$, such that $t, t_1, \ldots, t_n$ are in H, belong to B.

ii)   for each n-adic predicate symbol p, all the atoms $p(t_1, \ldots, t_n)$ such that $t_1, \ldots, t_n$ are in H, belong to B.

An interpretation I is a subset of B which has a consistent interpretation for functions, i.e.:

1)   if $f(t_1, \ldots, t_n) = t$ and $f(t_1, \ldots, t_n) = t'$ belong to I then $t \leq t'$ or $t' \leq t$.

2)   for each n-adic function symbol f, I contains all the ground atoms
       $f(t_1, \ldots, t_n) = \omega$.

These conditions state that a function, when applied to ground values, produces a unique value (possibly represented by its approximations). The value can always be undefined to model the case in which no approximation is required (see the atom elimination rule).

The notion of truth of a clause in an interpretation is the usual one. A model of a set of clauses C is an interpretation I such that, for each clause c_i in C, c_i is true in I.

The model intersection property of Horn clauses [14] holds and we can now define the *model theoretic semantics* as the minimal model of C, that is the intersection of all the models of C.

The *operational semantics* is based on the demand driven refutation procedure as defined in Section 4.4. The operational semantics is the set of all the elements of the Herbrand Base which are refutable.

The refutation procedure must be defined also for atoms containing the constant symbol ω. This extension requires atoms of the form $f(t_1, \ldots, t_n) = \omega$ to be refutable. This can be obtained by replacing, in each goal, all the atoms of the form $f(t_1, \ldots, t_n) = \omega$ by $f(t_1, \ldots, t_n) = v$ where v is a new variable.

It can be proved that the set of ground atoms defined by the operational semantics for a set of clauses is the minimal model.

The *fixpoint semantics* is based on the transformation $\Phi(C)$ which maps interpretations onto interpretations.

Let I be any interpretation and

$$c_i : A < -- B_1, \ldots, B_n$$

be a clause in C. c_i defines a transformation $\Phi(c_i)$ which maps I onto the interpretation I' defined as follows:

i)   for each instantiation λ of variables to terms of H, the atom $[A]_\lambda$ belongs to I' if all the atoms $[B_i]_\lambda$ belong to I;

ii) for each function symbol f occurring in C, all the ground atoms of the form $f(t_1, \ldots, t_n) = \omega$ (where $t_i \in H$) belong to I'.

$\Phi(C)$ is a transformation defined by all the clauses in C according to the above definition, i.e.

$$I' = \Phi(C)(I) = \bigcup_{c_i \in C} \Phi(c_i)(I)$$

It can be proved that the transformation $\Phi(C)$ on the set of interpretations (partially ordered by set inclusion) is monotonic and continuous. Hence, there exists the least fixpoint interpretation I^* such that $I^* = \Phi(C)(I^*)$.

I^* can be obtained by iteratively applying $\Phi(C)$ starting with the bottom element, $\perp$, of the partially ordered set of interpretations which contains all the ground atoms $f(t_1, \ldots, t_n) = \omega$ where f is a function symbol occurring in C and the t_i's belong to H.

219

The equivalence proof of the above defined semantics is similar to the proof given in [14].

5 THE PROCEDURAL COMPONENT OF LEAF

The procedural component of LEAF (LCA) is essentially the subset of LEAF corresponding to Kahn-McQueen's networks of processes. Namely,

- computations are deterministic,

- all the channels are directed, including the global output channels; as a consequence logical variables are not allowed and there is no back communication of data, and

- no multiple producers are allowed.

In addition, as is the case for functional languages, the network is acyclic.

LCA is obtained by a mode declaration mechanism (annotation). LCA procedures are defined by sets of rewrite rules, which are annotated Horn clauses, where each term is annotated either as an input term or as an output term. Annotated clauses allow one to define multi-output functions. A set of rewrite rules does not contain overlapping rules. Hence the rewriting system is deterministic.

A main program is a set of annotated atoms, which can be viewed as processes communicating through channels. Channels are directed from a producer (the only process where the variable occurs in an output term) to a set of consumers (the processes where the variable occurs in input terms). Syntactic constraints are imposed to guarantee that each channel has exactly one producer.

The demand driven refutation procedure is the one of the declarative component, suitably simplified because of the features not included in LCA. Moreover, the formal semantics of LCA [5] is exactly the one given in Section 4.5.

6 SOME REMARKS ON THE IMPLEMENTATION

LCA can very easily be mapped onto a demand driven architecture [37]. The parameter passing and return mechanism can be improved by compiling the set of clauses which define a procedure into a single clause, whose body is a conditional expression. The matching process can be replaced by parameter passing, if suitable predicates and selectors are inserted in the procedure body. Of course, data structure incremental evaluation is now caused by predicate and selector applications which perform "get" operations on the input channels. The resulting "intermediate" language is a first-order LISP-like language with user-defined lazy data structures and sub-expression sharing. The intermediate language can be efficiently executed on a reduction machine, whose main components are:

i)   a set of processors which perform input-output channel operations, provide for new process creation (rewriting) and send/receive control messages to implement the demand driven computation strategy;

ii) a processor which takes care of the assignment of processes to processors;

iii) a global channel environment and a shared garbage-collected dynamic storage.

Some of the machine components (typically, the dynamic storage) can also be used in the direct execution of declarative programs, which, however, is a much more complex process. That is, the direct execution of the declarative component requires the machine to be able to cope with the following additional aspects.

i)   Unification is the basic process used to build data structures and to process channels through put and get operations. An efficient concurrent hardware implementation of unification is crucial.

ii) Since there does not exist a partial ordering on processes, the machine contains a specific processor (the scheduler) which defines a suitable activation strategy.

iii) Nondeterminism must be efficiently handled by a hardware mechanism based on the notion of context [31], which defines the state of a specific deterministic computation. Each state component (process or channel) is indexed by its context. The same channel may have different states in different contexts.

The basic interpreter of the declarative component returns a (possibly infinite) stream of solutions, where each solution is the state of the output channels. In the next section we will show that the language integration problem can easily be solved by viewing the interpreter as a primitive LCA procedure.

7 PROCEDURAL AND DECLARATIVE PROGRAM INTEGRATION

Since the two languages share the same data structures (which are always Herbrand terms), the integration problem is essentially that of allowing mutual invocation. We will consider the two cases separately, starting with the occurrence of an LCA process (procedure invocation) within a declarative rule. Consider, for example the following clauses:

Family-income(x,y) < −− Not-married(x), Income(x,y)
Family-income(x,y) < −− Spouse-of(x,z),   Income(x,u),
                              Income(z,v), +(**in**: u,v; **out**: y)

which declaratively define the relation between a person and his or her total family income, which, if that person is married, is obtained by adding his or her own income with that of his or her spouse. The predicates Not-married, Income, Spouse-of are defined declaratively, while + is an LCA procedure.

It can easily be proved that LCA processes can occur in the body of a declarative clause without affecting declarativeness, but only if their input variables do not occur in the clause header.

For example the following clause

Plus(x,y,z) < −− +(**in**: x,y; **out**: z)

whose intent could be to transform a procedure + into a relation Plus, is not legal. The rationale for the above proposition is that procedures do not have logical variables. In the example, since the procedure + cannot compute any of its input arguments, the same limitation would be inherited by the relation Plus.

When LCA procedures are legally invoked in clause bodies, sets of LCA processes can occur in a goal statement and are handled by the LCA component of the machine in the standard way. The overall LCA output channels are consumed by the declarative language interpreter. A LCA process can only be rewritten when it has, on its input channels, the necessary information which can be produced by declarative processes. Coming back to our example, the goal:

222

< -- Family-income(George-Lewis,y)

will produce a single computation, while the goal:

< -- Family-income(x,25000)

could result in a non-deterministic computation. However, in each deterministic computation, the procedure + is applied only when both incomes have been determined. This would not be the case if a declarative relation Plus had been used.

The problem of invoking declarative procedures within LCA programs cannot be solved through simple syntactical constraints. In fact, a procedure whose body contains a declarative process will, in general, be nondeterministic and therefore, a non-legal LCA procedure. As is the case in POPLOG [30], a procedure body can contain a "closed" declarative atom, i.e. an atom containing only variables occurring in the inputs of the procedure header. This allows a procedure to invoke the declarative component to verify a condition.

A more general integration facility requires an interface between LCA and declarative processes. At the interface level a declarative process must explicitly return a (possibly infinite) set of results. The solution we propose consists of calling a declarative process through the declarative language interpreter, which, as already mentioned, behaves exactly as an LCA procedure. This, however, requires declarative programs to be considered as data for the procedural component. Clauses and goal statements, as well as run-time structures (typically, the declarative language output channels), must be represented by suitable Herbrand terms. Moreover, since the interface is necessarily concerned with the correspondence between channels in the two languages, LCA must have some knowledge about itself as well. In other words, LCA behaves like a metalanguage for the full procedural-declarative language. In the next section, we will consider some interesting consequences of the language-metalanguage relation. We will finally come back to the integration problem to define a precise interface.

8 TOOLS AND THE METALANGUAGE

LEAF must be supported by a set of interactive tools, which provide the standard functionalities of an integrated programming environment for program construction, modification, analysis and transformation. Tools are programs (typically procedures) which operate on (procedural and declarative) programs. The tool implementation language must have a complete knowledge about both the syntax and the semantics of the supported language. Then tools can properly be implemented in LCA, which embodies such a knowledge. The above solution allows the programming environment to be easily extended with new tools, which are defined in the procedural subset of the user language.

The traditional tools for controlled program execution (typically, symbolic debuggers) provide meta-analysis capabilities, which are very useful in an interactive inference-based programming environment. The user-tool interaction, in fact, is often achieved in terms of meta-objects such as the current state of the inference process, its history (the proof) and the content of the knowledge base.

LCA can also be used to implement a family of interpreters for the declarative component, so as to allow the definition of different evaluation strategies and/or different mechanisms for returning the result. We assume some basic functionalities (for example, to implement the resolution principle) are provided by the hardware machine. Only the external layer of the interpreters is defined in LCA. The following example, which illustrates our approach, uses several sorts (atom, clause, theory and goal) which are abstract data types modeling the various constructs of the declarative language. The following sorts are also used in the example.

env   which models a set of associations of variable names to terms.

state = goal × env
   which models computation states.

   The operations on states are:

sel-env : state → env
   which returns the environment component,

fail? : state → bool,

halt? : state → bool
   which recognize a failure or a successfully terminating state, respectively.

list(t: which is a parametric sort modeling homogeneous finite lists with the standard constructors NIL and CONS.

stream(t:
   which models (possibly infinite) homogeneous lists with the 0-adic function emptystream, the constructor mk-stream and the operation

append which acts as on standard lists.

The declarative interpreter:

decl-eval : stream(state) × theory → stream(env)

takes a set of clauses (theory) and a stream of states (which initially will contain a single state corresponding to the top level goal) and returns a stream of solutions, in terms of bindings of variables to terms.

```
decl-eval(emptystream,t) => emptystream
decl-eval(mk-stream(s,ss),t) =>
    if halt?(s)
        then mk-stream(sel-env(s),decl-eval(ss,t))
        else with choice(in: s,t; out: lf,slc)
                decl-eval(append(rewrite(s,lf,slc),ss),t).
```

Note that the arrow => implicitly defines the input/output terms for annotated functional atoms.

The procedure

choice : state × theory →
                list(atom) × stream(list(clause))

should be properly defined to encapsulate a specific proof strategy. It returns the list of atoms in the current state which have to be rewritten concurrently and generates, upon request, all the lists of clauses in the theory which can be used to perform the rewriting.

The procedure

rewrite : state × list(atom) × stream(list(clause)) → stream(state)

takes care of non-deterministic state transitions.

```
rewrite(s,lf,emptystream) => emptystream
rewrite(s,lf,mk-stream(lc,slc)) =>
    with resolve(s,lf,lc) => s' and rewrite(s,lf,slc) => ss'
        if fail?(s') then ss' else mk-stream(s',ss')
```

Finally, the procedure

resolve : state × list(atom) × list(clause) → state

is assumed to be directly provided by that component of the hardware machine which defines a state transformation obtained by concurrently applying each clause in the list to the corresponding atom.

Decl-eval returns a stream of environments, where each environment defines the variable bindings of a specific successful deterministic computation. Because of the LCA operational semantics, the way results will actually be computed will depend upon the procedures which will consume the output of decl-eval. It is worth noting that it is very easy to modify the procedures decl-eval and rewrite to modify the way results are returned, to maintain information about the proof or to implement specific versions of the underlying logic (typically, negation-as-failure).

Let us finally remark that the programming environment will also contain tools to transform declarative programs into procedural programs [6].

9 THE INTEGRATION INTERFACE AND SOME EXAMPLES

The integration interface will necessarily be concerned with the correspondence between values (Herbrand terms) and their representation at the metalanguage level. In the following, the prefix m will denote meta-objects. For example, an m-variable will be the Herbrand term used to represent a variable symbol (typically occurring in a declarative process).

The following functions define the mapping between the two representations

μ : term → m-term ρ : m-term → term.

Both μ and ρ are only defined for ground terms. Whenever μ is applied to a variable (ρ is applied to an m-variable) it will cause its evaluation. This is the basic demand driven mechanism to transfer values from LCA processes to declarative processes and vice versa.

The interface must explicitly define the correspondence between LCA channels and declarative channels. It is achieved by the LCA procedure

```
prove : theory × goal × list(m-variable) × list(term) ×
              × list(m-variable) → list(term)
```

```
prove(t,g,ilv,ilt,olv) =>
    set-output(decl-eval(mk-stream(
    mk-state(g,set-input(ilv,ilt)),emptystream),t),olv).
```

The initial environment is defined by

```
set-input : ilv: list(m-variable) × ilt: list(term) → env
```

which builds an environment, containing for each corresponding pair (v,t) of m-variables and terms in the lists ilv, ilt, a binding of v to the value $\mu(t)$. The variables in ilv are the declarative input channels, while the values in ilt are values computed by external LCA processes. μ will provide for the activation of such processes when required by the declarative interpreter.

Decl-eval is applied to the initial state consisting of the pair goal, initial environment and to the theory. Its value (which is a stream of environments) is given to the function set-output, together with the (output) list of m-variables olv. Set-output properly transforms the result, so as to make it usable by LCA processes, as follows:

```
set-output : se: stream(env) × olv: list(m-variable) → olt: list(term)
```

olv is the list of m-variables whose values have to be exported to LCA channels. The result olt is a list of terms, such that its i-th element is the (possibly infinite) stream of values, obtained by applying ρ to the values bound to the i-th m-variable of olv in the various environments computed by decl-eval. ρ will then activate the declarative interpreter (typically, for a new deterministic computation) when required by the consuming LCA processes.

The following simple example shows how declarative processes can be embedded into LCA procedures. Assume we have a declarative theory t, where the relations

Plumber(x: m-human)

and

227

Age(x: m-human,y: m-integer)

are defined.

The following LCA procedures allow us to compute a list of at least n plumbers, whose age is at least m, such that the list contains no plumber which is older than a plumber not in the list.

```
search-n(t:theory,n: integer,m: integer) =>
                select-n(search-all(t,m),n)

search-all(t: theory,m: integer) =>
    append(car(prove(t,< -- Plumber(x),Age(x,y),
            CONS(y,NIL),CONS(m,NIL),CONS(x,NIL))),
        search-all(t,S(m)))

select-n(mk-stream(x,s),0) => NIL
select-n(mk-stream(x,s),S(n)) => CONS(x,select-n(s,n))
select-n(emptystream,n) => NIL.
```

In the above example, m-terms are bolded. The third and fourth argument of prove define the input channel correspondence (i.e. the m-variable **y** is bound to the value of m), while the last argument asserts that the output will be a list consisting of a single stream, i.e. the values of the meta-variable **x**. The LCA semantics guarantees that new solutions will be demanded to the declarative interpreter only until necessary.

Our interface provides a mechanism very close to the one which is built into LOGLISP [34], i.e. the declarative interpreter is viewed as returning lists of values. A similar technique is used in the interface between and-relations and or-relations in PARLOG [13].

10 FINAL REMARKS

Our mechanism for integrating procedural and declarative programs allows us to write procedures which operate on meta-objects, such as declarative theories or sets of solutions of declarative programs. Of course it is also possible to write declarative programs containing invocations of LCA tools, which can be thought of as declarative meta-programs. Because of the constraints in section 4, our metareasoning facilities are less powerful than those provided in [9], where the declarative language itself is used as a metalanguage.

At the present time we have a software simulation of the machine which can run both procedural and declarative programs. We are now developing tools and looking into the problem of hardware realization.

REFERENCES

1.   Abramson, H. A Prological Definition of HASL a Purely Functional Language with Unification Based Conditional Binding Expressions. *New Generation Computing 2*, 1, (1984), 3-35.

2.   Asirelli, P., R. Barbuti, and G. Levi. Types and Declarative Static Type Checking in Logic Programming. IEI Internal Rep. B83-23, (1983).

3.   Barbuti, R., M. Bellia, G. Levi, and M. Martelli. On the Integration of Logic Programming and Functional Programming. Proc. 1984 Int. Symp. on Logic Programming, IEEE Comp. Society Press (1984) 160-166.

4.   Bellia, M., P. Degano, and G. Levi. The Call by Name Semantics of a Clause Language with Functions. In *Logic Programming*, K.L. Clark, and S.-A. Tarnlund, Eds., Academic Press, 1982, 281-295.

5.   Bellia, M., E. Dameri, P. Degano, G. Levi, and M. Martelli. Applicative Communicating Processes in First Order Logic. Proc. 5th Int. Symp. on Programming, Torino, 1982, *LNCS 137*, Springer-Verlag, 1-14.

6.   Bellia, M., G. Levi, and M. Martelli. On Compiling PROLOG Programs on Demand-driven Architectures. Proc. Logic Programming Workshop, Albufeira, 1983, 518-535.

7.   Bellia, M., E. Dameri, P. Degano, G. Levi, and M. Martelli. A Formal Model for Lazy Implementation of a PROLOG Compatible Functional Language. In *Implementations of PROLOG*, J.A. Campbell, Ed., Ellis Horwood, 1984, 309-326.

8.   Berkling, K., J.A. Robinson, and E.E. Sibert. A Proposal for a Fifth Generation Logic and Functional Programming System, Based on Highly Parallel Reduction Machine Architecture. Internal Rep. School of Computer and Information Science, Syracuse Univ., Nov. 1982.

9.   Bowen, K.A., and R.A. Kowalski. Amalgamating Language and Metalanguage in Logic Programming. In *Logic Programming*, K.L. Clark, and S.-A. Tarnlund, Eds., Academic Press, 1982, 153-172.

10.   Burstall, R.M., D.B. MacQueen, and B.T. Sannella. HOPE: An Experimental Applicative Language. Proc. LISP Conf., Stanford, 1980.

11.   Clark, K.L., and S. Gregory. A Relational Language for Parallel Programming. Proc. of ACM Functional Programming Language and Computer Architecture, Portsmouth, 1981, 171-178.

12.   Clark, K.L., F.G. McCabe, and S. Gregory. IC-PROLOG Language Features. In *Logic Programming*, K.L. Clark, and S.-A. Tarnlund, Eds., Academic Press, 1982, 253-266.

13.   Clark, K.L., and S. Gregory. PARLOG: A Parallel Logic Programming Language. Imperial College Research Rep. DOC 83/5, May 1983.

14.   vanEmden, M.H., and R.A. Kowalski. The Semantics of Predicate Logic as a Programming Language. *J. ACM 23*, 1976, 733-742.

15.   vanEmden, M.H., and G.T. de Lucena Filho. Predicate Logic as a Language for Parallel Programming. In *Logic Programming*, K.L. Clark, and S.-A. Tarnlund, Eds., Academic Press, 1982, 189-198.

16.   Falaschi, M., G. Levi, and C. Palamidessi. A Synchronization Logic: Axiomatics and Formal Semantics of Generalized Horn Clauses. *Information and Control 60*, 1984, 36-69.

17.   Fay, M. First-order Unification in an Equational Theory. Proc. 4th Workshop on Automated Deduction (1979), 161-167.

18.   Goguen, J.A., and J.J. Tardo. An Introduction to OBJ: A Language for Writing and Testing Formal Algebraic Program Specifications. Proc. IEEE Conf. on Specifications of Reliable Software, 1979, 179-189.

19.   Goguen, J.A., and J. Meseguer. Equality, Types, Modules and Generics for Logic Programming. Proc. 2nd Int. Logic Programming Conf., Uppsala, 1984, 115-125.

20.   Hansson, A., S. Haridi, and S.-A. Tarnlund. Properties of a Logic Programming Language. In *Logic Programming*, K.L. Clark, and S.-A. Tarnlund, Eds., Academic Press, 1982, 267-280.

21.   Hullot, J.-M. Canonical Forms and Unification. Proc. 5th Conf. on Automated Deduction, W. Bibel, and R.A. Kowalski, Eds., Springer-Verlag, *LNCS 87* (1980), 318-334.

22.   Jouannaud, J.-P., C. Kirchner, and H. Kirchner. Incremental Construction of Unification Algorithms in Equational Theories. Proc. ICALP 83, 1983, 361-373.

23.   Kahn, G., and D.B. McQueen. Coroutines and Networks of Parallel Processes. Information Processing 77, North-Holland, 1977, 993-998.

24.   Kornfeld, W.A. Equality for PROLOG. Proc. 7th IJCAI, 1983, 514-519.

25.   Kowalski, R.A. Predicate Logic as a Programming Language. Information Processing 74, North-Holland, 1974, 556-574.

26.   Kowalski, R.A. Algorithm = Logic + Control. *Comm. ACM 22*, 1979, 424-431.

27.   Levi, G., and F. Sirovich. Proving Program Properties, Symbolic Evaluation and Logical Procedural Semantics. Proc. MFCS 75, *LNCS*, Springer-Verlag, 1975, 294-301.

28.   Levi, G., and A. Pegna. Top-Down Mathematical Semantics and Symbolic Execution. *RAIRO Informatique Theorique 17*, 1983, 55-70.

29.   Lindstrom, G. Functional Programming and the Logical Variable. Proc. 12th ACM Symp. on Principles of Programming Languages, 1985.

30.   Mellish, C., and S. Hardy. Integrating PROLOG in the POPLOG Environment. In *Implementations of PROLOG*, J.A. Campbell, Ed., Ellis Horwood, 1984, 147-162.

31.   Montangero, C., G. Pacini, and F. Turini. Two-level Control Structures for Nondeterministic Programming. *Comm. ACM 20*, 1977.

32.   Moto-Oka, T., Ed. Proc. Int. Conf. on Fifth Generation Computer Systems. North-Holland, Amsterdam, 1982.

33.   Mycroft, A., and R. O'Keefe. A Polymorphic Type System for PROLOG. Proc. Logic Programming Workshop, Albufeira, 1983, 107-122.

34.   Robinson, J.A., and E.E. Sibert. LOGLISP: Motivations, Design and Implementation. In *Logic Programming*, K.L. Clark, and S.-A. Tarnlund,

Eds., Academic Press, 1982, 299-314.

35.   Shapiro, E.Y. A Subset of Concurrent PROLOG and its Interpreter. Technical Rep. TR-003, ICOT, 1983.

36.   Subrahmanyam, P.A., and J.-H. You. Conceptual Basis and Evaluation Strategies for Integrating Functional and Logic Programming. Proc. 1984 Int. Symp. on Logic Programming, IEEE Comp. Society Press (1984) 144-153.

37.   Treleaven, P.C., D.R. Browmbridge, and R.P. Hopkins. Data-driven and Demand-driven Computer Architecture. *ACM Comp. Surv. 14*, 1982, 93-143.

38.   Warren, D., L.M. Pereira, and F. Pereira. PROLOG. The Language and its Implementations Compared with LISP. Proc. Symp. on AI and Programming Languages, *SIGPLAN Notices 12,8* and *SIGART Newsletter 64*, 109-115.

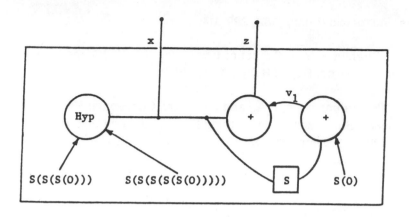

Figure 1

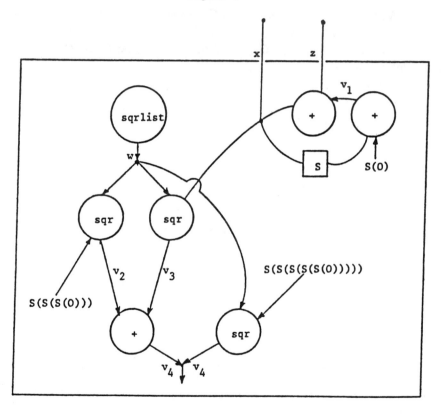

Figure 2

234

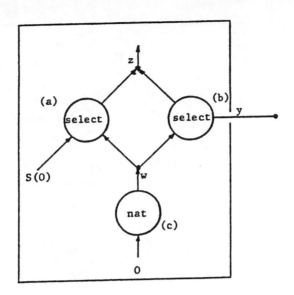

Figure 3

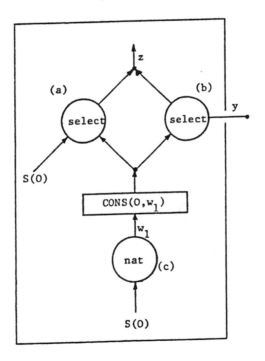

Figure 4

235

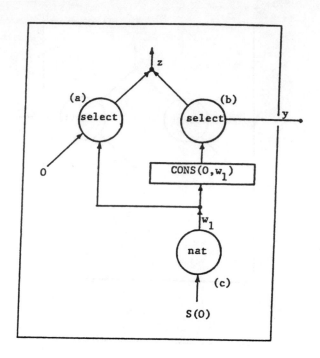

Figure 5

236

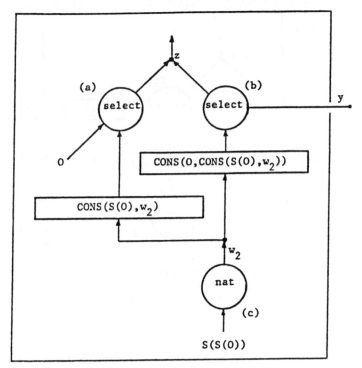

Figure 6

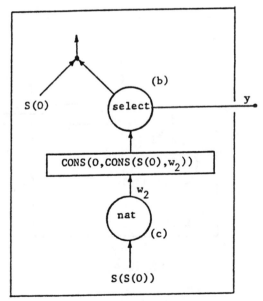

Figure 7

237

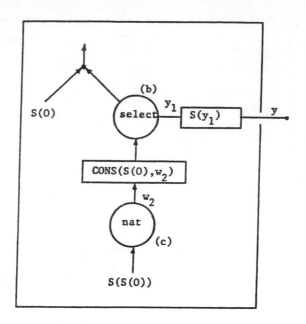

Figure 8

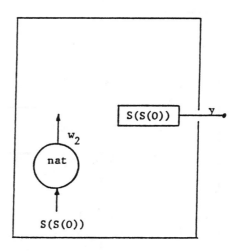

Figure 9

238

THE APPLOG LANGUAGE

Shimon Cohen

Schlumberger Palo Alto Research
3340 Hillview Avenue
Palo Alto, CA 94304[*]

ABSTRACT

The virtues of PROLOG and LISP are discussed, and the conclusion is reached that a mixture of these two languages is desirable. Toward that end, APPLOG, a combination of LISP and PROLOG, is described APPLOG is embedded within the PROLOG language with the facilities of PROLOG made available through a simple *goal* function. APPLOG is an applicative language, i.e. one whose primary composition method is the application of functions to arguments Variables in APPLOG are compatible with PROLOG variables, and serve as means for data transfer between APPLOG and PROLOG APPLOG supports *lambda* and *nlambda* function definitions and *one-to-one*, *one-to-many* and *mixed* binding mechanisms, in the manner of INTERLISP. The main advantage of APPLOG is the *simple* integration of LISP and PROLOG into one powerful language which incorporates, in our judgment, the best features of both languages. In particular APPLOG has the following advantages over traditional LISP languages: (i) pattern directed invocation; (ii) call by reference; (iii) an interface to PROLOG as a database query language; (iv) functions as operators (infix, prefix and postfix); (v) backtracking, and (vi) generators. APPLOG includes *aggregates* and *grouping* constructs, and has been extended to a simple relational database query language similar to Query-By-Example. An appendix includes a listing of the principal functions of the APPLOG interpreter.

---

[*]Part of this work was done while the author was a visitor at UC Berkeley [2]

1 INTRODUCTION

The idea of *logic programming* was proposed [6] as a new basis for programming languages. In so doing, Kowalski conceived a clear and simple deductive language which is based on the LUSH resolution of Horn clauses [5]. These ideas were first realized in the programming language PROLOG by [3]. Later it was shown [10] that PROLOG programs can run as fast as the equivalent LISP programs. Finally a compiler written in PROLOG [11] was demonstrated to compile Horn clauses into efficient machine code.

Although PROLOG is widely acknowledged to be useful in a large variety of applications, there are still some doubts concerning PROLOG's efficiency (e.g. in backtracking), and the "purity" of its mathematical background (when *cut, not*, etc. are included), especially in comparison to LISP. Other researchers [8] and [9] have, in dealing with these issues, proposed two other languages for programming in logic: QUTE and LOGLISP, both combinations of LISP and PROLOG. However, these two languages have been criticized as being too complicated, because to interface the logical and applicative components of the language, they introduce new syntax, special cases, and many new functions of questionable need. In APPLOG, the interface is practically *invisible*.

The goal of this paper is to show that a combination of LISP and PROLOG is *desirable* and can be *simply* achieved. The next section examines the nature of combining LISP and PROLOG, and then APPLOG is described in section 3.

In APPLOG, the LISP and PROLOG environments (variables, data structures, etc.) are "unified" and provide an easy way to express one's ideas in either an applicative or logical style. The main goal is to enable LISP and PROLOG users to write programs in their preferred language, while at the same time allowing them easy access to the power and virtues of the other language. The result is a more powerful and efficient language which provides such features as function application, logical inference, a relational database query language, and generators. The appendix contains a listing of the system as implemented in PROLOG. This definition (written in DEC-10 PROLOG) constitutes the operational semantics of APPLOG. In practice, if one has a

PROLOG system, one can load these definitions and then either (i) call top to enter the top loop interactor, or (ii) within any PROLOG clause invoke

eval(APPLOG form, Result).

The variable Result will be bound to the value of the form.

Here is a program solving the "eight queens" problem, which shows the general flavor of APPLOG. Suppose we wish to place eight queens on a chess board without having two of them on the same row, column or diagonal.

```
def(q8,
  lambda([Row, Board],
    if(Row = 0, Board,
        try(q8(Row - 1,  Board),
              or(1, 2, 3, 4, 5, 6, 7, 8)))))).

def(try, lambda([Board, Col],
        if(noaim(Board, Col, 1),
              cons(Col, Board), fail))).

def(noaim,
  lambda([Board, Col, Add],
    if(eq(Board, []), true,
        and(
          Col \== car(Board),
          Col+Add \== car(Board),
          Col-Add \== car(Board),
          noaim(cdr(Board), Col, Add+1)
        )))).
```

To call q8, evaluate q8(8, []) which means "try to place legally 8 queens on an empty board". The function try is called with a partially filled board and with a *generator* or which generates the numbers 1 to 8. At each stage, try attempts to place the next queen in the indicated column Col. If this is not possible, a failure occurs (see *fail* later), and or then generates a new possible Col number and try is re-attempted.

2 LISP VS. PROLOG

LISP and PROLOG are quite similar in intent, given that they both were designed to deal with natural language understanding, mathematical logic, algebraic manipulation and other artificial intelligence applications. Arguments made by PROLOG and LISP users in favor of their preferred language usually involve some of the following issues:

* mathematical basis;
* execution efficiency;
* programming styles supported;
* readability and clarity;
* the role of side effects, and
* special features such as unification and backtracking.

It is important to understand the basic advantages and utility of each of these language aspects. In the following pages we discuss the above issues at length.

2.1 Mathematical Background

PROLOG is based on the simple and well-investigated foundation of first-order logic theory. However, only the Horn clause subset of first-order logic is expressible in pure PROLOG Pure PROLOG does not include such features as evaluation control, logical negation and functional data objects (e.g. functions as arguments). PROLOG implementors have added a few "impure" control structures [1] which enable one to express functions which are otherwise not computable in pure PROLOG (e.g. cut, not and setof).

Pure LISP is based on the lambda calculus, which also has a well founded logical basis. It supports functionals and negation, and virtually any algorithm can be expressed in pure LISP. Although both pure PROLOG and pure LISP are based on a solid mathematical backgrounds, both of them need some practical changes and additions in order to make them usable as real vehicles in which to write programs.

2.2 Efficiency

In [11] the claim is made that PROLOG programs can be compiled and made to run as fast as LISP programs. That indeed is not a surprise if we heed appropriate pragmatic advice and, for example judiciously use cut in the programs. The use of cut makes the program deterministic in the sense that exponential search using backtracking can be curtailed. In addition one is recommended to specify each functor's input and output parameters. Although these additions are not "pure logic" they help to control backtracking, and thus enable PROLOG programs to run as fast as they might if written in LISP.

Another example illustrates this point: suppose we want to write a "program" that answers the following question: "Who is the father-of the wife-of the brother-of X?" In PROLOG we will naturally write:

```
query1(X, Y) :-
        father-of(Y, Z),
        wife-of(Z, W),
        brother-of(W, X).
```

This can result in a long search of the database, since it starts with the father-of relation. In the worst case PROLOG will search *all* the facts in the database about the father-of relation and for each Z it will search relation wife-of and then for each W it will try to determine whether W is the brother-of X. It would be much more efficient to write in LISP:

```
(lambda (X) (father-of (wife-of (brother-of X)))) 
```

or even in PROLOG:

```
query2(X, Y) :-
        brother-of(W, X),
        wife-of(Z, W),
        father-of(Y, Z).
```

The reason that the last two representations are more efficient is because the search is directed by a *key*; it starts

243

from X (which is known) and then finds the brother W and then the wife Z and finally the father Y. The point is that sometimes one has to "reverse" logical reasoning in order to gain efficiency. Consequently, efficient evaluation requires some understanding of the evaluation method being employed.

2.3 Programming Style and Readability

In the above example, the versatility of PROLOG is reflected in the query predicate (either version), which can be used:

* as a predicate (if both X and Y are instantiated);
* as a two way function (if only one is instantiated), and
* as a generator (if neither is instantiated).

A corresponding feature in LISP cannot be found. However, PROLOG requires a "flat" programming style, while LISP supports nested function calls. In PROLOG when one wishes to pass a value computed by one literal to the following literals, dummy variables must be introduced:

```
f3(X,Y), f2(Y,Z), f1(Z,W).
```

Here, Y is passed to f2, which passes Z to f3. In LISP, nested functions would be used, i.e. (f1 (f2 (f3))), and there would be no need for dummy variables. However, when one needs to pass the same value to more than one function, one needs to use lambda expressions such as:

```
((lambda (x) (f1 x (f2 x))) (f3 ...))
```

The value of (f3 ...) is bound to x and then x is passed both to f1 and f2. In PROLOG, one simply uses the same variable name in both places, e.g.

```
f1(I1, O1), f2(O1, O2), f3(O1, O3).
```

Thus O1 is passed from f1 to both f2 and f3. One of the main advantages of PROLOG over LISP is that it supports backtracking, while in LISP one has to explicitly code a backtracking mechanism. However, the implicit use of backtracking in

PROLOG may lead to an extensive use of cut. The reasons include (i) many programs are deterministic, and (ii) this is a means to imitate the if-then-else construct of applicative programming.

We conclude that some might prefer the explicit use of backtracking, and some its implicit use.

2.4 Side Effects

We argue that when one seeks to write efficient programs one might need some "dirty tricks" such as side effects. Indeed, logicians may hold that logic alone is adequate, but in some situations more practical concerns must be met. For example, is it really acceptable to use an unbalanced tree as a symbol table as proposed by Warren [11] for his compiler, when a hash table is clearly better? When one implements a window package is it acceptable to store a window as an applicative list of characters when a writeable character matrix is better?

Consider the following problem. Suppose we have a directed graph which is represented in PROLOG:

```
e(a, b). ; edge from a to b.
e(b, c). ; ...
...
```

We wish to define the relation path(X, Y, P) which is true if P is a path from X to Y.

```
path1(X, X, [X]).  ; trivial case
path1(X, Y, [X | Pz]) :-
        e(X, Z), path1(Z, Y, Pz).
```

This "perfect" definition (logically) might fail in reality because of cycles, for example if the graph consists of e(a, b). and e(b, a). To solve the problem we have to think a little bit more clearly and introduce a new relation path21.

```
path2(X, Y, P) :- path21(X, Y, P, []).
path21(X, X, [X], L).  ; trivial case
path21(X, Y, [X | Pz], L) :-
        e(X,Z), not(member(Z, L)),
        path21(Z, Y, Pz, [X | L]).
```

The fourth argument to path21 is the list of nodes already visited, i.e. those we wish not to revisit. The third parameter is also the list of nodes that we find along the path, however the third list is built when we return from the recursion and the fourth is built on the way in. Why can't we use only one list? The answer lies in PROLOG's special treatment of variables. PROLOG logical variables can be instantiated only once, but in this case we need the list not only as a result but also to compute the result. The way to overcome this inefficiency is to unify the list we build on our way down (the fourth parameter) with the variable carrying the result (the third parameter):

```
path3(X, Y, L) :- path31(X, Y, L, []).
path31(X, X, [X | L], L).
path31(X, Y, P, L) :-
        e(X, Z), not(member(Z, L)),
        path31(Z, Y, P, [X | L]).
```

Only at the end of the search (second clause) is the value of the fourth parameter assigned to the third. Note that the reverse list is generated (i.e. the list of nodes from Y to X).

This is not the end of the story, however. If one tries to run this particular program on a very large graph one will wait a long time before obtaining the result. The reason is that member consumes most of the time trying to determine if a particular node has already been encountered. In addition, when a node is considered that does not lead to the target, the program must backtrack away from it. There is no way to remember that this node is a "bad" one, so if this node is reached again using a different route, then the program will *retry the whole search again* from this node.

To overcome these problems side effects are needed (e.g. the imperative assert), and those nodes that have been visited must be stored in the database, as suggested in path4:

```
path4(X, X, [X]).
path4(X, Y, [X | Pz]) :-
        e(X, Z), try_edge(Z), path4(Z, Y, Pz).
try_edge(Z) :- was_visited(Z), !, fail.
try_edge(Z) :- assert(was_visited(Z)).
```

The first time node Z is visited assert is used to store this information in the database (via the fourth clause), so the next time Z is visited it will *fail* (via the third clause).

To solve the same problem in LISP, property lists are used as the database, and code for backtracking must be explicitly written, e.g.:

```
(def path (lambda (x y)
    (if (eq x y)
        (list x)
        (try_edges x y (get x 'edges)))))

(def try_edges (lambda (x y edges)
    (cond
      ((null edges) nil)
      ((get (first edges) 'was_visited)
       (try_edges x y (rest edges)))
      (t (putprop (first edges) 'was_visited)
         (try1 x y (path (first edges) y) edges)))))

(def try1 (lambda (x y nodes edges)
    (if (null nodes)
    (try_edges x y (rest edges))
    (cons x nodes))))
```

This definition is obviously less attractive than the corresponding PROLOG one. It is much more complicated and harder to understand, but this is not a surprise because LISP has no intrinsic mechanism for backtracking.

However, when speed is considered, the balance tips in the other direction. These programs were run interpretively on a

247

100 node graph with 1000 edges. The resulting timing relation-ships were:

LISP *vs.* path4   1:4
path4 *vs.* path3   1:4

Thus the pure logic program path3 is approximately sixteen times slower than the LISP program path. This is no surprise in that the LISP program is not pure, and contains more efficient data representations.

Hence a logic program is not necessarily an efficient program. Thus we conclude: (i) side effects can help one op-timize a program, and (ii) programming in high level languages such as LISP or PROLOG does not free the programmer from understanding the way the underlying system is working (If he or she requires the program to run efficiently).

2.5 PROLOG Special Features

Unification: No doubt "unification" is a more powerful tool than the simple binding mechanism of LISP. PROLOG proponents claim that one clause can replace several types of functions, e.g. constructors (like cons), modifiers (like rplaca) and predicates (like listp), and they are correct. Consider, for example, conscell([X | Y], X, Y):

conscell(C, 1, 2).   ; results in C = [1 | 2],
                          ; i.e. a constructor
conscell(C, 1, _).   ; will instantiate the car
                          ; of C (if not instantiated)
conscell(C, Car, Cdr).   ; selectors

PROLOG users also claim that unification helps to avoid repeated use of car, cdr combinations to decompose the structure of list (or other constructs). In the following example we show that this is not always the case.

The problem is to add two polynomials. We define the predicate add(P1, P2, P3), which is true if P3 is the sum of P1 and P2. Note each polynomial is represented as a list of terms of the form c(C, E), where C is the coefficient and E is the ex-

248

ponent. The first terms have smaller exponents and elements of the polynomial with zero coefficients do not appear.

```
1)  add([], P2, P2).

2)  add(P1, [], P1).

3)  add([c(C1, E1) | P1],
         [c(C2, E2) | P2],
         [c(C3, E2) | P3]) :-
              E1 == E2, !,   ; same exponent
              C3 is C1 + C2,
              add(P1, P2, P3).
                     ; recursive (loop on cdr chain) call

4)  add([c(C1, E1) | P1],
         [c(C2, E2) | P2],
         [c(C2, E2) | P3]) :-
              E2 < E1, !,
              add([c(C1,E1) | P1], P2, P3).

5)  add([c(C1, E1) | P1], P2, [c(C1, E1) | P3]) :-
         add(P1, P2, P3).
```

Note that in clauses 3, 4 and 5 we repeatedly unify the heads of the polynomials with the patterns. This is necessary since conditionals are not included in the PROLOG language.

In LISP we would write:

```
(defun polyadd(p q)
                    ; p = ((exp.coef)(exp.coef) ....)
                    ; same for q
     (cond
        ((null p) q) ; simple case
        ((null q) q) ; another simple case
        (t (prog (e1 e2 c1 c2) ; temp vars
             (setq c1 (caar p) e1 (cdar p)
                   c2 (caar q) e2 (cdar q))
```

```
(cond
  ((eq e1 e2)
     (cons (cons (plus c1 c2) e1)
              (polyadd (cdr p) (cdr q))))
  ((greaterp e1 e2)
     (cons (car q) (polyadd p (cdr q))))
  (t (polyadd q p)  ; switch p and q
))))))
```

Although this LISP function is not as elegant as the corresponding PROLOG code, it is likely to be more efficient since
it decomposes the structures only once with setq. This problem
can be solved by the compiler, which one hopes will generate
good code for unification and avoids multiple unifications.

Backtracking: In [1] Warren states: "A difficulty which
programmers new to PROLOG soon come up against is that they
need to combine information generated on alternative branches
of the program. However, in pure PROLOG, all information about
a certain branch of the computation is lost on backtracking to
an earlier point."

Warren suggested using a predicate setof, where setof(X,
P, L) is true if L is the set of instances of X that satisfy P. This
is a general mechanism; however, it does not allow one to
record information from a subset of branches. In LISP one can
record information using the dynamic environment and the
function setq to set free variables (global), while in PROLOG it is
quite impossible because variables are defined and used only
inside one clause.

2.6 LISP vs. PROLOG: a Summary

We summarize by reviewing the main issues.

Mathematical background: Drew McDermott put it
succinctly [7]: "Most published descriptions (of PROLOG) are
wretchedly misleading. The notion that programming in PROLOG
is programming in logic is ridiculous. Some simple clauses can
be thought of as first-order implications, but not most."

Efficiency: Pure recursive programs in LISP can be rewritten in PROLOG and run as efficiently as the corresponding LISP
program. In addition, certain types of programs (natural lan-

guage processing, relational databases, etc. as mentioned before) can be run effectively more efficiently in PROLOG. However, in many other cases, programs can become almost impossible to write efficiently in PROLOG.

Style: Also from McDermott: "It is often claimed that PROLOG programs can be used in more than one way, and simple ones can... Everyone *quickly* learns how seldom a program works this way. Use (of this style) will often introduce gross inefficiency or infinite loops. In practice this means programmers have to devote as much time to think about the different tasks a relation might do, as they would in writing a set of functions for these tasks in any other language."

Readability: There is no conclusive evidence that PROLOG programs are clearer or easier to understand than corresponding LISP programs, or vice versa. Typically arguments in this area are based on stylistic prejudice.

Side effects: There are ways to write side effect programs in PROLOG (assert, retract) and experience shows that they are often used for reasons of efficiency, simplicity and even clarity.

Special features: No doubt PROLOG has two important features (unification and backtracking) which are missing in LISP. It seems they are powerful and well incorporated into the language.

Thus both LISP and PROLOG are valuable tools for a variety of applications. In some applications (like natural language processing or relational database management) PROLOG is better than LISP, with its direct support for unification (pattern matching) and backtracking (for nondeterministic search). LISP, on the other hand, appears to be more general and applicable to a larger variety of applications. In one view, LISP can be thought of as the C of artificial intelligence where one has more control over one's computation, and PROLOG as the PASCAL of artificial intelligence where programs seem to be more pure and elegant.

The solution is perhaps to create one system which will support both LISP and PROLOG. In LOGLISP [8] the solution is to augment LISP with a package of functions (called LOGIC). The result is one system with two different languages living under the same roof.

The QUTE language [9] is another attempt to "amalgamate" LISP and PROLOG by introducing a new syntax and a new notion of variable. APPLOG is simpler and more straightforward: PROLOG remains exactly the same as a sublanguage, but is extended to embrace applicative expressions.

3 LANGUAGE DEFINITION

3.1 APPLOG Syntax

We now outline the syntax of APPLOG, which is substantially C-PROLOG syntax.

Atoms: Unlike traditional LISP, atoms in APPLOG are not variable names. Therefore, the value of an atom is the atom itself, and it need not be quoted.

Example: eval(aaaa) => aaaa.

Lists: The list syntax of APPLOG uses PROLOG's square brackets (to be compatible), and adjacent elements are separated by commas.

Examples: [1, 2, 3, 4, 5]
[1, 2, [4, 5, 6, 6], 7, 8].

Variables: APPLOG variables start with a capital letter, which is optionally followed by letters or digits or underscores. Like PROLOG, APPLOG variables can at any moment be uninstantiated (i.e. without a value) or instantiated (with a value). To determine this status we have the predicate var(X) which succeeds if X is uninstantiated (and returns X as its value).

Forms: APPLOG forms are written in the PROLOG style as *terms*.

Examples: cons(1, 2) => [1 | 2]
list(1, 2, 3, cons(3, 4)) =>
[1, 2, 3, [3 | 4]]

Transforming lists to terms: For this we use list_to_term(List) and conversely term_to_list(Term).

Examples: `list_to_term(list(a, 2, 3)) =>`
        `a(2, 3).`
    `term_to_list(quote(a(2, 3))) =>`
        `[a, 2, 3].`

Operators: Infix, prefix and even postfix operators are permitted in APPLOG forms:

Examples: `3*4 => 12`
    `3*2+(2+3) => 11`
    `cons(2+3, 3*5) => [5 | 15]`

Operators are APPLOG primitive functions which are stored as terms; thus the expression `2*3` is actually the term `*(2, 3)`. User defined functions can be declared as operators as well.

Success and failure: Unlike traditional LISP, the PROLOG notion of success and failure is adopted. Any function is also a predicate which can succeed or fail, where success means `true`, and failure means `false`. When a function succeeds, it always returns a value. Predicate functions, like eq, return the atom `true` when they succeed, but upon failure cause the failure of their containing form, rather than returning nil. This failure chain is stopped by conditional functions (e.g. `if`, `cond`), or predicates such as `and`, `or` etc. The effects of backtracking and generators can thereby be achieved (as in the ICON language [4]). Thus:

* `if(b(X), then_part(Y), else_part(Z))` means if `b(X)` succeeds, `then_part(Y)` is called, else (i.e. if `b(X)` fails) `else_part(Z)` is called.

* `or` behaves like a generator, i.e. `f(or(1, 2, 3, 4, 5))` causes the following effects. Function `f` is called with 1; if it fails then `or` generates 2, etc., until all the possibilities are exhausted, in which case `f` returns with a failure.

* `fail` explicitly causes a failure.

* `cond` generalizes `if-then-else` to have arbitrary number of arguments, e.g.

```
cond((eq(X, Y), Z)
     (X>Y,      X)
     (t,        Y)).
```

3.2 User-Defined Functions

Formal parameters are usually specified as a list of variables, but in APPLOG one can write any legal term as a formal parameter. The body of the function is any APPLOG expression. To define a function one writes:

```
def(Fn_name, lambda(Arg_list, Fn_body)).
```

Instead of lambda one can write nlambda to signal that arguments to this function are to be passed unevaluated. The following steps are used to evaluate the APPLOG expression f(a1, a2, a3):

1. The definition of f is consulted, and if it is a lambda function then the arguments a1, a2, a3 are evaluated; otherwise (the nlambda case), they are not.
2. The formal parameter list is *unified* with the actual parameter list.
3. The body of the function f is evaluated under the bindings that result from this unification.

The following is the actual code of the main part of the APPLOG interpreter, as written in PROLOG:

```
/* apply user functions */

eval(Form, Result) :-
     Form =.. [Fn | Args],   ; break expr apart
     do_args(Fn, Args, Vars, Body),
     eval(Body, Result).

do_args(F, A, V, B) :-
     def(F, lambda(V, B)), eval_args(A, V).
do_args(F, A, V, B) :-
     def(F, nlambda(V, B)), A=V.
```

```
eval_args([A1 | As], [X1 | Xs]) :-
    eval(A1, X1),
        ; also unify the formal parameter with the
        ; actual parameter
    eval_args(As, Xs).
eval_args([], []).
```

Note the absence of an explicit environment (e.g. an *alist*) because APPLOG exploits the environment of the underlying PROLOG system. APPLOG functions offer enhanced readability through operator notation and additional methods for parameter passing, e.g. by reference, pattern directed invocation, etc.

The following examples show how functions are written in APPLOG, and support the claim that APPLOG is *simple, readable* and *powerful* (observe the parameter passing methods, infix operators etc.).

1. The factorial function:

```
def(fact, lambda([X], if (X=1, 1, X*fact(X-1)))).
```

Note here the use of infix operators.

Example: fact(4) => 24

2. Appending two lists:

```
def(app, lambda([L1, L2],
        if(eq(L1, []), L2, cons(car(L1),
            app(cdr(L1), L2))))).
```

Example: app(list(1, 2, 3)), list(4, 5, 6)) =>
                    [1, 2, 3, 4, 5, 6].

3. Passing a term (structure) to an APPLOG function:

```
def(faaa, lambda([aaa(A, B), C], list(A, B, C))).
```

Note aaa is a record passed to faaa.

255

Example: `faaa(quote(aaa(4, 5)), 8) => [4, 5, 8].`

4. Call-by-reference: in the following example note how the variable B is the subject of a setq inside the function f4:

`def(f4, lambda([A, B], setq(B, A+A*A))).`

Example: `list(f4(2, X), X+1) => [6, 7].`

5. Fibonacci numbers:

```
def(fibo, lambda([N],
        if(N<2, 1, fibo(N-1) + fibo(N-2)))).
```

Compare here the APPLOG definition of fibo to a corresponding definition in LISP:

```
(def fibo (lambda (n)
        (if (lt n 2) 1
            (+ (fibo (- n 1)) (fibo (- n 2)))))).
```

6. Using a pattern argument to decompose a list:

`def(last, lambda([[X | L]], if(L=[], X, last(L)))).`

Note here the use of pattern-directed invocation: the first parameter of last must be a car-cdr pair, where X is bound to the car and L to the cdr. The same function in PROLOG would be:

```
last([X], X).
last([X | L], Y) :- last(L, Y).
```

7. A simple definition of the list function:

`def(mylist, lambda(L, L)).`

Note the one to many binding.

Example: `mylist(1, 2, 3, list(7, 8), 4, 5, 6) =>`
`[1, 2, 3, [7, 8], 4, 5, 6].`

8. Arguments passed unevaluated:

`def(f5, nlambda([A, B],`
`      list(A, B, eval(A), eval(B)))).`

Example: `f5(2*3, 5+6) => [2*3, 5+6, 6, 11].`

9. Variable length final arguments:

`def(f6, lambda([A, B | C], list(A, B, C))).`

Note C is a "catch all" variable, as in INTERLISP or \&rest as in ZETALISP.

`(lambda (A B . C) ...).`

Example: `f6(1, 2, 3, 4, 5) =>`
`[1, 2, [3, 4, 5]].`

3.3 APPLOG to PROLOG Interface

PROLOG is called from APPLOG using the goal function. There are two ways to use goal:

1. `goal(Goal, Form)`, where Goal is a PROLOG goal and Form is an APPLOG form. The Goal is satisfied by PROLOG and then the Form is executed by APPLOG. Recall that if the Form fails, it backtracks into the Goal and then if the Goal can be satisfied again, Form is evaluated again. Here are some simple examples.

* If the database contains `a(3)` then `goal(a(X), X+X)`. yields 6.
* Now, a backtracking example. Suppose the database contains `b(3, 4)`, `b(6, 7)`. Then `goal(b(X, Y), if(X>5, X+Y))` behaves as follows. Evaluation of `b(X, Y)` will find `b(3, 4)`, but when the if fails (because X is not larger than 5)

backtracking will occur, with b(6, 7) being found and 13 resulting.

2. goal(Goal), which means satisfy the Goal and deliver it as the returned value. Thus goal(a(X)) => a(3)

To enter new facts into the database use assert. Thus to insert the fact a(1, 2, 3) use assert(quote(a(1, 2, 3))) or assertq(a(1, 2, 3)).

3.4 PROLOG to APPLOG Interface

To call the APPLOG interpreter from PROLOG simply use:

eval(Form, Result).

3.5 System Utilities

The following facilities are provided in APPLOG.

1. *Top loop:* To call the friendly APPLOG top-loop function type top in PROLOG. History expressions can be re-executed by h(N). The history listing is obtained by h(From, To).

2. *Loading APPLOG programs:* Use load(File), where File may contain any APPLOG forms. The utility load reads and evaluates these forms (using APPLOG eval). To load PROLOG files perform goal(consult(File)).

3. *Pretty print:* Use pp(Term) or pp(Term, Linelength).

3.6 Relational Database Interface

We use PROLOG database and APPLOG evaluation methods to propose a simple extension of APPLOG as a relational database query language. We use "lazy evaluation" to access relations and thus save space. First we describe the simple functions rel and all.

1. rel *relation:* rel is a prefix operator (unary function) which behaves as a generator. It generates the tuples of relation relation. One can avoid the use of rel by declaring it as a relation, i.e.

def(<relation name>, relation).

and then only the relation name must be mentioned.

2. Func all Generator: all behaves almost like the LISP function maplist, in that it applies the function Func to *all* possible values which can be generated by Generator.

Here are examples of typical relational database operations, using the following database:

```
def(a, relation).
        a(1, 2).
        a(4, 1).
        a(2, 1).
        a(2, 3).

def(b, relation).
        b(2, 5).
        b(3, 5).
        b(3, 6).

def(d, relation).
        d(1, 2, 3, 4).
        d(5, 6, 7, 8).
        d(5, 8, 4, 3).

def(personal, relation).
        personal(john, male, 30000).
        personal(mary, female, 30000).
        personal(mike, male, 35000).
        personal(maria, female, 35000).

print(rel a(X, Y)). /* to print a single tuple of
                        relation a, or */
print(a(X, Y)). /* if a is defined as a relation
                        (see database). */
        will yield: a(1, 2).

print all a(X, Y). /* print all tuples of
                        relation a */
        will yield: a(1, 2). a(4, 1). a(2, 1).
                    a(2, 3).
```

```
print all a(X, Y) ? (X>Y) /* selection */
     will yield: a(4, 1). a(2, 1).

print all d(X, Y, Z, W) --> e(X, Z). /* project */
     will yield: e(1, 3). e(5, 7). e(5, 4).

print all a(X, Y) x b(Y, Z) --> c(X, Y, Z).
          /* will join the two relations a, b to form
               a third relation c */
     will yield: c(1, 2, 5). c(2, 3, 5).
          c(2, 3, 6).

sum(personal(Name, Sex, Salary), Salary).
          /* this aggregate function returns the sum
               of salaries from relation
               personal. */
     will yield: 130000.

sum(personal(Name, Sex, Salary), Salary, Sex).
          /* With grouping by sex, the functions sum
               is a generator */
     will yield: sum(male, 70000). and then
          sum(female, 70000).
```

3.7 Path Example Revisited

We conclude with an APPLOG solution to the problem of finding a path between two nodes in a graph, as discussed in section 2.4. Note the mixture of PROLOG and LISP features in the definition of path.

```
def(path, lambda([X, Y],
   if(eq(X, Y), list(X),
      cons(X, try_edges(e(X, Z), Y))))).

def(try_edges, lambda([e(X, Z), Y],
   if(was_visited(Z), fail,
     (assertq(was_visited(Z)),
      path(Z, Y))))).
```

```
def(e, relation).
def(was_visited, relation).
```

Note that relation **e** is a generator which generates all the edges going out from **X**. In **try_edges** we check if Z was visited and if so we fail. This failure causes backtracking to return to relation e which retrieves another edge and then **try_edges** is called again.

4 SUMMARY

It seems that both PROLOG and LISP are here to stay, each with its own group of proponents. This paper demonstrates how one can painlessly enjoy the virtues of both languages. As a proof we supply in the appendix the full listing of the APPLOG interpreter written in PROLOG, except for the **prettyprint** relations.

ACKNOWLEDGEMENTS

The author is indebted to the editors of this volume for their critical comments, and to Gary Lindstrom in addition for his extensive assistance in preparing the final version of this article.

APPENDIX: APPLOG INTERPRETER

Here is the listing of the APPLOG interpreter written in PROLOG (C-PROLOG 1.2). We believe any real PROLOG hacker will be able to adapt this version to his or her own system.

There are three files:

1. eval: the main interpreter;
2. rdb: the relational database interface, and
3. pp: the pretty printer of APPLOG expressions (omitted here).

Make sure the path names are correct in file eval (see instructions there).

```
/*


A  P  P  L  O  G     Interpreter          (file: eval)
-----------------------------------------


"LISP vs. PROLOG:
        If you can't fight them, JOIN them"

Written by: Shimon Cohen (April 1983).

NOTE: Before loading this file make sure all path
names are correct.  To do so, search for lines with
the string: "cohen" and insert the right PATH. Make
sure you have files rdb and pp in your directory.
*/
/* operators */
initop :-
        op(999, fx, is),
        op(998, fx, q).


:- initop.


/*      simple cases and special atoms      */

eval(X, Y)              :- var(X), !, X=Y.
eval(exit, R)           :- !, abort.
```

262

```
eval(fail, R)              :- !, fail.  /* cause failure */
eval(terpri, true)         :- !, nl.  /* cause newline */
eval(X, Y)                 :- (number(X); var(X); atom(X)),
                                   !, Y=X.
eval(value(X), Y)          :- !, Y=X.
eval((A, B), R)            :- !, eval(A, Ax), eval(B, R).
eval([A | B], R)           :- !, T =.. [A | B], eval(T, R).

 * arithmetic functions */

eval(A*B, C)               :- !, eval(A, Ae), eval(B, Be),
                                   C is Ae*Be.
eval(A-B, C)               :- !, eval(A, Ae), eval(B, Be),
                                   C is Ae-Be.
eval(A+B, C)               :- !, eval(A, Ae), eval(B, Be),
                                   C is Ae+Be.
eval(A/B, C)               :- !, eval(A, Ae), eval(B, Be),
                                   C is Ae/Be.
eval(A//B, C)              :- !, eval(A, Ae), eval(B, Be),
                                   C is Ae//Be.
eval(A mod B, C)           :- !, eval(A, Ae), eval(B, Be),
                                   C is Ae mod Be.
eval(A ^ B, C)             :- !, eval(A, Ae), eval(B, Be),
                                   C is Ae ^ Be.

eval(A>B, true)            :- !, eval(A, Ae), eval(B, Be),
                                   Ae>Be.
eval(A<B, true)            :- !, eval(A, Ae), eval(B, Be),
                                   Ae<Be.
eval(A=<B, true)           :- !, eval(A, Ae), eval(B, Be),
                                   Ae=<Be.
eval(A>=B, true)           :- !, eval(A, Ae), eval(B, Be),
                                   Ae>=Be.
eval(A==B, true)           :- !, eval(A, Ae), eval(B, Be),
                                   Ae==Be.
eval(A\==B, true)          :- !, eval(A, Ae), eval(B, Be),
                                   Ae\==Be.
eval(A=B, true)            :- !, eval(A, Ae), eval(B, Be),
```

Ae=Be.

```
/* basic LISP functions */

eval(cons(X, Y), [Xe | Ye]) :- !, eval(X, Xe),
                                  eval(Y, Ye).
eval(quote(X), Y)            :- !, X=Y.
eval(q X, Y)                 :- !, X=Y.
eval(setq(X, Y), Z)          :- !, eval(Y, Z), X=Z.
eval(X is Y, Z)              :- !, eval(Y, Z), X=Z.
eval(eq(X, Y), true)         :- !, eval(X, Xe),
                                  eval(Y, Ye),
                                  eqq(Xe, Ye).
eqq(A, B)                    :- (var(A); var(B)), !, A=B.
eqq(A, B)                    :- A==B.
eval(atom(X), X)             :- !, (var(X); atom(X)).
eval(car(X), Y)              :- !, eval(X, [Y | _]).
eval(cdr(X), Y)              :- !, eval(X, [_ | Y]).

/* eval, if functions */

eval(if(BoolExpr, ThenForm, ElseForm), Te)     :-
        eval(BoolExpr, Xe), !, eval(ThenForm, Te).
eval(if(BoolExpr, ThenForm, ElseForm), Ze)     :-
        !, eval(ElseForm, Ze).

eval(eval(Form), Result)     :-
        !, eval(Form, Z), eval(Z, Result).
eval(apply(FnExpr, Args), R) :- !,
        eval(FnExpr, Fn),
        NewExpr =.. [Fn | Args],
        eval(NewExpr, R).

/* IO */

eval(read(X), Y)     :- !, Read(X), Y=X.
eval(prin1(X), R)    :- !, eval(X, R), write(R).
eval(print(X), R)    :- !, eval(X, R), write(R), nl.
```

```
/* interface to PROLOG */

eval(goal(Goal, Body), Result)  :-
        !, Call(Goal), eval(Body, Result).
eval(goal(Goal), Goal)          :-
        !, Call(Goal).
eval(goalall(Goal), R)          :-
        !, setof(Goal, Goal, R).
eval(goalall(Goal, Body), true) :-
        !, doall(Goal, Body).
doall(G, B)                     :-
        call(G), eval(B, R), fail.
doall(G, B).
eval(assert(Fact), Xfact)       :- eval(Fact, Xfact),
                Assert(Xfact).
eval(assertq(Fact), Fact)       :- assert(Fact).

/* load relational database interface */

 :- consult('/na/doe/guest/cohen/prolog/lispl/rdb');
        true.

printall(G, B) :- eval(goal(G, B), R), write(R), nl,
                        fail.
printall(G, B).

/* history expression */

eval(h(N), Result)          :- !, history(N, Expr),
                                eval(Expr, Result).
eval(h(N1, N2), true)       :- !, h(N1, N2).
h(N1, N2)                   :- N1=<N2, history(N1, Expr),
                                write(N1), write(':   '),
                                write(Expr), nl,
                                Nx is N1 + 1, h(Nx, N2).
h(_,_).

/* def trace load */
```

```
eval(load(File), File)    :- !, see(File), nofileerrors,
                                 doload.
doload                    :- read(E), !, doE(E).
doE(E)                    :- E == end_of_file,!.
doE(E)                    :- eval(E, R), doload.
doload                    :- seen.

eval(trace(Fn), Fn)       :- !, (trace(Fn);
                                 assert(trace(Fn))).
eval(untrace(Fn), Fn)     :- !, Retract(trace(Fn)).
eval(def(F, L), F)        :- !, dodef(F, L).
dodef(F, L) :- putq(L, Lq),
               (retract(def(F, Autoload(_))); true),
            assert(def(F, Lq)).

eval(Cond, Result)        :- functor(Cond, Cond, N),!,
                             Cond =.. [cond | Clauses], !,
                                 evcond(Clauses, Result).
evcond([C1 | Cr], R)      :- C1 =.. [Stam, P | E],
                             eval(P, Px),!, evand(E, R).
evcond([(P) | Cr], R)     :- eval(P, R).
evcond([C1 | Cr], R)      :- evcond(Cr, R).
evcond([], []).

/* list or and functions */

eval(List, Result)        :- functor(List, list, N), !,
                             List =.. [list | El],
                             evlist(El, Result).
evlist([], []).
evlist([E1 | Er], [X1 | Xr]) :- eval(E1, X1),
                                evlist(Er, Xr).
eval(Term, Result)        :- functor(Term, term, N),!,
                        Term =.. [term | El], evlist(El, Ex),
                             !, Result =.. Ex.
/* term <--> list */

eval(list_to_term(L), R)     :- !, eval(L, Lx),
```

```prolog
                                             R  =.. Lx.
eval(term_to_list(T), R)        :- !, eval(T, Tx),
                                             Tx =.. R.


eval(Or, Result)                :- functor(Or, or, N), !,
                                   Or =.. [or | Er],
                                   evor(Er, Result).
evor([E1 | Er], Result)         :- eval(E1, Result).
evor([E1 | Er], Result)         :- evor(Er, Result).


eval(And, Result)               :- functor(And, And, N),!,
                                   And =.. [and | Er],
                                   evand(Er, Result).
evand([E], R)                   :- eval(E, R).
evand([E1 | Er], Result)        :- eval(E1, Stam), !,
                                   evand(Er, Result).


/* apply user functions */

eval(Form, Result)      :-
                Form =.. [Fn | Args],
                do_args(Fn, Args, Vars, Body),
                enter_trace(Fn, Vars, L),
                eval(Body, Result),
                exit_trace(Fn, Result, L).


/* binding(B, B).  isn't it simple ??? */

/* arguments evaluation if lambda */

do_args(F, A, V, B)  :- def(F, lambda(V, B)),
                                   eval_args(A, V).
do_args(F, A, V, B)  :- def(F, nlambda(V, B)), A=V.
do_args(F, A, V, B)  :- def(F, Autoload(File)),
                        consult(File), (retract(def(F,
                                Autoload(File)))); true),
                                do_args(F, A, V, B).
```

```
do_args(F, A, V, B)  :-
        def(F, Relation), eval_args(A, V),
        T =.. [F | V], B =.. [goal, T].


def(pp,    autoload('/na/doe/guest/cohen/prolog
                /lispl/pp')).
def(pplen, autoload('/na/doe/guest/cohen/prolog
                /lispl/pp')).

eval_args([A1 | Al], [X1 | Xl]) :-
        eval(A1, X1), eval_args(Al, Xl).
eval_args([], []).

/* trace printout */

enter_trace(F, X, L)   :- trace(F), !,
                          (retract(trace_lvl(F, N));
                          N=0), L is N + 1, tab(L),
                          assert(trace_lvl(F, L)),
                          write(' -enter- '), write(F),
                          write('     ARGS  : '),
                          write(X), nl.
enter_trace(F, X, L).

exit_trace(F, R, L)    :-  trace(F), !,
                          retract(trace_lvl(F, N)),
                          tab(L),
                          L1 is L - 1,
                          Assert(trace_lvl(F, L1)),
                          write(' -exit - '), write(F),
                          write('     RESULT: '),
                          write(R), nl.
exit_trace(F, R, L).

/* avoid re-evaluation of vars */

putq(A, A)    :- (atom(A); integer(A)), !.
```

```
putq(A, value(A)) :- var(A), !.

/* The first argument of sp_fn functions is not
        "valued" */

putq(A, B)     :- A=.. [F, X1 | Xs],
        sp_fn(F), !,
        doputq(Xs, Y),
        B=.. [F, X1 | Y].

/* simple functions */

putq(A, B)     :- A=.. [F | X],
        doputq(X, Y),
        B=.. [F | Y].

sp_fn(setq).
sp_fn(is).
sp_fn(goal).
sp_fn(goalall).
sp_fn(q).
sp_fn(quote).
sp_fn(lambda).
sp_fn(nlambda).
sp_fn(assertq).

doputq([], []) :- !.
doputq([C | D], [Cq | Dq]) :- putq(C, Cq),
                              doputq(D, Dq).

/* friendly top loop */

top :- abolish(history, 2), top(1).
top(N) :-
        repeat, Abolish(trace_lvl, 1),
        write('-'), write(N), write('- '),
        write('APPLOG: '),
        read(E),
```

```
      ((functor(E, def, 2), Eq=E);putq(E, Eq)), !,
         assert(history(N, Eq)),
         ((eval(Eq, R), write('RESULT IS: '), write(R));
          write(' F A I L ')),
         nl, N1 is N + 1, !, top(N1).


   /*
```

```
A P P L O G    Interpreter         (file: rdb)
----------------------------

"LISP vs. PROLOG: If you can't fight them, JOIN them"

Written by: Shimon Cohen (April 1983).

Relational Data Base Interface
-----------------------------        */

eval(rel(R), Tuple)    :-
      !, reval(R, Tuple),Call(Tuple).

eval(rjoin(R1, R2, R3), T) :-
      !, eval(R1, T1), eval(R2, T2), reval(R3, T).

eval(rselect(R, Cond), T) :-
      !, eval(R, T),  eval(Cond,_).

eval(rproject(R, T),  T) :-
      !, eval(R, T1), reval(T1, T).

eval(all(Fn, R), T1)      :- !, rall(R, Fn, T1).

rall(R, Fn, T) :-
      eval(R, T), Action =.. [Fn, value(T)],
      rall1(Action).
rall(R, Fn, T).

rall1(A) :-   eval(A,_), !, fail.
rall1(A).

reval(value(T), T).
reval(R, T) :- R =.. L, evlist(L, Vs), T =.. Vs.

/* end relational database  */

initoprdb :-
```

271

```prolog
 op(980, xfx, all),
 op(970, xfx, -->),
 op(970, xfx, <--),
 op(960, yfx, x  ),
 op(950, yfx, '?'),
 op(950, yfx, '!'),
 op(940, fx, rel).
:- initoprdb.

eval(find(R), Tuple)  :-
       !, reval(R, Tuple), Call(Tuple).
eval(rel R,  Tuple)  :-
       !, reval(R, Tuple), Call(Tuple).


eval(insert(R), Tuple)  :-
       !, eval(R, Tuple), Assert(Tuple).

eval(R1 --> T1, T)  :- !, eval(R1,_), reval(T1, T).
eval(T1 <-- R1, T)  :- !, eval(R1,_), reval(T1, T).

eval(R1 x R2, T2)   :- !, eval(R1, T1), eval(R2, T2).

eval(R ? Cond, T)   :- !, eval(R, T),  eval(Cond,_).

eval(R ! T1,  T)    :- !, eval(R,_), reval(T1, T).

eval(Fn all R, T1)    :- !, rall(R, Fn, T).
eval(count(R), N)     :- !, Count(R, N).

eval(sum(R, Field, Group), GG) :-
       !, Aggr_group(R, plus2, Field, Group, GG).
eval(sum(R, Field), S)         :-
       !, Aggr_group(R, plus2, Field, All,
       Group(all, N, S)).

eval(max(R, Field, Group), GG) :- !,
       Aggr_group(R, max2, Field, Group, GG).
eval(max(R, Field), Min)   :-
```

```
        !, Aggr_group(R, max2, Field, All,
        Group(all, N, Min)).

eval(min(R, Field, Group), GG) :-
        !, Aggr_group(R, min2, Field, Group, GG).
eval(min(R, Field), Min)   :-
        !, Aggr_group(R, min2, Field, All,
        Group(all, N, Min)).

eval(count(R, Group), group(G1, N)) :-
        !, aggr_group(R, plus2, 1, Group,
        Group(G1, N, S)).

eval(avr(R, Field, Group), group(G1, N, A)) :- !,
        aggr_group(R, plus2, Field, Group,
        Group(G1, N, S)), A is S / N.
eval(avr(R, Field), A) :- !,
        aggr_group(R, plus2, Field, All,
        Group(all, N, S)), A is S / N.
eval(sort_g(R), Y) :- !, do_sorty(R, Y).

do_sorty(R, Y) :-
        get_unq_number(U), !,
        U1 is 97 + (U mod 26),
        name(Unq_name, [97, 95, 95, 95, U1]),
        do_sort(R, Unq_name),
        A =.. [Unq_name, X], !,
        setof(A, A, L),
        B =.. [Unq_name, Y], !,
        list_to_g(B, L, Y).

/* generate tuples */
list_to_g(B, [B | L], Y).
list_to_g(B, [_ | L], Y) :- list_to_g(B, L, Y).

do_sort(R, Un) :-
   eval(R, Rx),
   T =.. [Un, Rx],
```

```
        assert(T),
        fail.
do_sort(R, Un).


/* dirty stuff to support aggregates */

max2(A, B, B) :- B>A, !.
max2(A, B, A).
min2(A, B, A) :- A<B, !.
min2(A, B, B).
plus2(A, B, C) :- C is A + B.


unq_number(1).
get_unq_number(U) :-
        !, Retract(unq_number(U)), U1 is U + 1,
        assert(unq_number(U1)).


count(X, N) :-
        get_unq_number(U),
        assert(count_yy(U, 0)),
        !, do_count(U, X), !,
        count_yy(U, N).
do_count(U, X) :- eval(X, Res), Add1_count(U), fail.
do_count(U, X).
add1_count(U) :-
        retract(count_yy(U, N)),
        N1 is N + 1,
        assert(count_yy(U, N1)), !.
/* Generator - generates tuples
   F2 - PROLOG axiom which return a value.
   Field - to act upon this field.
   Grouping - do aggregate according to groups.
*/
aggr_group(Generator, F2, Field, Grouping,
           group(Gnow, N, Result)) :-
                get_unq_number(U),
                !, do_aggr(U, Generator, F2, Field,
                Grouping), !,
```

```
                count_gg(U, Gnow, N, Result).

do_aggr(U, Generator, F2, Field, Grouping) :-
      eval(Generator, R),
      eval(Field, Fld),
      eval(Grouping, Groupy),
      do_aggr1(U, F2, Fld, Groupy),
      fail.

do_aggr(U, Generator, F2, Field, Grouping).

do_aggr1(U, F2, Field, Grouping) :-
      retract(count_gg(U, Grouping, N, R)), !,
      Act =.. [F2, R, Field, R2],
      call(Act), !,
      N1 is N + 1,
      assert(count_gg(U, Grouping, N1, R2)).

do_aggr1(U, F2, Field, Grouping) :-
      assert(count_gg(U, Grouping, 1, Field)).
```

REFERENCES

1. Warren, D. H. D. "High order extensions to PROLOG: are they needed?". *Machine Intelligence 10* (1982).

2. Cohen, S. The APPLOG language: PROLOG vs. LISP, if you can't fight them, join them. UCB/CSD 84/179, Computer Science Department, Univ. of Calif. at Berkeley, May 1984.

3. Colmerauer, A., H. Kanousi, R. Pasero and P. Roussel. Un systeme de communication homme-machine en francais. Groupe d'Intelligence Artificial, U.E.R. de Luminy, Universite' d'Aix-Marseille, 1973.

4. Griswold, R. E. and M. T. Griswold. *The ICON Programming Language.* Prentice-Hall, 1983.

5. Hill, R. LUSH resolution and its completeness. DCL Memo NO. 78, Dept. of Artificial Intelligence, Univ. of Edinburgh, 1974.

6. Kowalski, R. A. Predicate Logic as Programming Language. Congress Proceedings 1974, IFIP, 1974.

7. McDermott, D. "The PROLOG phenomenon." *SIGART Newsletter 72* (1980), 16-20.

8. Robinson, J. A. and E. E. Sibert. "LOGLISP: An alternative to PROLOG." *Machine Intelligence 10* (1982).

9. Sato, M. and T. Sakurai. QUTE: A PRLOG/LISP type language for logic programming. Proc. of 8th International Conference, IJCAI, Karlsruhe, West Germany, August 1983.

10. Warren, D. H. D., L. M. Pereira and F. Pereira. "PROLOG- The language and its implementation compared with LISP." *SIGPLAN Notices 12*, 8 (1977), 109-115. Proc. of Symp. on AI and Pro- gramming Languages; also appeared as SIGART Newsletter number 64.

11. Warren, D. H. D. "Logic Programming and Compiler Writing." *Software Practice and Experience 10* (1980), 97-125.

Part IV:

Programming with Equality

EQUALITY FOR PROLOG [1]

William A. Kornfeld

Quintus Computer Systems, Inc.
2345 Yale Street
Palo Alto, California 94306

ABSTRACT

An extension of the language Prolog, called "Prolog-with-Equality", is presented which allows the inclusion of assertions about equality. When an attempt is made to unify two terms that do not unify syntactically, an equality theorem may be used to attempt to prove the two terms equal. If it is possible to prove that the two terms are equal, the unification succeeds with the variable bindings introduced by the equality proof. It is shown that this mechanism significantly improves the power of Prolog. Sophisticated data abstraction with the advantages of object-oriented programming becomes available. Techniques for passing partially instantiated data are described that extend the "multi-use" capabilities of the language, improve the efficiency of some programs, and allow the implementation of arithmetic relations that are both general and efficient. The modifications to standard Prolog are simple and straightforward and in addition the computational overhead for the extra linguistic power is believed to not be significant. Equality theorems may play an important role in future logic programming systems.

---

[1]Originally published in *Proceedings of The Eighth International Joint Conference on Artificial Intelligence,* Karlsruhe, West Germany, August, 1983, pp. 514–19. Copyright 1983 by IJCAI, Inc. All rights reserved. Used by permission of IJCAI Inc. and the author.

1 Introduction

Prolog is a computer language based on Horn clause resolution. The basic resolution procedure does not allow statements about equality. We cannot, for example, express that $6 = successor(5)$ and then be able to unify $P(6)$ with $P(succesor(5))$. We have adapted a Lisp-based Prolog system [5] so that it is possible to specify theorems about equality. The unification algorithm has been modified so that if the unification of two terms fails, an assertion is sought that will prove the two terms are equal. As with any application of the unification procedure, the proof of equality of the two terms may cause the binding of variables in either or both of the terms.

Our Prolog-with-Equality is a natural extension to standard Prolog. We have found several applications for it that extend the power, expressibility, and generality of Prolog. These principally fall into two categories—extensible datatypes and greater opportunities to pass partially specified data objects. The former turns out, surprisingly, to augment Prolog with all the flexibility of "object-oriented" languages typified by Smalltalk [4]. The second major application area is a greatly improved facility for passing partially instantiated data objects as an alternative to a backtracking-based enumeration of possible bindings. These turn out to be quite easily implemented in Prolog-with-Equality. Moreover, the effect on efficiency in interpreted Prolog is minimal and there is every reason to suppose that most computational overhead that is introduced can be eliminated in compilation.

The notion of equality theorems is very similar to the demodulation rule [2].

2 Example—Rational Number Datatype

We will create a rational number datatype as an example of the use of equality theorems. Rational numbers will be represented by a term made up of the functor `rat` with two arguments, the numerator and denominator respectively. There is a distinguished predicate symbol `equals` which is used to specify the equality axioms.

We add the following assertion to our database: [2]

---

[2]Our Prolog syntax is not standard and should be briefly explained. A term is represented as a Lisp list whose first element is the functor and the remaining elements are the arguments. A literal prefaced by the symbol "_" is a variable;

```
(equals (rat _num1 _denom1) (rat _num2 _denom2)) :-
        (times _num1 _denom2 _intermediate)
        (times _num2 _denom1 _intermediate)
```

This expresses the usual cross-multiplication rule for deciding if two rationals are equal to one another.

Our augmented unification rule works as follows: When the interpreter attempts to unify two objects Φ and Ψ using standard unification and fails, it will establish the goal (equals Φ Ψ). If this demonstration succeeds, the unification succeeds with the new variable bindings. If this fails, it will attempt to prove (equals Ψ Φ). An attempt to unify (rat 2 3) with (rat _X 3) will succeed because standard unification succeeds. An attempt to unify (rat 2 3) with (rat _X 6) will cause the goal

```
(equals (rat 2 3) (rat _X 6))
```

to be posed by the system. This will succeed with the variable _X bound to 4. The original computation continues with this binding and it is placed in the trail for undoing on backtracking.

We have not yet told the system how to match rationals with any other kind of object. We wish to express a method to decide if a rat is the same as an integer. The following assertion is added:

```
(equals (rat _num _denom) _n)   :-
      (type _n integer)
      (if (and (variable _num)
               (variable _denom))
          (and (= _num _n) (= _denom 1))
          (times _denom _n _num))
```

If both the numerator and the denominator are uninstantiated it succeeds by unifying the numerator with the integer, otherwise it proves the multiplicative relationship that must hold for the equality to hold.

The following little program will now succeed 3 times:

---

case is not significant. Non-unit clauses are represented using the ":-" notation.

```
(member (rat 4 _x)
        [2 3 (cons _y _z) (rat _r _w) (rat 2 7)])
_x = 2
_r = 4, _x = _w
_x = 14
```

We will also wish to specify the behavior of this new datatype for several additional relations. The > relation for rationals is implemented with the following assertion:

```
(> (rat _n1 _d1) (rat _n2 _d2)) :-
    (times _n1 _d2 _x)
    (times _d1 _n2 _y)
    (> _x _y)
```

This rule could of course work in a Prolog without equality theorems when comparing two terms beginning with the functor rat. Now, however, if we try to prove the goal (> (rat 3 2) 1), the attempt to unify this goal with the head of this assertion will cause an attempt to prove that 1 equals (rat _n2 _d2) which will succeed with the appropriate bindings (n2=1, d2=1), allowing the > goal to succeed. In other languages this might be called "automatic type coercion."

3 Extensible Datatypes and Generic Operations

Equality theorems allow us to gain the modularity advantages of generic operations and class structuring as are found in object-oriented languages like Smalltalk. The important contributions of this class of languages are two:

1. One can specify methods for computing facts about whole classes of objects and then have those methods automatically inherited by subclasses.

2. A given operation will have different effects on different data, in a manner determined by a datum's class. It is decided at run time rather than compile time.

282

The paradigm of logic programming is very different from the paradigm of message passing systems. We do not have "objects" which receive "messages." The role of objects is played by terms; the role of messages by relations. The concept of "class" has no formal analog in Prolog-with-Equality. The effect of class structuring is accomplished by the use of equals assertions. A subclass relationship is indicated by a single equals assertion containing terms for the sub- and super-class. The pattern of variables between the two terms and the body of the assertion express the relationship between the two classes.

As an example, we might have the class `regular-polygon`. All regular polygons have four attributes, an X and Y location, a side length, and the number of sides. In Prolog we might want to specify a method for computing the areas of regular polygons. This would be done as follows:

```
(area (regular-polygon (_x _y _side-number _length))
    _area)                                               :-
  (quotient 180 _side-number _theta)
  (cotangent _theta _cotangent)
  (times _length _length _length-squared)
  (times _length-squared _side-number _prod1)
  (times _prod1 _cotangent _prod2)
  (quotient _prod2 4 _area)
```

We could then have a functor `equilateral-triangle` that is defined to be equal to a `regular-polygon` with three sides:

```
(equals (equilateral-triangle _x _y _length)
        (regular-polygon _x _y 3 _length))
```

Then if we attempt to prove the goal

```
(area (equilateral-triangle _ _ 100) _ans)
```

the attempt to unify it with the head of the `area` assertion will result in an attempt to show the term with functor `equilateral-triangle` is equal to a term with functor `regular-polygon`. This will succeed with _side-number bound to 3 and the goal will succeed with _ans bound to 150. We could, of course, ask the question: "How long does the side of an equilateral triangle have to be to have an area of 150?" This would be:

```
(area (equilateral-triangle _ _ _length) 150)
```

This goal will succeed with _length bound to 100.

We could also have area assertions for other kinds of objects such as ellipses:

```
(area (ellipse _x _y _minor-axis _major-axis) _area) :-
```

This will not interfere in any way with goals asking for the areas of triangles because there is no theorem that allows us to show Triangles and Ellipses are equal.

We could define a circle by saying:

```
(equals (circle _x _y _radius)
        (ellipse _x _y _diameter _diameter)) :-
   (times 2 _radius _diameter)
```

that will then allow the use of theorems about ellipses for answering questions about circles.

There is one sense in which we have more flexibility in Prolog-with-Equality than can be achieved with object-oriented languages. As with other aspects of Prolog, we are able to leave many aspects of our computation undetermined and still carry out the computation. Within object-oriented languages an object's class is known at object instantiation time. This is not true for terms in Prolog-with-Equality. Suppose we have the goal:

```
(and (= _obj (regular-polygon (_ _ _side-number _length)))
     (= _side-number 3)
     (predicate _obj))
```

The variable obj is unified with a regular-polygon of an indeterminate number of sides. Side-number is later unified with 3 and predicate is called. If predicate has assertions that will allow proofs about triangles then we will succeed because obj will unify with triangles.

A fanciful example involves the term closed-figure with two argument, a perimeter and an area. We can state the following equality assertion:

```
(equals (closed-figure _perimeter _area)
        (circle _ _ _radius))                :-
   (times 6.2831853 _radius _perimeter)
   (times _radius _radius _squared-radius)
   (times 3.14159265 _radius-squared _area)
```

284

expressing the fact that if the perimeter of a closed figure is $2\pi r$ and the area is πr^2 for some r, then it is a circle. A closed-figure described in this way, if instantiated to be a circle, can be used in any proof that was defined using the circle functor.

The code above is most unlikely to appear as part of a practical program. When things are left so undetermined, simple programs can take very long because there may be very esoteric ways of doing proofs. It is important, however, to see that such generality is available. Moreover, the uses of equality theorems that model the class-structuring idea are very efficiently implemented. We discuss these issues briefly in section 7.

4   Partially Specified Objects

One of the desirable features of Prolog is its ability to deal with partially instantiated data objects. One way to look at this is that the partially instantiated data object stands for a non-singleton subset of the Herbrand Universe corresponding to our Prolog program. If we were not able to pass such objects freely in our programs the control structure of Prolog (or any logic programming language remotely like it) would require us to successively generate bindings of the variable to ground objects for consideration by the remainder of the proof. This is the power that unification gets us and also the principle difference between Prolog and the language Micro-Planner [8] which preceded it but was otherwise similar. We find that our inclusion of equality proofs in Prolog extends the range of possibility for passing partially instantiated data. In some cases this can significantly improve the efficiency of programs by replacing an otherwise expensive enumeration of ground terms with backtracking. In other cases it makes possible a program that would not be possible otherwise because there is no convenient way to enumerate the space.

We define a binary functor called omega which will represent an arbitrary, partially specified object. The first argument to an omega term is a variable that is uninstantiated when the term is introduced. The second argument is a relation that must hold for all terms in the subset of the Herbrand Universe that this omega term represents; it is expressed in terms of the uninstantiated variable. For example, if we execute the goal (> _x 3) where the variable x is at this point uninstantiated, we will succeed with the binding for x: (omega _num (> _num 3)). This represents (and will unify with) all numbers that are greater than three. When this is unified with a number (e.g., 5) the variable num is unified with 5 and the unification succeeds of the relation succeeds (which it does because five is greater than three).

The equals relation for omega terms is defined as follows:

```
(equals (omega _obj _relation) _thing) :-
   (instantiate _thing _value)
   (= _obj _value)
   _relation

(equals (omega _obj1 _relation1) (omega _obj2 _relation2)) :-
     (and  (not-instantiated _obj1)
           (not-instantiated _obj2)
           (conjoin-relations _obj1 _relation1
                              _obj2 _relation2
                              _obj _relation)
           (= _obj1 _obj2)
           (= _obj2 (omega _obj _relation))))
```

The predicate instantiate succeeds if its argument is instantiated, i.e. that it is neither a variable nor an uninstantiated omega term; when it succeeds, the second argument is bound to the instantiated value. The first assertion declares that an omega term is equal to something if the item the omega functor represents (obj) is equal to the thing's instantiated value and the constraining relation is true. The second assertion applies if two omega terms are unified and neither has yet been instantiated. Both omega terms are made equal to one another and to another omega term whose relation is the conjunct of the two previous relations. This new term represents the intersection of the space of possible ground terms of the two omega terms that were unified.

The code for > is as follows: [3]

```
(> _m _n)  :-
   (cases ((and (instantiate _m _m1)
                (instantiate _n _n1))
           (lisp-> _m1 _n1))
          ((instantiate _m _m1)
           (= _n (omega _num (> _m1 _num))))
          ((instantiate _n _n1)
           (= _m (omega _num1 (> _num1 _n1))))
          ((= _n (omega _num (> _m _num)))
           (= _m (omega _num1 (> _num1 _n))))))
```

If we had the Prolog goal:

```
(and (> _x 3) (member _x [2 4 6 _y]))
```

we would succeed 3 times with the bindings 4, 6, and

```
(omega _num1 (> _num1 3))
```

the last of which is also bound to y.
   The goal

```
(and (> _x _y) (= _x 3) (= _y 2))
```

succeeds, while the goal

```
(and (> _x _y) (= _x 3) (= _y 4))
```

does not.
   The basic arithmetic functions are defined in a similar way, and have the property of not failing if any or all of their arguments are not instantiated.

---

[3]The preponderance of the impure **instantiate** relation is necessary only when data is to be passed to evaluable predicates (such as **lisp->**). Our > relation is a true Prolog predicate in that it is not required that its arguments be instantiated when called. Our goal is to be able to bury such impure evaluable predicates inside logically sound relations.

The definition of the times predicate is:

```
(times _arg1 _arg2 _result) :-
  (cases
    ((instantiate _arg1 _ans1)
     (cases ((instantiate _arg2 _ans2)
             (lisp-value _result (* _ans1 _ans2)))
            ((instantiate _result _ans)
             (lisp-value _arg2 (// _ans _ans1)))
            ((= _result
                (omega _ans (times _ans1 _arg2 _ans)))
             (= _arg2
                (omega _ans2 (times _ans1 _ans2 _result))))))
    ((instantiate _arg2 _ans2)
     (cases ((instantiate _result _ans)
             (lisp-value _arg1 (// _ans _ans2)))
            ((= _result
                (omega _ans (times _arg1 _ans2 _ans)))
             (= _arg1
                (omega _ans1 (times _ans1 _ans2 _result))))))
    ((instantiate _result _ans)
     (= _arg1 (omega _ans1 (times _ans1 _arg2 _ans)))
     (= _arg2 (omega _ans2 (times _arg1 _ans2 _ans))))
    ((= _arg1 (omega _ans1 (times _ans1 _arg2 _result)))
     (= _arg2 (omega _ans2 (times _arg1 _ans2 _result)))
     (= _result (omega _ans (times _arg1 _arg2 _ans))))))
```

The definition of times determines which arguments are instantiated and takes an appropriate action. If two or three are instantiated it executes an evaluable predicate corresponding to a Lisp function call. Otherwise it creates omega terms that express the arithmetic constraints on the value of the variable. Other arithmetic functions are defined analogously. Prolog programs written using these relations have the property that the relations can be in any order and the program will find the answer without any backtracking. For example, the goal

```
(and (times _x _y _z)
     (plus _a 3 _x)
     (plus 1 _a 2)
     (= _z 12))
```

will succeed with correct bindings for all the variables. This is accomplished with sequential evaluation of the predicates and no backtracking.

288

Arithmetic expressed in this way can solve systems of equations that are not simultaneous. [4] It is a very efficient way of doing arithmetic, and will work for floating point as well as integer computations. [5]

Arithmetic expressions are an example where it is impossible in a practical sense to generate each of the possible bindings as ground terms. However there are other situations where we may wish to use omega terms as an alternative to enumerating the bindings.

Consider the following goal:

```
(and (member _x _very-long-list)
     (pred _x))
```

where on entry very-long-list is instantiated to a very long list and x is uninstantiated. Suppose that pred is true of only a few of those elements. In this case, using the standard Prolog definition of member, the relation would become a generator of succesive elements from the list. An alternative way of writing member would be that, if x is not instantiated upon entry into the member relation, the relation would instantiate x to:

```
(omega _element (member _element _very-long-list))
```

This would effectively save the constraint that x be a member of the list until there was some item under consideration. Then, and only then, would the constraint be checked.

It is far from clear how one would characterize the conditions under which omega terms will be preferable to using a predicate as a generator. Yet this does seem an important tool. It is distinct from, yet compatible with, extralogical control annotation as in IC-Prolog [3].

5   Functional Notation

Many people are uncomfortable with the flat relational style of Prolog as opposed to the functional notation and Lisp and most other languages. Lisp syntax allows the composition of functions without the need to introduce temporary variables to glue successive relations together as in

---

[4]This is equivalent in power to constraint propagation in constraint network formalisms [1].

[5]IC-Prolog [3] provides arithmetic on integers by building the integers using successor. This is very general, but not efficient for practical problems.

the above example for computing the area of a polygon. We can straight-forwardly augment Prolog with functional notation by using equality theorems:

```
(equals (%times _x _y) _z) :=
   (times _x _y _z)

(equals (%plus _x _y) _z) :-
   (plus _x _y _z)

(equals (%difference _x _y) _z) :-
   (difference _x _y _z)

(equals (%quotient _x _y) _z) :-
   (quotient _x _y _z)
```

Notice that we distinguish the function %plus from the relation plus. It makes no sense in (logic or) Prolog to unify a relation and a function. Using these new functors we can define a temperature converter relation that expresses the relationship between the Fahrenheit and centigrade scales. The relation is a "one-liner":

```
(temp-converter _f (%times (%difference _f 32) (rat 5 9)))
```

This is like the "executable pattern" of [6].

6   Equality Assertion Invocation

Prolog constructs can be understood in either a declarative or procedural sense. Thus far we have not considered the precise procedural semantics of Prolog-with-Equality. Certain care must be exercised in defining the procedural semantics to avoid infinite loops or otherwise unacceptably wasteful searches. Our solution yields a system which is far from complete in the logical sense, yet is sufficient for the classes of examples in this paper. It has a further desirable property that allows the compiler to precompute certain information that will allow most failing unifications to fail in *constant time*. Such a property is critical if this mechanism is to find its way into practical programs.

The first restriction we put on unification via equality assertions is that the assertions can be used only *one way.* Suppose we attempt to match (foo 1) with (bar 2). This will cause the unifier to generate a goal of the form:

(equals (foo 1) (bar 1))

Now suppose we had an equality theorem whose head was:

(equals (bar _n) _s)

An attempt to unify the goal with this assertion head would cause a recursive goal of (equals (foo 1) (bar 1)). This will lead to an infinite computation. To avoid this problem we require that in matching the *first* term of the equals goal with its counterpart in the head of the assertion the functors must be the same. The unification of the second argument may recursively create new equality assertions. This allows for chains of equality matches (but not cycles).

Unification in Prolog-with-Equality, as in standard Prolog, is deterministic—it can succeed only once. For normal Prolog there is no problem because there can be only one most general unifier. However, in consideration of models other than the standard Herbrand model it is possible for there to be no unique most general unifier. To properly handle such cases would require introducing a backtracking point in the unification itself. For the class of applications I have looked at so far there does not seem to be any compelling reason for doing so, yet this is a possible route to be taken in the future. One way this could be understood within the class hierarchy paradigm is that there may be more than one most general unifier because there is more than one way to view the first as an instance of the second.

7 Efficiency Considerations

It is critically important from the efficiency point of view that one of the functors must be explicitly present as the first functor of an equals assertion. Thus equals assertions can be grouped in much the same way that assertions with the same first predicate are grouped in the implementation. If one tries to match two terms, neither of which has equals assertions for it, the match can fail quickly. In the event that one or both have assertions associated with them a series of equals derivations may ensue that is potentially costly. A compiler can do much to eliminate this whenever the terms are not relatable by figuring the chains of functors statically from the code. If neither functor can be reached by a chain of equals assertions from the other the two can definitely not be unified. By using hash tables to store this information most failures can be discovered in constant time. In particular, the use of equality to model object-oriented languages requires no backtracking and a small, constant overhead to determine failure.

8 Conclusions

My experience with Prolog-with-Equality to date has been very encouraging. The modifications necessary to the interpreter to make equality theorems possible was done in one evening of programming. The basic paradigms explored (extended datatyping, partially instantiated omega terms) appear quite natural and general. Moreover, the added features do not impinge on the efficiency of basic Prolog. I am hopeful that new paradigms for using equality will emerge as more experience is gained.

9 Bibliography

1. Borning. A., *Thinglab—A Constraint-Oriented Simulation Laboratory*, Xerox PARC report SSL-79-3, July 1979.
2. Chang. C., R. Lee, *Symbolic Logic and Mechanical Theorem Proving*, Academic Press, 1973.
3. Clark. K., *IC-Prolog Language Features*, in Clark & Tärnlund, *Logic Programming*, Academic Press, 1982.
4. Ingalls *The Smalltalk-76 Programming System: Design and Implementation*, Fifth Annual ACM Symposium on Principles of Programming Languages, Tucson, Arizona, January 1978.
5. Kahn. K., *Unique Features of LM-Prolog*, unpublished manuscript.
6. Nakashima, H. *Prolog K/R language feature*, First International Logic Programming Conference, Marseille, September 1982.
7. Siekmann, J., P. Szabó, *Universal Unification and a Classification of Equational Theories*, 6th Conference on Automated Deduction, New York, June 1982.
8. Sussman. G., T. Winograd, E. Charniak, *Micro-Planner Reference Manual*, MIT Artificial Intelligence Laboratory memo 203, 1970.
9. Sussman. G., G. Steele, *Constraints* MIT Artificial Intelligence Laboratory memo 502, November 1978.
10. Warren. D., *Implementing Prolog—Compiling Predicate Logic Programs*, University of Edinburgh Department of Artificial Intelligence Report No. 39.

EQLOG:

EQUALITY, TYPES, AND GENERIC MODULES

FOR LOGIC PROGRAMMING

Joseph A. Goguen and José Meseguer

SRI International, Menlo Park CA 94025

and

Center for the Study of Language and Information

Stanford University, Stanford CA 94305

ABSTRACT

This paper presents Eqlog, a logic programming language that unifies (predicate-based) Horn clause relational programming with (equality-based) functional programming. The unification seems quite natural, since it is based on the smallest logic having both Horn clauses and equality, namely Horn clause logic with equality. Rather than force functions to be viewed as predicates, or predicates to be viewed as functions, Eqlog allows using both functions and predicates as convenient. Furthermore, Eqlog computes differently with functions than with predicates: functions are computed by term rewriting, while queries to predicates are computed in the usual Prolog-like fashion with unification and backtracking (but with unification modulo equations, implemented by narrowing in general, and by more efficient methods for built-in types). In fact, narrowing does much more than this, since it allows solving for the values of logical variables that occur in equations. This gives Eqlog very powerful capabilities as a "constraint language", using narrowing and Prolog-style backtracking to solve constraints over user-defined abstract data types, and using efficient built-in algorithms for solving constraints over built-in types (such as numbers). With the usual Church-Rosser assumptions, Eqlog's operational semantics is logically complete. In effect, this paper shows how to extend the paradigm of logic programming with a number of features that are prominent in current programming methodology, without any sacrifice of logical rigor. Beyond simple functional programming, Eqlog also

This is a substantially revised version of the paper, "EQLOG: Equality, Types and Generic Modules for Logic Programming," by J. Goguen and J. Meseguer appearing in the *Journal of Logic Programming,* 1984, Vol. 1, No. 2, pp. 179–209, © Elsevier Science Publishing Co., Inc., 1984.

provides strong typing, user definable abstract data types, and generic (i.e., "parameterized") modules, using methods developed for the specification language Clear. A very useful refinement is "subsorts," which provide polymorphic operators and an inheritance relation on types of data. We show that our logic admits "initial models" having properties that generalize those of minimal Herbrand models for ordinary Horn clause logic. All of these features are given a rigorous semantics in terms of the underlying logic, and illustrated with a number of examples, including the well-known Missionaries and Cannibals problem and some natural language processing problems.

1 Introduction

The original vision of Logic Programming called for using pure predicate logic as a programming language [58, 88]. Prolog only partially realizes this vision, since it has many features with no corresponding feature in logic, and it also lacks important features of logic (such as semantic equality). A main feature of the system described in this paper, hereafter called Eqlog, is the way it unifies relational programming (i.e., the technology of Prolog, including unification and backtracing) with functional programming (in this case, the technology of OBJ, an efficient first order rewrite rule implementation) to yield more than just their sum: in addition to querying predicates and computing functions, Eqlog can also solve for the values of logical variables in equations, over user-defined abstract data types (hereafter, ADTs); this is logically described by unifying the logics that underlie relational and functional programming, namely first order Horn clause logic and many-sorted equational logic, to get many-sorted first order Horn clause logic with equality; an operational semantics is provided by so-called narrowing. This gives Eqlog much of the power of so-called "constraint languages", since in particular, narrowing and Prolog-style backtracking can solve constraints over user-defined ADTs, while built-in efficient algorithms can solve constraints over built-in types. In addition, generic (i.e., parameterized) modules are available with a rigorous logical foundation, and Eqlog also has a subsort facility that greatly increases its expressive power.

We believe that the many advantages claimed for logic programming, including

296

- simplicity,
- clarity,
- understandability,
- reusability and
- maintainability,

are all compromised to the degree that the logic underlying the programming language is not a pure logic. Consequently, the goal of our research has been to *extend* the facilities available in pure logic programming so as to better support the requirements of truly practical programming. The extension proposed in this paper, as embodied in Eqlog, do not solve all the problems. We believe that we have significantly advanced the state of the art by eliminating the need for *ad hoc* facilities to forcing evaluation of built-in functions (such as Prolog's is), as well as by providing generic modules, logical variables in equations *via* narrowing, and a capability for handling partial functions and errors *via* subsorts. But much further research remains to be done, particularly in areas such as control and database facilities.

1.1 What is Logic Programming?

There is considerable current controversy about the semantics of programming languages. This very informal subsection is intended to provide a sort of rhetorical background for our design of Eqlog; it consists of polemic and jargon, but should at least enable the reader to know where we stand; of course, you can always skip it.

We take the broad view that a *logic programming language* is one whose programs consist of sentences in a well-understood[1] logical system, and whose operational semantics is *deduction* in that system; this is entirely consistent with the original vision of logic programming [58, 88]. In particular, logic programming in this sense includes:

---

[1]In particular, there should be reasonably simple notions of deduction and model, and a completeness theorem.

- **relational** (i.e., predicate, i.e., Horn clause) **programming**[2], where the associated logic is first order Horn clause logic, and
- **functional** (i.e., equational) **programming**, where the logic is equational logic, i.e., the logic of substitution of equals for equals.

There is another requirement that we argue should also be imposed on logic programming languages: every program should have an initial model. For those not familiar with this terminology, an initial model is (at least for the usual logics) characterized (uniquely up to isomorphism) by the property that only what is provable is true, and everything else is false (in effect this is Occam's famous razor); also, there is a standard initial model construction that is closely related to the minimal Herbrand universe given as a model for pure Horn clause programming by [88]; see Theorem 1 and the discussion in Section 2 for further information about how this applies to Eqlog. The initial model provides a foundation for database manipulations, since you know exactly what is true; in fact, the "closed world" that the program is talking about is exactly the initial model. It has been proven (see [86, 60, 61, 63]) that the largest sublanguage of first order logic such that all sets of sentences have initial models, is Horn clause logic. This result extends to many-sorted logic and/or logic with equality, and gives us a pretty good idea of just how far we can go with logic programming and still provide the programmer with a good intuition for what his program is about (namely, exactly what is in the initial model).

Note that equational logic need not be first order; for example, Backus' "Algebra of Programs" for FP [2] consists of higher order equations among a number of basic functions, many of which are higher order. The phrase **applicative programming** is often used to refer to programs in which the dominant mode of construction is to apply a function (or functional, i.e., higher order function) to some arguments. FP, pure Lisp and the lambda calculus are therefore all applicative; and in fact, all functional programming languages are applicative. We reject the views that "logic programming"

---

[2]Of course many people restrict their use of "logic programming" to this case, or even to just Prolog, but we feel that this is no longer appropriate, in view of the many alternative forms of logic programming (in our broader sense) that are now available.

refers only to Prolog, or only to relational programming, as well as the view that it includes any language whose syntax contains significant bits of logic, such as conjunction, implication or quantifiers.

Not only does logic programming in our broad sense include both relational and functional programming, but we will attempt to convince the reader that a very natural way to unify relational and functional programming is just to unify their logics, i.e., to take the smallest sublogic of first order logic that contains both Horn clause logic and equational logic; this is, of course, Horn clause logic with equality. Both relational and functional programming, as well as our proposed unification, have a rigorous model-theoretic semantics, so that there is no need for a denotational semantics. In fact, we would claim that denotational semantics is only really *needed* for languages like (impure) Lisp, (impure) Prolog, Ada, PL/I, Pascal, etc., that are not logic programming languages in our sense.

Closely related to logic programming are **declarative languages**, whose statements (loosely speaking) describe desired conditions without explicitly indicating how to achieve them. All logic programming languages are declarative, but not conversely. In fact, declarative languages need not be executable; they could be used for specifications, designs, or requirements, and statements in a declarative language could even be sentences in English. The idea of declarative programming is also very close to that of abstract data types (hereafter, ADTs), in that both advocate abstracting away lower level "how to do it" considerations. In fact, functional programming languages that are based on first order equational logic can easily provide user-definable ADTs [25], and Eqlog acquires this capability through its equational sublanguage.

Eqlog permits solving a wide variety of constraints, and in particular, it permits solving for the values of logical variables in equations. There are two main mechanisms for this: built-in procedures for built-in data types, particularly the various kinds of numbers; and a general purpose "narrowing" procedure for user-defined ADTs, which are provided by Eqlog's generic modules. This makes Eqlog a very powerful user-extendable **constraint language**, that is, users can define their own data abstractions, which might be missionaries, cannibals, boats, graphical entities like charts, spread sheets, or VLSI circuits, and then solve them for values satisfying the constraints that they have specified on those abstractions. This makes Eqlog a suitable language for solving various problems and puzzles, since (in many cases) the problem statement is actually executable, and gives the solution; Section 8 illustrates this with the well-known "Missionaries and Cannibals" problem, and some problems for natural language processing. We believe that this capability is the ideal to which logic programming languages should aspire; of course, no real language will be able to entirely achieve this ideal behavior.

1.1.1 Imperative Programming Considered Harmful

Imperative programming refers to programs that compute by modifying states, often in the form of global variables, generally using some form of assignment. We claim that imperative programming is *harmful, inefficient, and unnecessary.* Of course, these claims are exagerated in terms of current technology, but they do clearly express certain goals of logic programming, as explained further in the following three paragraphs:

1. The complexities of Hoare axioms and of denotational semantics clearly demonstate that imperative programming is much more complicated than it seems at first; for example, students have a hard time understanding and accepting even the relatively simple Hoare axiom for the assignment statement (with its backward substitution), let alone such monsters as Hoare axioms for procedure calls; [69] gives several examples of published axioms that are actually incorrect. Denotational definitions of standard programming languages commonly run to thousands of lines of hard to digest higher order semantic equations, and are almost certainly wrong in detail, since they have never been mechanically tested. This complexity helps explain why imperative programs are so very hard to debug, and indicates what we mean by "harmful."

2. Imperative programming embodies the so-called "von Neumann bottleneck" [2] in the way it handles assignment, memory, and control; in fact, all are essentially sequential. This implies that imperative programming cannot be made really efficient on massively parallel machines without careful hand coding, for example, explicitly declaring

300

all processes and writing explicit synchronization for them[3]; but this is not practical when one wants to use thousands of processors! Two commonly proposed "answers" to this problem include parallel assignment and so-called SIMD (Single Instruction Multiple Data) programming; but these have been found very wasteful of processor power, except on very special problems (although some of these problems are important). Another proposed solution is compiling from imperative languages to parallel machines; but the problems involved here are far too difficult for a compiler to solve except by magic. This explains what we mean by saying imperative programming is "inefficient".

3. Of course, logic programming does not yet provide a sufficiently powerful alternative to imperative programming; projects like Eqlog will require many more man-years before they succeed in this sense. In particular, it will take further research to handle operations like database updates and input/output within pure logic programming; however, we think we know how to provide modules with local states in an essentially functional way, following ideas in [36], and we believe that this can be used to solve these problems. Another problem that will have to be solved is how to control control; it appears likely, however, that some form of annotation can be given a precise semantics and still be sufficiently powerful for practice.

1.1.2 Impure Logic Programming Considered Harmful

As mentioned before, we believe that the advantages of logic programming, including its

- simplicity,
- clarity,
- understandability,
- reusability and
- maintainability,

are all compromised to the degree that the logic underlying the programming

---

[3]E.g., as with Concurrent Prolog's "read only" variables [81], which, by the way, have a very complex semantics when examined in detail

language is not a pure logic. In general, the compromises tend in the direction of imperative programming, and give rise to the problems described in the previous subsection. Our approach has been to attempt to provide as much practical programming power as possible, without in any way compromising the underlying logic. Thus, we have attempted to extend the logic in such a way as to encompass a greater range of programming language features, while preserving reasonable efficiency. To be more precise, our general research strategy is to adhere to pure logic programming, in the general sense of our definition in Section 1.1, but be willing to extend the logic involved; in particular, we insist on our underlying logic having initial models, since this seems necessary for supporting database applications (where queries should have unique answers[4]) and also for efficient parallel processing[5]. Eqlog is based on many-sorted[6] first order Horn clause logic with equality. We note again that the most general sublogic of first order logic with equality having initial models is Horn clause logic with equality [86, 61]. Eqlog also uses subsorts, but we show how to reduce this enriched logic to standard many-sorted Horn clause logic with equality.

1.1.3 Higher Order *vs.* First Order Logic

We have deliberately limited Eqlog to first order logic, because we believe that first order logic is better than higher order logic in some important ways. In particular, we believe that **first order programming** is

- easier to understand,
- easier to interpret and compile,
- easier to parallelize,
- has a simpler logic, with a well-known completeness theorem,

---

[4]Of course, a *set* of answers is acceptable as a unique entity, but we hold that a *disjunctive* answer (such as "either Tom or Harry") should not be acceptable since one cannot determine a unique individual.

[5]If either disjunction or (classical) negation are allowed in clauses, the algorithms for answering queries are much less efficient. Thus, there seems to be a strong connection between the existence of efficient implementations and the existence of initial models.

[6]From here on, we usually use the word "sort" instead of "type" to avoid confusion among the many uses of the word "type"; two exceptions are the phrases "abstract data type" and "strong typing".

and, although it is less expressive, we claim that we can get the power of higher order (or at least second order) logic by using generic modules, as discussed in Section 6. However, we do not get all the convenience of higher order logic in this way, and there remains some doubt about whether this loss is worth what Eqlog gains in its better control of scoping. We note that it seems clear that there should be some special cases of higher order logic that are more tractable than the full general case, and there have recently been some encouraging theoretical results in this direction. An interesting related topic is reflexive languages.

1.2 Combining Relational and Functional Programming

There has been a good deal of work on combining relational and functional programming. For example, Kornfeld [57] gives several interesting examples (some of which inspired examples in this paper), but gives no theoretical justification for his implementation of equality; in fact, it is not complete (i.e., it can sometimes fail to find the right answer when one does exist). Moreover, the ADT and object-oriented facilities are less general than might be desired, since neither modularity nor strong typing are provided, and functions are not carefully distinguished from predicates. In addition to combining logic and functional programming, the Funlog language [85] also provides infinite data structures, lazy evaluation, and non-determinism; however, no formal logic is given for these features, either model-theoretic or proof-theoretic, and Funlog's "semantic unification" algorithm is also incomplete. A natural deduction technology is used by Hansson, Haridi and Tarnlund [48] to implement a superset of Horn clause logic with equality that includes negation and explicit universal quantifiers; the system also handles infinite data structures by lazy evaluation; however, we are not aware of a formal semantic theory for the language. FPL [3] is a logic programming notation for what is essentially a functional programming language; a rigorous semantics is given, but it does not support logical variables, or solve systems of equations containing them; also, the model theory is completely different from that of first order logic. LOGLISP [78] combines Horn clause programming with Lisp, but Robinson concludes in later work that it is not desirable to have two different logical systems, and also that it would be better to have some form of pure logic programming.

The present paper approaches the problem of unifying relational and functional programming by first unifying their logics by taking many-sorted[7] first order Horn clause logic with equality as its basis, and then shows that many useful "impure" features of Prolog can be made "pure" within this context. In fact, both pure Prolog and OBJ2 are "sublanguages" of Eqlog; that is, both Horn clause programming and first order functional programming are provided, and one also gets logical variables in equations, generic modules, ADTs, subsorts, and other goodies. The paragraphs below informally discuss these and other aspects of Eqlog.

1.2.1 Functional Programming by Term Rewriting

There are many cases where computational intuition is essentially functional rather than relational, and for such cases it is convenient to use functional programming. The well-known append function is a good example. In Prolog, it is usual to treat it as a 3-place predicate, append(X,Y,Z), defined by clauses that express the obvious recursion. In Eqlog, we can declare append to be a binary, associative, infix constructor for lists in just one line,

```
_ _ : List List -> List (assoc id: nil)
```

which all at the same time actually defines Lists, gives append the optimal "empty" syntax, and introduces nil as a formal identity. In general, Eqlog evaluates ground terms by term rewriting (i.e., reduction), but the built-in data structure for associative operators gives a very efficient implementation in which append is computed by moving a single pointer; these implementation details follow those of OBJ2 [25]. Of course, solution of predicates by the usual Prolog method is also available in Eqlog, but it seems to us highly undesirable, if not actually absurd, for append to be a predicate requiring linear computation time, when such a simple alternative is available. For more details on term rewriting, see [52, 67, 68].

---

[7]There is nothing essential about the use of many sorts, and those who do not like strong typing can use unsorted Horn clause logic with equality and still get most of what this paper offers.

1.2.2 Subsorts

In addition to its use of many-sorted logic, Eqlog also has a powerful subsort facility, which is a simplified, generalized, and extended version of the "Order Sorted Algebra" (hereafter, OSA) of [31]; see [38] for details of the theory, and [41] for details of its operational semantics. This approach supports:

1. Polymorphism and overloading;
2. Error recovery as well as error definition and detection;
3. Multiple inheritance in the sense of object-oriented programming;
4. Selectors even when there are multiple constructors; and
5. Sort constraints, which permit users to define what would otherwise be partial functions as total functions on equationally defined subsorts.

We have found subsorts to be enormously helpful in practical examples in the OBJ language [25]. This paper later indicates both a model-theoretic semantics and a first order equational axiomatization of Eqlog's subsort concept.

A major motivation has been to correctly handle erroneous and meaningless expressions, such as the top of an empty stack or division by zero. This has been seen as important from the earliest days of the "initial algebra" approach to abstract data types, and for example, was treated rather awkwardly in [43]. Two subsequent attempts at a better approach, [30] and [31], were both more complicated than necessary. We now believe that OSA provides a fully satisfactory and very flexible solution to this problem.

It is rather widely believed that partiality and subsorts are appropriate tools for treating erroneous and meaningless expressions. The following is a brief survey of various approaches styles of using partiality and subsorts:

1. **Partial Operators** -- here operators are defined on only part of what might normally be considered their domain; for example, tail is only defined for non-empty lists. There have been many different approaches to partial operators:

    a. **Partial Algebras** -- here one attempts to extend the theory of abstract data types to algebras that have partially defined operators; this has been advocated by [75], [6], [55] and others (also see [62] for a survey of various approaches from logic). In our view, the mathematical theory involved with this approach is more complex than necessary; for example, the right definitions of homomorphism and of satisfaction for equations may not be clear. Perhaps more importantly, this approach is incompatible with error messages and error recovery. For example, one cannot return the information that a certain index in an array has no value stored there; if the get operator is modelled as a partial function, then the computation simply dies, without giving any indication of why it died; this would prevent modelling many important aspects of applications like database query handling.

   b. **Domain Subsorts** -- here one restricts operators to a domain on which they are intrinsically meaningful by defining an explicit subsort for this domain; for example, one might declare NeList < List to be the sort of non-empty lists and then declare tail : NeList -> List. This style is supported by OSA and is used in OBJ2 [25] and [27] as well as Eqlog; the approach of Reichel [75] can also be seen in this light.

   c. **Sort Constraints** -- a generalization of the "declarations" of [31], these greatly increase the power of the OSA approach by allowing definition of new subsorts from predicates; these new suborts can even be subsorts of a product of sorts. This new concept gives us essentially all the power of the approaches of Reichel [75] and Gabriel and Ulmer [26].

2. **Error Values** -- these are special values for operators to return in evaluating erroneous or meaningless situations. Among the approaches using this style are the following:

   a. **Explicit error values** of the same sort as normal or "OK" values -- this approach was suggested by [43, 47, 46] and others, but it has many difficulties, particularly the tediousness of writing out such specifications rigorously, as shown by the formalization in [43]. The requirement that operators "preserve errors" is also limiting.

   b. **Special error sorts** for error values that are disjoint from "OK sorts" for ok values -- this approach is formalized in the theory of error algebras of [30], has been implemented in OBJT [40] andOBJ1 [42], and is studied deeply in [72]. It takes an "innocent until proven guilty" philosophy toward errors, but unfortunately it fails to have initial algebras for all presentations.

c. **Explicit error supersorts** -- this approach involves creating new supersorts for standard sorts; for example, one might have List < ErrList with tail : List -> ErrList and tail(nil) = tailess where tailess is an error message of sort ErrList not of sort List. This style is supported by OSA, and is also used in the tradition of [20] and [28]; [20] provides an operational semantics using rewrite rules that embodies this idea, but without giving a corresponding mathematical semantics.

3. **Recovery Operators** -- these are operators from a sort that may contain errors to one that doesn't. Note that it is impossible to recover from an error that is modelled by an operator being undefined; recovery is also precluded by the discipline of "error preserving" operators used by [43] and [30].

a. **Retracts** -- these are right inverses to "coercions", which are inclusions of a subsort into a supersort; retracts permit contingent parsing of expressions which would otherwise be ill-formed; for example s(4 / 2) with s the successor function on the naturals, will recover.

b. **Error Handlers** -- more general recovery operators than retracts are possible in OSA, for example, reinitializing a stack that has overflown.

The choice among these options is largely a matter of style and taste; moreover, certain of these choices are very closely related to one another. For example, Eqlog supports styles 1b., 1c., 2a., 2c., and 3. in a simple and elegant manner, since a coercion and a retract are automatically provided for every subsort pair; in particular, both error supersorts and domain subsorts have associated retracts; styles 1c. and even 2a. are also supported.

There is an interesting distinction between handling errors in the syntax and handling them in the semantics. Approaches 1b. and 1c. treat errors *syntactically*, in the sense that an expression like tail(nil) is just considered not well-formed. But note that sometimes this cannot be determined at parse-time and must be left for runtime; for example, (-4 / -2)! turns out after evaluation to be 2 ! and thus is OK, while (2 / 4)! turns out to be a rational rather than a natural, and is thus erroneous. Our operational semantics handles this by inserting retracts (see 3a.) at run-time; if the expression is erroneous, these retracts remain after evaluation, and provide a very informative error message. In constrast, the approaches under 2. treat errors *semantically*, by imposing special equations or even using a special kind of algebra.

Two recent papers that relate to the operational semantics of order-sorted algebra are [14] and [90]. The first shows that there need not be a most general unifier when the sorts form a lattice; the second shows that there are most general unifiers when the sorts form a tree and there is not overloading of operations. Both papers discuss algorithms for unification and [90] argues for the utility of subsorts in connection with resolution and paramodulation. The work of [89] and [45] should also be mentioned in connection with order-sorted algebra. [89] describes a system called "classified algebra" that seems to be a version of order-sorted algebra with a "universal" (maximum) sort; the theory of "multi-target" operations in [45] combines aspects of the partial algebra and the explicit error sort approaches.

1.2.3 Relational Programming and Solving for Logical Variables

Eqlog uses the standard Prolog evaluation mechanism (e.g., [13] and [10]) to solve for values of logical variables in relations. This can be seen as a special kind of resolution based on unification [77], with backtracking on failure to ensure completeness; however, we may have to take account of the equations in performing this unification, i.e., to do "universal unification." For this, our Eqlog evaluation algorithm draws on results from the theory of rewrite rules about "narrowing" [53, 23] to get a complete implementation of equality; this approach can be seen as arising from the work on combining equations and resolution [74], [79], [83]. In fact, narrowing is just the alternation of unification and rewriting. It should be noted that our evaluation mechanism correctly handles conditional equations, in both term rewriting and narrowing, and in particular, can solve for the values of logical variables in programs consisting of Horn clauses that have equations anywhere within them.

Related work has also been done by Sato [80] on Qute (which really is cute, although it is higher order) and by Fribourg [24] on SLOG, which suggests some very interesting strategies for speeding up narrowing. There is also some relevant work by Dershowitz, e.g. [17].

1.2.4 Modular Programming

We believe that **modular programming** is essential for writing large programs, since it permits grouping together statements that create, modify, access, and interrogate common data structures. Then we can

- compile modules separately,
- verify them once and for all, and
- reuse them freely.

Going a little further, we get generic (parameterized) modules, with interface declarations that contain semantic information, as discussed in Section 6. Strong typing is also very helpful for large programs, especially in conjunction with subtypes (see Section 7.1).

Combining many-sorted logic with modules provides a very convenient treatment of data abstraction, inspired by our experience with the rewrite rule based language OBJ [25, 42, 40].

Since our approach to generic modules relies on very general results from the logical foundations of specification languages [34], it should apply at least to other variants of pure logic programming as well as to ordinary unsorted Prolog, although it is not clear to what extend it would apply to more impure dialects such as Concurrent Prolog [82].

1.2.5 Completeness and Control

Completeness is a very important property for the evaluation algorithm underlying a logic programming language; without it, a user cannot be sure that what he writes will eventually produce the result that the logic says it should! However, there seems to be a trade-off between generality and efficiency: highly expressive complete languages are not necessarily efficient; thus, the challenge of designing a good logic programming language is to reach a suitable compromise between efficiency and generality (with completeness).

Tablog [64] is an example of a language that tries to sacrifice completeness for efficiency, but still fails to attain an efficient language.

We suggest that a good logic programming style is to identify inefficient subcases and try to avoid them, except perhaps during initial exploratory development of a program. In Eqlog, assuming custom hardware which we are now in the process of developing, this means doing as much as possible functionally, and using relations primarily for control rather than computation.

There is actually a good deal to say about the issue of control in logic programming. Let us first quote the logic programming slogan "Program = Logic + Control" which argues for a clean separation between the logic of a program (describing what it computes) and the control of how it does its computation. Prolog, of course, provides the impure primitive "cut"; it can be used in a relatively harmless way to cut down on search spaces; but it can also be used in drastically nonlogical ways, such as in defining negation-by-failure. There have been a number of proposals for annotating logic programs with control information in order to improve their efficiency; we have not committed Eqlog to any particular one of these, pending the outcome of debates currently going on; but one should be able add to Eqlog nearly any desired method for controlling control.

2 The Underlying Logic

First order Horn clause logic without equality underlies ordinary Prolog. But there are many other logics, some of which have distinct advantages. Thus, first order logic with equality supports user definable ADTs; and many-sorted logic gives strong typing. Pure equational logic can also give rise to programming languages. One such language is OBJ [25, 42, 40], which supports user definable ADTs by regarding the defining equations as rewrite rules; Hoffman and O'Donnell [50] describe another such language. Other languages that are systematically based upon some kind of logic are pure Lisp, CDS [5] which is based on the lambda calculus, and the language of the "Prolog technology" theorem prover of Stickel [84], which is the full first order predicate calculus.

We now briefly review many-sorted Horn clause logic with equality. Here, one has a set S of **sorts**, plus **signatures** Π and Σ which give the predicate and function symbols, respectively. Each predicate symbol Q has an **arity** which is a string of sorts that serves to indicate the number and sort of arguments that it can take; thus, arity $s_1 s_2 s_1$ indicates that Q takes three arguments, of which the first and third must be of sort s_1, and the second of sort s_2. Similarly, each function symbol has a **rank** consisting of a string w of sorts (its **arity**) and a sort s (its **value** sort). Equality enters as a distinguished binary predicate symbol $=_s$ for each sort s, which we will write with infix notation, and usually without the subscript. Sentences are Horn clauses in the usual sense, but may involve the distinguished equality predicate; that is, they are of the form

    P :- P_1, ..., P_n .

where each P and P_i is a positive atomic formula of the form $Q(t_1, \ldots, t_n)$, and each t_i is a term of sort s_i when $s_1 \ldots s_n = w$ is the arity of Q; these terms may include variables, which will of course be "logical variables"; also P and/or any P_i may be an equation, since it can use an equality predicate. P is called the **head** of the clause, and $P_1, \ldots, P_n$ constitute its **tail**.

A simple Eqlog[8] program for calculating the population density of countries is

    density(C) = pop(C) / area(C) .

In ordinary Prolog, this would be given by the clause

    density(C,D) :- pop(C,P), area(C,A), D is P/A .

using the impure is feature, which is a weak analog of Lisp's eval function. In case, for some reason, one really wants density, pop and area to be predicates rather than functions, one can still write

    density(C,D) :- pop(C,P), area(C,A), D = P / A .

in Eqlog. Furthermore, the three tail clauses can be given in any order.

---

[8]We use the convention that variables names begin with a capital letter, while both function and predicate names are all lower case. In particular, constants like "china" arc all lower case, since they are regarded as null-ary function symbols.

Similarly, we can compute the temperature in Fahrenheit from that in Centigrade by the usual formula,

f(C) = (9 / 5)* C + 32.

where f is a rational (abbreviated Rat) valued function and C is a Rat-sorted variable (assuming the rationals are available; otherwise, one could use floating point numbers)[9]. However, we can still write the query

eval f(C) = 77.

and get the right answer

as Int: C = 25

where Int indicates that the answer is an integer.

We now sketch how to get the rationals from the integers by using equality; further details are given in Section 5. The basic idea is to use a greatest common divisor function to insure that equality of rationals can be determined just by examining their reduced forms; the relevant equation is

X / Y = (X / gcd(X,Y)) /(Y / gcd(X,Y)) :- gcd(X,Y) ≠ 1.

where / is a Rat-valued function symbol denoting division, and X, Y are variables of sort Int (for integer)[10]. The above clause (plus a bit more, including some declarations; see Section 5) will enable an Eqlog user to define the rationals for himself; by contrast, [57] uses logical variables in a non-obvious way. This also guarantees that queries like that above about temperature will actually yield reduced fractions.

For typical interesting cases, we can build in decision procedures that yield most general unifiers using techniques like Gaussian elimination (see Section 3), so that Eqlog can automatically handle most computations that result from this definition of the rationals. For example, we can define * and + as usual in mathematics, by

---

[9]Compare this with [57], which uses functions like $times having bizarre definitions that seem to involve putting arbitrary Lisp functions inside clauses.

[10]Actually, Y must be restricted to non-zero values; as shown in Section 6.5, this can be done using the subsort mechanism described in more detail in Section 7.1.

$$(X / Y) * (Z / W) = (X * Z) / (Y * W).$$

and

$$(X / Y) + (Z / W) = ((X * W) + (Z * Y)) / (Y * W).$$

and then get the expected behavior.

Logical precision requires specifying the intended models. For first order many-sorted logic with equality, these have one set for each sort s, together with a predicate among those sets for each predicate symbol, such that the sorts of its arguments match its arity; similarly, with a function among those sets corresponding to each function symbol, such that the argument and values match those of the sorts in its rank. It is also assumed that equality predicates are always interpreted as *actual identity* in the models. In addition, there may be a number of sort, function, and predicate symbols that have a fixed interpretation. Thus, for reasons of efficiency, it is desirable to build in the integers; in terms of model theory, this means taking a fixed interpretation for the sort Int and for all the associated functions and predicates.

A model M **satisfies** a clause of the form

$$P :- P_1, \ldots, P_n.$$

iff for every assignment α of values in the model M to variables in the clause (such that sort restrictions are satisfied), αP holds in M whenever αP_i holds in M for all i. A model M **satisfies** a set C of clauses iff it satisfies every clause in C. But for programming, we are not really interested in *all* models satisfying all the clauses in C; rather, we are interested in the standard model of C, which we now explain. Given signatures Σ and Π of function and predicate symbols (respectively) and a set C of Horn clauses (including equality predicates), the **standard model**, denoted $T_{\Sigma,\Pi,C}$, has as its elements equivalence classes of ground terms[11] under the equivalence relation

$$t \equiv t' \text{ iff } C \vdash t =_s t',$$

---

[11]I.e., terms without variables that are built up from the constants and operator symbols in Σ.

where $\vdash$ is the provability relation for many-sorted first-order logic with equality. Let [t] denote the equivalence class of t under this relation. Then function symbols are interpreted in the usual way, and predicate symbols are interpreted by:

$P([t_1],...,[t_n])$ is true in $T_{\Sigma,\Pi,C}$ iff $C \vdash P(t_1,...,t_n)$;
and is false otherwise.

$T_{\Sigma,\Pi,C}$ is like the Herbrand universe, except that it consists of equivalence classes of terms instead of individual terms.

The basic facts about this situation are as follows: $T_{\Sigma,\Pi,C}$ satisfies C; also, if M is any other model satisfying C, then there is a unique Σ,Π-homomorphism h: $T_{\Sigma,\Pi,C} \to M$, where a Σ,Π-**homomorphism** h: $M \to M'$ is a many-sorted function preserving the function and predicate symbols in the signatures, in the sense that

$h(f_M(a_1,...,a_n)) = f_{M'}(h(a_1),...,h(a_n))$, and
$Q_M(a_1,...,a_n)$ implies $Q_{M'}(h(a_1),...,h(a_n))$,
for each f in Σ and Q in Π.

A model satisfying C such that there is a unique Σ,Π-homomorphisms from it to any other satisfying C, is called an **initial** Σ,Π,C-model [29, 43, 44]. Initial Σ,Π,C-models are unique up to Σ,Π-isomorphism. This approach is, we think, an attractive alternative formulation of the "minimal Herbrand model" approach; it characterizes the construction at a level of abstraction that is independent of representation details, and has many pleasant properties, as shown by

Theorem 1: Let C be a set of Horn clauses with equality, using function and predicate symbols from the signatures Σ and Π respectively. Then:

1. $T_{\Sigma,\Pi,C}$ satisfies C;
2. if M is any other model satisfying C, there is a unique Σ,Π-homomorphism h: $T_{\Sigma,\Pi,C} \to M$ (where a Σ,Π-homomorphism is a many-sorted function preserving the function and predicate symbols in the signatures), i.e., $T_{\Sigma,\Pi,C}$ is an **initial** Σ,Π,C-model;
3. any model initial among those satisfying C is isomorphic to $T_{\Sigma,\Pi,C}$; and
4. an n-ary predicate Q is satisfied by elements $[t_1],...,[t_n]$ of $T_{\Sigma,\Pi,C}$ iff $Q(t_1,...,t_n)$ is provable from C; in particular, two Σ-terms denote the

same element of $T_{\Sigma,\Pi,C}$ iff they can be proved equal using the clauses in C.

Proof: We will prove the above assertions in order.

1. Let P :- $P_1,...,P_n$ be a clause in C with variables $Y_1,...,Y_k$, and assume that $P_1,...,P_n$ are satisfied in $T_{\Sigma,\Pi,C}$ for a given assignment of values $[t_1],...,[t_k]$ to the variables $Y_1,...,Y_k$. Then

$$C \vdash P_i(t_1,...,t_n)$$

for i=1,...,n (we can use the same representatives t_i by the substitutivity for equality) and so by substitution and *modus ponens*,

$$C \vdash P(t_1,...,t_k) ,$$

and therefore $P([t_1],...,[t_k])$ is true in $T_{\Sigma,\Pi,C}$. (Note that P and the P_i may contain the equality predicate or any other predicate symbol.)

2. Let Γ be the set of all ground equations derivable from C. Then every model M satisfying C is a (Σ,Γ)-algebra. Therefore $T_{\Sigma,\Pi,C}$ is also a (Σ,Γ)-algebra, and is initial by construction [43]; thus, there is a unique Σ-homomorphism h: $T_{\Sigma,\Pi,C} \to M$. It remains to check that h preserves predicates. Assuming $Q([t_1],...,[t_k])$ is true in $T_{\Sigma,\Pi,C}$, we know that $Q(t_1,...,t_k)$ is provable from C; therefore, it must hold in M, i.e.,

$$M \models Q(t_1,...,t_k)$$

which by definition means that $Q_M(h[t_1],...,h[t_k])$ is true in M, as desired.

3. This follows from a very general result in category theory, that any two initial objects are isomorphic; it is also not hard to prove the result directly.

4. This is just a restatement of the fact that for ground terms,

$$T_{\Sigma,\Pi,C} \models Q(t_1,...,t_k) \text{ iff } C \vdash Q(t_1,...,t_k) , \text{ and}$$

$$t \equiv t' \text{ iff } C \vdash t =_s t' . \quad \square$$

From these results, we get the following

Corollary 2: (Herbrand's Theorem) For Q a predicate symbol and $t_1,...,t_n$ Σ-terms in variables $Y_1,...,Y_m$ one has

$$C \vdash (\exists Y_1,...,Y_m) Q(t_1,...,t_n)$$

iff there is a substitution σ sending the Y_i to ground terms such that $Q([\sigma(t_1)],...,[\sigma(t_n)])$ is true in $T_{\Sigma,\Pi,C}$.

Proof: If there is a substitution σ mapping $Y_1,\dots,Y_m$ to ground terms such that $Q([\sigma(t_1)],\dots,[\sigma(t_k)])$ is true in $T_{\Sigma,\Pi,C}$, then

$$C \vdash Q(\sigma(t_1),\dots,\sigma(t_k)) \ ,$$

and by m applications of $\exists$ introduction rule, we get

$$C \vdash (\exists Y_1,\dots,Y_m)\, Q(t_1,\dots,t_k) \ .$$

Conversely, if

$$C \vdash (\exists Y_1,\dots,Y_m)\, Q(t_1,\dots,t_k) \ ,$$

since $T_{\Sigma,\Pi,C}$ satisfies C, there is an assignment $[\sigma]\colon Y_i \mapsto [t_i']$ of values in $T_{\Sigma,\Pi,C}$ to the variables in Y_i such that $[\sigma]Q(t_1,\dots,t_k)$ is true in $T_{\Sigma,\Pi,C}$. By definition, this means that

$$C \vdash Q(\sigma(t_1),\dots,\sigma(t_k)) \ , \text{ for } \sigma \text{ the substitution mapping } Y_i \text{ to } t_i',$$

i.e., that $Q([\sigma(t_1)],\dots,[\sigma(t_k)])$ is true in $T_{\Sigma,\Pi,C}$ for such a σ. $\Box$

All this is closely related to the so-called "Closed World" assumption for the initial model $T_{\Sigma,\Pi,C}$. In the language of [9], this model has "no junk" and "no confusion." **No junk** means that every element of the model can be denoted by a term using the given function symbols. **No confusion** means that a predicate holds of some elements iff it can be proved to hold using the axioms; in particular, two elements are identified iff they can be proved equal using the given axioms. In fact, these two conditions together are equivalent to initiality. It is worth noting that the full first order predicate calculus does not admit initial models in the above sense. This appears to be closely connected with the difficulties associated with extending both "circumscription" [66] and Prolog to full first order logic.

Coercions are treated by [57] in a complex manner involving the use of impure Prolog predicates like var. However, coercions can be handled much more easily using subsorts. Thus, we can just declare[12]

    Int < Rat

and then assert

---

[12]This really means Int $\leq$ Rat, but we use the simpler notation because it can be done with just one keystroke.

`N / 1 = N.`

to get the desired effect. The basic idea is to use a logic having a partial ordering on its set of sorts. Actually, subsorts are traditional in theorem proving and go back at least to Herbrand [49]. The model-theoretic semantics of subsorts simply requires that if $s < s'$ then the set that interprets s is a subset of the set that interprets s'. The proof theory is a little more complicated; see Section 7.1. Subsorts are easily implemented in a logic programming language, and in fact are part of the OBJ language [40, 25]; sorts form an acyclic graph under the subsort relation, so that a form of "multiple inheritance" is provided. Note that polymorphic operators are also supported. For example, _+_ is binary operator for both Int and Rat.

3 Solving Equations over Built-in Sorts

Assume that we are given a signature Σ of function symbols and a reachable[13] Σ-model M. Now let E be a set of Σ-equations over a set X of variables. Then a **ground solution** of E in M is an assignment α from the variables in X to values in M such that $\alpha(E)$ is satisfied in M. Now letting $T_\Sigma(Y)$ denote the Σ-terms with variables from Y, we define a **solution** of E in M to be an assignment σ from X to terms in $T_\Sigma(Y)$ such that $\alpha(\sigma(E))$ is satisfied in M for every assignment α from Y to M. A **complete solution** of E in M is a set L of solutions such that every solution of E in M is a substitution instance of one in L; i.e., such that for any solution τ (from variables X to $T_\Sigma(Y)$) there is a solution σ in L and a substitution ρ from the variables in Y to $T_\Sigma(Y)$ such that $\tau = \rho(\sigma)$. (Note that these definitions do *not* require most general substitutions.)

For example, let **N** be the natural numbers with only the function +, so that Σ contains elements of **N** as constants and +. Let us consider just linear equations, regarding 3X as an abbreviation for (X + X + X). Thus, the equations

---

[13]This means that every element of M is denoted by some Σ-ground term, i.e., there is no junk.

$$3X + Y + 2Z = 1$$
$$X - 2Y = 3$$

have a ground solution $\sigma(X) = 7$, $\sigma(Y) = 2$, $\sigma(Z) = -11$, and have a complete solution given by $\sigma(X) = 3+4V$, $\sigma(Y) = 2V$, $\sigma(Z) = -4 -7V$, where V is a parameter variable. It is a general theorem that any set of linear equations over the integers has either no solution, or else a complete solution consisting of just one substitution.

One can also get a complete solution over the naturals for any equation of the form

$$a_1 * a_2 = a_3 * a_4$$

where a_1, a_2, a_3, a_4 are either variables or constants, and are not necessarily distinct. For example,

$$X^2 = 2Y$$

has the complete solution $\sigma(X) = 2V$, $\sigma(Y) = 2V^2$, and

$$X*Y = 0$$

has a complete solution $\{\sigma, \tau\}$, where $\sigma(X) = V$, $\sigma(Y) = 0$, and $\tau(X) = 0$, $\tau(Y) = V$, while

$$X^2 = Z*W$$

has an infinite complete solution.

Note that for some theories over built-in sorts like Int, things are very inefficient to decide, while others have no complete decision procedure. For example, a user should not expect to get an answer very soon from

```
fermat :- X ** N + Y ** N = Z ** N, N >= 3.
eval fermat.
```

since the query will halt iff Fermat's Last Theorem is false. Similarly, there is no decision procedure for arbitrary equations in + and *, by Matijasevic's negative solution to Hilbert's tenth problem [65, 16]. Section 7.3 considers solving equations over user defined sorts and Section 4 describes a sublogic within which equations over user defined sorts can be made solvable with reasonable efficiency.

318

Complete solutions do not necessarily exist; also, just because a complete solution exists does not mean that it is recursively enumerable, i.e., that there is an algorithm that will produce all the substitutions in it. Moreover, even if a recursively enumerable complete solution exists, the algorithm can still fail to terminate when faced with a case for which no solution exists. Let us say that we have a **totally complete solution** in case there is an algorithm that will explicitly fail if there is no solution, and otherwise will enumerate a complete solution. Similarly, let us say we have a **r.e. complete solution** in case there is an algorithm that will enumerate a complete solution when there is one, and say we have a **finite solution** if we have a totally complete solution that is always finite. More algorithmically, we will assume that SOLN(E) produces substitutions in the solution of E, if any exist, one at a time on request until there are no more.

A further desirable property of a complete solution L of E in A is that it should be **most general**, in the sense that for any solution substitution σ, there is a unique member τ of L and a unique substitution ρ such that $\rho \circ \tau = \sigma$. It can be shown that any two most general solutions are essentially the same. Unfortunately, there are cases where totally complete solutions exist, but no most general solution exists [22]. However, the examples given above do have most general solutions; in fact, the (non-ground) solutions given are most general.

The most classical case in the present context, of course, is that where the model is the set of terms over some signature Σ, and the functions are just those in Σ. Then Robinson's unification algorithm gives a finite solution (it is totally complete and always consists of just one most general unifier). A more complex case is that of integer linear programming, because of the inequality predicates that are involved. Solution algorithms for built-in sorts provide Eqlog with all the power of so-called "constraint languages," and narrowing provides a powerful capability for handling equational and logical constraints over user-defined ADTs.

319

4 Computing in Horn Clause Logic with Equality

This section considers how to solve for the values of logical variables over user definable ADTs within Horn clause logic with equality. We begin with a simple basic logic and then extend it in two steps to the full general case of Horn clause logic with equality. The basic sublogic assumes that all clauses are of two types, either a pure equation, or else a clause whose head is not an equation. Let $\mathcal{E}$ denote the set of equations and $\mathcal{P}$ the set of Horn clauses whose head clause is not an equation; thus, $\mathcal{C} = \mathcal{E} \cup \mathcal{P}$. To unify two positive atomic formulae, say $Q_1(t_1,...,t_n)$ and $Q_2(u_1,...,u_m)$, we must of course have that Q_1 is Q_2, the arity w_1 of Q_1 is the arity w_2 of Q_2 so that n=m, and we must also solve the system

$$t_1 = u_1, \; ..., \; t_n = u_n$$

of simultaneous equations modulo the equations given in $\mathcal{E}$; this is called $\mathcal{E}$-**unification**, or **universal unification**. Under this assumption about the structure of clauses, those in $\mathcal{P}$ can have no influence on finding an $\mathcal{E}$-unifier.

The computation algorithm of ordinary Prolog has been described clearly but informally by Warren [91]:

> To *execute* a goal, the system searches for the first clause whose head *matches* or *unifies* with the goal. The *unification* process finds the most general common instance of the two terms, which is unique if it exists. If a match is found, the matching clause instance is then *activated* by executing in turn, from left to right, each of the goals of the body (if any). If at any time the system fails to find a match for a goal, it *backtracks*, i.e., it rejects the most recently activated clause, undoing any substitutions made by the match with the head of the clause. Next it reconsiders the original goal which activated the rejected clause, and tries to find a subsequent clause which also matches the goal.

The assumption that the set $\mathcal{C}$ of clauses decomposes into disjoint sets $\mathcal{E}$ of equations and $\mathcal{P}$ of predicate-headed clauses has the desirable effect of isolating the solution of equations into a separate $\mathcal{E}$-unification algorithm SOLN, which is then called by the Prolog search algorithm described above. Of course, SOLN must be called in a way that can be backtracked and is fair, in the sense that every substitution gets tried. This gives a semidecision procedure that may not halt; but if SOLN is r.e. complete, then a general proof of completeness of the algorithm can be given along standard lines [74, 1]. As shown in Section 7.3, a complete SOLN using narrowing always exists if the equations in $\mathcal{E}$ are confluent and terminating.

We now consider some extensions of the basic case $C = \mathcal{E} \cup P$. There are not any essential difficulties with these extensions; rather, the problem is that we lack useful sufficient conditions to verify completeness. Now our three extensions, arranged in order of increasing generality:

1. $C = \mathcal{E} \cup P$, with $\mathcal{E}$ a set of confluent and terminating rewrite rules. Then SOLN can be computed by narrowing, and the usual Knuth-Bendix algorithm can be used to check confluence.

2. $C = \mathcal{E} \cup P$, with $\mathcal{E}$ a set of confluent and terminating *conditional* rewrite rules. Everything works just as in case 1., but methods for establishing confluence are not yet as well developed[14].

3. The fully general case has C an arbitrary set of Horn clauses, within which equality predicates may occur anywhere. Our basic evaluation algorithm remains the same, but now SOLN and the Prolog-like algorithm may call each other recursively. If the clauses having equations in their heads are confluent and terminating, then narrowing (see Section 7.3) will compute SOLN. However, techniques for establishing confluence for this case are not yet available[15].

Several of the examples in this paper belong to the more general cases 2. and 3.

Notice that user queries can also be equations, to be solved using the SOLN algorithm. In addition, terms can be evaluated, i.e., reduced to normal form. Reduction to normal form is a completely general and very powerful paradigm

---

[14]There has been important recent progress on checking confluence for conditional rewrite rules [76, 73, 56], so that really practical algorithms might be available in the near future.

[15]One approach to proving confluence is to translate case 3. into case 2. (with P empty), by viewing predicates as boolean-valued functions. However, it remains unclear how effective this will be in practice. Notice that this is not the same as translating 3. into 2. for evaluation, where questions of efficiency, control and naturalness would also arise.

for functional computations [67, 25]. To illustrate this, if we declare a function symbol ! on the natural numbers, write the equations

```
0 ! = 1.
(succ(N))! = succ(N) * (N !).
```

and then write an expression like

```
eval (3 !)*(3 !).
```

that contains no variables, Eqlog will apply the given equations as rewrite rules, until it can go no further, in this case, producing the answer 36. We could similarly have defined binomial coefficients, Fibonacci numbers, or more interestingly, non-numerical ADTs like SET, BAG and QUEUE with their associated functions, as will be shown later. More complex functions, such as sorters and parsers, can also be defined; in fact, any general recursive function can be defined equationally [4, 67].

5 User Defined Abstract Data Types

There is much work on providing user defined ADTs in programming languages (e.g., OBJ [40, 32, 25], Clu [59], Ada[16] [18]), and on the logical basis for this in purely equational logic (e.g., [43, 67]). The essential idea is to allow users to introduce modules that define new sorts and their associated functions and give axioms in Horn clause logic with equality as rules of computation; it can also be very helpful to have available subsorts and their associated predicates, as we will see. The intended model-theoretic semantics of a module is the standard or initial model of its associated theory in Horn clause logic with equality. A purely syntactic notion of module has been given for Mprolog by [19].

We now give an Eqlog module RAT defining the rationals, using the built-in module INT of integers[17] Note that Eqlog keywords are underlined, that

---

[16]Ada is a registered trademark of the U.S. Government (Ada Joint Program Office).

[17]The approach to defining the rationals used in this example is inspired by a similar example in OBJ developed jointly with J.-P. Jouannaud.

module names are all capitals, while variable names begin with a capital and that relation, function and constant names are all lower case. Also note that Eqlog provides built-in types as modules; for example, the module INT has sort Int with subsorts NzInt of nonzero integers, Nat of naturals and NzNat of nonzero naturals (modules, especially generic modules, are discussed in more detail in Section 6). "Attributes" can be given for operators; for example, assoc, comm, and idp indicate that a binary operator is associative, commutative, and idempotent, respectively; and id: e indicates that it has e as its identity. The associative and commutative properties of functions can be built into unification algorithms; these attributes also have important syntactic implications.

Eqlog "mix-fix" notation permits any desired ordering of keywords and arguments for operators; this is declared by giving a syntactic "form" consisting of a string of keywords and underbar characters "_", followed by a ":", followed by the arity as a string of sorts, followed by "->", followed by the value sort of the function; if there are no underbars, then the usual parentheses-with-comma notation must be used. Similar conventions are used for predicates. An expression is considered "well-formed" in this scheme iff it has exactly one parse; the parser can interactively help the user to satisfy this condition[18]. Now we define the rationals; notice that nzint is used as a predicate; intuitively, it is true if its argument has the sort NzInt; Section 7.1 gives more information on such predicates; notice also that there is a disequality[19]

$$gcd(X,Y) \neq 1.$$

in the body of one of the clauses. This violates the purity of the language only in appearance, since Section 7.4 shows how to reduce the semantics of disequality to that of equality.

---

[18]The parser is greatly helped if spaces always separate the keywords declared in the form of a function, and this paper follows that convention throughout; but since parentheses are also delimiters, they do not need to be separated by spaces. These and many other syntactic conventions follow those of OBJ2 [25].

[19]We prefer the word "disequality" to "inequality" because of the ambiguity of the latter.

```
module BASICRAT using INT is
  sorts Rat
  subsorts Int < Rat
  fns
    _/_ : Int,NzInt -> Rat
    _*_ : Rat,Rat -> Rat (assoc comm id: 1)
    _+_ : Rat,Rat -> Rat (assoc comm id: 0)
  vars
    N,X,Z : Int
    Y,W : NzInt
    A : NzNat
  axioms
    nzint(Y * W).
    N / 1 = N.
    0 / Y = 0.
    N / (- A) = (- N) / A.
    X / Y = (X / gcd(X,Y)) / (Y / gcd(X,Y)) :- gcd(X,Y) ≠ 1.
    (X / Y)+(Z / W) = ((X * W) + (Z * Y))/(Y * W).
    N + (X / Y) = ((N * Y) + X) / Y.
    (X / Y)*(Z / W) = (X * Z)/(Y * W).
    N * (X / Y) = (N * X) / Y.
endmod BASICRAT
```

Here the keyword using indicates that the sorts, subsorts, predicates, functions, and axioms of the listed modules are imported into the module being defined. We refer to the relationship between modules being defined and being used as the **using hierarchy**. We now enrich BASICRAT to define division and the subsort of nonzero rationals.

```
module RAT using BASICRAT is
  sorts NzRat
  subsorts NzInt < NzRat < Rat
  fns
    _/_ : Rat,NzRat -> Rat
  vars
    X : Int
    Y,Z,W : NzInt
  axioms
    nzrat(X / Y) :- nzint(X).
    (X / Y)/(Z / W) = (X * W)/(Y * Z).
    X / (Z / W) = (X * W) / Z.
```

```
        (X / Y) / Z = X / (Y * Z).
    endmod RAT
```

It is easy to define new types in the same style; for example:

```
    module SET-OF-INT using INT is
       sorts Set-of-int
       fns
          Ø  : Set-of-int
          {_} : Int -> Set-of-int
          _U_ : Set-of-int,Set-of-int -> Set-of-int
               (assoc comm idpt id: Ø)
       preds
          _∈_ : Int,Set-of-int
          empty : Set-of-int
       vars
          N : Int
          S : Set-of-int
       axioms
          N ∈ S :- { N } U S = S.
          empty(S) :- S = Ø.
    endmod SET-OF-INT
```

Although this definition is algebraically elegant, it is actually not the most efficient or convenient approach; a better definition of a generic set module is given in Section 6.

It is a bit tedious to repeat such a definition every time one wants to define sets or bags of some new sort. One way to avoid this tedium is to use polymorphic sorts; but we prefer parameterization, as explained in the next section.

We have already noted that the sorts and subsorts currently defined form an acyclic graph (thus supporting so-called "multiple inheritance"). This motif is repeated at the module level, with another acyclic graph under the using hierarchy. In fact, the subsort hierarchy and the using hierarchy interact, since subsorts are declared inside of modules: At a given node M of the using hierarchy, the set of curently defined sorts is the union of those declared in M with all those declared in nodes below M in the using hierarchy (i.e., all those

325

related to M by the transitive closure of the <u>using</u> relation); similarly, the subsort relation applicable at M is the union of the subsort declarations in M with those from all modules below M. Thus, the subsort graph of a lower level module is a subgraph of that of a higher level module. (All this has already been implemented in OBJ and has been found very natural and helpful.)

6 Generic Modules

Reusability is a major goal of modern software engineering. In order to achieve this goal, it is necessary that software be broken into components that are as reusable as possible; parameterization is a technique that can greatly enhance the reusability of components [32]. For example, Bag-of and Set-of, which have caused considerable controversy in the *Prolog Digest*, can easily be defined as generic ADTs, and then automatically implemented using rewrite rules. Generic modules also greatly ameliorate the otherwise odious need for defining abstractions whenever they are used. Without some such facility, strong typing would not be tolerable to use in practice. (Interactive syntax also helps greatly, by allowing menu selection instead of keyword typing.)

6.1 Requirement Theories

Before giving details, we consider how to specify a parameterized module's interface, especially the **requirements** that an actual parameter should satisfy in order for the instantiation to make sense. We express these requirements in the form of a logical **theory**, that is, a set of axioms, that the actual must satisfy. Such a theory may include sort, subsort, predicate and function declarations, declaring what the actual parameter must provide to the parameterized module, as well as axioms declaring what properties must be satisfied. For example, a generic sorting module might have the theory of partially ordered sets as its requirement theory; this means that an actual must provide a designated sort and a transitive binary relation on it. In Eqlog, this theory is given as follows:

```
theory POSET is
  sorts Elt
  preds _<_ : Elt,Elt
```

```
     vars A,B,C : Elt
     axioms
       A < C :- A < B, B < C.
       ~(A < A).
     endth POSET
```

where ~ denotes negation. Theories are not intended to be used for computation, but only for declaring the properties of interfaces. The idea is that before an instantiation of a generic module can be "certified" it must be shown that the actual parameter does in fact have the properties required by the theory. Because computations do not use the axioms given in theories, but only those in modules, there is no reason to restrict the form of the axioms in theories, and in fact, we allow arbitrary first order axioms; otherwise we could not have axioms like the second one in POSET. Difficulty only arises when one has to prove that the axioms hold of some particular module; then, one needs a first order theorem prover like that of Stickel [84] or Hsiang [51], and, of course, the simpler the axioms the better the chance of actually getting the proof[20].

Here is an even simpler theory, the one that is actually used for the generic SET example:

```
     theory TRIV is
       sorts Elt
     endth TRIV
```

This theory requires nothing except that a particular sort be designated.

We now give an example illustrating Eqlog's syntax for generics, a generic LIST module:

```
     module LIST[X :: TRIV] using NAT is
       sorts List, Nelist
       subsorts Elt < Nelist < List
       fns
         _ _: List, List -> List (assoc id: nil)
         head : NeList -> Elt
         tail : NeList -> List
```

---

[20]Note that certain axioms may require induction for their proof.

```
    #_ : List -> Nat
  vars
    X : Elt
    L, L' : List
  axioms
    nelist(X L).
    head(X L) = X.
    tail(X L) = L.
    # nil = 0.
    # X = 1.
    #(L L') = # L + # L'.
endmod LIST
```

After the name of the generic module comes a left square bracket, indicating that what follows is the formal parameter name, X in this case, and then after the :: comes the name of the theory that it is required to satisfy, TRIV in this case; the interface declaration is then closed by a right square bracket. Eqlog also allows more than one formal parameter - requirement theory pair in an interface declaration, although this is not illustrated in this paper.

In this example, subsorts provide a way of dealing with functions that are not defined on the entire collection of data items of some sort. For example, head and tail are only defined on nonempty lists. The approach is simply to define a subsort Nelist < List of nonempty lists; the head and tail are functions with domain Nelist rather than all of List. This approach is discussed in more detail in Section 7.1.

Now the generic sorting module, which uses the generic LIST module, and has POSET as its requirement theory:

```
module SORTING[ELT :: POSET] is
  extending LIST[ELT]
  relns sorted : List
  fns sorting : List -> List
  vars E E' : Elt
    L L' : List
  axioms
    sorted(nil).
    sorted(E).
```

328

```
                sorted(E E' L)  :- E < E', sorted(E' L).
                sorted(E E L)  :- sorted(E L).
                sorting(L E E' L') = sorting(L E' E L')  :- E' < E.
                sorting(L) = L :- sorted(L).
         endmod SORTING
```

6.2 Views and Instantiations

To instantiate a generic module, one must provide an actual parameter A; but more than this is actually needed. Since both modules and theories can involve more than one sort, we need to say just which sorts in the actual correspond to those declared in the requirement theory T of the generic; similarly, we need to say which functions and predicates in an actual A correspond to those required by the theory. Following [32] and ideas developed for use in Clear [7, 8], this correspondence is given by a **view**, which consists of:

1. a function σ from the sorts of the theory T to those of A;
2. a function ϕ from the functions of T to those A; and
3. a function π from the predicates of T to those of A,

such that

1. the subsort relation is preserved, in the sense that s $<$ s' in T implies $\sigma(s) < \sigma(s')$ in A;
2. the sorts of functions and predicates are preserved, in the sense that if function f in T has arity $s_1...s_n$ and value sort s in T then $\phi(f)$ has arity $\sigma(s_1)...\sigma(s_n)$ and value sort $\sigma(s)$ in A; and similarly for predicates; and
3. the translations of the equations and axioms in T to equations and axioms about A are in fact true of the initial model of A.

Note that one sometimes wants to consider views where A is a theory rather than a module, in which case the translated equations and axioms need only follow from the axioms given for A. Thus, when A is a theory, one can use ordinary first order logic (with equality) to prove the third condition, which in that case only needs that the translated axioms follow from the axioms of A, but when A is a module, more than this may also be needed, e.g., induction, since the translated axioms need only hold for the initial model. Also note that in practical large scale programming, one may wish to settle for less than a formal proof of the third condition; for example, an informal proof might be acceptable. In the language of [34], a view is a "theory morphism" between "data theories"; see Section 7.2 for a bit more about this.

In many cases, it is obvious how to construct a view of A as T; this is formalized by the notion of a **default view** in [32, 25]. In other cases, there is only one appropriate view in the current environment, and of course that is the one to apply. In such cases, it is not necessary to indicate what view is intended, one can just write the name of the actual module. For example, in order to construct SET-OF-INT, we just say

> make SET-OF-INT is SET[INT] endmake

since there is a default view of INT as a TRIV. In other cases, it may be necessary to include a view in the make statement. For example,

> make SORTING-OF-INT-DIV is SORTING[INT-AS-DIV-POSET] endmake

instantiates a generic SORTING module with the poset of integers ordered by the relation of (non-reflexive) divisibility. When it is not necessary to give the instantiated module a name, we can just write, e.g., SET[INT].

Views also provide an elegant form of declaration at the module level. In ordinary sequential programming, "assertions" can be inserted after a statement to indicate that the program's state is supposed to satisfy some property after the execution of that statement. In Eqlog, a view from a theory to a module serves to indicate that the module (i.e., its sorts, functions and predicates) satisfies certain axioms. It should be noted that one can also compose generics. For example, one can form SET[LIST[INT]]; this is a so-called "module expression" [32, 25].

Of course, there is nothing special about the details of the features and the syntax described here for Eqlog modules and generics; what is special is the underlying semantic ideas. Unfortunately, there is not room in this paper for a full exposition of this semantics, which is based on ideas from the Clear specification language [8]. The ideas are not really difficult, but they use some comparatively advanced mathematics. Some discussion is given in Section 7.2. The application of these ideas to the equational logic programming language OBJ is described in [32] and [25], and to an Ada library system in [33].

6.3 Sets

We now develop the example of generic sets in some detail, beginning with a generic BASICSET module, providing only symmetric difference, ⊎, and intersection; later we will define the rest of the set functions from these.

```
module BASICSET[ELT :: TRIV] is
  sorts Set
  fns
    ∅,Ω : Set
    { } : Elt -> Set
    _⊎_ : Set,Set -> Set (assoc comm id: ∅)
    _∩_ : Set,Set -> Set (assoc comm idp id: Ω)
  vars S,S',S" : Set, Elt,Elt' : Elt
  axioms
    S ⊎ S = ∅.
    { Elt } ∩ { Elt' } = ∅ :- Elt ≠ Elt'.
    S ∩ ∅ = ∅.
    S ∩(S' ⊎ S") = (S ∩ S')⊎(S ∩ S").
endmod BASICSET
```

This way of defining finite sets follows Hsiang's [51] approach to the propositional calculus; Ω is the "universal" set, i.e., the set of all things of sort Elt. In many cases, this definition will execute faster than more conventional axiomatizations[21]; furthermore, since Hsiang has shown that it is confluent and terminating modulo associativity and commutativity, and Fages [21] has proven correctness of a unification algorithm modulo these equations, we know that narrowing will work [54]. This observation will be important in some later examples. It should be noted that the BASICSET module provides not only all finite subsets of the set given as actual parameter, but also all **cofinite** sets (i.e., sets whose complement is finite). As in the RAT example, there is a disequality

```
{ Elt } ∩ { Elt' } = ∅ :- Elt ≠ Elt'.
```

in one of the axioms violating the purity of the language only in appearance (see Section 7.4).

---

[21] It is fast for conjunctions, but slow for disjunctions.

331

We now enrich the generic BASICSET module given earlier (recall that it provided symmetric difference and intersection) to provide union, difference and cardinality functions, plus some of the usual predicates.

```
module SET[X :: TRIV] using NAT, BASICSET[X] is
  fns
    _U_  : Set,Set -> Set
    _-_  : Set,Set -> Set
    #_   : Set -> Nat
  preds
    _∈_  : Elt,Set
    _⊆_  : Set,Set
    empty : Set
    _∉_  : Elt,Set
  vars X : Elt, S,S′,S″ : Set
  axioms
    S ∪ S′ = (S ∩ S′)⊎ S ⊎ S′.
    S - S′ = S ∩(S ⊎ S′).
    empty(S) :- S = ∅.
    X ∈ S :- { X } ∪ S = S.
  z[3] S :- { X } ∩ S = ∅.
    S ⊆ S′ :- S ∪ S′ = S′.
    # ∅ = 0.
    #({ X } ⊎ S) = pred(# S) :- X ∈ S.
    #({ X } ⊎ S) = succ(# S) :- X ∉ S.
endmod SET
```

Although # does not yield the answer ∞ for infinite sets, it does work reasonably. For example in the case of SET[INT], # Ω is just # Ω again, a reduced term rather than a non-terminating computation. In case Ω is a finite set, say {1, 3, 5}, one should add an equation explaining this,

Ω = { 1 } ∪ { 3 } ∪ { 5 }.

and in case Ω is an infinite set, one may want to add the equations

succ(# Ω) = # Ω.
pred(# Ω) = # Ω.

in order to get the expected behavior in all cases.

We can also enrich a module without giving the enrichment an explicit name; this can be useful if some constants are being defined for a single query or example. Another feature illustrated by the following module is that when the requirement theory is TRIV, a view can be determined just by giving a sort name (provided that the sort only occurs in one module in the current environment). If the sort name does not occur in any module in the current environment, then it serves to declare a new sort and apply the generic to it; we shall call this a declaration "on the fly." For example,

```
module using SET[Country] is
   fns pop150, area3 : Set
   vars C : Country
   axioms
     C ∈ pop150 :- pop(C) >= 150.
     C ∈ area3 :- area(C) >= 3.
endmod
```

We can now pose queries such as

```
eval china ∈ pop150.
eval china ∈ pop150 ∩ area3.
eval india ∈ pop150 - area3.
```

and get the expected answers: whether or not china has a population greater than (or equal to) 150 (million people); whether or not china has both a population greater than 150 and an area greater than (or equal to) 3 (million square miles); and whether or not india has a population greater than 150 and an area not greater than 3. We can also, of course, use logical variables in queries such as

```
X ∈ area3 - pop150.
```

6.4 Fractions

We now sketch a general parameterized version of the construction that yielded the rationals from the integers. To avoid excessive detail we give a somewhat weaker construction, and then indicate how it can be strengthened to a parameterized construction that will yield exactly the rationals when applied to the integers. We first give a standard definition from algebra, the theory of rings:

```
theory RING is
```

```
    sorts Ring
    fns
      _+_ : Ring,Ring -> Ring (assoc comm id: 1)
      -_ : Ring -> Ring
      _*_ : Ring,Ring -> Ring (assoc comm id: 0)
    vars
      X,Y,Z : Ring
    axioms
      X + (- X) = 0.
      X *(Y + Z) = (X * Y) + (X * Z).
  endth RING
```

Our general parameterized fraction construction requires that the elements that can appear as denominators be specifically designated by a subsort. In many cases this subsort denotes the nonzero elements; for example, with the integers, and with polynomials over the integers. But the general construction only requires a set of elements that contains 1 and is closed under multiplication. The following theory expresses this requirement.

```
  theory MULT using RING is
    sorts Mult
    subsorts
      Mult < Ring
    vars
      X,Y : Ring
    axioms
      mult(1).
      mult(X * Y) :- mult(X), mult(Y).
  endth MULT
```

Now we are ready for the general parameterized construction. It is very close to our previous construction for the rationals, except for not reducing fractions to canonical form and requiring a multiplicatively closed subsort denoted Mult. In addition, we define a subsort Invertible of fractions that can be inverted.

```
  module FRACTION[M :: MULT] is
    sorts Invertible, Fract
    subsorts Ring < Fract, Mult < Invertible < Fract
    fns
```

```
    _/_ : Ring,Mult -> Fract
    _*_ : Fract,Fract -> Fract (assoc comm id: 0)
    _+_ : Fract,Fract -> Fract (assoc comm id: 1)
     -1 : Invertible -> Invertible
  vars
    Y,W : Mult
    X,Z : Ring
  axioms
    X / 1 = X.
    0 / Y = 0.
    (X / Y)+(Z / W) = ((X * W) + (Z * Y))/(Y * W).
    X + (Z / W) = ((X * W) + Z)/W.
    (X / Y)*(Z / W) = (X * Z)/(Y * W).
    X * (Z / W) = (X * Z)/W.
    invertible(X / Y) :- mult(X).
    (W / Y)-1 = (Y / W).
    Y -1 = 1 / Y.
endmod FRACTION
```

In order to apply this, one says, for example,

make RAT is FRACTION[INT] endmake

to get the rationals (without fraction simplification, but see below) from the integers. Of course, this needs a view of INT as MULT, and we shall assume that the usual one, assigning NzInt to Mult, has been provided in the environment. This view looks like

```
view NZINT-AS-MULT is INT as MULT by
          Int is Ring
          NzInt is Mult
endview
```

so that the explicit form of the application of FRACTION to INT given above is

make RAT is FRACTION[NZINT-AS-MULT] endmake

To add fraction simplification to the previous parameterized construction one would have to strengthen the requirement theory MULT in two ways by:

1. asserting that the subsort Mult coincides with the nonzero elements
2. asserting the existence of a gcd à la Euclid;

the requirement theory so obtained would be that of Euclidean Domains (as defined in [87]).

335

6.5 Higher Order Capability

We now illustrate how generic modules confer the power of higher order functions in Eqlog. Our first example is a general "map" function (called "mapcar" in many dialects of Lisp) which applies a given function to each member of a list of elements; this occurs in a MAP module. The interface theory of this module says that we need to supply a unary function:

```
theory FN is
  sorts Elt
  fns f : Elt -> Elt
endth FN
```

Now the module that supplies the map function:

```
module MAP[X :: FN] is
  using LIST[X]
  fns map_ : List -> List
  vars X : Elt ; L : List
  axioms
    map nil = nil.
    map X L = f(X) map L.
endmod MAP
```

Next, here is how to apply MAP to the actual INT, which we assume supplies a square function, to get a function that squares each member of a list of integers.

```
module SQLIST is MAP[square of INT] * [map is sqlist] endmod
```

Finally, here is how this looks when you run it (assuming we are in a context that includes the SQLIST module):

```
eval sqlist(2 -3 4)
   as Nat: 4 9 16
```

For our second illustration, we give a general iteration function, such that special cases are summing a list of numbers, and taking their product. First the interface theory, which just says that we need a binary associative function with an identity:

```
theory MONOID is
  sorts Elt
```

```
    fns _*_ : Elt Elt -> Elt (assoc id: 1)
  endth MONOID
```

Next, the module that defines the generic iteration function:

```
  module ITER[M :: MONOID] is
    using LIST[M]
    fns iter : List -> Elt
    vars E : Elt ; L : List
    axioms
        iter(nil) = 1.
        iter(E L) = E * iter(L).
  endmod ITER
```

And now we instantiate it to get a module PI that takes the product of a list of numbers ("PI" is to suggest the traditional Π notation):

```
  module PI is ITER[INT] * [iter is prod] endmod
```

Here is a test case showing how it works:

```
  eval prod(2 4 6).
    as Int: 48
```

We can also instantiate ITER to produce a module SUM which sums a list of numbers, as follows:

```
  module SIGMA is ITER[INT, * is +, 1 is 0] * [iter is sum]
  endmod
```

Here is how it executes:

```
  eval sum(2 4 6).
    as Int: 12
```

7 Logical Foundations

This section discusses in more detail four issues regarding the foundations of Eqlog: subsorts, generics, narrowing, and disequality.

7.1 Subsorts

Many of our examples use subsorts and subsort predicates. We now explain why this is not an impure feature, but rather an expressive shorthand for a specification in standard Horn clause logic with equality. We also describe some conditions that insure valid use of subsort predicates; these conditions could be enforced syntactically. Although more permissive uses of subsort predicates are possible and certainly worth exploring, the one presented here is already very general.

Whenever a subsort $s < s'$ is declared, a corresponding unary predicate $s(\_)$ of sort s' also becomes available; intuitively, this predicate is true of a term iff that term lies in the subsort. Users can give axioms involving the subsort predicate; but these should only assert that certain functions restrict (and constants belong) to the subsort. For example, the subsort NeList < List of nonempty lists can be characterized by the clause

```
nelist(X L)
```

asserting that concatenation of an element X with a list L yields a nonempty list.

Our reconstruction of subsorts within standard Horn clause logic with equality involves giving ordinary signatures Σ and Π, and a set C of Horn clauses, such that the initial model $T_{\Sigma,\Pi,C}$ is isomorphic to the model intended for the subsort declarations and their corresponding predicates. The first step is to introduce a new ordinary sort for each subsort. We then force that in all models, the new sort s is identified with a subset of the sort s' whenever $s < s'$ by introducing a new function symbol $j: s \rightarrow s'$ that is made to play the role of an inclusion by satisfying the axiom

```
j(X) = j(Y) :- X = Y.
```

Similarly, we can express the fact that certain functions or constants restrict to a subsort by introducing new function symbols for these functions and constants such that their value sort is the subsort; equations are then given to insure their relationship to the functions and constants in the supersort. For example, from NeList < List and the clause above, we would get a function

```
    _ _  : Elt List -> NeList
```

and an equation

```
    j(j'(X) L) = X L.
```

where j : NeList -> List and j' : Elt -> List are the function symbols associated to the sort inclusions NeList < List and Elt < List.

In order to get the unary predicate s(_) of sort s', which is nelist(_) in the present example, we need give just one clause,

```
    s(j(Y)) ,
```

where the variable Y has sort s. This clause makes the predicate true in the initial model iff the element belongs to the subsort. (A more detailed discussion of these issues will appear in [38].)

We now illustrate this technique with two other previously given examples. In the definition of the requirement theory MULT, the clause

```
    mult(X * Y) :- mult(X),mult(Y).
```

for the subsort Mult < Ring can be translated as introducing the new function symbol

```
    _*_ : Mult,Mult -> Mult
```

and the equation

```
    j(X * Y) = j(X) * j(Y).
```

Similarly, for the subsort Invertible < Fract in the FRACTION module, the axiom

```
    invertible(X / Y) :- mult(X).
```

corresponds to introducing a new function

```
    _/_ :  Mult,Mult -> Invertible
```

and an equation

```
    j(X) / Y = j'(X / Y).
```

where j : Mult -> Ring and j' : Invertible -> Fract represent the inclusions. It should be noted that we can introduce a "top" sort ⊤ such that s < ⊤ for all sorts s, and then define all the sort predicates s(_) to be unary predicates of sort ⊤. It should also be noted that our approach to subsorts supports polymorphic operators, which can either be declared explicitly (as was _+_ in RING and FRACT), or implicitly by sort predicates (as was _*_ for MULT and RING); for more on this, see [38].

7.2 Putting Theories together

The module, theory, view and instantiation features of Eqlog support generic (i.e., parameterized) programming, a form of programming-in-the-large that permits an unusually high degree of reusability. All these features can be defined for any logical system satisfying some very simple and reasonable axioms that make it an **institution** [34]. In particular, it has been shown that the logic of Horn clauses with equality is an institution, so the general machinery can be applied directly to this case, giving a semantics for the parameterization features in Eqlog.

This approach relies on category-theoretic concepts like colimit, and therefore to explain it in detail here would require substantially greater prerequisites of the reader. However, we can give the flavor of the approach by considering in somewhat more detail the example given in Section 6.2, of applying the generic SORTING[M :: POSET] to the actual INT to get a program for sorting lists of integers. The first thing to notice is that the requirement theory POSET can be considered a subtheory of the generic module body SORTING; this is because SORTING can also be considered a theory, since it contains of a set of axioms. Notice also that LIST is another subtheory of SORTING, used to introduce the new sort List of lists of integers. Now there is a significant difference in the intended (model-theoretic) interpretations for these theories: we allow *any* interpretation for POSET, but we only allow interpretations for SORTING such that the sort List is *free* over the (arbitrary) sort Elt; i.e., the lists are uniquely determined once the elements are given. This is a kind of *relative* closed world assumption, and is explained technically by the notion of a "data constraint" in [34]. Let us denote the inclusion of POSET into SORTING by I.

340

The next thing we need is a view from POSET to INT; it is just the obvious one that maps Elt to Int; let us denote it V. Thus, we have two views whose source is the theory POSET. In the language of category theory, what we want is the "pushout" of these two theory morphisms; this is a kind of "least upper bound" theory which contains both of the target theories (namely SORTING and INT) but identifies the parts that they are supposed to share, as given by POSET (or more accurately, by the two views from POSET); see Figure 1.

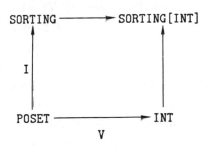

Figure 1: Application of SORTING to INT

From an implementation point of view, all that needs to be done to get the new module SORTING[INT] is to take the text for SORTING and substitute the text for INT (or appropriate pointers, in case INT is actually built-in, as of course it should be) for the text of POSET, making exactly the changes indicated by the view V; one could regard V as instructions for how to "edit" SORTING to get SORTING[INT], but of course, these instructions are given in a very structured form, and are guaranteed (by the additional semantic conditions that must be fulfilled by views) to give a meaningful new module SORTING[INT]. Thus, it is also important to implement at least the syntactic checks that are implied by the notion of view; however, the semantic checks involve theorem proving, so that users may well want to put them off, or even omit them entirely. Nevertheless, users should be aware that if the semantic conditions are in fact not satisfied, then the instantiation will have some unexpected properties.

The theory of "institutions" of [34] gives general sufficient conditions for when such pushouts can be calculated, also taking account of any "data constraints" that may occur in the theories involved. It may be worth remarking that the subsystem of Horn clause logic with equality consisting of pure equations (or conditional equations) plus Horn clauses whose heads are not equations, is also an institution; these restrictions on the syntax of clauses were mentioned in Section 4.

7.3 Narrowing

An equational theory is given by a pair $\langle \Sigma, T \rangle$ where Σ is an S-sorted signature of function symbols and T is a set of Σ-equations. The rules of many-sorted equational deduction [35] define an equivalence relation $=_T$ between Σ-terms with variables, namely that of being provably equal using the equations in T. If X denotes an S-sorted set containing an infinite supply of variables of each sort, and if $T_\Sigma(X)$ stands for the Σ-algebra of terms with variables in X, then a **substitution** is an S-sorted function $\alpha: X \to T_\Sigma(X)$; such a function extends to a unique Σ-homomorphism from $T_\Sigma(X)$ to itself that we also denote by α. A substitution α is said to have **domain** $Y = \{Y_s\}$ when $Y_s = \{x \in X_s \mid \alpha_s(x) \neq x\}$; we then write $Y = \text{dom}(\alpha)$. The set of variables **introduced** by α is the S-sorted $\text{int}(\alpha)_s = \cup\{\text{vars}(\alpha(x)) \mid x \in \text{dom}(\alpha)_s\}$, where vars(t) denotes the set of variables occurring in a term t.

Given an S-sorted set of variables $Y \subseteq X$ and substitutions α and β, we write $\alpha =_T \beta$ [Y] iff $\alpha(x) =_T \beta(x)$ for each x in Y. Similarly, we write $\alpha \leq_T \beta$ [Y] iff there is a substitution γ such that $\beta =_T \gamma \circ \alpha$ [Y]. A T-**unifier** of two terms t and t' is a substitution α such that $\alpha(t) =_T \alpha(t')$. Given terms t and t' with $Y = \text{vars}(t) \cup \text{vars}(t')$, a set L of T-unifiers of t and t' is called a **complete set of T-unifiers** of t and t' iff for each T-unifier γ of t and t' there is an α in L with $\alpha \leq_T \gamma$ [Y]. (This was called a most general complete solution in Section 3.) Without loss of generality we may assume, for technical reasons, that $\text{dom}(\alpha) \subseteq Y$ and $\text{int}(\alpha) \cap Y = \emptyset$ for each α in L.

Given an equational theory T, a **complete T-unification algorithm** SOLN is an algorithm such that if started with any two terms t and t', SOLN generates a complete set of T-unifiers for t and t'; SOLN is **finite** if, in addition, it always terminates with a finite set. Particular unification algorithms for theories T of frequent use, such as associativity and commutativity, have been given in the literature. For the general case when T consists of a confluent and terminating set $\mathcal{R}$ of rewrite rules, a unification algorithm using narrowing has been given by Fay [23] and improved in order to give a termination criterion by Hullot [53]. When $\mathcal{R}$ is confluent and terminating, then for any two terms one has $t=_T t'$ iff $\text{can}(t)=\text{can}(t')$, where $\text{can}(t)$ is the canonical form of the term t, obtained after exhaustive rewriting by applications of the rules $\mathcal{R}$.

The one step narrowing relation is defined as follows: Let t be a term; by renaming of variables (or some other convention) we can always assume that the variables occurring in t do not occur in any of the rules. Let t_0 be a nonvariable subterm of t that unifies (in the ordinary sense) with the left hand side t_1 of a rule $t_1=t_2$ in $\mathcal{R}$, with α the most general unifier. Let t' be the term obtained by replacing in $\alpha(t)$ the subterm $\alpha(t_0)=\alpha(t_1)$ by $\alpha(t_2)$. Then we say that t' is a **one step narrowing** of t, and we write $t \Rightarrow t'$. The **narrowing relation** is the reflexive and transitive closure of one step narrowing, and contains the rewriting relation as a subset. The following algorithm then provides a complete set of T-unifiers.

Theorem 3: [23, 53]. Let $T=\mathcal{R}$ be a confluent and terminating set of rewrite rules. Given a pair t,t' of terms, introduce a new function symbol[22] τ and consider all the narrowing chains that begin with $\tau(t,t')$. If such a chain ends with a term of the form $\tau(t_n,t'_n)$ such that t_n and t'_n are unifiable by a substitution α, then compose α with the substitutions obtained at the previous narrowing steps in the chain, and add this composition to the set of unifiers already generated. The set so obtained is a complete set of T-unifiers for t and t'. □

This algorithm has been extended to handle the more general situation when the equations in T can be partitioned into a set of rewrite rules $\mathcal{R}$ and a set of equations $\mathcal{E}$ in such a way that $\mathcal{R}$ is terminating and confluent "modulo $\mathcal{E}$". Many common examples fall into this category. Some important cases were treated by Hullot [53], while a general answer is given in [54], generalizing Theorem 2 by showing that if there is a finite $\mathcal{E}$-unification

---

[22]The reader may find it helpful to construe this symbol as a formal equality symbol.

algorithm, then narrowing modulo $\mathcal{E}$ still provides a complete $T = \mathcal{R} \cup \mathcal{E}$-unification algorithm. The idea, in this case, is to have part of the T-unification work done by a built-in $\mathcal{E}$-unification algorithm, and the rest by $\mathcal{E}$-narrowing. Both [53] and [54] give sufficient conditions for termination of their algorithms.

Now a simple example showing how a query involving an equation is evaluated by narrowing; for illustrative purposes, this example does not use the built-in natural number type, but rather provides its own, of sort Nat1, with successor function succ; also, notice there is no nil list here.

```
module LIST[ELT :: TRIV] is
  sorts Elt, List, Nat1
  subsorts Elt < List
  fns
    0 : Nat1
    succ : Nat1 -> Nat1
    _*_ : List,Elt -> List
    length : List -> Nat1
  vars Elm : Elt, Lst : List
  axioms
    length(Elm) = succ(0).
    length(Lst * Elm) = succ(length(Lst)).
endmod LIST
```

The sort Elt is a parameter, and is empty in the Herbrand universe; however this causes no problem if a suitable modification of the rules of deduction is used (see [35] for the equational case). Figure 2 shows how the query

eval length(Lst') = succ(succ(succ(0))).

evaluates to

as List: length((Elm″ * Elm') * Elm) = succ(succ(succ(0)))

by accumulating the substitutions associated with the narrowings from the root length(Lst') to the expression succ(succ(succ(0))).

Let us follow this in more detail. First of all, since the term succ(succ(succ(0))) is a canonical form ground term, it cannot be narrowed any further. Thus the narrowings of τ(length(Lst'),succ(succ(succ(0))))

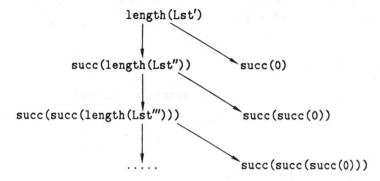

Figure 2: Narrowing on the Length Function

are exactly those of the subterm length(Lst'). The term length(Lst') unifies with the left hand side length(Elm) by the substitution

α_1(Lst') = Elm

giving the narrowing

length(Lst') $\Rightarrow$ succ(0)

which is a failure node since succ(0) cannot be narrowed any further and does not unify with succ(succ(succ(0))). The term length(Lst') also unifies with the left hand side length(Lst * Elm) by the substitution

β_1(Lst') = (Lst" * Elm) ,
β_1(Lst) = Lst"

giving the narrowing

length(Lst') $\Rightarrow$ succ(length(Lst")) .

In the same way we get a narrowing

succ(length(Lst")) $\Rightarrow$ succ(succ(0))

leading to another failure node, and a narrowing

succ(length(Lst")) $\Rightarrow$ succ(succ(length(Lst'")))

with substitution

345

$$\beta_2(\text{Lst}'') = (\text{Lst}''' * \text{Elm}'),$$
$$\beta_2(\text{Elm}) = \text{Elm}', \quad \beta_2(\text{Lst}) = \text{Lst}''' .$$

One more step of narrowing

$$\text{succ}(\text{succ}(\text{length}(\text{Lst}'''))) \Rightarrow \text{succ}(\text{succ}(\text{succ}(0)))$$

gives a success node with substitution

$$\alpha_3(\text{Lst}''') = \text{Elm}'' .$$

The corresponding unifier is the substitution

$$\gamma = \alpha_3 \circ \beta_2 \circ \beta_1$$

which finally gives the solution

$$\text{length}((\text{Elm}'' * \text{Elm}') * \text{Elm}) = \text{succ}(\text{succ}(\text{succ}(0))) .$$

Now that we have discussed narrowing, let us return to the question of sufficient conditions for completeness of our Eqlog evaluation algorithm. Recall that we need to call the function SOLN in order to get the unifications needed by the Prolog-like part of the evaluation algorithm, and that we propose to use narrowing to implement SOLN for user defined modules. However, if there are equations that are conditioned by predicates, then we will need to use Prolog-like evaluation just to see whether or not we can apply such equations during the narrowing process. Thus, in order for SOLN to do narrowing on a term t by means of the equation

$$t_1 = t_2 :- P_1, \ldots, P_n.$$

the goals $\sigma(P_1), \ldots, \sigma(P_n)$ have to be solved (where σ is the substitution unifying t_1 with a subterm of t), and this will yield another substitution σ'. It seems clear that the standard proof of correctness for the standard Prolog evaluation algorithm will genealize to the case where the set of clauses having equations as their heads is confluent and terminating as a set of rewrite rules. The only difficulty is in verifying confluence; however, recent rapid progress in this area gives grounds for optimism, and in any case, the problem is not worse than that of avoiding non-termination in standard Prolog, since the programmer is likely to have a good intuition about what he writes.

346

7.4 Equality and Disequality

The use of negation for arbitrary predicates gives rise to difficulties. However, perhaps surprisingly, it is not so difficult to treat the negation of equality, which we will call **disequality**. For example, the BASICSET module of Section 6 contains the axiom

{ Elt } ∩ { Elt' } = ∅ :- Elt ≠ Elt'

which appears to lie outside the realm of Horn clause logic with equality. However, this is only an appearance, because the semantics of disequality can be reduced to that of equality. The equational part of any Eqlog module should define a **computable** abstract data type. This is implicit in our requirement that the equations form a confluent and terminating set of rewrite rules (perhaps modulo some decidable equations such as associativity, commutativity, etc.) since it has been shown that any computable data type can be presented that way [4, 67]. Equality and disequality of ground terms is then built in, since one can just compute the canonical forms of the terms in question and see whether or not they are equal. Moreover, as shown in [67], a data type is computable if and only if its equality is finitely axiomatizable by confluent and terminating equations. This means that we can always axiomatize equality for each sort s as a function _≡_ : s,s -> Bool, by means of a finite set of equations. Bool is a new sort having two constants, true and false, such that for any two ground terms t,t' we have:

- t=t' (in the data type) iff (t≡t')=true (in the equational equality enrichment); and similarly,
- t ≠t' (in the data type) iff (t≡t')=false (in the equational equality enrichment).

In this way, disequality is reduced to equality.

Given a disequality t≠t', the Eqlog system will then:

1. compute it by rewriting if both t and t' are ground terms; and
2. otherwise, requiring the existence of an equationally defined equality, ≡, for the sort in question, translate the disequality into the equation

t≡t' = false ,

and then solve this equation by using narrowing.

8 Some Applications

This section discusses some applications of Eqlog, showing the power of generic modules, subsorts, functions and predicates, overloading, and of course narrowing. The first subsection gives a complete solution to the famous Missionaries and Cannibals problem. The second subsection is a "prospectus," arguing that techniques like those provided by Eqlog should be very useful for natural language processing.

8.1 The Missionaries and Cannibals Problem

This subsection shows how some standard generics (which of course would be taken from the Eqlog library), plus subsorts, functions and predicates, solve a general Missionaries and Cannibals problem (hereafter, MAC); once the parameters are instantiated, Eqlog solves MAC by $\mathcal{E}$-narrowing, for $\mathcal{E}$ a set of equations including associativity and commutativity for the set functions.

We begin with a theory MACTH of the preconditions for MAC: there are two disjoint sets of persons, m0 of missionaries and c0 of cannibals. Later we instantiate MACTH to the usual case of three missionaries and three cannibals. MACTH uses a generic SET module to get set difference, union, and cardinality. By convention, a module with a "principal" sort has the same name as that sort (unless explicitly indicated otherwise); e.g., the sort of PSET is Pset.

```
theory MACTH[PERSON :: TRIV] is
   using SET, PSET = SET[PERSON]
   fns
      m0 : Pset
      c0 : Pset
   axioms
      m0 ∩ c0 = ∅.
endth MACTH
```

The MAC module also uses a generic LIST module that provides the empty list nil, the length function #, and concatenation *. The new sort Trip is introduced "on the fly" (see Section 6) in the submodule TRIPLIST.

We now briefly discuss the intuition behind this specification. A solution is

348

a list of trips having certain "good" properties, where a trip is a boat containing a set of persons; odd numbered trips go from the left bank to the right, and even trips go from the right to the left. Missionaries and cannibals are persons. The predicate boatok indicates that a boat has an ok number of persons; the predicate good is true if a list of trips never allows there to be more cannibals than missionaries on a bank; the predicate solve indicates that a trip list is a solution to the problem. The functions lb and rb give the sets of persons on the left and right banks, respectively, and the functions mset and cset extract the subsets of missionaries and cannibals (respectively) from a set of persons.

```
module MAC[T :: MACTH] is
  using NAT, TRIPLIST = LIST[Trip]
  preds
    boatok : Trip
    solve,good : Triplist
  fns
    boat : Pset -> Trip
    lb,rb : Triplist -> Pset
    mset,cset : Pset -> Pset
  vars PS : Pset, L : Triplist, P : Person, T : Trip
  axioms
    boatok(boat(PS)) :- # PS = 1.
    boatok(boat(PS)) :- # PS = 2.
    lb(nil) = m0 ∪c0.
    mset(PS) = PS ∩ m0.
    cset(PS) = PS ∩ c0.
    rb(nil) = ∅.
    lb(L * boat(PS)) = lb(L) - PS :- even # L.
    rb(L * boat(PS)) = rb(L) ∪ PS :- even # L.
    rb(L * boat(PS)) = rb(L) - PS :- odd # L.
    lb(L * boat(PS)) = lb(L) ∪ PS :- odd # L.
    good(L * T) :-
      # cset(lb(L * T)) =< # mset(lb(L * T)),
      # cset(rb(L * T)) =< # mset(rb(L * T)),
      good(L), boatok(T).
    good(nil).
    solve(L) :- good(L), lb(L) = ∅.
endmod MAC
```

Now the constants to instantiate MAC to the usual case.

```
module EX1 using SET[ID] is
  axioms
    m0 = { taylor, helen, william }.
    c0 = { umugu, nzwawe, amoc }.
endmodule EX1
```

The notation {a, b, c} is shorthand for { a } ∪ { b } ∪ { c }. We can now instantiate MAC and ask Eqlog to solve the resulting problem with

```
make MAC[EX1] endmake
eval solve(L).
```

using the default view of EX1 as MACTH, and not bothering to give the resulting module a name.

Of course, what we have written will produce a crude depth first search by ℰ-narrowing, and the program should be annotated with some form of control information to make this more efficient (we do not consider this problem in this paper, but argue that it should yield to solutions like those currently being developed for Prolog).

8.2 Applications to Natural Language Processing

This subsection argues that features like those provided by Eqlog should be very useful for applications to natural language processing. We do not try to develop the theme in detail, but only to show the particular relevance of narrowing and subsorts. Some familiarity with computational linguistics will probably be needed.

Logic programming provides very convenient ways to describe both the syntax and semantics of natural language. For example, in Prolog we can easily write things like

```
sentence(s(NP,VP),S0,S) :- noun-phrase(NP,N,S0,S1),
    verb-phrase(VP,N,S1,S).
```

to say that a sentence (as a string of symbols running from S0 to S) may consist of a noun phrase NP (from S0 to S1) and a verb phrase NP (from S1 to S), each having "number" N (i.e., both NP and VP must be "singular", or both must be "plural").

There is much good work in this area, e.g. [12, 70, 15]; in particular, Definite Clause Grammar [71] provides a good notation in which, for example, the above would be written simply as

```
sentence(s(NP,VP)) → noun-phrase(NP,N), verb-phrase(VP,N).
```

We will now indicate how a language like Eqlog can do this kind of thing even more naturally. First, we define a "yield" function

y: **Parses** → **Sentences**

which, given a parse, returns the sentence, which will just be the frontier of the parse tree. Then we can express the parsing problem as follows: given a sentence S, we want a parse P such that

```
y(P) = S .
```

This is, of course, a simple example showing that functional notation can be a bit simpler and more natural; but what makes this formulation particularly nice is that narrowing can automatically solve the above equation for the parse P, given S and equations and clauses that define Fy. Moreover, the approach generalizes in a natural way to "interpretations", which we take to be parse trees annotated with additional information, such as number; for example,

```
y(sent(NP, VP, Number)) = NP VP if #(NP) = #(VP) = Number .
```

expresses the Prolog clause that we started with above.

However, we can do an even better job of this using subsorts. For example, if we have the following

```
sorts Sent, Parse
subsorts
    N ≤ NP
    MassN, FemN, NeuN ≤ N
    SingN, PlN ≤ N
    V ≤ VP
    SingV, PlV ≤ V
fns
    sent : SingN, SingV → Parse
    sent : PlN, PlV → Parse
```

```
        y : Parse → Sent
      axioms
        y(sent(NP,VP)) = NP VP .
```

Now we can solve things like

```
      y(sent(NP,VP)) = John runs.
```

and get the parse together with the number information. Notice that we no longer have number as a indexical; instead, it has been absorbed into the type structure.

For another example, we can solve

```
      y(sent(NP,VP)) = Boys run.
```

and get the right result, but

```
      y(sent(NP,VP)) = John run.
```

will fail, as desired.

This approach can be further extended into semantics. In fact, we have already demonstrated, using OBJ, that one can write axioms for a programming language and then automatically get an interpreter for it [39]; We can even get a theorem proving capability for that language, e.g., using REVE (see [25]). The technique of partial interpretation could be used to make this a very efficient interpreter; or one could use it to make particular programs efficient. It seems clear that similar things can be done for natural language semantics.

9 Future Research and Conclusions

There is some interesting recent work that can be viewed as providing ways to reduce all logic programming to equational logic. For example, Dershowitz [17] encodes predicates as boolean-valued fuctions and turns queries into equations of the form

```
      t(x₁, ... ,xₙ) = true
```
$$t(x_1, \ldots, x_n) = true$$

that are solved by a method essentially equivalent to narrowing. Of course

Eqlog can do that too, but we adopt a different philosophy. Rather than trying to encode all functions as predicates or all predicates as functions, Eqlog provides queries for predicates, solutions for equations, and evaluation for terms, as different options within a unified framework, in the conviction that both programmer's intuition and efficiency considerations will, for each particular problem, make some combinations of options preferable and more natural than others. The current state of the art seems to be that some experimentation is needed to determine which of the various available options are best for various kinds of problem; relevant measures are efficiency, control mechanisms, expressiveness, understandability, etc. We prefer to have a language in which all options are available, since this will support the necessary experimentation.

The work of Hsiang [51] is also of great potential interest, since it provides an entirely algebraic paradigm for theorem proving by means of rewrite rules (also encoding predicates as boolean valued functions, and doing unification modulo the boolean equations). However, his present approach does not provide an explicit way to get the substitution that answers a query; rather, a refutation is proved by completing associated rewrite rules until true → false is generated. Another approach for dealing with the full power of first order predicate calculus is presented by Stickel [84]. It would be very interesting to explore how these three approaches might be combined with that presented in this paper.

Most of the language features that we have presented for Eqlog have already been implemented in Prolog, OBJ or Clear, and quite recently there have been some experiments with the mechanism that joins the predicate logic and equational logic features, namely narrowing, for example by Fribourg [24]. This is something that we very much wish to do in the near future. In fact, once unification and term rewriting are available, it is very little extra effort to provide narrowing, since it is just a combination of these two. Most of the work would actually lie in implementing solution algorithms for the built-in types, including good incremental implementations of built-in unification algorithms for frequently used theories. This will enable us to explore the important open question of the efficiency of narrowing. Clearly, narrowing can be very inefficient for some cases, and very efficient for others. Therefore it would be very useful to have simple and general sufficient conditions (on the form of ADT definitions) that would guarantee the effiency of narrowing.

The many advantages that have been claimed for logic programming, including simplicity, clarity, understandability, reusability and maintainability, are all seriously compromised to the extent that the logic used in the programming language is not pure. Thus, it is highly desirable to extend the logic in such a way as to encompass a greater range of programming language features. This paper has shown how many-sorted logic supports strong typing and, with a little extra effort, subsorts. We also show how some results from the theory of institutions support very powerful features for programming with generic modules, including instantiation with views. Moreover, we have shown how Hsiang's [51] axiomatization of Boolean algebra provides a convenient implementation of finite (and cofinite) set theory that supports narrowing. Finally, we have provided a number of examples showing the power of the various language features, including a very simple program for the Missionaries and Cannibals problem.

It is worth emphasizing certain fundamental points. Eqlog combines pure predicate logic programming with first order functional programming; that is, predicates are predicates, functions are functions, and the programmer does not have to encode either one in terms of the other. However, Eqlog is based on the logic of Horn clauses (with equality), rather than the full first order predicate calculus (with equality). This means that any set of clauses has a unique (up to isomorphism) standard (i.e., initial) model in which there is "no junk" (i.e., all its elements are namable) and "no confusion" (i.e., a predicate holds iff it is provable from the given clauses, and in particular, two terms are equal iff that is provable). This amounts to a Closed World assumption [11]. Eqlog also supports arbitrary user definable generic modules, including abstract data types. Finally, we wish to emphasize that narrowing seems to provide a very elegant unification of relational logic and functional programming.

We have taken very seriously the idea that *pure* logic programming has many advantanges, and that these advantages are diminished to the extent that purity is compromised. Consequently, we have designed Eqlog as a pure logic programming language, based upon first order Horn clause logic with equality. However, we have attempted to provide as much programming power as possible within this framework, and although many interesting problems remain, we believe that we have succeeded in eliminating the need for *ad hoc* mechanisms to force evaluation of built-in functions (such as Prolog's is), in providing user-definable generic modules, and in providing powerful facilities for handling partial functions, errors and exceptions with the subsort mechanism.

Acknowledgements

We extend our most sincere thanks to Jean-Pierre Jouannaud and Fernando Pereira for their extensive comments on this paper, and for their help and encouragement while it was being imagined and then constructed. The research reported here was supported in part by Office of Naval Research Contract No. N00014-82-C-0333, by National Science Foundation Grant No. MCS8201380, and by a gift from the System Development Foundation; this paper is a substantially expanded revision of [37].

References

1. Apt, K. R. and van Emden, M. H. "Contributions to the Theory of Logic Programming." *Journal of the ACM 29*, 3 (1982), 841-862.

2. Backus, J. "Can Programming be Liberated from the von Neumann Style?" *CACM 21*, 8 (1978), 613-641.

3. Bellia, M., Degano, P. and Levi, G. The Call by Name Semantics of a Clause Language with Functions. In *Logic Programming*, Clark, K.L. and Tarnlund, S.-A., Eds., Academic Press, 1982, pp. 281-295.

4. Bergstra, J. A., and Tucker, J. V. A Characterization of Computable Data Types by Means of a Finite Equational Specification Method. In *Automata, Languages and Programming, Seventh Colloquium*, J. W. de Bakker and J. van Leeuwen, Eds., Springer-Verlag, 1980, pp. 76-90.

5. Berry, G. and Currien, P. L. The Applicative Language CDS: its Denotational and Operational Semantics. In *Algebraic Methods in Semantics*, M. Nivat and J. Reynolds, Eds., Cambridge University Press, 1984.

6. Broy, M. and Wirsing, M. "Partial Abstract Types." *Acta Informatica* *18* (1982), 47-64.

7. Burstall, R. M. and Goguen, J. A. "Putting Theories together to Make Specifications." *Proceedings, Fifth International Joint Conference on Artificial Intelligence 5* (1977), 1045-1058.

8. Burstall, R. M., and Goguen, J. A. The Semantics of Clear, a Specification Language. In *Proceedings of the 1979 Copenhagen Winter School on Abstract Software Specification*, Springer-Verlag, 1980, pp. 292-332.

9. Burstall, R. M. and Goguen, J. A. Algebras, Theories and Freeness: An Introduction for Computer Scientists. In *Proceedings, 1981 Marktoberdorf NATO Summer School*, Reidel, 1982.

10. Byrd, L., Pereira, F. and Warren, D. A Guide to Version 3 of DEC-10 Prolog. DAI Occasional Paper 19, University of Edinburgh, Department of Artificial Intelligence,1980.

11. Clark, K. L. Negation as Failure. In *Logic in Data Bases*, H. Gallaire and J. Minker, Eds., Plenum Press, 1978, pp. 293-322.

12. Colmerauer, A. Metamorphisis Grammars. In *Natural Language Communication with Computers*, L. Bolc, Ed.,Springer-Verlag, 1978.

13. Colmerauer, A., Kanoui, H. and van Caneghem, M. Etude et Realisation d'un Systeme Prolog. Groupe d'Intelligence Artificielle, U.E.R. de Luminy, Universite d'Aix-Marseille II,1979.

14. Cunningham, R. J. and Dick, A. J. J. Rewrite Systems on a Lattice of Types. Imperial College, Department of Computing,1983.

15. Dahl, V. Un Systeme Deductif d'Interrogation de Banques de Donnees en Espagnol. These de 3eme, Universite d'Aix-Marseille II, Faculte de Sciences de Luminy.

16. Davis, M, Matijasevic, Y. V. and Robinson, J. Hilbert's Tenth Problem: Diophantine Equations: Positive Aspects of a Negative Solution. In *Mathematical Developments Arising from Hilbert Problems*, AMS, 1976, pp. 323-378.

17. Dershowitz, N. Computing with Rewrite Rules. ATR-83(8478)-1, The Aerospace Corp.,1983.

18. United States Department of Defense. Reference Manual for the Ada Programming Language. ANSI/MIL-STD-1815 A.

19. Domolki, B. and Szeredi, P. Prolog in Practice. In *Information Processing 83*, Mason, R. E. A., Ed.,Elsevier, 1983, pp. 627-636.

20. Engels, G., pletat, U. and ehrich, H.-D. Handling Errors and Exceptions in the Algebraic Specification of Abstract Data Types. Heft 3, Reihe Informatik, Fachbereich Mathematik, Universitat Osnabruck,1981.

21. Fages, F. Associative Commutative Unification. These de 3eme Cycle; to appear in *Proceedings*, 1984 Conference on Automatic Deduction.

22. Fages, F. and Huet, G. Unification and Matching in Equational Theories. In *Proceedings, Fifth Conference on Trees, Algebra and Programming*, Springer-Verlag, 1983.

23. Fay, M. "First-order Unification in an Equational Theory." *Proceedings, Fourth Workshop on Automated Deduction 4* (February 1979), 161-167.

24. Fribourg, L. Handling Function Definitions through Innermost Superposition and Rewriting. 84-69, Institut de Programmation, Université Paris 7,Decembre, 1984.

25. Futatsugi, K., Goguen, J., Jouannaud, J.-P., and Meseguer, J. Principles of OBJ2. In *Proceedings, 1985 Symposium on Principles of Programming Languages*, ACM, 1985, pp. 52-66.

26. Gabriel, P. and Ulmer, F.. *Lokal Präsentierbare Kategorien*. Springer-Verlag, 1971. Springer Lecture Notes in Mathematics, vol. 221.

27. Gogolla, M. Algebraic Specifications with Partially Ordered Sorts and Declarations. 169, Universitat Dortmund, Abteilung Informatik,1983.

28. Gogolla, M. and Drosten, K. and Lipeck, U. and Ehrich, H.D. Algebraic and Operational Semantics of Specifications Allowing Exceptions and Errors. In *Proceedings, 6th GI Conference on Theoretical Computer Science*, Springer-Verlag Lecture Notes in Computer Science, Volume 145, 1983, pp. 141-151.

29. Goguen, J. A. Semantics of Computation. In *Proceedings, First International Symposium on Category Theory Applied to Computation and Control*, University of Massachusetts at Amherst, 1974, pp. 234-249.

30. Goguen, J. A. Abstract Errors for Abstract Data Types. In *IFIP Working Conference on Formal Description of Programming Concepts*, MIT, 1977, pp. 21.1-21.32.

31. Goguen, J. A. Order Sorted Algebra. UCLA Computer Science Department,1978.Semantics and Theory of Computation Report No. 14.

32. Goguen, J. A. "Parameterized Programming." *Transactions on Software Engineering SE-10*, 5 (September 1984), 528-543.Originally appeared, *Proceedings, Workshop on Reusability in Programming*, edited by Biggerstaff, T. and Cheatham, T., ITT, pages 138-150, 1983; also, revised version as Technical Report CSLI-84-9, Center for the Study of Language and Information, Stanford University, September 1984.

33. Goguen, J. A. LIL: A Library Interconnection Language for Ada. SRI International,1984.Prepared for Ada Joint Program Office.

34. Goguen, J. A. and Burstall, R. M. Introducing Institutions. In *Proceedings, Logics of Programming Workshop*, E. Clarke and D. Kozen, Ed.,Springer-Verlag, 1984, pp. 221-256.

35. Goguen, J. A. and Meseguer, J. "Completeness of Many-sorted Equational Logic." *SIGPLAN Notices 16*, 7 (July 1981), 24-32.Also appeared in *SIGPLAN Notices*, January 1982, vol. 17, no. 1, pages 9-17; extended version as SRI Technical Report CSL-135, May 1982; final version as Technical Report CSLI-84-15, Center for the Study of Language and Information, Stanford University, September 1984, and to be published in *Houston Journal of Mathematics*.

36. Goguen, J. A. and Meseguer, J. Universal Realization, Persistent Interconnection and Implementation of Abstract Modules. In *Proceedings, 9th ICALP*, Springer-Verlag, 1982.

37. Goguen, J. and Meseguer, J. "Equality, Types, Modules and (Why Not?) Generics for Logic Programming." *The Journal of Logic Programming 1*, 2 (1984), 179-210.Also appears in *Proceedings, 1984 Logic Programming Symposium*, Upsala, Sweden, pp. 115-125; and Report CSLI-84-5, Center for the Study of Language and Information, Stanford University, March 1984.

38. Goguen, J. and Meseguer, J. Order-Sorted Algebra I: Partial and Overloaded Operations, Errors and Inheritance. To appear, SRI International, Computer Science Lab,1985.Given as lecture at Seminar on Types, Carnegie-Mellon University, June 1983.

39. Goguen, J. A. and Parsaye-Ghomi, K. Algebraic Denotational Semantics using Parameterized Abstract Modules. In *Formalizing Programming Concepts*, J. Diaz and I. Ramos, Eds., Springer-Verlag, Peniscola, Spain, 1981, pp. 292-309.

40. Goguen, J. A. and Tardo, J. An Introduction to OBJ: A Language for Writing and Testing Software Specifications. In *Specification of Reliable Software*, IEEE Press, 1979, pp. 170-189.

41. Goguen, J., Jouannaud, J.-P. and Meseguer, J. Operational Semantics of Order-Sorted Algebra. In *Proceedings, 1985 International Conference on Automata, Computation and Programming*, Springer-Verlag, 1985.

42. Goguen, J. A., Meseguer, J., and Plaisted, D. Programming with Parameterized Abtract Objects in OBJ. In *Theory and Practice of Software Technology*, D. Ferrari, M. Bolognani and J. Goguen, Eds., North-Holland, 1983, pp. 163-193.

43. Goguen, J. A., Thatcher, J. W. and Wagner, E. An Initial Algebra Approach to the Specification, Correctness and Implementation of Abstract Data Types. RC 6487, IBM T. J. Watson Research Center,October, 1976.Reprinted in *Current Trends in Programming Methodology, IV*, ed. R. Yeh, Prentice-Hall, 1978, pp. 80-149.

44. Goguen, J. A. , Thatcher, J. W., Wagner, E. and Wright, J. B. "Initial Algebra Semantics and Continuous Algebras." *Journal of the Association for Computing Machinery 24*, 1 (January 1977).

45. Guiho, G. Multioperator Algebras. In *Proceedings, 2nd Workshop on Theory and Applications of Abstract Data Types*, Universitat Passau, Germany, 1983.

46. Guttag, J. "Notes on Type Abstraction." *IEEE Transactions Software Engineering SE-5* (1980), 13-23.

47. Guttag, J., Horowitz, E., and Musser, D. "Some Extensions to Algebraic Specifications." *SIGPLAN Notices 12*, 3 (March 1977), 63-67.

48. Hansson, A., Haridi, S. and Tarnlund, S.-A. Properties of a Logic Programming Language. In *Logic Programming*, Clark, K.L. and Tarnlund, S.-A., Eds., Academic Press, 1982, pp. 267-280.

49. Herbrand, J. "Recherches sour la Theorie de la Demonstration." *Travaux de la Soc. des Sciences et des Lettres de Varsovie, Classe III 33*, 128 (1930).

50. Hoffman, C. M. and O'Donnell, M. J. "Programming with Equations." *ACM Transactions on Programming Languages and Systems 1*, 4 (1982), 83-112.

51. Hsiang, J. Refutational Theorem Proving using Term Rewriting Systems. Ph.D. Thesis, Univeristy of Illinois at Champaign-Urbana.

52. Huet, G. and Oppen, D. Equations and Rewrite Rules: A Survey. In *Formal Language Theory: Perspectives and Open Problems*, R. Book., Ed.,Academic Press, 1980.

53. Hullot, J.-M. Canonical Forms and Unification. In *Proceedings, 5th Conference on Automated Deduction*, W. Bibel and R. Kowalski, Eds., Springer-Verlag, Lecture Notes in Computer Science, Volume 87, 1980, pp. 318-334.

54. Jouannaud, J.-P., Kirchner, C., Kirchner, H. Incremental Construction of Unification Algorithms in Equational Theories. Automata, Languages and Programming, Barcelona, 1983., 1983, pp. 361-373.

55. Kamin, S. and Archer, M. Partial Implementations of Abstract Data Types: A Dissenting View on Errors. In *Semantics of Data Types*, G. Kahn, D. MacQueen and G. Plotkin, Eds., Springer-Verlag, 1984, pp. 317-336.

56. Kaplan, S. Fair Conditional Term Rewriting Systems: Unification, Termination and Confluence. 194, Universite de Paris-Sud, Centre d'Orsay, Lab. de Recherche en Informatique,Novembre, 1984.

57. Kornfeld, W. A. "Equality for Prolog." *Proceedings, Seventh International Joint Conference on Artificial Intelligence 7* (1983), 514-519.

58. Kowalski, R. Logic for Problem Solving. DCL Memo 75, Department of Artificial Intelligence, University of Edinburgh,1974.

59. Liskov, B. H., Moss, E., Schaffert, C., Scheifler, B., and Snyder, A. CLU Reference Manual. MIT, Lab for Computer Science,1979.

60. Mahr, B. and Makowsky, J. A. An Axiomatic Approach to Semantics of Specification Languages. In *Proceedings, 6th GI Conference on Theoretical Computer Science*, Springer-Verlag, 1983.

61. Mahr, B. and Makowsky, J. A. "Characterizing Specification Languages which Admit Initial Semantics." *Theoretical Computer Science 31* (1984), 49-60.

62. Majster, M. E. Treatment of Partial Operations in the Algebraic Specification Technique. In *Specification of Reliable Software*, IEEE Press, 1979, pp. 190-197.

63. Makowsky, J. A. Why Horn Formulas Matterin Computer Science: Initial Structures and Generic Examples. Department of Computer Science, Technion, Haifa, Israel, 1985.

64. Malachi, Y., Manna, Z. and Waldinger, R. TABLOG: The Deductive-Tableau Programming Language. Technical Note 328, SRI International, Artificial Intelligence Center, 1984.

65. Matijasevic, Y. V. Diophantine Representation of Recursively Enumerable Predicates. In *Proceedings, Second Scandinavian Logic Symposium*, North-Holland, 1971, pp. 171-177.

66. McCarthy, J. "Circumscription - A Form of Non-Monotonic Reasoning." *Artificial Intelligence 13*, 1,2 (1980), 27-39.

67. Meseguer, J. and Goguen, J. A. Initiality, Induction and Computability. In *Algebraic Methods in Semantics*, M. Nivat and J. Reynolds, Eds., Cambridge University Press, 1985, pp. 459-540.

68. O'Donnell, M. J.. *Lecture Notes in Computer Science*. Volume 58: *Computing in Systems Described by Equations*. Springer-Verlag, 1977.

69. O'Donnell, M. J. "A Critique of the Foundations of Hoare-style Programming Logic." *Communications of the ACM 25*, 12 (1982), 927-934.

70. Pereira, F. Logic for Natural Language Analysis. Technical Note 275, Artificial Intelligence Center, SRI International,1983.

71. Pereira, F. and Warren, D. F. D. "Definite Clause Grammars for Language Analysis - A Survey of the Formalism and a Comparison with Augmented Transition Networks." *Artificial Intelligence 13* (1980), 231-278.

72. Plaisted, D. An Initial Algebra Semantics for Error Presentations. SRI International

73. Plaisted, D. Semantic Confluence Tests and Completion Methods. manuscript.

74. Plotkin, G. "Building-in Equational Theories." *Machine Intelligence 7* (November 1972), 73-90.

75. Reichel, H. "Initially Restricting Algebraic Theories." *Springer Lecture Notes in Computer Science 88* (1980), 504-514.Mathematical Foundations of Computer Science

76. Remy, J. L. *Etude des Systemes de Reecriture Conditionnels et Application aux Types Abstraits Algebriques.* Ph.D. Th., Centre de Recherche en Informatique de Nancy,1982.

77. Robinson, J. A. "A Machine-oriented Logic Based on the Resolution Principle." *Journal of the Association for Computing Machinery 12* (1965).

78. Robinson, J. A. and Sibert, E. E. LOGLISP: Motivation, Design and Implementation. In *Logic Programming*, Clark, K. L. and Tarnlund, S.-A., Ed.,Academic Press, 1982, pp. 299-314.

79. Robinson, G. and Wos, L. T. Paramodulation and First Order Theorem Proving with Equality. In *Machine Intelligence*, Meltzer, B. and Michie, D., Eds., Edinburgh University Press, 1969, pp. 135-150.

80. Sato, M. Qute: A Functional Language Based on Unification. 84-09, University of Tokyo,September, 1984.

81. Shapiro, U. A Subset of Concurrent Prolog and its Interpreter. Weizmann Institute of Science,1983.

82. Shapiro, E. Systems Programming in Concurrent Prolog. In *Proceedings, Symposium on Principles of Programming Languages*, ACM, 1984, pp. 93-105.

83. Slagle, J. R. "Automated Theorem-Proving for Theories with Simplifiers, Commutativity, and Associativity." *Journal of the ACM 21*, 4 (October 1974), 662-642.

84. Stickel, M. A Prolog Technology Theorem Prover. In *International Symposium on Logic Programming*, ACM, 1984.

85. Subrahmanyam, P. A. and You, J.-H. Pattern Driven Lazy Reduction: a Unifying Evaluation Mechanism for Functional and Logic Programs. In *Proceedings, Symposium on Principles of Programming Langagues*, ACM, 1984, pp. 228-234.

86. Tarlecki, A. Abstract Algebraic Institutions which Strongly Admit Initial Semantics. CSR-165-84, University of Edinburgh, Computer Science Department,1984.

87. van der Waerden, B.L.. *Moderne Algebra, 1.* Julius Springer, 1930. First edition.

88. van Emden, M. H. and Kowalski, R. A. "The Semantics of Predicate Logic as a Programming Language." *Journal of the Association for Computing Machinery 23*, 4 (1976), 733-742.

89. Wadge, W. Classified Algebras. Report Number 46, University of Warwick,October, 1982.

90. Walther, C. A Many-sorted Calculus Based on Resolution and Paramodulation. In *Eighth International Joint Conference on Artificial Intelligence*, W. Kaufman (Los Altos CA), 1983, pp. 882-891.

91. Warren, D. "Logic Programming and Compiler Writing." *Software - Practice and Experience 10* (1980), 97-125.

TABLOG:
A NEW APPROACH
TO LOGIC PROGRAMMING

Yonathan Malachi
Zohar Manna

Computer Science Department
Stanford University
Stanford, California 94305

Richard Waldinger

Artificial Intelligence Center
SRI International
Menlo Park, California 94025

ABSTRACT

TABLOG [12] is a programming language based on first-order predicate logic with equality that combines relational and functional programming. In addition to featuring both the advantages of functional notation and the power of unification as a binding mechanism, TABLOG also supports a more general subset of standard first-order logic than PROLOG and most other logic-programming languages.

The Manna-Waldinger *deductive-tableau* [13,14] proof system is employed as an interpreter for TABLOG in the same way that PROLOG uses a resolution proof system. Unification is used by TABLOG to match a query with a line in the program and to bind arguments. The basic rules of deduction used for computing are a nonclausal resolution rule that generalizes classical resolution to arbitrary first-order sentences and an equality rule that is a generalization of narrowing and paramodulation.

This is a substantially revised version of the paper "TABLOG: A New Approach to Logic Programming," by Y. Malachi and R. Waldinger appearing in *Proceedings of the Symposium on Lisp and Functional Programming,* 1984, pp. 323–30, © ACM, 1984.

In this article we describe the basic features of TABLOG and its (implemented) sequential interpreter, and we discuss some of its properties. We give examples to demonstrate when TABLOG is better than a functional language like LISP and when it is better than a relational language like PROLOG.

1 INTRODUCTION

Logic programming [8] attempts to improve programmer productivity by using predicate logic, a human-oriented language, as a programming language. PROLOG, the most widely known logic-programming language is based on a resolution proof system and has a restricted syntax. In TABLOG we take the view (shared by other works described in this volume) that logic programming is not to be regarded as synonymous with PROLOG.

A TABLOG program is a list of *assertions* in (quantifier-free) first-order logic with equality that allows one to mix freely functional and relational styles of programming. The use of this richer and more flexible syntax overcomes some of the shortcomings of PROLOG's syntax and makes programming in TABLOG a more intuitive process. For instance, many examples introduced in [15] as mathematical definitions of functions and predicates can be directly executed as TABLOG programs.

The procedural (proof theory) semantics of TABLOG is based on the *deductive-tableau* proof system [13,14]. This powerful proof system, which is described in Section 6, can be applied to arbitrary quantifier-free first-order sentences and therefore does not require the conversion of logic statements into a restricted special form (such as Horn clauses). The execution of a program corresponds to the proof of a *goal*, which produces the desired output(s) as a side effect. When the proof system is used as an interpreter for programs in the TABLOG language, the theorem prover is restrained. Since a particular algorithm is specified by the programmer and since the proof taking place is always a proof of a special case of a theorem—the case for the given input—the program interpreter does not need the full set of deduction rules available in the original deductive-tableau proof system. The theorem prover can thus

be more directed, efficient, and predictable than a theorem prover
used for program synthesis or for any other general-purpose deduction. When the theorem prover is restricted in order to get these
properties, we unfortunately lose the completeness that the general framework enjoys; this fact is briefly treated in the discussion
section at the end of the article.

We will first define the syntax of TABLOG and give its flavor
using a few simple examples. Before going into more details of
TABLOG we will contrast the language with PROLOG and LISP.
Later, after giving the proof-theory background in Section 6, we
will describe the semantics and execution of TABLOG programs.
We will close the article with a brief comparison to other works
and a general discussion of our approach. More detailed exposition
of TABLOG and its properties can be found in [11].

2 TABLOG SYNTAX

2.1 Syntactic Objects

TABLOG uses the language of the quantifier-free first-order
predicate logic with equality. The basic building blocks are:

- truth values: *true, false.*
- connectives: $\wedge$, $\vee$, $\neg$, $\equiv$, $\rightarrow$ (*implies*), $\leftarrow$ (*if*),
  if-then-else.
- variables such as u, v, x_1, y_{25}.
- constants such as a, b, $[\,]$, 5.
- predicates such as $=$, **prime**, $\in$, $\geq$.
- functions such as **gcd**, **append**, $+$.

We assume the standard definition in logic of *terms* and *formulas* (atomic and compound); an *expression* is either a term or
a formula. We do, however, extend these definitions by using the
if-then-else construct, both as a connective for formulas, e.g.,

$$\text{if } u = [\,] \text{ then } \mathbf{empty}(u) \text{ else } \mathbf{sorted}(u)$$

and as an operator generating terms, e.g.,

$$\mathbf{gcd}(x, y) = \text{if } x \geq y \text{ then } \mathbf{gcd}(x-y, y)$$
$$\text{else } \mathbf{gcd}(x, y-x).$$

In the rest of this article we use the term *logic* to refer to the quantifier-free first-order predicate logic extended as above, unless explicitly stated otherwise.

2.2 Programs

A program is a list of *assertions* (formulas in the language), specifying an algorithm. Variables are implicitly universally quantified.

Here is a very simple program, for appending two lists:

$$\textbf{append}([\,], v) \; = \; v.$$
$$\textbf{append}(x \circ u, v) \; = \; x \circ \textbf{append}(u, v).$$

The $\circ$ symbol denotes the list insertion operator (**cons** in LISP), $[\,]$ denotes the empty list (**nil** in LISP), and **append** is a function symbol whose semantics is defined by this program.

The inclusion in the syntax of the *if-then-else* construct together with $\leftarrow$ (reverse implication) enables the programmer to write LISP-style as well as PROLOG-style programs.

A call to a program is a *goal* (or query) to be proved. Like the assertions, goals are formulas in logic, but variables are implicitly quantified existentially. The bindings of these variables are recorded throughout the proof and become the outputs of the program upon termination.

For example, a call to the **append** program above might be

$$z \; = \; \textbf{append}([1, 2, 3], [3, 2]).$$

The result of the execution of this program call will be binding z to the output

$$[1, 2, 3, 3, 2].$$

The list construct e.g., $[1, 2, 3]$, is used for convenience in expressing input and output, and is actually an abbreviation for $1 \circ (2 \circ (3 \circ [\,]))$.

3 EXAMPLES

The following examples demonstrate a style of programming in TABLOG. The correctness of these programs does not depend on the order of assertions in the program. It is possible, however, to write programs that do take advantage of the known order of the interpreter's goal evaluation, as will be explained later.

In principle, most of the examples described in the other articles in this volume could be executed in TABLOG when written in the appropriate syntax. In particular any PROLOG program that does not use *cut* and does not depend on negation as failure can be trivially converted into an equivalent program directly executable by a TABLOG interpreter.

In the examples, we use x and y (possibly with subscripts) for variables intended to be assigned atoms (integers in most of the examples); u and v (possibly with subscripts) are variables used for lists.

Although we have not as yet described the semantics of TAB-LOG programs, these examples can be intuitively understood based on the standard meaning of predicate logic.

3.1 Deleting a List Element

The following program deletes all (top-level) occurrences of an element x from a list:

$$\textbf{delete}(x, [\,]) \;=\; [\,].$$
$$\textbf{delete}(x, y \circ u) \;=\; \big(\text{if } x = y \text{ then } \textbf{delete}(x, u)$$
$$\text{else } y \circ \textbf{delete}(x, u)\big).$$

This program demonstrates the use of equality, *if-then-else*, and recursive calls. If one does not like the explicit conditional *if-then-else*, the last equality assertion can be replaced by the two assertions:

$$\textbf{delete}(x, x \circ u) = \textbf{delete}(x, u).$$
$$x \neq y \;\rightarrow\; \textbf{delete}(x, y \circ u) = y \circ \textbf{delete}(x, u).$$

To remove all occurrences of a from the list $[a, b, a, c]$, the goal

$$z = \textbf{delete}(a, [a, b, a, c])$$

is given to the interpreter.

3.2 Quicksort

Here is a TABLOG program that uses the quicksort algorithm to sort a list of numbers. It combines a PROLOG-style relational subprogram for partitioning with a LISP-style functional subprogram for sorting.

1. $\mathbf{qsort}([\,]) = [\,]$.

2. $\mathbf{qsort}(x \circ u) = \mathbf{append}(\mathbf{qsort}(u_1), x \circ \mathbf{qsort}(u_2))$
   $\leftarrow \mathbf{partition}(x, u, u_1, u_2)$.

3. $\mathbf{partition}(x, [\,], [\,], [\,])$.

4. $\mathbf{partition}(x, y \circ u, y \circ u_1, u_2)$
   $\leftarrow y \leq x \,\wedge\, \mathbf{partition}(x, u, u_1, u_2)$.

5. $\mathbf{partition}(x, y \circ u, u_1, y \circ u_2)$
   $\leftarrow x < y \,\wedge\, \mathbf{partition}(x, u, u_1, u_2)$.

The assertions in lines 1 and 2 form the sorting subprogram. Line 1 asserts that the empty list is already sorted. Line 2 specifies that, to sort a list $x \circ u$, with head x and tail u, one should append the sorted version of two sublists of u, u_1 and u_2, and insert the element x between them; the subprogram **partition** generates these two sublists, u_1 and u_2, by collecting the elements of u less than or equal to x and greater than x, respectively.

The assertions in lines 3 to 5 specify how to partition a list according to a partitioning element x. Line 3 deals with the partitioning of the empty list, while lines 4 and 5 treat the case in which the list is of the form $y \circ u$. Line 4 is for the case in which y, the head of the list, is less than or equal to x; therefore, y should be inserted into the list u_1 of elements not greater than x. Line 5 is for the opposite case.

The **append** function for appending two lists was defined earlier.

4 COMPARISON WITH PROLOG

4.1 Functions and Equality

While PROLOG programs must be defined as relations, TABLOG programs can be either relations or functions. The availability of functions and equality makes it possible to write programs more naturally. The functional programming style frees the programmer from needing to introduce many auxiliary variables.

We can compare the PROLOG and TABLOG programs for quicksort. In TABLOG, the program uses the unary function **qsort** to produce a value, whereas a corresponding PROLOG program is defined as a binary relation **qsortp**, in which the second argument is needed to hold the output.

The second assertion in the TABLOG program is

$$\mathbf{qsort}(x \circ u) = \mathbf{append}(\mathbf{qsort}(u_1), x \circ \mathbf{qsort}(u_2))$$
$$\leftarrow \mathbf{partition}(x, u, u_1, u_2).$$

The corresponding clause in the PROLOG program would be something like

$$\mathbf{qsortp}(x \circ u, z) \leftarrow \mathbf{partition}(x, u, u_1, u_2) \wedge$$
$$\mathbf{qsortp}(u_1, z_1) \wedge$$
$$\mathbf{qsortp}(u_2, z_2) \wedge$$
$$\mathbf{appendp}(z_1, x \circ z_2, z).$$

The additional variables z_1 and z_2 are required to store the results of sorting u_1 and u_2. This demonstrates the advantage of having functions and equality in the language. Note that, although function symbols exist in PROLOG, they are used only for constructing data structures (like TABLOG's primitive functions) and are not reduced.

Since TABLOG includes all the features of (pure) PROLOG, logic-programming techniques like the *difference list* notation or multi-mode (backward) use of relational programs are immediately available in TABLOG.

Recently there have been attempts to add equality to PROLOG. Some of these proposals are described in section 8 on related research, while others are described in other articles in this volume.

4.2 Negation and Equivalence

In PROLOG, negation is not available directly; it is simulated by finite failure. To prove $not(P)$, PROLOG attempts to prove P; $not(P)$ succeeds if and only if the proof of P fails. In TABLOG, negation is treated like any other connective of logic. Therefore, we can directly solve queries such as $\neg\textbf{member}(1,[2,3])$.

The TABLOG **union** program uses both equivalence and negation:

$$\textbf{union}([\,],v) = v.$$

$$\textbf{union}(x \circ u, v) = \ \text{if } \textbf{member}(x,v)$$
$$\text{then } \textbf{union}(u,v)$$
$$\text{else } (x \circ \textbf{union}(u,v)).$$

$$\neg\textbf{member}(x,[\,]).$$

$$\textbf{member}(x, y \circ u) \equiv (x = y) \vee \textbf{member}(x,u).$$

Here is a possible PROLOG program of the same algorithm:

$$\textbf{unionp}(x \circ u, v, z) \leftarrow \textbf{memberp}(x,v) \wedge \textbf{unionp}(u,v,z).$$

$$\textbf{unionp}(x \circ u, v, x \circ z) \leftarrow \textbf{unionp}(u,v,z).$$

$$\textbf{unionp}([\,],v,v).$$

$$\textbf{memberp}(x, x \circ u).$$

$$\textbf{memberp}(x, y \circ u) \leftarrow \textbf{memberp}(x,u).$$

Changing the order of the first two clauses in the PROLOG program will result in an incorrect output; the second clause is correct only for the case in which x is not a member of v. The TABLOG assertions can be freely rearranged; this suggests that all of them can be matched against the current goal in parallel, if desired. If in the PROLOG example we add the condition $not(\textbf{memberp}(x,v))$ as the first conjunct in the body of the second clause, the program will become less order-sensitive but then in many cases $\textbf{memberp}(x,v)$ will be evaluated twice, once for the first clause and once for the second.

4.3 The Alpine Club Puzzle

The next example shows that some problems are very hard to encode (and solve) when we restrict ourselves to the language of Horn clauses. In addition to negation and equivalence this example also utilizes disjunction.

The following puzzle was the subject of discussion by a few contributors to the PROLOG (electronic) mailing list.

> Tony, Mike and John belong to the Alpine Club. Every member of the Alpine Club is either a skier or a mountain climber or both. No mountain climber likes rain, and all skiers like snow. Mike dislikes whatever Tony likes and likes whatever Tony dislikes. Tony likes rain and snow.

> Is there a member of the Alpine Club who is a mountain climber but not a skier?

One of the solutions in PROLOG was offered by R. O'Keefe:

$$\textbf{alpinist}(\text{Tony}).$$
$$\textbf{alpinist}(\text{Mike}).$$
$$\textbf{alpinist}(\text{John}).$$
$$\textbf{likes}(\text{Tony}, \text{rain}, \text{yes}).$$
$$\textbf{likes}(\text{Tony}, \text{snow}, \text{yes}).$$
$$\textbf{likes}(\text{Mike}, x, \text{yes}) \leftarrow \textbf{likes}(\text{Tony}, x, \text{no}).$$
$$\textbf{likes}(\text{Mike}, x, \text{no}) \leftarrow \textbf{likes}(\text{Tony}, x, \text{yes}).$$
$$\textbf{likes}(x, \text{rain}, \text{no}) \leftarrow \textbf{climber}(x).$$
$$\textbf{nonskier}(x) \leftarrow \textbf{likes}(x, \text{snow}, \text{no}).$$
$$\textbf{climber}(x) \leftarrow \textbf{alpinist}(x) \wedge \textbf{nonskier}(x).$$

To solve the puzzle in this form the query

$$\textbf{alpinist}(x) \wedge \textbf{climber}(x) \wedge \textbf{nonskier}(x).$$

should be given to the PROLOG system.

To make sure that the solution is consistent with the original statement of the puzzle we also have to independently show the unprovability of the query

$$\mathbf{likes}(x, y, \text{yes}) \ \land \ \mathbf{likes}(x, y, \text{no}).$$

In principle we should also assert in the program

$$\mathbf{likes}(x, y, \text{yes}) \ \lor \ \mathbf{likes}(x, y, \text{no}).$$

However, since the predicate **likes** does not appear in the program or the goal with an uninstantiated third argument, this assertion can be omitted.

Other solutions in PROLOG proposed in the discussion were even less satisfactory as they did not encode the puzzle accurately.

The syntax of TABLOG makes solving this puzzle much more straightforward:

1. $\mathbf{alpinist}(\text{John}) \land \mathbf{alpinist}(\text{Tony}) \land \mathbf{alpinist}(\text{Mike}).$
2. $\mathbf{skier}(x) \lor \mathbf{climber}(x) \leftarrow \mathbf{alpinist}(x).$
3. $\neg\mathbf{climber}(x) \leftarrow \mathbf{likes}(x, \text{rain}).$
4. $\neg\mathbf{skier}(x) \leftarrow \neg\mathbf{likes}(x, \text{snow}).$
5. $\mathbf{likes}(\text{Tony}, \text{rain}) \land \mathbf{likes}(\text{Tony}, \text{snow}).$
6. $\mathbf{likes}(\text{Mike}, y) \equiv \neg\mathbf{likes}(\text{Tony}, y).$

The puzzle is solved by proving the goal

$$\mathbf{alpinist}(z) \land \mathbf{climber}(z) \land \neg\mathbf{skier}(z).$$

The solution produced by the interpreter is $z = \text{Mike}$.

Note that in line 4 of the program, the procedural interpretation of TABLOG forces us to use the contrapositive

$$\neg\mathbf{skier}(x) \leftarrow \neg\mathbf{likes}(x, \text{snow})$$

rather than the direct form

$$\mathbf{skier}(x) \rightarrow \mathbf{likes}(x, \text{snow})$$

which is regarded as a definition for **likes**. This is the only transformation applied to the original specification.

4.4 Occur Check

The unification procedure customarily built into PROLOG is not really unification (e.g., as defined in [22]); it does not fail in matching an expression against one of its proper subexpressions since it lacks an *occur check*. When a theorem prover is used as a program interpreter, the omission of the occur check makes it possible to generate cyclic expressions that may not correspond to any concrete objects (and might take infinite amount of time to print).

For example, look at the following program specifying the **parent** relation:

$$\textbf{parent}(\textbf{father}(x), x).$$

If this program is called with the goal

$$\textbf{parent}(z, z)$$

a PROLOG interpreter will succeed but with the binding

$$\{z \leftarrow \textbf{father}(z)\}$$

i.e.,

$$\{z \leftarrow \textbf{father}(\textbf{father}(\textbf{father}(\cdots)\cdots))\}$$

which is cyclic and cannot be printed unless a special notation for such cases is introduced. This answer is also wrong because logically the program does not imply the truth of the goal. The fact that everyone's father is his or her parent does not imply that someone is his or her own parent.

The unification used by the TABLOG interpreter does include an occur check, so that only theorems can be proved. This choice is orthogonal to the other design decisions in the implementation of TABLOG; if future implementors think that the cost of this test is too high they will be able to use unification without the occur check and pay by losing soundness for some cases. TABLOG allows using nested function calls, and hence programs tend to have fewer repetition of variables than the corresponding PROLOG programs; since the occur check is necessary only if there is at least one variable that occurs more than once in one of the unified expressions (assuming renaming of variables to preserve their locality) this observation can lead to a more efficient unification with restricted application of the occur check.

In the QUTE language [23], the omission of the occur check is essential to the way recursive definitions are introduced. Since QUTE is not based on resolution theorem proving, this does not compromise its soundness.

5 COMPARISON WITH LISP

LISP programs are functions, each returning one value; the arguments of a function must be bound before the function is called. In TABLOG, on the other hand, programs can be either relations or functions, and the arguments need not be bound; these arguments will later be bound by unification.

We can illustrate this with the quicksort program again, concentrating on the partition subprogram. In TABLOG, we have seen how to achieve the partition by a predicate with four arguments, two for input and two for output:

$$\textbf{partition}(x, [\,], [\,], [\,]).$$
$$\textbf{partition}(x, y \circ u, y \circ u_1, u_2)$$
$$\leftarrow \; y \leq x \; \wedge \; \textbf{partition}(x, u, u_1, u_2).$$
$$\textbf{partition}(x, y \circ u, u_1, y \circ u_2)$$
$$\leftarrow \; x < y \; \wedge \; \textbf{partition}(x, u, u_1, u_2).$$

The definition of the program **partition** is much shorter and cleaner than the corresponding LISP program:

$$\textbf{highpart}(x, u) \quad \Leftarrow$$

if $\textbf{null}(u)$ then $\textbf{nil}$
else if $x \geq \textbf{car}(u)$ then $\textbf{highpart}(x, \textbf{cdr}(u))$
else $\textbf{cons}(\textbf{car}(u), \textbf{highpart}(x, \textbf{cdr}(u)))$

$$\textbf{lowpart}(x, u) \quad \Leftarrow$$

if $\textbf{null}(u)$ then $\textbf{nil}$
else if $x \geq \textbf{car}(u)$
    then $\textbf{cons}(\textbf{car}(u), \textbf{lowpart}(x, \textbf{cdr}(u)))$
else $\textbf{lowpart}(x, \textbf{cdr}(u))$.

We can generate the two sublists in LISP simultaneously, but this will require even more pairing and decomposition. Modern LISP systems include provisions for functions with more than one output. Although the syntax for using this feature is somewhat complex, we can get a nicer solution to this problem using multi-valued functions.

Note that unification also gives us "free" decomposition of the list argument into its head and tail; in the LISP program, even if multi-valued functions are used, this decomposition requires explicit calls to the functions $\textbf{car}$ and $\textbf{cdr}$. This feature is available as a syntactic sugar in some modern functional languages like SASL [26] and ML [17].

Unification is even more powerful than is indicated by this example. For example, we can generate partially computed results by using a logical variable before it is evaluated, with the concrete value later communicated by the unification. This feature is nicely demonstrated by Reddy's address translation example [19] but it is not limited to relational programs and can be used in a functional language with unification.

6 THE DEDUCTIVE-TABLEAU PROOF SYSTEM

The deductive-tableau proof system [13,14] is a general framework for theorem proving that was originally utilized for program synthesis. LISP and PROLOG implementations of it as a part of interactive systems are described in [10], [1], and [27]. Stickel [24] combines the nonclausal resolution rule of this proof system with connection graphs to yield an automatic theorem prover that has been incorporated into a natural-language understanding system.

In this section, we describe the version of the proof system that is used as the TABLOG interpreter; only the deduction rules actually employed by this interpreter are detailed. For a better description of the theory of the general proof system please refer to the original articles. For even more details await [16].

A *deductive tableau* consists of a set of rows, each containing either an *assertion* or a *goal*. The assertions and goals (both of which we refer to by the generic name *entries*) are first-order logic formulas. The tableau is valid if and only if under every interpretation some instance of at least one of the assertions is false or some instance of at least one of the goals is true.

To prove a theorem we enter it as the initial goal; if we want to prove that a sentence is implied by some assumptions we enter the assumptions as assertions and the implied sentence as the goal. In most cases the assertions will specify properties of the data domain. In contrast to standard resolution proof system we do not have to manipulate the negation of the given theorem (using a refutation procedure) and we do not have to convert any sentence to clausal form.

A proof in this system is constructed by adding new goals to the tableau, using deduction rules, in such a way that the final tableau is semantically equivalent to the original one. In the version of the tableau used for the TABLOG interpreter, we follow an affirmation procedure and the proof is complete when we have generated the goal *true*. In general a proof within the tableau can also succeed by refutation (i.e., producing the assertion *false*) rather than by affirmation. Standard resolution and Stickel's implementation of nonclausal resolution use a refutation procedure.

Logically there is duality between assertions and goals: an assertion can be replaced by a goal containing its negation and *vice versa*. By using both assertions and goals we can preserve the intuitive meaning of the sentences.

6.1 Deduction Rules

As mentioned before, not all the deduction rules supported by the deductive-tableau proof system are used in the interpreter for TABLOG. The soundness of the inference rules can be justified by case analysis, showing that introducing a new goal in each case will not make the tableau valid unless it was valid before the addition. The basic rules used for the program execution task are the following:

- *Nonclausal Resolution*: This generalized resolution rule allows removal of a subformula P from a goal $\mathcal{G}[P]$ by means of an appropriate assertion $\mathcal{A}[\hat{P}]$. (Note that the use of square brackets here is in the metalanguage and is not related to the list notation). Resolving the goal

$$\mathcal{G}[P]$$

with the assertion

$$\mathcal{A}[\hat{P}],$$

provided that P and $\hat{P}$ are unifiable, i.e., $P\theta = \hat{P}\theta$ for some (most-general) unifier θ, we get the new goal

$$\neg \mathcal{A}'[false] \ \wedge \ \mathcal{G}'[true],$$

where $\mathcal{A}'[false]$ is $\mathcal{A}\theta$ after all occurrences of $P\theta$ have been replaced by *false*, and similarly for $\mathcal{G}'[true]$.

This form of the rule is called *goal-assertion resolution*; another form used in TABLOG is the *assertion-goal resolution* that changes the role of the subformulas replaced by *false* and *true*. For example, for the assertion and goal above, assertion-goal resolution will generate the new goal

$$\neg \mathcal{A}'[true] \ \wedge \ \mathcal{G}'[false].$$

The choice of the unified subformulas is governed by the *polarity strategy*. A subformula has *positive* polarity if it occurs within an even number of (explicit or implicit) negations, and has *negative* polarity if it occurs within an odd number of negations. Assertions are positive and because of duality every goal has an implicit negation applied to it. A subformula can occur both positively and negatively in a formula. According to the polarity strategy, the instance $\hat{P}\theta$ of the subformula $\hat{P}$ will be replaced by *false* only if $\hat{P}$ occurs with positive polarity; dually, (the instance $P\theta$ of) the subformula P will be replaced by *true* only if P occurs with negative polarity.

Murray [18] proves that nonclausal resolution system is complete for first order logic even under the restriction of the polarity strategy. Note that the version used by TAB-LOG is not complete because we do not use the versions of the rule that match two assertions or two goals. The version used here always unifies a pair of subformulas while the general rule allows unifying sets of subformulas (and thus takes care of factoring).

- *Equality Rule*: This rule uses an asserted (possibly embedded in a larger formula) equality of two terms to replace one of the terms with the other in a goal. If the asserted equality is conditional, the conditions are added to the resulting goal as conjuncts.

  Thus, suppose the assertion is of the form

  $$\mathcal{A}[s = t],$$

  with the equation $s = t$ occuring in positive polarity, and the goal is

  $$\mathcal{G}[\hat{s}],$$

  where s and $\hat{s}$ are unifiable, i.e., $s\theta = \hat{s}\theta$ for some unifier θ. Then we get the new goal

  $$\neg \mathcal{A}'[\textit{false}] \;\wedge\; \mathcal{G}'[t'],$$

where $\mathcal{A}'[false]$ is $\mathcal{A}\theta$ after all occurrences of the equality $s\theta = t\theta$ have been replaced by *false*, and where $\mathcal{G}'[t']$ is $\mathcal{G}\theta$ after all occurrences of the term $s\theta$ have been replaced by $t\theta$.

The general version of this rule allows matching against the left-hand side or the right-hand side of the equality; in TABLOG however we use this rule in directional way and we always use it to replace the left-hand side by the right-hand side (after the appropriate unification, of course).

- *Equivalence Rule*: This rule replaces one subformula by another asserted to be equivalent to it. This is completely analogous to the equality rule except that we replace atomic formulas rather than terms, using equivalence rather then equality.

While nonclausal resolution and the equivalence rule can be performed unifying arbitrary subformulas, the TABLOG interpreter applies these deduction rules unifying atomic subformulas only.

Each of the above inference rules is followed by *simplification*: a formula is replaced by an equivalent but simpler formula. Both propositional and basic arithmetic simplification are performed automatically by the TABLOG interpreter immediately following every deduction step.

7 PROGRAM SEMANTICS

Every line in a program is an assertion in the tableau; a call to the program is a goal in the same tableau. The logical interpretation of a tableau, containing the assertions of a TABLOG program and a goal calling it, is the logical sentence associated with that tableau: the conjunction of the universal closures of the assertions implies the existential closure of the goal.

The desired goal is reduced to *true* by means of the assertions and the deduction rules. The variables are bound when subexpressions of the goal (or derived subgoals) are unified with subexpressions of the assertions. The order of the reduction is explained in the next section. The output of the program is the final binding of the variables of the original goal.

The function symbols of TABLOG are grouped according to their intended use: *constructor* function symbols serve to build data structures in the language; for example, ∘ is a predefined constructor. *Basic* (or *built-in* functions have attached procedures hard-wired into the implementation to define their semantics; basic arithmetic functions like + and **min** are predefined built-in functions. *Defined functions* are those that are defined by the assertions of a TABLOG program. The constructor and basic functions are called *primitive* functions, while the basic and defined functions are called *reducible* functions. The difference between the two kinds of reducible functions is the way they are reduced: basic functions are reduced by the built-in simplifier while defined functions are reduced by the equality rule. Although there are no constructor predicates we do distinguish between *basic* (primitive) predicates and *defined* predicates. The *primitive operators* include the primitive functions, primitive predicates the logical connectives and the *if-then-else* construct (in both usages). A *primitive expression* is an expression that does not contain defined (i.e., nonprimitive) operators; a *ground expression* is a variable free primitive expression. For example, the term $[(2 + x + 5)]$ (i.e., $(2 + x + 5) \circ [\,]$) is a primitive (but not ground) expression (with constructor function ∘, and primitive built-in function +), and will be automatically simplified to $[(x + 7)]$.

As in PROLOG, variables are local to the assertion or goal in which they appear. Renaming of variables is done automatically by the interpreter when there is a collision of names between the goal and assertion involved in a derivation step.

The variables of the original goal are the *output variables*. The interpreter records their bindings throughout the derivation and their final binding is the output of the computation.

8 PROGRAM EXECUTION

The tableau system provides deduction rules but does not specify the order in which to apply them. To use this proof system as a programing language, we must devise a *proof procedure* that employs the rules in a predictable and efficient manner.

The proof system is used to execute programs in a way analogous to the inversion of a matrix by linear operations on its rows, where we simultaneously apply the same transformations to the matrix to be inverted and to the identity matrix. In the program execution process, we start with a tableau containing the assertions of the program and a goal calling this program; we apply the same substitutions (obtained by unification) to the current subgoal and to the binding of the output variables. A matrix inversion is complete when we reduce the original matrix to the identity matrix; in TABLOG we are done when we have reduced the original goal to *true*. At this point, the result of the computation is the final binding of the output variables.

Although in the declarative (logical) semantics of the tableau the order of entries is immaterial, the procedural interpretation of the tableau as a program takes this order into account; changing the order of two assertions or changing the order of the conjuncts or disjuncts in an assertion or a goal may lead to different computations and results.

The user must specify an algorithm by employing the predefined order of evaluation of the tableau; the next subsection describes this evaluation order.

8.1 Order of Evaluation

At each step of the execution, one *simple expression* (a nonvariable term or an atomic formula) of the current goal is reduced. The expression to be reduced is selected by scanning the goal from left to right. The first (leftmost-outermost) simple expression is chosen and reduced, if possible. The reduction is done by applying an appropriate inference rule: the equality rule for a term, and nonclausal resolution or the equivalence rule for an atomic formula.

If the reduction fails the choice of the simple expression is suspended and a subexpression of it is chosen instead. If no such subexpression exists, a form of backtracking takes place as will be described later.

If the atomic formula is an equality and its two sides do not contain any *defined* functions, the equality is reduced by unifying the two sides and replacing the equality by *true*; if this is not the case or if the unification fails, the choice is suspended and the two sides are searched for the next simple expression.

If the operator (function or predicate) of the chosen expression is primitive it gets special treatment. Operators with built-in semantics (in the form of attached procedures) are evaluated when they have appropriate arguments; otherwise they are treated like failed reductions, i.e., the choice is suspended. Since constructors are not reducible, the choice of a term with a constructor function as the main operator is suspended immediately and subexpressions are reduced.

Formulas generally occur as the outermost expressions; therefore resolution and equivalence rules are in most cases tried first. Only if they cannot be applied do we reduce the terms inside the formulas; this is very similar to the way narrowing is applied in other approaches. Note however that this is not always the case; for example, we can have formulas inside the terms (as the condition of an *if-then-else* expression) and we also have the notion of suspension.

The order of evaluation described here is essentially *lazy evaluation*, as arguments are not computed unless their values are needed. Given the left-to-right order of evaluation between (for example) conjuncts in the goal, we can force the evaluation of an argument by using an auxiliary variable (this is similar to the way [4] removes nested function calls).

Before we demonstrate this with an example, it is important to emphasize again that the matching of the selected expression against program assertions is done in order of appearance. This order dependence makes it possible to guide the control of execution of the program and achieve a more efficient program.

All of the order dependence of programs is part of the sequential model for TABLOG execution. A parallel model does not require programs to be order-dependent.

8.2 An Example: Quicksort

Now we will try to illustrate and clarify the description of the last subsection via an instance of a call to the **quicksort** program of section 3.2.

To sort the list $[2, 1, 4, 3]$ using quicksort, we write the goal

$$z = \mathbf{qsort}([2, 1, 4, 3]).$$

Since the right-hand side of the equality contains the defined function **qsort**, the unification of the two sides is delayed and the simple expression chosen for reduction will be the term $\mathbf{qsort}([2, 1, 4, 3])$, i.e., $\mathbf{qsort}(2 \circ [1, 4, 3])$. This term unifies with the leftmost term $\mathbf{qsort}(x \circ u)$ in the second assertion of the quicksort program,

$$\mathbf{qsort}(x \circ u) = \mathbf{append}(\mathbf{qsort}(u_1), x \circ \mathbf{qsort}(u_2))$$
$$\leftarrow \mathbf{partition}(x, u, u_1, u_2).$$

According to the equality rule, it will be replaced by the corresponding instance of the right-hand side of the equality; this is done only after the unifier

$$\{x \leftarrow 2, \ u \leftarrow [1, 4, 3]\}$$

is applied to both the goal and the assertion. The occurrence of the equality

$$\mathbf{qsort}(2 \circ [1, 4, 3]) = \mathbf{append}(\mathbf{qsort}(u_1), 2 \circ \mathbf{qsort}(u_2))$$

is replaced by *false* in the (modified) assertion; the occurrence of the term

$$\mathbf{qsort}(2 \circ [1, 4, 3])$$

is replaced by the term

$$\mathbf{append}(\mathbf{qsort}(u_1), 2 \circ \mathbf{qsort}(u_2))$$

in the (modified) goal, and a conjunction is formed, obtaining

$$not(\textit{false} \ \leftarrow \ \mathbf{partition}(2, [1, 4, 3], u_1, u_2)) \ \wedge$$
$$z = \mathbf{append}(\mathbf{qsort}(u_1), 2 \circ \mathbf{qsort}(u_2)).$$

This formula can be reduced by the simplifications

$$(false \leftarrow P) \implies not\ P$$

and

$$not(not\ P) \implies P$$

to obtain the new goal

$$\textbf{partition}(2, [1, 4, 3], u_1, u_2) \land$$
$$z = \textbf{append}(\textbf{qsort}(u_1), 2 \circ \textbf{qsort}(u_2)).$$

Continuing with this example, we now have a case in which the expression to be reduced is an atomic formula, namely,

$$\textbf{partition}(2, [1, 4, 3], u_1, u_2).$$

This atomic formula is unifiable with a subformula in the second assertion of the **partition** subprogram (with variables renamed to resolve collisions)

$$\textbf{partition}(x, y \circ u, y \circ u_3, u_4)$$
$$\leftarrow\ y \leq x \land \textbf{partition}(x, u, u_3, u_4).$$

Nonclausal resolution is now performed to further reduce the current goal. The unifier

$$\{x \leftarrow 2,\ y \leftarrow 1,\ u \leftarrow [4, 3],\ u_1 \leftarrow 1 \circ u_3,\ u_2 \leftarrow u_4\}$$

is applied to both the assertion and the goal; the formula

$$\textbf{partition}(2, [1, 4, 3], 1 \circ u_3, u_4)$$

is replaced by *false* in the (modified) assertion and by *true* in the goal. Once again a conjunction is formed and the new goal generated (after simplification) is

$$\textbf{partition}(2, [4, 3], u_3, u_4) \land$$
$$z = \textbf{append}(\textbf{qsort}(1 \circ u_3), 2 \circ \textbf{qsort}(u_4)).$$

After a sequence of resolutions to compute the partition of the input list we get the goal

$$z = \textbf{append}(\textbf{qsort}([1]), 2 \circ \textbf{qsort}([4,3]))$$

which leads to the selection of the whole right-hand side of the equality as the expression to reduce. None of the two assertions defining **append** can be used to reduce this term; therefore the selection is suspended and the term **qsort**([1]) is chosen instead and gets reduced successfully.

Eventually we reach the subgoal

$$z = [1,2,3,4],$$

where the right-hand side of the equality contains only primitive functions and constants. The execution then terminates and the desired output is

$$[1,2,3,4].$$

Note that some functions and predicates (e.g., $\circ$ in this example) are predefined to be primitive; an expression in which such a symbol is the main operator is never selected to be reduced, although its subexpressions may be reduced.

8.3 Backtracking

If the selected expression cannot be reduced, the search for other possible reductions is done by backtracking.

In PROLOG each goal is a conjunction, so all the conjuncts must be proved; this means that, when facing a dead end, we have to undo the most recent binding and try other assertions.

In TABLOG the situation is more complex: each goal (and each assertion) is an arbitrary formula, so it is possible to satisfy it without satisfying all its atomic subformulas. Therefore, when the TABLOG interpreter fails to find an assertion that reduces some basic expression, it tries to reduce the next expression that can allow the proof to proceed. If the expression that cannot be reduced

387

is "essential" (for example, a conjunct in a conjunctive goal), no other subexpression will be attempted and backtracking will occur.

During backtracking, the goal from which the current goal was derived becomes the new current goal, but the next plausible assertion is used. This is similar to the backtracking used in PROLOG.

8.4 The Implementation

A prototype interpreter for TABLOG has been implemented in MACLISP. The implemented system serves as a program editor, debugger, and interpreter. All the examples mentioned in this paper have been executed on this interpreter.

The user must declare the variables, constants, functions, and predicates used in the program; some primitive constants, functions, and predicates (such as 0, $[]$, $+$, $-$, $\geq$, **odd**) are predefined.

Because the interpreter is built on top of a versatile theorem-proving system, the execution of programs is relatively slow. The simplifier built into the interpreter now handles complicated cases that might arise in a more general theorem-proving task, but will never occur in TABLOG. We hope that performance will be improved considerably by tuning the simplifier and utilizing tricks from PROLOG implementations to make the binding of variables faster.

9 RELATED RESEARCH

Logic programming has become a fashionable research topic in recent years. Most of the research relates to PROLOG and its extensions. We mention here some of the work that has been done independently of TABLOG to extend the capabilities of PROLOG.

While the deductive-tableau theorem prover used for TABLOG execution is based on a generalized resolution inference rule, [4], [5], and [3] describe a programming language based on a natural-deduction proof system. They do allow quantifiers and other connectives in their language. The language is very general and its execution uses forward as well as backward reasoning. Instead of having the equality rule, all formulas are converted to a *basic form* by eliminating all nested functions. We do not know about the status of implementations for this language. This is the only approach that actually adds all the connectives to logic programming.

Kornfeld [7] extends PROLOG to include equality: asserting equality between two objects in his language causes the system to unify these objects when regular unification fails. This makes it possible to unify objects that differ syntactically. Kornfeld treats only Horn clauses and does not introduce any substitution rule either for equality or for equivalence.

Tamaki [25] extends PROLOG by introducing a reducibility predicate, denoted by ▷. This predicate has semantics similar to the way TABLOG uses equality for rewriting terms. This work also includes *f-symbols* and *d-symbols* that are analogous to TABLOG's distinction between defined and primitive functions. The possible nesting of terms is restricted and programs must be in Horn clause form.

The works of [20], [2], and [9] extend functional programming to have logical variables and unification. By either adding relations or encoding them using functions these languages essentially have most of the power of TABLOG. While EQLOG [2] also contains Horn clauses Reddy's language [20] is essentially functional and [9] takes an even more cautious approach: each function symbol can occur exactly once on the left-hand side of a definition.

There are PROLOG systems, such as LOGLISP [22] and QLOG [6], that are implemented within LISP systems. These systems allow the user to invoke the PROLOG interpreter from within a LISP program and vice versa. In TABLOG, however, LISP-like features and PROLOG-like features coexist peacefully in the same framework and are processed by the same deductive engine.

10 DISCUSSION

The TABLOG language is a new approach to logic programming: instead of patching up PROLOG with new constructs to eliminate its shortcomings, we suggest a more powerful deductive system.

The combination in TABLOG of unification as a binding mechanism, equality for specifying functions, and first-order logic for specifying predicates creates a rich language that is logically clean. As a consequence, programs more directly correspond to our intuition and are easier to write, read, and modify. We can mix LISP-style and PROLOG-style programming and use whichever is more convenient.

By restricting the general purpose deductive-tableau theorem prover and forcing it to follow a specific search order, we have made it suitable to serve as a program interpreter; the specific search order makes it both more predictable and more efficient than attempting to apply the deduction rules in arbitrary order.

When the theorem prover is restricted to achieve predictability and efficiency, we do lose its completeness. The reasons for losing completeness include: absence of *factoring* or its equivalent in the restricted form of the resolution rule; the omission of *goal-goal* and *assertion-assertion* resolution, and the directionality of using equivalence and equality to define functions and predicates. The absence of completeness does not however affect the examples that we have tried. Furthermore, whenever the programs are restricted to Horn clause form we still enjoy all the completeness properties of this sublanguage.

While the theorem prover supports reasoning with quantified formulas [16, 1], the ramifications of including quantifiers in the language are still under investigation. Quantifiers would certainly enhance the expressive power of TABLOG, but we believe that they are more suited to a specification language than a programming language. If for example we have a universally quantified formula in the condition of an *if-then-else*, in order to evaluate its truth value we have to check the validity of the matrix of the formula. This can be done if we have decision procedures for the data domain of the program, which is reasonable for a general theorem proving system but too expensive for a program interpreter. On the other hand quantifiers may be introduced as an iteration operator. This can be done if we restrict every quantifier to be bounded by some predicate (e.g., membership in a set).

It seems very natural to extend TABLOG to parallel computation. The inclusion of real negation and the conditional *if-then-else* makes it possible to write programs that do not depend on the order of assertions.

The extension of TABLOG to support concurrent programs is being pursued. If the conditions of the assertions are disjoint, several assertions can be matched against the current subgoal in parallel. In addition, disjunctive goals can be split between processes. If there are no common variables, conjuncts can be solved in parallel; otherwise some form of communication is required.

The *or-parallelism* and *and-parallelism* suggested for PROLOG are applicable for TABLOG as well. The or-parallelism of PROLOG corresponds to matching against many assertions; in TABLOG or-parallelism is also possible within every goal, since, for example, goals can be disjunctive. In TABLOG, other forms of parallelism can be applied to nested function calls.

We believe that TABLOG offers a significant advance over PROLOG in allowing more direct expression of the programmer's intentions. If PROLOG is destined to become the FORTRAN of the year 2000, we can hope that TABLOG will become at least its PASCAL.

ACKNOWLEDGMENTS

Thanks are due to Martin Abadi, Yoram Moses, Oren Patashnik, Jon Traugott, and Joe Weening for comments on various versions of this paper. We are especially indebted to Bengt Jonsson and Frank Yellin for reading many versions of the manuscript and providing insightful comments and suggestions.

This research was supported in part by the National Science Foundation under grants MCS-82-14523, MCS-81-11586, and MCS-81-05565, by the United States Air Force Office of Scientific Research under Contract AFOSR-81-0014, and by Defense Advanced Research Projects Agency under Contract N0039-82-C-0250.

The first author gratefully acknowledges the support by an IBM predoctoral fellowship and an HTI fellowship during early stages of this research.

REFERENCES

1. Bronstein, A. "Full quantification and special relations in a first-order logic theorem prover," unpublished report, Computer Science Department, Stanford University, 1983.

2. Goguen, J.A., and J. Meseguer, "EQLOG: Equality, types, and generic modules for logic programming," this volume.

3. Hansson, Å., S. Haridi, and S.-Å. Tärnlund, "Properties of a logic programming language," in *Logic Programming*, K.L. Clark and S.-Å. Tärnlund (editors), Academic Press, 1982.

4. Haridi, S. "Logic programming based on a natural deduction system," PhD Thesis, Department of Telecommunication Systems and Computer Science, The Royal Institute of Technology, Stockholm, Sweden, 1981.

5. Haridi, S., and D. Sahlin, "Evaluation of logic programs based on natural deduction," Technical report RITA-CS-8305 B, Department of Telecommunication Systems and Computer Science, The Royal Institute of Technology, Stockholm, Sweden, 1983.

6. Komorowski, H.J. "QLOG: The Programming Environment for PROLOG in LISP," in *Logic Programming*, K.L. Clark and S.-Å. Tärnlund (editors), Academic Press, 1982.

7. Kornfeld, W. "Equality for PROLOG," this volume.

8. Kowalski, R. *Logic for Problem Solving*, North-Holland, 1979.

9. Lindstrom, G. "Functional Programming and the logical variable," in *Proceedings of the Twelfth ACM Symposium on Principles of Programming Languages*, New Orleans, Louisiana, January 1985.

10. Malachi, Y. "Deductive programming," unpublished report, Department of Computer Science, Stanford University, December 1982.

11. Malachi, Y. "Nonclausal Logic Programming," PhD Dissertation, Computer Science Department, Stanford University, forthcoming.

12. Malachi, Y., Z. Manna and R. Waldinger, "TABLOG—the deductive-tableau programming language" in *Proceedings of the ACM Symposium on Lisp and Functional Programming*, Austin, Texas, August 1984.

13. Manna, Z., and R. Waldinger, "A deductive approach to program synthesis," *ACM Transactions on Programming Languages and Systems*, Vol. 2, No. 1, pp. 92–121, January 1980.

14. Manna, Z., and R. Waldinger, "Special relations in automated deduction," Technical Report, Department of Computer Science, Stanford University, May 1985. Also, Technical Note 355, Artificial Intelligence Center, SRI International. To appear in *Journal of the ACM*.

15. Manna, Z., and R. Waldinger, *The Logical Basis for Computer Programming, Volume 1: Deductive Reasoning*, Addison-Wesley, 1985.

16. Manna, Z., and R. Waldinger, *The Logical Basis for Computer Programming, Volume 2: Deductive Systems*, Addison-Wesley, to appear.

17. Milner, R. "A proposal for standard ML," *Proceedings of the ACM Symposium on Lisp and Functional Programming*, Austin, Texas, August 1984.

18. Murray, N.V. "Completely nonclausal theorem proving," *Artificial Intelligence*, Vol. 18, No. 1, pp. 67–85, 1982.

19. Reddy, U. "On the relationship between logic and functional languages," this volume.

20. Reddy, U. "Narrowing as the operational semantics of functional languages," to appear.

21. Robinson, J.A. "A machine-oriented logic based on the resolution principle," *Journal of the ACM*, Vol. 12, No. 1, January 1965, pp. 23–41.

22. Robinson, J.A., and E. E. Sibert, "LOGLISP: An alternative to PROLOG," in *Machine Intelligence 10*, J. E. Hayes, D. Michie, and Y-H Pao (editors), Ellis Horwood Ltd., Chichester, 1982.

23. Sato, M., and T. Sakurai, "QUTE: A Functional language based on unification," this volume.

24. Stickel, M.E. "A nonclausal connection-graph resolution theorem-proving program," *Proceedings of the National Conference on Artificial intelligence*, Pittsburgh, Pennsylvania, August 1982.

25. Tamaki, H. "Semantics of a logic programming language with a reducibility predicate," *Proceedings of the IEEE Logic Programming Conference*, Atlantic City, February 1984.

26. Turner, D.A. "SASL language manual," Computer Laboratory, University of Kent, Canterbury, England, 1976 (revised August 1979).

27. Yellin, F. "PROLOG based program synthesis," unpublished report, Computer Science Department, Stanford University, 1983.

Part V:

Augmented Unification

CONSTRAINING-UNIFICATION

AND THE PROGRAMMING LANGUAGE

UNICORN*

Robert G. Bandes

Computer Science Department, FR-35
University of Washington
Seattle, Washington 98195

ABSTRACT

Up to this point, direct implementations of axiomatic or equational specifications have been limited because the implementation mechanisms are incapable of capturing the full semantics of the specifications. The programming language Unicorn was designed and implemented with the intention of exploring the full potential of programming with equations. Unicorn introduces a new language mechanism, called *constraining unification*. When coupled with *semantic unification*, constraining-unification closely models the semantics of equational specifications thereby allowing for the implementation of a wider class of specifications. Unlike the language mechanisms of rewrite-rule and logic programming, constraining-unification is free of order dependencies. The same results are produced regardless of the order in which the axioms are stated. The use of *viewpoints* contributes to the flexibility of the Unicorn language. Preconditions for partial operations can be specified without added machinery.

*Originally published in <u>Proceedings</u> <u>of</u> <u>the</u> <u>11th</u> <u>Annual</u> <u>ACM</u> <u>Symposium</u> <u>on</u> <u>Principles</u> <u>of</u> <u>Programming</u> <u>Languages</u>, Salt Lake City, Utah, January 1984. Reprinted by permission of the Association for Computing Machinery, Inc.

397

1 INTRODUCTION

Unicorn represents a new approach to the implementation of equational specifications. It employs a new language mechanism, called *constraining-unification*. In constraining-unification an axiom is thought of as stating constraints on the result of applications of the operations mentioned in the axiom. With the aid of *semantic unification*, this mechanism is capable of capturing much of the semantics of equational specifications. At the same time, constraining-unification solves the problem of order dependency that occurs in logic and rewrite-rule programming, languages which have both been used to implement equational specifications.

Unicorn also incorporates a new concept called *viewpoints*. A viewpoint is used to give an interpretation of the axioms that insures termination of the implementation. The examples in section 5 demonstrate the flexibility provided by viewpoints. The first example shows how the same specifications can be used to define preconditions for partial operations that must be checked by the user and preconditions that are automatically checked by Unicorn.

An interpreter for Unicorn has been written in Prolog [11] that implements all the features mentioned here.

1.1 Relations to Previous Work

OBJ [4] and AFFIRM [9] explore a particular approach into the implementation of algebraic specifications, that of treating the axioms as rewrite-rules. In this technique, axioms are used in a left-to-right manner to perform pattern matching reductions. An input expression is successively transformed by finding an axiom whose left-hand-side unifies with some subexpression of the input expression and then replacing the matched subexpression with the corresponding right-hand-side of the axiom. Prolog has also been used for the implementation of algebraic specifications [1]. The approach is essentially the same; the axioms are translated into Prolog clauses which mimic the rewrite-rule approach. Hoffman and O'Donnell use the rewrite-rule approach for the implementation of equational programming [7]. They show that the resulting language is useful for, among other things, the concise description of programming language interpreters and data abstractions.

However, it is not possible to implement all algebraic specifications (or equational programs) by treating the axioms (or equations) as rewrite-rules. Thus this implementation technique is only suitable for a subset of the possible equational programs. For example, the axiom square(square-root(X)) = X says as much about the definition of the operation square-root as it says about the definition of the operation square. However, the rewrite-rule implementation technique would only treat this as part of the definition of the operation square.

Constraint programming languages, such as those developed by Borning [2] and Steele [12], also deal with axioms. In constraint languages, axioms are treated as producing constraints on the values of the variables mentioned in those axioms. Thus, in a constraint language, the axiom

```
Fahrenheit =
        plus(32, times(9, divide(Centigrade, 5)))
```

is treated as a constraint on the values of the variables Fahrenheit and Centigrade. It says as much about the value of Centigrade as it does about the value of Fahrenheit. Variables in constraint languages, however, have a different status from variables in equational languages. In constraint languages the scope of a variable may extend beyond the given constraint, while in equational languages the scope of a variable is the axiom in which it is used.

The principal difference between constraining-unification and the mechanisms used in constraint languages is that in constraining-unification, an axiom is treated as producing constraints on the **operations** rather then the **variables** mentioned in the axioms. Thus the equivalent statement for temperature conversion in Unicorn would be

```
centigrade(X) =
        fahrenheit(plus(32, times(9, divide(X, 5)))).
```

This axiom states the desired relationship between quantities of the form centigrade(X) and fahrenheit(Y). Note that

399

we could treat this axiom as a rewrite-rule to convert from centigrade to fahrenheit. But the rewrite-rule approach would be useless if we wanted to use this axiom to convert from fahrenheit to centigrade.

Semantic unification allows constraints to be produced in situations that would normally not be considered in standard unification. In Unicorn we could use the above axiom to transform the expression `fahrenheit(32)` since it is possible to find a value for the variable `X` such that `plus(32, times(9, divide(X,5)))` transforms to 32. This is similar to the way that equality theorems are used in Prolog-with-Equality [8] (the differences will be discussed in section 3). In Prolog-with-Equality, if two terms do not unify syntactically then an attempt is made to use equality assertions to prove that the two terms are equal. If this attempt succeeds, then the original unification succeeds with the variable bindings introduced by the equality proof. In standard Prolog, one would make explicit use of a predicate to perform the conversion between centigrade and fahrenheit. The following is an example of such a Prolog predicate:

```
convert(C, F):-
        var(F) -> (nonvar(C), F is 32+(9*(C/5)));
        C is ((F-32)/9)*5.
```

In Unicorn, preconditions can be specified for the definition of partial operations. This technique, which has been advocated by Guttag [5], is an alternative to the use of complicated error algebras [3] for totalizing partial operations. Guttag introduces a special construct for the specification of preconditions. This is not necessary in Unicorn. As is demonstrated in section 5, preconditions for partial operations can be succinctly stated in the existing language.

2 CONSTRAINING-UNIFICATION

In constraining-unification, axioms are used to constrain the possible transformation of input expressions to result expressions. Given a particular input expression and set of axioms, constraining-unification produces a set of constraints, called *transformation constraints*, that any allowable transformation of the input expression must satisfy. There may be more than one expression that satisfies the transformation constraints. In this way nondeterministic operations are permitted. On the other hand, if the transformation constraints are inconsistent, then no expression can satisfy all of the constraints: hence there will be no allowable transformation of the input expression.

We now describe how an input expression and set of axioms combine to produce a set of transformation constraints, and how these transformation constraints can be used to find allowable transformations of the input expression. A transformation constraint is produced by unifying the input expression with a subexpression of some axiom and then replacing the matched subexpression with a special variable. There is no restriction as to where in the axiom the unification can be made. For example, the input expression $square\text{-}root(4)$ unifies with the subexpression $square\text{-}root(X)$ in the axiom $X = square(square\text{-}root(X))$ thereby producing the transformation constraint $4 = square(V)$, where V is a special variable not occurring elsewhere in the transformation constraint. Each possible unification with each axiom produces exactly one transformation constraint, and the same special variable is used in each constraint. If a value can be found for the special variable such that all of the transformation constraints are simultaneously satisfied, then that value is an allowable transformation of the original input expression. Referring to the above example, any value of V for which $square(V)$ transforms to 4 satisfies the transformation constraint and is therefore an allowable transformation of the original input expression $square\text{-}root(4)$.

A transformation constraint is satisfied by recursively transforming both sides of the transformation constraint and then checking that the the results are identical. The problem with this definition is that, in general, there is no end to the recursive transformation of the sides of the transformation constraints.

This problem is solved in section 4 by introducing the concept of a *viewpoint*.

If the expression to be transformed contains variables, there may be more than one possible set of transformation constraints depending on the bindings of the variables. For example, suppose we wish to transform the expression plus(A, succ(zero)) given the peano axioms:

1) plus(zero, X) = X
2) plus(succ(X), Y) = succ(plus(X, Y))

Two sets of transformation constraints are produced. The first set consists of the singleton V1 = succ(zero), produced by unifying with the left-hand-side of axiom 1, where zero has been substituted for the variable A. The second set consists of the singleton V2 = succ(plus(X,succ(zero))), produced by unifying with the left-hand side of axiom 2, where succ(X) has been substituted for the variable A. When more than one set of transformation constraints exists, the sets are checked in parallel. Within a particular set, the transformation constraints must be simultaneously satisfied. Thus, the ordering of axioms 1 and 2 is irrelevant. This checking of transformation constraints for different values of the variables in the expressions to be transformed replaces the order-dependent evaluation schemes of logic and rewrite-rule programming.

In logic and rewrite-rule programming, results may vary depending on the order in which clauses or rewrite-rules are stated. For example, in standard Prolog the equivalent definition of addition would be:

```
plus(zero, X, X).
plus(succ(X), Y, succ(Z)) :- plus(X, Y, Z).
```

Evaluation of the predicate plus(A, succ(zero), Z) succeeds with the bindings A = zero and Z = succ(zero) by unifying with the first clause. If the order of the clauses had been reversed, however, no results whatsoever would have been produced.

Besides the fact that constraining-unification involves no order dependency, transformation in constraining-unification generalizes the notions of evaluation used in logic and rewrite-rule programming. The expression to be transformed may contain variables (as in logic programming) and in performing a transformation it may be decided to first transform subexpressions (as in rewrite-rule programming). In rewrite-rule programming, different results may be obtained depending on the order in which subexpressions are evaluated. This problem is avoided by assuming a fixed evaluation strategy, such as an innermost or outermost strategy [10]. In Unicorn we use an outermost transforming strategy in which the outermost possible subexpression is always transformed first.

3 SEMANTIC UNIFICATION

Semantic unification in Unicorn differs from equality in Prolog-with-Equality [8] (see section 1.1) in two ways. Firstly, in Unicorn, two expressions are considered semantically unifiable if their principal functors (their outermost operators) are identical and if corresponding arguments transform to identical primitive expressions. In Prolog-with-Equality, two expressions are considered equal if one of the expressions unifies with the left-hand side of an equality assertion having identical principal functor and it is possible to show that the corresponding right-hand side of the equality assertion is equal to the other expression. Thus, a one-way chain of equality assertions is used to relate the two expressions.

The other difference is that in Unicorn, semantic unification may be used to produce transformation constraints only when transformation is otherwise impossible. Since transformation in general is undecidable, semantic unification is undecidable as well. When semantic unification is used there may be more than one semantic unification attempted before transformation can proceed, since all transformation constraints must be simultaneously satisfied. Some of these semantic unifications may terminate while others may not. If any of these semantic unifications is non-terminating, this would cause non-termination of the entire transformation. However, transformation without the use of semantic unification may be possible, hence avoiding the non-terminating semantic unifications. In practice, the cases where this has been beneficial have outweighed the cases where a violation of intended semantics occurs.

4 VIEWPOINTS

It is useful to think of a viewpoint as a mapping from equational specifications to Unicorn programs. Two different viewpoints map a specification onto different, but usually related, Unicorn programs. A viewpoint gives more specific information for each axiom about which operations are being defined. Visualize the viewpoint as overlaying an equational specification with marks that highlight the operations being defined. A new viewpoint is established by overlaying the specification with a new set of marks. This is essentially how viewpoints are implemented in Unicorn. A particular occurrence of an operation that is marked within the current viewpoint is called a *marked operation*. Any subexpression of any axiom whose principal functor is a marked operation is called a *marked subexpression*. Those operations that appear in the equational specification but are nowhere marked within the viewpoint are called *primitive operation*. A *primitive expression* is any expression consisting of only primitive operations and variables.

When producing transformation constraints, the expression to be transformed may only be unified with marked subexpressions. Therefore primitive expressions can never be transformed. Transformation proceeds until the constraints are expressed in terms of primitive expressions only. Thus, under a particular viewpoint, the axioms demonstrate how any expression can be represented in terms of the primitive operations. The concept of primitive operations corresponds very closely to the concept of constructor operations in algebraic specifications [6]. Note that if the viewpoint being used marks only the principal functor of the left-hand side of each axiom, then, except for the lack of order dependency, the result is a Unicorn program that behaves in the same way as a rewrite-rule implementation of the same specification.

As defined so far, the set of possible transformations of an input expression might contain non-primitive as well as primitive expressions. Those transformations that produce primitive expressions are the transformations that are of interest. By allowing only those unifications that substitute primitive expressions for variables, we guarantee that only those transformations of interest are generated.

5 EXAMPLES

It turns out that the viewpoint technique lends itself quite nicely to the definition of preconditions for partial operations [5] without the need for added machinery. Consider the stack specification appearing in Figure 1.

1) pop(push(S, X)) = S
2) top(push(S, X)) = X
3) notempty(new) = false
4) notempty(push(S, X)) = true
5) pre(pop(S)) = notempty(S)
6) pre(top(S)) = notempty(S)
7) pre(X) = true

Figure 1: Stack specification with preconditions.

Say that in our viewpoint, pre is the only marked operation in axioms 5 and 6, and that no operations are marked in axiom 7. Then it is up to the user to make use of the operation pre to insure that only legal calls to the operations pop and top are made. However, if in our viewpoint pop and top as well as pre are marked in axioms 5 and 6, and pre is marked in axiom 7, then the preconditions will be maintained automatically by Unicorn. For example, suppose we want to transform the expression top(new). This expression unifies with axiom 6 producing the transformation constraint pre(V) = notempty(new). Because of axiom 7, the left-hand side of this transformation constraint transforms to the primitive expression true. Because of axiom number 3, the right-hand side of this transformation constraint transforms to the primitive expression false. Thus, there is no way to satisfy the transformation constraint and hence there are no allowable transformations of the original input expression top(new). Note that we excluded pre(V) from unifying with either of the expressions pre(pop(S)) or pre(top(S)) in axioms 5 and 6 since that would involve the substitution of a non-primitive expression for the variable V.

Suppose we want to transform the expression top(push(new, apple)). This expression unifies with both axioms 2 and 6 producing the two transformation constraints V = apple and pre(V) = notempty(push(new, apple)). Since these constraints are simultaneously satisfied by the substitution of the primitive expression apple for the special variable V, apple is an allowable transformation of the input expression top(push(new, apple)). So, depending on the viewpoint that we use, the same specification can be used to define preconditions that must be checked by the user, or preconditions that are automatically checked by the system. In order to define a precondition on a predicate in standard Prolog, in general one would be forced to make an explicit call to the precondition in each clause defining that predicate.

As another example of the flexibility provided by the use of viewpoints, consider the specification appearing in Figure 2. Axioms 1 through 4 provide some temperature data for the substances ammonia and krypton. Our viewpoint considers the operations boilingpoint, freezingpoint and meltingpoint to be the marked operations in these axioms. Axiom 5 provides another way to access this data; info is the marked operation in our viewpoint. Depending on the viewpoint that we use for axioms 6 and 7, we can have our results expressed in terms of either centigrade, fahrenheit, or kelvin. The fahrenheit viewpoint would consider centigrade to be the marked operation in axiom 6 and kelvin to be the marked operation in axiom 7. The centigrade viewpoint would consider fahrenheit to be the marked operation in axiom 6 and kelvin to be marked operation in axiom 7. The kelvin viewpoint would consider fahrenheit to be the marked operation in axiom 6 and centigrade to be the marked operation in axiom 7.

```
1) boilingpoint(ammonia) = centigrade(-33)
2) boilingpoint(krypton) = kelvin(121)
3) freezingpoint(ammonia) = fahrenheit(-103)
4) meltingpoint(krypton) = centigrade(-157)

5) info(X) =
        tuple(tuple(boilingpoint, boilingpoint(X)),
        tuple(freezingpoint, freezingpoint(X)),
        tuple(meltingpoint, meltingpoint(X)))

6) centigrade(X) =
        fahrenheit(plus(32, times(9, divide(X, 5))))
7) centigrade(minus(X, 273)) = kelvin(X)
```

Figure 2:   Temperature data and conversion factors.

If we transform the expression info(ammonia) using the kelvin viewpoint, we get the result

```
        tuple(tuple(boilingpoint, kelvin(240)),
        tuple(freezinpoint, kelvin(195)),
        tuple(meltingpoint, meltingpoint(ammonia))).
```

However, if we transform the expression info(krypton) using the fahrenheit viewpoint, we get the result

```
        tuple(tuple(boilingpoint, fahrenheit(-238)),
        tuple(freezingpoint, freezingpoint(krypton)),
        tuple(meltingpoint, fahrenheit(-247))).
```

This example has demonstrated the general technique for using viewpoints to tailor the form of transformation results. Viewpoints may also be used to alter the algorithms used for obtaining results. For example, different viewpoints might be used to switch from an abstract implementation to a more concrete implementation of the same abstraction.

6 CONCLUSIONS

We have given an informal description of Unicorn, a programming language based on the technique of constraining-unification. Although constraining-unification is a generalization of the mechanisms used in logic and rewrite-rule programming, the order dependency problems inherent in those languages are avoided. Constraining-unification closely models the semantics of equational specifications. As a result, it is possible to implement equational specifications of nondeterministic operations in Unicorn. The use of viewpoints and semantic unification in conjunction with constraining-unification results in an expressive and flexible programming language. Preconditions for partial operations can be specified in Unicorn. By employing different viewpoints, the same specification can be used to require the user to check the preconditions or to have Unicorn automatically maintain the preconditions. In addition, Unicorn would be suitable for a parallel processing implementation, since transformation constraints can be concurrently checked.

ACKNOWLEDGEMENTS

Thanks are due to Professor Alan Borning for making helpful comments on earlier versions of this and related papers. He was initially responsible for stirring my interest in logic and constraint programming and specification languages in general.

This research was supported in part by a gift from Atari, Incorporated, and in part by National Science Foundation Grant No. MCS-8202520.

[*Editors' note:* Robert Bandes died in a skydiving accident on August 21, 1983, shortly after this paper was written.]

REFERENCES

1. Bandes, R.G. Algebraic specification and Prolog. 82-12-02, Department of Computer Science, University of Washington, December, 1982.

2. Borning, A.H. "The programming language aspects of ThingLab, a constraint-oriented simulation laboratory". *ACM Trans. on Programming Lang. and Systems 3*, 4 (October 1981), 353-387.

3. Goguen, J.A. Abstract errors for abstract data types. In *Formal Description of Programming Concepts*, E.J. Neuhold, Ed., North Holland, 1978, pp. 491-525.

4. Goguen, J.A., and J.J. Tardo. An Introduction to OBJ: A Language for Writing and Testing Formal Algebraic Program Specifications. Proc. Conference on Specification of Reliable Software, IEEE, 1979, pp. 170-189.

5. Guttag, J.V. "Notes on type abstraction (version 2)". *IEEE Transactions on Software Engineering SE-6*, 1 (January 1908), 13-23.

6. Guttag, J.V., and J.J Horning. "The algebraic specification of abstract data types". *Acta Informatica 10* (1978), 27-52.

7. Hoffman, C.M., and M.J. O'Donnell. "Programming with equations". *ACM Trans. on Programming Lang. and Systems 4*, 1 (January 1982), 83-112.

8. Kornfeld, W.A. Equality for prolog. Proc. Eighth International Joint Conference on Articicial Intelligence, Karlsruhe, 1983. Also appears in this volume.

9. Musser, D.R. "Abstract data type specification in the AFFIRM system". *IEEE Transactions on Software Enginering SE-6*, 1 (January 1980), 24-32.

10. M.J. O'Donnell. *Lecture Notes In Computer Science. Volume 58: Computing in Systems Described by Equations.* Springer, 1977.

11. Pereira, L.M. User's guide to DECsystem–10 Prolog. Divisio de Informatica, Lab. Nac. de Engenharia, Lisbon, 1977.

12. Steele, G.L. *The Definition and Implementation of a Computer Programming Language Based on Constraints*. Ph.D. Th., Dept. Electrical Engineering and Computer Science, M.I.T., August 1980.

UNIFORM

A LANGUAGE BASED UPON UNIFICATION

WHICH UNIFIES (much of)

LISP, PROLOG, and ACT 1

Kenneth M. Kahn

Xerox PARC
Intelligent Systems Laboratory
3333 Coyote Hill Road
Palo Alto, CA 94304

ABSTRACT

Uniform is an AI programming language based upon augmented unification. It is an attempt to combine, in a simple coherent framework, the most important features of Lisp, actor languages such as Act 1 and SmallTalk, and logic programming languages such as Prolog. Among the unusual abilities of the language is its ability to use the same program as a function, an inverse function, a predicate, a pattern, or a generator. All of these uses can be performed upon concrete, symbolic, and partially instantiated data. Uniform features automatic inheritance from multiple super classes, facilities for the manipulation of programs, and a unification-oriented database.

This is a substantially revised version of two previously published papers appearing in *Progress in Artificial Intelligence*, edited by L. Steels and J. Campbell, pp. 129–45, Ellis Horwood, 1985, and in *Proceedings of the Seventh International Joint Conference on Artificial Intelligence*, 1981, Copyright 1981 by IJCAI, Inc.

1 A Language Based upon Unification

Uniform is based upon the idea of an extensible unification procedure. All programs are extensions to the unification process. Unification plays the roles of pattern matching, evaluation, message passing, inheritance, and symbolic evaluation. In the process of unifying the factorial of 3 with an integer **n**, **n** is unified with 6. The concatenation of **x** and the list **(c d)** unifies with the list **(a b c d)**, resulting in **x** being unified with the list **(a b)**. Unifying the **n**th element of the list of all prime numbers with 5 results in **n** unified with 3. Unifying the reverse of a list consisting of the variables **x** and **y** with a list **z** unifies **z** with a list consisting of **y** and **x**. Unifying a member of set **x** with a member of set **y** yields a member of the intersection of **x** and **y**. Unifying a description of red chairs with a description of big chairs produces a description of big red chairs. And so on.

1.1 Unification --- What It Is

Unification was invented for use in resolution theorem provers [24] and has since been used in a few programming languages. Two well-known examples are Prolog, which is a programming language based upon resolution theorem proving [29], and Qlisp [25]. In these languages unification is only one computational mechanism among others. In Uniform unification is augmented so that it subsumes other mechanisms such as resolution or evaluation.

Unification is the process of generating the most general common instance of a set of descriptions. It is implemented as a process that returns a "unifier" which if applied to any of the original descriptions produces the sought after instance. In the most common case, the unifier is simply an environment describing variable bindings, and it is applied to a description by substituting its values for the variables in the description. It is the use of unifiers rather than actually constructing instances which makes the unification process computationally feasible, in much the same way that environments emulate lambda substitution in Lisp. As an example, **(unifier-of (foo x 'a r) (foo 'b y r))** produces **{(= x 'b) (= y 'a)}** which if substituted into either description produces the instance **(foo 'b 'a r)**. (As in Lisp, Uniform follows the convention that constants are numbers or quoted symbols and variables are unquoted symbols.) Unification is defined to produce the *most general* common instance, which means that the instance produced must unify with all other possible instances. From an implementation viewpoint, producing the most general instance is the same as generating the weakest set of bindings such that the descriptions become equal when bindings are substituted in each of the instances.

Another way of thinking about unification is that the descriptions being unified describe sets, and unification is the process of generating a description of the intersection of the sets. This view is preferable when considering extensions to unification beyond *syntactic* notions of instances and descriptions.

Pattern matching, which has played such a large role in most AI languages, is a special case of the unification of two descriptions. The pattern is a description containing variables which is matched against a description without any variables. If the match succeeds, the unifier produced is a set of match bindings which when substituted into the pattern produces the other description.

1.2 How Unification is Augmented in Uniform

Unification is a syntactic process. Its only concerns are that descriptions have the same type, that their arguments unify pairwise, that corresponding constants are equal and recursively that their parts unify. (It is also concerned with preventing circular structures via an "occur check". This aspect of unification is discussed later.) A syntactic unifier cannot unify the sum of x and 3 with 7 by unifying x with 4. Unification is augmented in Uniform so that two descriptions unify if they unify syntactically, if at least one of the descriptions is primitive and the primitive "succeeds", or if the equivalence of the descriptions can be deduced from

413

assertions stating what is equal to what. The deduction is based upon the reflexivity and transitivity of equality as well as the rule that two descriptions are equal if they are of the same type and the corresponding elements can be shown to be equal. In addition in Uniform one can state second-order equalities about the equivalence of statements about the equality of descriptions.

The only constraint upon augmentations to the unification of two descriptions is that the resulting unifier produce equivalent descriptions when applied. It is the current set of assertions which determine the equivalence of descriptions. Different notions of equivalence for different purposes are handled by different sets of assertions. For example, the unifier describing x as 4 when applied to 7 and the sum of x and 3 produces 7 and the sum of 4 and 3. Either the sum of 4 and 3 is considered equivalent to 7 or else the augmentation that produced the unifier is invalid.

A few of the primitive descriptions stretch this view of unification. There are primitives for dynamically creating unification variables and descriptions for enforcing sequentiality (critical in situations involving input-output), for determining if two things are the exact same object (Lisp's **EQ**, critical when dealing with circular structures and important for efficiency), and the logical connectors **and**, **or**, and **not**. The primitive description **(print)** unifies with anything and prints the other description as a side effect. It is unclear if primitives such as **print** need to be done this way. I/0 can be performed using streams in a logical fashion as has been done in Concurrent Prolog [26].

1.3 How Uniform Uses Augmented Unification

The top level loop of Uniform is, analogous to Lisp, a "read unify print" loop. The user types a description which is unified with the user's assertions. If the relation is either " = " (are they equivalent?) or **"unify"** (return the most general common instance) then the unification algorithm is applied to the arguments. Two descriptions unify if there is an assertion stating their equivalence or if they are of the same type and the corresponding arguments unify (unless there is an assertion stating that they are not equal). If an assertion has constraints (a body) they are checked. If the unification is successful the unifier produced is applied to the user's query and the resulting instance is printed. If several assertions are applicable then the user can demand to see more solutions. If the unification fails then a description of the failure is returned.

Here is a short sample session:

```
User:     (unify (foo x) (foo 'a))
Uniform: (foo 'a)
User:     (= (plus x 3) 7)
;;this is computed by the primitive plus
Uniform: (= (plus 4 3) 7)
User:     (= (foo 3) (foo 4))
Uniform:
    (or ;;this fails because either the
        ;;arguments of foo don't unify
        (failure 'arguments-do-not-unify
                 (foo 3)
                 (foo 4))
        ;;or because 3 and 4 don't unify
        (failure 'constants-do-not-unify
                 3
                 4))
```

The last query failed because there were no assertions about how to unify **foo**. The user can extend unification by presenting assertions. For example, the following is how unification can be extended to handle factorial given augmentations for integer subtraction and multiplication.

```
(assert (= (factorial 0) 1))
(assert (= (factorial n)
           (* n (factorial (- n 1)))))
```

The first assertion extends unification so that anything which unifies with factorial of 0 is unifiable with anything which unifies with 1. The second clause states that anything that unifies with factorial of anything, which is called **n**, also

415

unifies with anything which unifies with the product of that thing called **n** and factorial of one minus that thing called **n**.

This definition of factorial can be used in many ways as illustrated below. For example, it can be used as a function as follows:

```
User:     (= (factorial 3) (integer m))
Uniform:  (= (factorial 3) (integer 6))
```

Uniform computed this by searching (by default in a breadth first manner) for an assertion linking descriptions of factorials with descriptions of integers. The base case of **factorial** is one such assertion but it fails since **0** does not unify with **3**. Next the path from **factorial** to integer multiplication of integers is tried. The **n** of a copy of the other **factorial** assertion is unified with **3** and the subproblem of unifying **(* 3 (factorial (- 3 1)))** with **(integer m)** is explored. Integer multiplication then creates the subproblem of unifying **(factorial (- 3 1))** with **(integer y)**. After a few more cycles the problem becomes one of unifying **(factorial (- (- (- 3 1) 1) 1))** with **(factorial 0)**. This succeeds enabling its superiors to succeed causing **m** to unify with **6**.

If we unified **(factorial 3)** with **m** in the above example then **m** would have been unified with **(factorial 3)** instead of **6**. The use of **integer** gives the user greater control over the unification at the price of having to explicitly mention the type. To alleviate this the type **primitive** can be used which unifies only with primitive types. Such use of the **primitive** type corresponds to evaluation in Lisp.

Our description of **factorial** can be used as an inverse function.

```
User:     (= (factorial m) 24)
Uniform:  (= (factorial 4) 24)
```

The system first tries to unify this problem with the base case of **factorial** and fails since **24** does not unify with **1**. Then the path from the other factorial assertion and integer multiplication is tried. The problem **(= (* n (factorial (- n 1))) 24)** is taken care of by integer multiply. It has the rule that if the problem is the product of two unknowns unified with a known integer then unify one of the unknowns with the description **(a-divisor-of** <the product>**)** and the other with the appropriate quotient of the other two. This causes the unification of **(factorial (- (a-divisor-of 24) 1))** and **(quotient 24 (a-divisor-of 24))** to be attempted. The base case of **factorial** is tried and fails. We then apply the recursive assertion for **factorial** and get the subproblem of unifying **(* (- (a-divisor-of 24) 1) (factorial (- (- (a-divisor-of 24) 1) 1))** with **(quotient 24 (a-divisor-of 24))**. Here integer multiplication tries to unify one if its arguments with an integer (to make some progress). The description **(- (a-divisor-of 24) 1)** generates the stream of integers 0, 1, 2, 3, 5, 11, 23, -1, -2, -3, -5, -11, and -23. The number 3 works and m becomes unified with 4.

Inverse **factorial** is partial and fails while trying to intersect two virtual sets.

```
User:     (= (factorial n) 5)
Uniform: (failure 'no-elements-in-common
           (a-divisor-of 5)
           (- (a-divisor-of 5) 1)))
```

Factorial of a constant can be used as a pattern without necessarily being evaluated. The following fails after 2 steps.

```
User:  ( = (factorial 1000000) 17)
Uniform:
    (failure 'constraint-unsatisfiable
        (= (* 1000000
              (factorial
                (- 1000000 1)))
           17)
        (= (*-inverse 17 1000000)
           (factorial
             (- 1000000 1)))
        (failure 'evaluation-error
              *-inverse
              (17 1000000)))
```

This failure was generated by the unification of **(* 1000000 (factorial (- 1000000 1)))** with **17**. Integer multiplication when faced with unifying a product of an integer and an unknown with another integer, unifies the unknown with the integer *-**inverse** of the product and the known multiplicand. *-**inverse** is a function for integer division which raises an error if there is a remainder as was the case here.

Definitions can be single stepped, as illustrated below:

```
User:     (= (factorial 1000000)
          (* (integer x)
          (factorial (integer y))))
Uniform: (= (factorial 1000000)
          (* 1000000
          (factorial 999999)))

User:     (more)
     ;another answer to the last problem
Uniform: (= (factorial 1000000)
          (* 999999000000
          (factorial 999998)))
```

1.4 What is Interesting about Unification

Uniform was developed both to produce a simple yet powerful AI language and to explore unification. Unification is interesting not only as a basis for computation but as a source of insight into questions about specialization, generalization, object merging, inheritance and multiple super classes.

Traditional unification is concerned with creating the most general *syntactic* instance of a set of descriptions. Class and instance are defined purely via the description of the terms. The more instantiated versions of a class are its instances. From an AI point of view, the semantic, not syntactic, instances are what is interesting. A description of a particular equilateral triangle is a semantic instance of the prototype equilateral triangle, regular polygon, triangle, closed figure, line drawing, geometrical figure and so on. The semantic unification of regular polygons and triangles should produce equilateral triangles. Unification not only generates an instance of two descriptions but produces a

418

unifier, i.e. a description of a viewpoint under which the two descriptions are the same. For syntactic unification, the viewpoint is an environment giving bindings and constraints to the variables in the descriptions. A view of polygons and triangles that makes them the same is a description of equal-sidedness and three-sidedness. A viewpoint is not the same as the instance. An equilateral triangle is more than equal-sided and three-sided, it is also a closed geometrical figure. Obtaining this kind of semantic unification is a direction in which this research is headed.

As another example, consider the unification of two trivial Lisp programs: **(cons head tail)** with **(list first second)**. The common instance of the two programs can be described in four ways **(cons first (list second))**, **(cons head (list second))**, **(list first (car tail))** and as **(list head (car tail))**. What is often of more interest than the instance is the viewpoint (or unifier) which produced it. In this example, the viewpoint identifies **first** with **head**, **tail** with **(list second)**, and **second** with **(car tail)**.

Unification can be used to dynamically determine who is an instance of whom. Suppose descriptions **x** and **y** unify to produce a common instance **z**. If **z** equals **x** but not **y**, then **x** is an instance of **y**. If **z** equals both **x** and **y** then **x** and **y** are equal.

The augmentations of unification in Uniform are almost always stated as equivalences between programs. For example, consider a definition of **append** in Uniform.

```
(assert (= (append () back)
           back))
(assert
  (= (append (cons first rest) back)
     (cons first (append rest back)))))
```

Occasionally an augmentation of unification will explicitly describe an instance. This is expressed as a second-order unification as illustrated in the following example,

```
(assert
  (= (unify (a-divisor-of n)
            (a-divisor-of m))
     (a-divisor-of
       (greatest-common-divisor m n))))
```

This example is computationally interesting since it can be used in appropriate cases to intersect virtual sets very efficiently. (a-divisor-of 6), for example, is logically, but not computationally, equivalent to (a-member-of (set 1 -1 2 -2 3 -3 6 -6)).

1.5 Unification and Circularity

Another of Uniform's extensions of unification deals with the handling of circularity. Traditionally unification is defined to perform an "occur check" on every variable binding. The check causes a failure if a variable is bound to something which contains that variable. Because of the expense of making such a check most implementations of Prolog do not make the check. In Uniform's augmented unification, the user can specify for each type of description whether or not the occur check should be performed. For example, **plus** does not perform the check since there is nothing wrong with unifying x with the sum of x, y and z provided the sum of y and z can unify with 0. In general, if the check is not performed the system needs to be able to unify circular structures. In the following example **cons** does not do the check. The variable x is bound to 'a consed with itself while y is bound to 'a consed with a cons of 'a and itself. The two structurally different infinite lists of a's unify successfully.

```
(and (= x (cons 'a x))
     (= y (cons 'a (cons 'a y)))
     (= x y))
```

What is difficult about unifying x and y above is avoiding an infinite recursion. The unification algorithm is extended to check first if the two descriptions are identical. If not, then before recursing on the components of the descriptions, the

420

descriptions are temporarily made identical. If the descriptions were circular then if the same problem reappears recursively, the unification will succeed because they have been made identical. If the descriptions were not circular then no harm was done making them temporarily identical. Several logic programming languages have recently incorporated the ability to unify circular structures (e.g., Prolog II [7] and LM-Prolog [4]).

Circular structures occur naturally in situations where objects need to refer to themselves. Sometimes objects need to know about their parts which in turn need to know what it is they are a part of. The squares in a Monopoly game can conveniently be represented as a list that repeats after 40 elements.

Occur checks can also be used to prevent certain types of inconsistencies. Consider the following example from Peano arithmetic:

```
;a successor of any x is greater than x
(assert (> (successor x) x))
```

Given the query (> y (successor y)), Uniform will try to bind y to (successor (successor y)). If this is considered an inconsistency, then successor should perform the occur check to prevent it.

2 Relationships with Other Languages

Uniform was designed and developed with the initial goal of incorporating the most important features of Lisp, Act 1, and Prolog into a single coherent framework. My basic research strategy begins with the belief that many existing languages and systems contain very general and powerful facilities, but each one has only a small subset of the union of these facilities. Furthermore, a simple coherent union of these facilities is both possible and desirable. Boley's research on the FIT language shares this research strategy [2]. FIT, however, is based upon a generalized notion of variables, assignment, pattern matching and demons. Loops is a language which is also based upon the belief that there are important ideas in procedural, object-oriented, and rule-based systems that need to be combined in a coherent framework [28]. The unification of these facilities is much stronger in Uniform, resulting in a simpler, more elegant system. As discussed later, the major disadvantage of Uniform is that it is very difficult (and perhaps not even possible) to implement it *efficiently*.

2.1 Uniform and Lisp

Uniform was built upon MacLisp and, through the use of an escape mechanism, incorporates all of Lisp. However, in using this escape one loses the ability to run programs symbolically or on partial descriptions or backwards. A more interesting way in which Uniform incorporates Lisp is the ability to write Uniform programs that look very much like Lisp. For example, one can write **append** in Uniform as follows,

```
(assert
    (= (append front back)
       (cond ((null front) back)
             ((cons (first front)
                    (append (rest front)
                            back))))))
```

This program does not mean the same as the corresponding Lisp program. It states an equivalence not an evaluation step. Unification does not have **eval**'s sense of direction or notion of simplification. Instead of evaluation, a description is unified with a variable constrained to be of a particular data type, such as integer or s-expression, or constrained to consist of only primitive data types. This corresponds closely to lazy evaluation in Lisp. Lacking the control information implicit in Lisp, Uniform's interpreter is in general slower. In return, the **append** program above can be executed symbolically, used in pattern matching, run backwards, be used to append any kind of list, and be used in judging program equivalence.

The reason the **append** program looks like Lisp is that the primitives **null**, **first**, **rest**, and **cond** can be written in

Uniform. The primitives of Lisp that are difficult to write include those that perform side-effects such as **setq**, **rplaca** and array operations. One promising solution to overcoming the lack of side-effects in Uniform is to implement logical but mutable structures as in LM-Prolog's implementation of mutable arrays [9]. The basic idea is to provide primitives that look as if they are creating new copies of objects but hidden in the implementation side-effects are being performed upon shared structures. Other possibilities for implementing side-effects in Uniform are to use tail-recursion optimization as is done in Concurrent Prolog [26] or reference counts to know when it is safe to re-use the current structure rather than copy.

The most essential property of Lisp, the ability to run large programs efficiently, is lacking in Uniform. Uniform will remain a toy language until a compiler is written for it. Compilers for SmallTalk [11], Director [15], Prolog [29], and LM-Prolog [4] contain relevant techniques. Also very promising are partial evaluators which can be used for compilation [8] [17]. Another area of research which shows some promise of leading to an acceptable level of efficiency is work within logic programming languages on describing and using control or meta-level information [5] [10].

2.2 Uniform and Actor Languages

Computer languages based upon computational entities called "actors" offer modularity, parallelism, full extensibility of both data and functions and a simple but powerful computational semantics. An early version of Uniform was attempted in Act 1 [20], a language that takes the idea of actors to the extreme. Many of the facilities of Act 1 would have been available in Uniform under this implementation, including its excellent primitives for describing concurrent computation. Unfortunately the implementation of Act 1 is too slow to build a practical interpreter upon it.

Act 1 is a message passing language based upon the convention that actors be able to respond to "eval" and "match" messages. Uniform can be viewed as a language in which descriptions pass "unify" messages between themselves and their parts. As we saw in the previous section, unification subsumes evaluation. Unification clearly subsumes the match messages in Act 1 since pattern matching is just the special case of unification where one of the descriptions contains no variables.

One of the important features of actor languages is the ability to describe a new data type and be able to use old programs on the new type. This is a consequence of the fact that programs depend only upon the behavior of data in response to messages. A list is any actor which can answer **first** and **rest** messages. The analogous statement about Uniform is that a list is any description that can unify with **(cons x y)**. For example, suppose we want to define a new kind of list which efficiently represents lists of successive integers. The description **(list-of-integers 1 100)** is equal to a list of the first 100 integers. To define such lists we need only describe how they unify with descriptions of conses as follows.

```
(assert
 ;;if the end is less than the beginning
 ;;then its an empty list
 (= (list-of-integers begin
                      (less-than begin))
    ()))
```

```
(assert
 ;;if the beginning is less than the end
 ;;then its just the beginning consed
 ;;onto a new list of integers
    (= (list-of-integers
          begin
          (and end
               (greater-than-or-equal
                 begin)))
       (cons begin
             (list-of-integers
                (plus begin 1)
                end))))
```

Notice that this way of implementing lists as anything that can unify with a cons of two variables subsumes the method inheritance mechanism in languages like SmallTalk and Director. A method can be applied to an object if there

424

is a way of unifying the type of the method with the object. If nothing is known about how to do some operation upon a particular kind of list then the same operation upon lists in general will be used. The query

```
(= (append (list-of-integers 1 100)
           (list-of-integers 101 200))
   (is-list list))
```

will unify list with the list of the first 200 integers. (is-list has one argument which is a list; e.g. (is-list (cons 1 nil)) and (is-list (list 'a 'b 'c)) are valid lists.) The list is described as (is-list (cons 1 (cons 2 ... (list-of-integers 101 200)))). This is because the only path from **append** to **is-list** is via the **cons** in the definition of **append** given earlier. One could provide the equivalent of a method for appending lists of integers as follows so that list becomes (is-list (list-of-integers 1 200)).

```
(assert
  (= (append
       (list-of-integers start middle)
       (list-of-integers
          (plus middle 1)
          end))
     (list-of-integers start end)))

;;The following declares that
;;list-of-integers is a list.
(assert
  (= (list-of-integers start end)
     (is-list
        (list-of-integers start end)))))
```

Uniform's breadth-first search will use the above to find solutions long before the general "method" for **append** is used. Since in general we want to be able to find all solutions, it is difficult to indicate that the general method should not be considered if the special one succeeds. One clearly needs a rich control language.

Subclasses can be defined in the same manner as we used to define classes. A trivial subclass of **list-of-integers** which always starts with 1 can defined as follows.

425

```
(assert (= (first-n-integers n)
           (list-of-integers 1 n)))
```

This same mechanism works for multiple super classes. If we define how horizontal-dashed-lines unify with both horizontal-lines and with dashed-lines then operations upon either one can be applied to horizontal-dashed-lines. If the control strategy is breadth-first then the multiple super classes are searched in a breadth-first fashion.

One very important part of some of the actor languages is their user definable control structures and the ability to compute in parallel [14] [20]. The absence of such facilities is a serious deficiency of Uniform. One could add such information as *advice* to the interpreter and compiler as to how to go about doing the unifications. This approach is similar to one taken in Metalog [10]. The appeal of separating logic from control is that a user can develop and test the logic or competence of a program before adding control information to improve its performance [19] [23]. Also, different uses of the same program may be helped by different control information.

2.3 Uniform and Logic Programming

In recent years a number of logic programming languages have appeared. Most notable is Prolog. Programs in Prolog are statements in the first-order predicate logic restricted to Horn clauses. Programs are executed by a resolution theorem prover. What is special about Prolog is that it is intended as a general purpose programming language meant to compete with compiled Lisp as well as with Planner-like languages. (It may well be that Prolog's success in this regard over Planner-like languages is its use of unification as the principle way of constructing and tearing apart structures as well as binding variables.) The objection to logic as being an excessively constrained manner of reasoning is irrelevant to its worth as a programming language. One would not want to build AI programs upon a Lisp whose interpreter did "informal" reasoning. The objection to logic that it is not concerned

426

with control over the use of knowledge is a serious one. This is an active area of research in logic programming.

When compared with Lisp, Prolog has many advantages and a few very serious disadvantages. Prolog shares with Uniform the ability to use the same program in many ways. For example, the Prolog definition of **append** can be used not only to compute the result of appending two lists together but can also be used as a predicate to verify that the result of appending two lists is a third list, as a generator of pairs of lists that append to a particular list, as a way of finding the difference between two lists, and as a generator of triples of lists such that the first two append to form the third.

Prolog has a few other features which Lisp lacks. Among them are the ability to compute with partially instantiated structures, a convenient way to handle multiple outputs, and the use of pattern matching instead of explicit list construction and selection. On the negative side, Prolog implementations are the result of a much smaller implementation effort than the major Lisp dialects and correspondingly lack good programming environments, I/O facilities, adequate arithmetic, and the like. The Japanese fifth generation project or attempts to embed Prolog in Lisp (e.g. LM-Prolog [4]) may alleviate this.

Uniform was developed with the goal of capturing and improving these positive aspects of Prolog. Uniform supports all the uses of a definition that Prolog does and an additional few. For example, Uniform's definition of **append** is equivalent to Prolog's and can also be used as an implementation of segment patterns. For example, the Uniform description **(append (list first) (append middle (list last)))** will unify with any list whose first element is **first** and last element is **last** and whose middle is a possibly empty list called **middle**. Unlike Prolog, this can be used inside a description. For example, the following program relates two lists with swapped ends.

```
(assert
   (= (swap-ends
        (append (list first)
                (append middle
                        (list last))))
      (append (list last)
              (append middle
                      (list first)))))
```

Because **append** is so generally useful Uniform provides a read macro to allow the above to be expressed as follows.

```
(assert
   (= (swap-ends [first !middle last])
      [last !middle first]))
```

In Uniform one can augment the unification of relations other than the = relation. If desired one can write in Prolog's relational style. The following is a Uniform program for defining the **grandparent** relation (which can be used as the **grandchild** relation too).

```
(assert
   (grandparent-of grandchild grandparent)
   ;;the above is true if
   ;;the following holds
   (parent-of a-parent grandparent)
   (parent-of grandchild a-parent))
```

The program says that two variables are in the grandparent relation if a child of the first variable unifies with a parent of the second. As in Prolog the variables **grandparent** and **grandchild** are universally qualified and **a-parent** is existential (by virtue of not being in the "head"). It is equivalent to the Prolog program:

```
grandparent-of(Grandchild, Grandparent)
:-
parent-of(A-parent, Grandparent),
parent-of(Grandchild, A-parent).
```

Some extensions to Prolog augment unification in ways similar to Uniform. Prolog II [7] and LM-Prolog [4] have the ability to put "constraints" upon variables (by "freezing" goals). These constraints are ordinary Prolog statements which are executed when they are unified with other objects. Kornfeld [18] has incorporated equality directly into Prolog and has shown how this subsumes "freeze". His addition of equality to Prolog has many limitations, primarily because its search is severely limited for the sake of efficiency. Term re-writing systems also have a built-in directionality in their use of equivalences.

3 A Detailed Example

As a simple example that illustrates many of Uniform's features let us consider an implementation of association lists. It is a typical example of how the same program can be used to construct a data structure and to compute with the same data structure. Besides reducing the amount of programming it impossible for accessing programs to be based upon a mistaken notion of how the structure is constructed since the accessing programs are also used to construct the structures.

The following is an implementation of association lists:

```
(assert
 ;;association pair is in the front
 ;;of the list
 (= (association-of
        key
        (cons (list key value) rest))
     value))
(assert ;otherwise "cdr" down the list
 (= (association-of
        key
        (cons first rest))
     (association-of key rest)))
```

This program can best be understood by seeing how it can be used. First let us build a list of associations between objects and colors. We can associate **sky** with **blue** in a list **colors** by unifying (**association-of** 'sky colors) with the symbol **blue**. The variable **colors** is unified with **(cons (list 'sky 'blue) rest-1)** or in an alternative syntax **[['sky 'blue] !rest-1]**. In other words, **colors** is a list whose first element is a list of **sky** and **blue** and the rest is an unbound variable. If we next associate **grass** with **green** and **ocean** with **blue**, the **colors** list will be bound to **[['sky 'blue] ['grass 'green] ['ocean 'blue] !rest-3]**. Were we to add any of the associations already in colors it would succeed without making any new bindings.

The association list can be used in many ways. If we associate **grass** with the variable **grass-color**, it will be bound to **green**. Or if we associate the variable **blue-thing** with **blue**, **blue-thing** will be bound to **sky**. If that fails later, or other alternatives are desired, then **blue-thing** will be unified with **ocean**.

If that alternative fails, a weakness of Prolog is revealed. The problem of unifying **(association-of blue-thing colors)** with **'blue** is interpreted as "is it possible that **blue-thing** is associated with **blue** and if so how". If we reject an answer it is interpreted as "is it possible in some other way". If an association list "ends" with a variable, then the answer is always yes. The first answer was "yes if **blue-thing** is **sky**", the second answer was "yes if **blue-thing** is **ocean**" and the next answer was "yes if **colors** is **[['sky 'blue] ['grass 'green] ['ocean 'blue] [blue-thing 'blue] !rest-4]**. In other words, "yes, if **colors** is an association list with the variable **blue-thing** associated with **blue**". This is a reasonable answer and sometimes exactly what was meant by the question, but the more common question "given what you currently know about colors, what is associated with blue" cannot be expressed in logic programming languages (without finding and binding all the variables in **colors** to unique constants).

Uniform has a primitive relation to distinguish the two interpretations. The default is "is it possible". "Is it known" is indicated by using the relation "known". It marks the incoming unifier so that a failure results if any of its unbound variables are unified. Unifying **(known (= (association-of blue-thing colors) 'blue))"** would prevent **rest-3** inside of **colors** from being bound. The variable **blue-thing** will be

430

bound to **sky**, then **ocean**, and then the unification would fail.

This problem was revealed when in answer to the question "what can be blue", Uniform replied, "the sky, the ocean and any blue thing". It was the question that was at fault, not the answer. It should have been "what is known to be blue". A strength of Uniform is that one can define and use an association list which has variables in it. Dealing with partial knowledge is very important in AI. One can express, for example, that John's apple is either red, green or yellow by associating John's apple with a variable for the color of John's apple and unifying that variable with the disjunction of red, green, and yellow. Later if we learn more about the color of John's apple we can specify it further, in the meanwhile we can use what is known about his apple.

4 Implementation Issues

At the time of this writing, the implementation does not run all the examples in this paper. The unification algorithm, the primitive types, and the top-level work. The implementation is capable of running examples such as **append**, **association-of**, and **grandparent**. The clever integer multiply for **factorial** and the **known** primitive do not yet work. Examples involving them have been hand-simulated.

Uniform was implemented twice during 1980 and 1981. (The second implementation is described in [16].) Both implementations were excessively slow. This is due partly to two questionable design decisions: the first problem is that Uniform's unification algorithm works on sub-problems independently and then combines the results. This may possibly be implemented efficiently on a massively parallel machine but it is excessively slow on sequential hardware. Partial results need to be communicated between subproblems to achieve an acceptable level of efficiency. The other questionable, poor design decision is that failures are represented by complex descriptions of why something failed. For some applications this may be extremely useful but it is very expensive. These descriptions often grow very large as they become a disjunction of all the things that failed along the way.

More fundamentally Uniform has so little control and so much power that it is often forced into combinatorial searches. Consider the unification of (f <term1> <term2>) and (g <term3> <term4>). The unifier needs to see if there is an assertion or a chain of assertions between f of two arguments and g of two arguments. For each one of the form (= (f <term5> <term6>) (g <term7> <term8>) the system must attempt to unify <term1> with <term5>, <term2> with <term6>, <term3> with <term7> and <term4> with <term8>. Because Uniform, unlike Prolog with equality [18], can on demand generate all solutions, it is forced into a combinatoric search. There are various solutions to this problem:

(1) We can provide a control facility that allows the user to write programs which give guidance of various degrees of specificity. The guidance can describe where to search, how to index assertions, how to represent descriptions, as well as what not to do. The original programs are left alone and the user, to the degree desired or necessary, provides control information to increase the effectiveness of the computation. The idea is that the programs work, but too slowly, and the programmer provides guidance that changes only their speed. Wherever there is a choice within the interpreter there should be a corresponding hook in the control language. Research on control languages for Prolog is being carried out by, among others, [10] and [5]. In addition to providing a control language, the user needs tools to monitor the execution of programs to see where guidance is needed.

(2) The incorporation of general heuristics is also possible. When faced with an arbitrary choice of which step to take next, the system could take into account the number and degree of instantiation of variables in each of the alternatives, database statistics, the current recursion depth of the proof, whether the step can lead to a proof or a disproof of the goal, and so on.

(3) Another solution is to automatically eliminate bad paths and to exploit special representations of descriptors,

equivalences, and assertions. Certain paths that will never lead to a solution can be recognized and need never be considered. Other paths contain a series of steps that accomplish something that can always be accomplished by a series of fewer steps and so can be eliminated. Solutions can be sketched out and worked out at successive levels of abstraction. Certain very common relations or assertions can be built into the mechanisms and representations of the interpreter. Intermediate results can be indexed around the objects involved for fast retrieval. Promising paths can be followed while less promising ones delayed until the promising paths no longer are so promising. All of these techniques were incorporated into the second implementation of Uniform in the attempt to provide a reasonable default behavior in the absence of control information.

(4) Another possibility is to make use of a "partial evaluator" to automatically generate more efficient specialized versions of Uniform's unifier. These specialized versions could then be used when appropriate. [17]

5 Conclusions and Future Research

A surprising result of this research is that unification, a process of generating the most general instance of a set of descriptions, can be such a powerful basis for a programming language. Unification unifies the essence of Lisp, Act 1, and Prolog into a simple coherent framework.

Uniform is far from complete. Some of the major avenues of future research include:

(1) Developing and incorporating the dual of unification, generalization, into the language. The duality between unification and generalization is striking and their implementations may share a lot of mechanism. Generalization is a process of finding the most specific description of a set of descriptions such that all the descriptions are instances of the generalization. This is the dual of the view of unification as a process finding the most general instance common to a set of descriptions.

(2) A shortcoming of Prolog is its inability to use negative information. In the previous example of association lists we might want to prevent a key from having more than one association. Uniform should be able to use the following:

```
(assert
   (not (= (association-of
            key
            (cons (list key value)
                  rest))
         (not value))))
```

This would cause the unification to fail if the key is found but the values do not unify. Negative information can be used in a default strategy which concurrently tries to unify two descriptions and to show that they are not unifiable.

(3) In the process of unification a variable may acquire multiple constraints. As a default, Uniform simply conjoins them. If later an attempt is made to give the variable a value, then the constraints disappear if the value satisfies them, otherwise it fails. Inconsistent constraints do not cause failure unless there is an attempt to use them. If the constraints have a unique solution then only that value can unify with them, but the system does not compute that value. The unification of constraints appears to be a natural place to use some of the constraint satisfaction techniques found in systems such as Thinglab [3], and Steele and Sussman's constraint system [27]. These systems provide evidence for the general usefulness of describing much of computation in terms of constraints.

(4) We have explored the unification of descriptions of programs. Exploring the unification of other complex structures such as frames, scripts, and units should be equally valuable. Much of what systems such as FRL, XPRT, SAM and KRL do is match complex declarative structures with others. Unification, a more general and powerful process than pattern matching, promises to be very useful for dealing with these structures.

(5) As has been pointed out elsewhere [21] [13] [23] [19] there is much to be gained by separating the control and logic components of an algorithm. Uniform programs have

434

much less control information in them than equivalent Lisp or Act 1 programs. A general search strategy is used as a default so that the factual or competence component of programs can be developed and tested without the added complexity of being concerned with efficiency. The efficiency can be put in later and kept lexically separate from the rest of the program.

(6) Theoretical work needs to be done connecting Uniform's notion of augmented unification with work on higher-order unification and theories of equality.

(7) It is very difficult to evaluate the worth of computer language based solely upon small programs. A serious implementation is sorely needed. Concurrent with the research suggested above, Uniform needs to be tested by writing large complex programs in it. In this respect Uniform is way behind Lisp, Prolog, and actor systems.

REFERENCES

1 Attardi, G. and M. Simi. "Consistency and Completeness of OMEGA, A Logic for Knowledge Representation", IJCAI-81, August 1981.

2 Boley, H. "Five Views of FIT programming", Fachbereich Informatik, University of Hamburg, Nr. 57, September 1979.

3 Borning, A. "ThingLab -- A Constraint-Oriented Simulation Laboratory", Xerox Palo Alto Research Center report SSL-79-3, July 1979.

4 Carlsson, M. and K. Kahn. "LM-Prolog User Manual", UPMAIL, Uppsala University, Sweden, Technical Report No. 24, November 1983.

5 Clark K. and F. McCabe. "IC-Prolog - Language Features" in [6].

6 Clark, K. and S-A. Tarnlund. *Logic Programming*, Academic Press, 1982.

7 Colmerauer, A. "Prolog and Infinite Trees", in [6].

8 Emanuelson, P. "Performance enhancement in a well-structured pattern matcher through partial evaluation", Ph.D. thesis, Software Systems Research Center, Linkoeping University, 1982.

9 Eriksson, L-H. and M. Rayner. "Incorporating Mutable Arrays into LM-Prolog", Proceedings of the Second International Conference on Logic Programming, Uppsala Sweden, July 1984.

10 Gallaire, H. and C. Lasserre. "A Control Metalanguage for Logic Programming" in [6].

11 Goldberg, A. and D. Robson. *SmallTalk-80: The Language and its Implementation,* Addison-Wesley, Reading, MA. 1983.

12 Hansson A., S. Haridi and S-A.Tarnlund. "Some Aspects of a Logic Machine Prototype" in [6].

13 Hayes, P. "Computation and Deduction", Proc. Symp. Math. Found. of Comp. Sci., Czech Acad. of Sciences, 1973.

14 Hewitt, C. "Viewing Control Structures as Patterns of Passing Messages" *Artificial Intelligence*, Vol 8. No. 3, June 1977, pp. 323-364.

15 Kahn, K. "Director Guide", MIT AI Memo 482B, December 1979.

16 Kahn, K. "The Implementation of Uniform -- A Knowledge-Representation/Programming Language based upon Equivalence of Descriptions", ECAI-82, Orsay France, 1982.

17 Kahn, K. and M. Carlsson. "Compilation of Prolog Programs without the use of a Prolog Compiler", The Proceedings of the FGCS'84, Tokyo, November 1984.

18 Kornfeld, W. "Equality for Prolog", IJCAI-83, Karlsruhe, West Germany, August 1983. Also appears in this volume.

19 Kowalski, R. "Algorithm = logic + control", *Communications of the ACM*, Vol. 22, no. 7, 1979.

20 Lieberman, H. "A Preview of Act 1", MIT AI Laboratory Memo 625, June 1981.

21 McCarthy, J. "Programs with Common Sense", in *Semantic Information Processing*, Minsky, M. ed., MIT Press, Cambridge, Mass. 1968.

22   Minker, J.   "A Set-Oriented Predicate Logic Programming Language", University of Maryland, Computer Science Center TR-922, July 1980.

23 Pratt, V. "The Competence/Performance Dichotomy in Programming", MIT AI Memo 400, January 1977.

24 Robinson, J. A Machine-oriented Logic Based on the Resolution Principle, *Journal of the ACM*, Vol. 12, no. 1, January 1965.

25 Sacerdoti E.,   R. Fikes., R. Reboh, D. Sagalowicz, R. Waldinger, M. Wilber. "Qlisp: A Language for the Interactive Development of Complex Systems", SRI Technical Note 120, 1976.

26 Shapiro, E. "A Subset of Concurrent Prolog and Its Interpreter", ICOT Technical Report, TR-003, ICOT, Tokyo 1983.

27 Steele G.   "The definitions and implementation of a computer programming language based on constraints", MIT AI Lab TR-595, August 1980.

28   Stefik, M., D. Bobrow,   S. Mittal, and L. Conway. "Knowledge Programming in Loops: Report on an Experimental Course", The AI Magazine, Fall 1983.

29 Warren, D. "Implementing Prolog -- compiling predicate logic programs", Department of Artificial Intelligence, University of Edinburgh, 1977.

Part VI:

Semantic Foundations

LOGIC PROGRAMMING LANGUAGE SCHEME

Joxan Jaffar

Department of Computer Science
Monash University
Clayton, Victoria 3168
Australia.

Jean-Louis Lassez†
Michael J. Maher†

Department of Computer Science
University of Melbourne
Parkville, Victoria 3052
Australia.

ABSTRACT

Numerous extended versions of PROLOG are now emerging. In order to provide greater versatility and expressive power, some versions allow functional programming features, others allow infinite data structures. However, there is concern that such languages may have little connection left with logic. In some instances, various logical frameworks have been proposed to solve this problem. Nevertheless, the crucial point has not been addressed: the preservation of the unique semantic properties of logic programs. The significance of our effort here is twofold: (1) There is a natural logic programming language scheme wherein these properties hold. (2) Formal foundations for extended versions of traditional PROLOG can be obtained as instances of this scheme. They automatically enjoy its properties.

---

†Current address: I.B.M. Thomas J. Watson Research Center, Yorktown Heights, NY 10598, USA

1 INTRODUCTION

Logic formalisms have become attractive for programming language designers. The two relevant aspects of logic are model theory and proof theory: model theory corresponds to specification and other declarative notions, and proof theory corresponds to operational semantics and implementations. In other words, model theory is used to formalize *what* we want to be computed and proof theory is used to formalize *how* to compute it. The meaning we give to a program is the set of logical consequences, that is the set of formulas which are true in every model of the program. We expect the program to tell us when a given formula is true in all models.

Much of automatic theorem proving is based on the clausal form of predicate logic, allowing reasoning to be performed in the purely syntactic context of Herbrand bases and Herbrand models. Resolution is used to compute the syntactic part of logical consequence, i.e. it tells us when a formula is true in all Herbrand models. This is sufficient to determine that it is true in all models. However speeds of execution that are expected of programming languages cannot be achieved in that general framework.

The restriction to definite clauses, which leads to a loss of expressive power, has nevertheless distinct advantages. It allows the use of SLD resolution, which is sufficiently efficient to form a basis for the implementation of a programming language. Furthermore, the declarative semantics have a remarkable property: logical consequence can be determined by examining a single model. Indeed, SLD resolution tells us when a formula is true in the least model. This is sufficient to determine that the formula is true in all models. Finally, complete logic programs have been proposed to regain some of the lost expressive power at no cost in execution time. All this forms a theoretical basis for the language PROLOG.

PROLOG is considered by many to be a kernel language. Consequently, much of the present research in logic programming concentrates on extensions of PROLOG. A major issue is the integration of the essential concepts of functional programming and logic programming.

LISP is the earliest and the most common system implementing a functional programming concept. Thus it is not surprising that efforts have been made to amalgamate LISP and PROLOG. Some examples include LOGLISP [29] and QLOG [17], these being PROLOG systems implemented within LISP wherein the PROLOG interpreter can be invoked from within a LISP program and vice versa. A version of QUTE [33] was developed achieving a similar amalgamation, but here the motivating factor was an already existing formal foundation: the domain of symbolic expressions [32].

There are approaches to functional programming in logic programming other than using LISP. FUNLOG [37, 38, 39], for example, uses a pattern-driven reduction method to replace the conventional unification process in logic programming systems. [40], on the other hand, uses a "reducibility predicate" to allow user-defined reductions within a conventional logic programming framework. LCA [4] interprets its predicate and function definitions by means of procedures executed by rewriting mechanisms. A more recent version of QUTE [34] uses traditional unification as a common evaluation method for both its functional and logic programming features. A central mechanism involves reducing sets of equations over QUTE expressions.

Some systems concentrate on using equations, particularly for defining data types. UNIFORM [16] and UNICORN [3] handle equality inside their respective unification algorithms. PROLOG-WITH-EQUALITY [18], on the other hand, allows the user to augment the traditional unification algorithm by means of a distinguished PROLOG procedure where equality is defined. The main motivation was to gain the modularity advantages of generic operations and class structuring as are found in object-oriented languages such as SMALLTALK. [10] treats these issues more systematically in the language EQLOG. They provide user-definable abstract data types and parameterized modules and propose a category-theoretic interpretation.

[7] essentially abandons first order logic as a foundation for PROLOG II. The formal basis is instead a rewriting system over the domain of rational trees. In particular, this provides an infinite data structure for the language. Both FUNLOG and LCA allow the use of another infinite data structure, streams, which can be used to incorporate the notion of processes.

In summary, these extensions are focused upon the inter-related concepts of equations, data types, infinite data structures and functions.

As indicated above, some of the systems have accompanying proposals for formal frameworks. In general, the choice of the exact framework is dictated by the particular extension of PROLOG in question. Consequently, there is concern that these extensions and their accompanying frameworks have little connection left with logic. In fact, the very nature of the concepts in these extensions is such that it is not difficult to accommodate them in standard logic or some variant thereof. For example, [10] proposes many-sorted first-order Horn clause logic with equality. [11] and [8] re-interpret an aspect of the term rewriting based PROLOG II in standard logic by showing the soundness of successful derivations.

The crucial point we address here is not, however, just the issue of formalization within or without logic. After all, the various formalisms should be considered as complementary rather than competing. Our main concern is the preservation, in the extensions, of the semantic properties of traditional logic programming which make the latter so simple and powerful. We achieve this essentially by introducing equality theories and generalized unification. The proofs of the various results we will mention can be obtained from [14].

In the following section, we explain how the desirable model theoretic and fixpoint properties can be extended naturally to logic programs with equality. The third section contains a discussion of the corresponding computational methods. The results of soundness and completeness are given. In the fourth section we show how, by completing the equality theory, we can preserve the soundness and completeness of negation-as-failure. The definition of our proposed logic programming language scheme is given in the final section. Any extension to logic programming which is an instance of this scheme will automatically enjoy all the previously discussed properties. We illustrate a use of the scheme by outlining its application to PRO-LOG II.

Appropriate background information on automatic theorem-proving can be found in [5], and on logic programming in [19]. [8] established the existence of a least model for definite clause programs and its least fixpoint characterization. [1] provided a treatment of the soundness and completeness of SLD resolution and characterized SLD finite failure using fixpoint techniques. [20] extended the model-theoretic and fixpoint semantics and the results of [1] on finite failure by using the notions of closure and fairness. Further related results can be found in [21]. A formal treatment of negation-as-failure and the definition of a complete logic program were given by [6]. [13] established the completeness of the negation-as-failure rule for complete logic programs. A self-contained account of most of these results can be found in [23] and a further treatment [22] is forthcoming. Additional references are contained in

444

the extensive bibliography [2].

2 DECLARATIVE ASPECTS

2.1 Logic Programs

Model theory is a rich and natural formalism for the declarative aspects of programming languages. We obtain a model by assigning a meaning to all the constructs of a logic program and truth values to logic formulas such that the logic program itself is assigned the value true. A logic program has, in general, infinitely many models. A particular formula may be true in some models and false in others. This simply means that the program does not contain enough information to force a particular truth value upon this formula. Of particular interest are those formulas, called logical consequences, which are true in all models of the programs. We give a declarative semantics to a logic program by assigning it its associated set of logical consequences. In other words, we view a logic program as defining a database of facts whose truth value is guaranteed regardless of the meanings assigned to the various constructs (provided the meanings are consistent with the program itself being assigned the value true).

The importance of working within the clausal form of predicate logic stems from the following facts: (1) there is a canonical syntactic domain and functional assignment which facilitates symbolic computation, and (2) to prove that a ground atom is a logical consequence, we can restrict ourselves to proving that it is true in the models associated with this syntactic domain. This domain, called the Herbrand universe, will be denoted by $\tau(\Sigma)$ where Σ is the alphabet. The associated models are called Herbrand models. In summary, this is formalized as

Proposition 1. $P \models q$ iff $P \models_{\tau(\Sigma)} q$

where P is in clausal form, q is a ground atom, and $\models_D$ denotes logical implication in the context of a fixed domain and functional assignment; in this case, D is the Herbrand domain and functional assignment.

By restricting attention to definite clausal formulas, we can, at the expense of foregoing full expressive power, obtain some remarkable semantic properties. One of them is the existence of a *canonical* Herbrand model M, known as the least Herbrand model, such that

445

Proposition 2. $P \models q$ iff $M \models q$

where P is in definite clause form and q a ground atom. Thus M characterizes the set of ground atomic logical consequences of P. Another semantic property concerns the fixpoint formalization of the usual informal semantics of logic programs based on a bottom-up production system. Associating with a definite clause formula P a function T_P which maps from and into Herbrand interpretations, we have the following link between T_P and M.

Proposition 3.   The least fixpoint of T_P is the least Herbrand model M.

2.2 Logic Programs with Equality

A major shortcoming of using Herbrand universes is that the notion of equality is accommodated only via syntactic identity. One easy solution is to consider those quotient universes $\tau(\Sigma)/R$ where R is a congruence relation consistent with the intended equality theory E. In general, there are an infinite number of such models R of E. There is a result, in this context, analogous to Proposition 1:

Proposition 4. $P, E \models q$ iff $P \models_{\tau(\Sigma)/R} q$ for all R

We desire, however, a result along the lines of Proposition 2, i.e. the existence of a canonical model for the equality theory. In other words, we wish the existence of a congruence R such that

Proposition 5. $E \models s = t$ iff $[s] = [t]$

where $[s]$ and $[t]$ denote the R-congruence classes of the ground terms s and t respectively. But this can be achieved *only* if the theory E has a finest congruence relation R. This motivates our choice of using *Horn equality clauses* in our framework presented below.

We use the symbols V, Σ and Π to denote the sets of variables, function symbols and non-logical predicate symbols respectively. (Note that constants are functions of arity 0.) Thus the latter set does not contain the symbol $=$. $\tau(\Sigma)$ and $\tau(\Sigma \cup V)$ denote respectively the ground terms and the terms possibly containing variables.

446

As usual, *equations* are of the form s = t where s and t are terms over $\tau(\Sigma \cup V)$.

A *definite clause logic program* is defined to be a finite set of definite clauses

$$A \leftarrow e_1, e_2, \ldots, e_n, B_1, B_2, \ldots, B_m$$

where A is an atom, i.e. not an equation, each e_i is an equation and each B_i is an atom.

A *Horn equality clause* takes one of two forms:

$$e \leftarrow e_1, e_2, \ldots, e_m$$

or

$$\leftarrow e_1, e_2, \ldots, e_m$$

where $m \geq 0$ and all the e_i's therein are equations. As usual, variables in Horn equality clauses are implicitly universally quantified. We define a *Horn clause equality theory* to be a possibly infinite set of Horn equality clauses. (See e.g. [35] for some properties of definite clause equality theories.) A given consistent Horn clause equality theory E defines a logic programming language whose programs, called *logic programs*, are the pairs (P, E) where P is a definite clause logic program.

The results given here are for the simple extension of the class of logic programs defined in [14] obtained by allowing equations in the body of clauses. The corresponding proofs are easily adapted from the proofs in that paper.

Proposition 6. Each consistent Horn equality theory generates a finest Σ-congruence over $\tau(\Sigma)$.

The proof of this proposition follows easily from Proposition 2. We thus may now write $\tau(\Sigma)/E$ to denote this finest congruence. As a consequence

Proposition 7. $(P, E) \models q$ iff $P \models_{\tau(\Sigma)/E} q$

Let $\bar{t}$ denote a sequence of terms $t_1, t_2, \ldots, t_n$, $n \geq 0$. We now give definitions with respect to a given logic program (P, E). The *E-base* is $\{p(\bar{d}): \bar{d} \in (\tau(\Sigma)/E)^n, p \in \Pi, p \text{ is n-ary}\}$. An *E-interpretation* I is a subset of the E-base. We write [s] to denote the element in $\tau(\Sigma)/E$ assigned to the ground term s. Similarly, $[\bar{t}]$ is a element of $(\tau(\Sigma)/E)^n$ and $[p(\bar{t})]$ is an element of the E-base. Where S is a set of ground terms, [S] denotes $\{[s]: s \in S\}$. We are now in a position to give the declarative semantics of logic programs with equality as a natural extension of the declarative semantics of traditional logic programs. There is a least E-model of (P, E), M, and

Theorem 1. $(P, E) \models q$ iff $M \models q$.

Note that Proposition 2 is a trivial instance of this theorem: syntactic identity corresponds to the empty Horn equality theory.

   We now consider the fixpoint formalization of an intuitive semantics of our logic programs. $T_{(P, E)}$ maps from and into E-interpretations and is defined as follows:

$$T_{(P,E)}(I) = \{p(\bar{d}): \text{there is a ground instance of a clause in P}$$

$$p(\bar{s}) \leftarrow e_1, \dots , e_n, B_1, \dots , B_m$$

$$\text{such that } [\bar{s}] = \bar{d}$$

$$E \models e_k \text{ for } 1 \leq k \leq n \text{ and}$$

$$[B_k] \in I \text{ for } 1 \leq k \leq m\}$$

   Intuitively, $T_{(P, E)}(I)$ is the set of facts deducible in one step from the facts in I. Thus $T_{(P, E)}^n(\emptyset)$ is the set of facts deducible from the program (P, E) in n or fewer steps. Call this set $T_{(P, E)} \uparrow n$. Then the set of all facts deducible from (P, E) is $\bigcup_{n=0}^{\infty} T_{(P, E)} \uparrow n$; we call this $T_{(P, E)} \uparrow \omega$.

   We now have two semantics for (P, E), one being its least E-model and the other $T_{(P, E)} \uparrow \omega$. That these two sets are in fact identical follows from a well-known fixpoint theorem which can be phrased as follows: if L is a complete lattice and $f : L \rightarrow L$ is a continuous function, then f has a least fixpoint lfp(f) which can be characterized in two ways:

$$\text{lfp}(f) = \bigcup_{n=0}^{\infty} f^n(\bot) \text{ where } \bot \text{ is the least element of L}$$

and

$$\text{lfp}(f) \;=\; \cap \; \{x \colon f(x) \subseteq x\}$$

Since the class of E-interpretations forms a complete lattice (under the inclusion ordering), since $T_{(P,\,E)}$ is continuous over this class, and since the class of E-models is given by $\{I \colon T_{(P,\,E)}(I) \subseteq I\}$, a simple application of the above theorem gives

Theorem 2. $M = T_{(P,\,E)} \!\uparrow\! \omega.$

where M is the least E-model of (P, E).

3 OPERATIONAL ASPECTS

The two major constituents of an interpreter for logic programming are a unification algorithm and an implementation of SLD resolution. In this section we consider the generalization of these two processes to accommodate the integration of a Horn clause equality theory in logic programs.

3.1 Equality and Unification

We consider here generalized unification (e.g. [36]), i.e. unification of terms in equality theories. The theoretical foundation of incorporating equality into the unification process of theorem-proving was given by [26]. The major result there was that for a set of clauses augmented with an equational theory, one can work on the clauses alone and yet have a complete inference system in a theorem-prover using a generalized unification algorithm, which respects the equational theory in question, and the usual resolution and paramodulation inference rules. As argued in both the above mentioned papers and [30], the study of generalized unification can have a tremendous practical significance.

Generalized unification is defined here with respect to a consistent Horn equality theory E. Our definitions below are compatible with those in the literature, e.g. [12], [36]. (However, such works usually consider only equational theories, i.e. universal closures of equations.) A *substitution* is defined to be a mapping from the set of variables V into the set of terms $\tau(\Sigma \cup V)$. In what follows we sometimes (a) use obvious generalizations of substitutions to maps from terms into terms and atoms into atoms, and (b) speak of

449

substitutions as equations, e.g. the substitution $\{x/t, y/u\}$ can be regarded as the set of equations $\{x = t, y = u\}$. Where E is a consistent Horn equality theory, an *E-unifier* for two terms s and t is a substitution θ such that $E \models s\theta = t\theta$.

E-unification can be viewed as the process of solving equations within the theory E. An E-unifier represents a solution. Of particular concern is the problem of finding a finite representation for the set of all solutions. In the traditional case, the most general unifier provides this finite representation. Indeed, every solution is a particular instance of the most general unifier and, conversely, every instance of the most general unifier is a solution. In other cases, for instance the theory of a commutative function (i.e. $E = \{f(x,y) = f(y,x)\}$), the set of all solutions can be represented by a finite set of maximally general E-unifiers; every solution is a particular instance of one maximally general E-unifier and, conversely, every instance of any maximally general E-unifier is a solution. For example, in unifying $f(g(x),y)$ and $f(g(a),g(z))$ within E, we obtain two maximally general E-unifiers: $\{x/a, y/g(z)\}$ and $\{x/z, y/g(a)\}$. In general, however, there is no finite representation of the set of all solutions via the concept of maximally general E-unifiers since there may be zero or infinitely many maximally general E-unifiers.

In traditional logic programming, a goal may have infinitely many solutions which can be effectively enumerated. This important property is retained in the general framework of Horn equality theories. In other words, the possibility of having an infinite number of unifiers does not prevent an effective enumeration of all solutions.

In practice, we seldom require the full power of the theorem-proving ability, let alone the generation of all E-unifiers, from the E-unification algorithm. For example, the "function call equations" of FUNLOG restrict the unification problem to the case where one side of the equality is a variable, the other a term. In this case the unification algorithm is used to simplify this term. A similar restriction is placed on the *is* predicate of some PROLOGs.

The existence of normal forms may help reduce the problem of equality of two terms to a much simpler case. For example, in a queue data type, the two terms add(c, add(a, remove(add(b, emptyQ)))) and add(c, remove(add(a, add(b, emptyQ)))) both have the normal form add(c, add(a, emptyQ)).

3.2 Derivations

We now define the appropriate generalizations of derivation sequences, success and finite failure sets for our logic programs. We point out here that while these sets are defined in an operational manner, we do not address in this paper the issue of corresponding computational methods implementing them. In what follows, we write $\bar{t} = \bar{u}$ to mean $t_1 = u_1 \wedge t_2 = u_2 \wedge ... \wedge t_n = u_n$. Similarly $\exists \bar{x}$ A means $\exists \bar{x}_1 \exists \bar{x}_2 ... \exists \bar{x}_n$ A. Thus we say $\bar{t}$ E-unifies with $\bar{u}$ to mean that $E \models \exists \bar{x} \, (t_1 = u_1 \wedge ... \wedge t_n = u_n)$. We observe here that an immediate consequence of Theorem 1 is that $\bar{s}$ E-unifies with $\bar{t}$ iff $[\bar{s}] = [\bar{t}]$ when $\bar{s}$ and $\bar{t}$ are ground.

A *(P, E)-derivation sequence* is a (finite or infinite) sequence of *goals* $G_0, G_1, G_2, ...$ such that (a) G_i is a multiset of the form

$$e_1, ... , e_k, ... , e_K, B_1, ... , B_m, ... , B_M$$

where $0 \le k \le K$, $0 \le m \le M$, each e_j is an equation and each B_j is an atom, (b) there is a collection of $m \ge 0$ clauses

$$A^{(1)} \leftarrow D_1^{(1)}, \cdots , D_{n_1}^{(1)}$$

$$A^{(2)} \leftarrow D_1^{(2)}, \cdots , D_{n_2}^{(2)}$$

$$\cdots$$

$$A^{(m)} \leftarrow D_1^{(m)}, \cdots , D_{n_m}^{(m)}$$

where each clause above is a clause from P with variables renamed to names never before used in the derivation and each $D_q^{(p)}$ is either an atom or an equation, (c) there is an E-unifier θ_i of the equations

$$e_1, ... , e_k, B_1 = A^{(1)}, ... , B_m = A^{(m)},$$

where $\{e_1, ... , e_k, B_1, ... , B_m\}$ is called the *selected subgoal* of G_i, and finally (d) G_{i+1} is

$$\left(e_{k+1}, ..., e_K, B_{m+1}, ..., B_M, D_1^{(1)}, \cdots , D_{n_1}^{(1)}, \cdots , D_1^{(m)}, \cdots , D_{n_m}^{(m)}\right)\theta_i$$

A (P, E)-derivation sequence is *successful* if some G_i is empty. A (P, E)-derivation sequence is *finitely failed* with length i if θ_i cannot be formed, that is, the selected subgoal of G_i does not satisfy (c)

451

above. Note that a (P, E)-derivation sequence is either successful, finitely failed or infinite.

We may remark that in the standard case implementations use the most general unifier for θ_i for all derivation steps. This allows a more compact representation, as potentially infinitely many (P, E)-derivation steps can be written as a single one. Similarly, in the general case maximally general unifiers can be used whenever they exist.

A *selection rule* determines, for all (P, E)-derivation sequences, the selected subgoal in each derivation step. We say that a (P, E)-derivation sequence is *fair* if it is finite, or for every equation or atom D in G_i, D (or some further instantiated version of D) is in the selected subgoal of G_j, for some $j \geq i$. We thus say that a selection rule is fair if every (P, E)-derivation sequence formed using this rule is fair.

The standard selection rule in PROLOG is not fair. The use of unfair selection rules may result in otherwise avoidable infinite derivations [20]. In that respect, all fair selection rules are equivalent, and there exists a canonical one, the breadth-first selection rule, where all elements in the goal are selected simultaneously. In [27], fairness is linked to lazy evaluation.

The following defines the success, finite failure and general failure sets, denoted SS(P, E), FF(P, E) and GF(P, E) respectively, for a given logic program (P, E). Let $\bar{s}$ denote ground terms.

SS(P, E) = {$p(\bar{s})$: there exists

 a successful (P, E)-derivation sequence of $p(\bar{s})$}

FF(P, E) = {$p(\bar{s})$: for any fair selection rule, there exists

 a number n such that all (P, E)-derivation sequences of $p(\bar{s})$

 are finitely failed with length $\leq$ n}

GF(P, E) = {$p(\bar{s})$: for any fair selection rule,

 all (P, E)-derivation sequences of $p(\bar{s})$ are finitely failed}

These definitions relate closely to resolution-like implementations of logic programming systems.

General failure is, in general, different from finite failure because there can be a ground atom which does not have an infinite derivation sequence and yet there is no number n such that all derivation

452

sequences of this atom are finitely failed with length $\leq n$. This possibility arises because E can be such that there is an infinite set of maximally general E-unifiers for some pair of terms s and t. For example, take $E = \{f(x, f(y, z)) = f(f(x, y), z)\}$, the theory of an associative function. Noting that the equation $f(y, a) = f(a, y)$ has an infinite number of maximally general E-unifiers $\{y/a\}$, $\{y/f(a, a)\}$, $\{y/f(f(a, a), a)\}$, ... , the program P:

$$p(a) \quad \leftarrow q(f(a, y), f(y, a))$$
$$q(x, x) \quad \leftarrow r(x)$$
$$r(f(a, x)) \leftarrow r(x)$$

is such that $FF(P, E) \neq GF(P, E)$. This is easily verified by considering the initial goal $p(a)$. However, if E is such that for all pairs of terms s and t, there is a finite set of maximally general unifiers which subsume all the E-unifiers of s and t, then $FF(P, E)$ is identical to $GF(P, E)$.

In the traditional framework, the success and finite failure sets have also been defined inductively. We give the appropriate generalizations here. Let $\bar{t}$ denote ground terms, e_j an equation and B_j an atom.

$SS_0(P, E) = \{\}$

$SS_{i+1}(P, E) = \{p(\bar{t})$: there is a ground instance of a clause in P

$$p(\bar{u}) \leftarrow e_1, \dots , e_n, B_1, \dots , B_m$$

such that $\bar{t}$ E-unifies with $\bar{u}$,

e_k is E-unifiable for all $1 \leq k \leq n$, and

$B_k \in SS_i(P, E)$ for all $1 \leq k \leq m\}$

$$SS(P, E) = \bigcup_{i=0}^{\infty} SS_i(P, E)$$

$FF_0(P, E) = \{\}$

$FF_{i+1}(P, E) = \{p(\bar{t})$: for each ground instance of a clause in P

$$p(\bar{u}) \leftarrow e_1, \dots , e_n, B_1, \dots , B_m$$

either $\bar{t}$ does not E-unify with $\bar{u}$, or

e_k is not E-unifiable for some $1 \leq k \leq n$, or

$B_k \in FF_i(P, E)$ for some $1 \leq k \leq m\}$

453

$$FF(P, E) = \bigcup_{i=0}^{\infty} FF_i(P, E)$$

In fact, the inductively defined SS(P, E) is the set of all ground atoms which have a successful ground (P, E)-derivation. Similarly, the inductively defined FF(P, E) is the set of all ground atoms such that all their ground (P, E)-derivations are finitely failed. As in the standard case, we have

Proposition 8.

(a) The two definitions of SS(P, E) define the same set.
(b) The two definitions of FF(P, E) define the same set.

We therefore might suspect that a corresponding (transfinite) inductive definition can be made for the set GF(P, E). Let GGF(P, E) (to suggest generalized failure at the ground level) denote the set given by the inductive definition below. If α and β denote not necessarily finite ordinals,

$GGF_0(P, E) = \{\}$

$GGF_\alpha(P, E) = $ *if* $(\alpha \neq 0$ and α is not a limit ordinal) *then*

$\{p(\bar{t}):$ for each ground instance of a clause in P

$p(\bar{u}) \leftarrow e_1, \dots , e_n, B_1, \dots , B_m$

either $\bar{t}$ does not E-unify with $\bar{u}$, or

e_k is not E-unifiable for some $1 \leq k \leq n$, or

$B_k \in GGF_{\alpha-1}(P, E)$ for some $1 \leq k \leq m\}$

else

$\bigcup_{\beta < \alpha} GGF_\beta(P, E)$

GGF(P, E) is such that $A \in GGF(P, E)$ iff $A \in GGF_\alpha(P, E)$ for some ordinal α.

Unfortunately, this inductive definition is *not* equivalent to the definition of GF(P, E). Take the empty theory $E = \emptyset$ (thus we are in the traditional case) and the following simple program P

$$p(a) \leftarrow q(x)$$
$$q(s(x)) \leftarrow q(x)$$

The initial goal p(a) gives rise to an infinite (P, E)-derivation; it is easy to verify, however, that every *ground* (P, E)-derivation with initial goal p(a) is finitely failed, that is, $p(a) \in GGF(P, E)$. Thus while we may use either one of the definitions for SS(P, E) and FF(P, E), we have only one definition of generalized failure, GF(P, E), in this paper. The problem of finding an inductive definition for GF(P, E) remains.

We are now in a position to relate these operational notions to the declarative notions of the previous section. The formal proofs of the following results can be obtained from [14]. There the results were proved for derivations which are an interesting specialized version of the (P, E)-derivations defined above. This specialization is obtained by simply enforcing one selection rule: in every derivation step the selected subgoal equals the entire goal. Nevertheless it is important to note that no generality is lost. For example, we obtain the same success, finite and general failure sets regardless of this specialization. The selection rule in the specialization is automatically fair.

We begin by establishing the desired result relating ground atoms and the canonical domain $\tau(\Sigma)/E$, which allows us to abstract the equality theory from the reasoning about success and failure:

Proposition 9. Let $\bar{t}$ denote a list of ground terms. Then

(a) $p(\bar{t}) \in SS(P, E)$ iff $[p(\bar{t})] \in [SS(P, E)]$.

(b) $p(\bar{t}) \in FF(P, E)$ iff $[p(\bar{t})] \in [FF(P, E)]$.

(c) $p(\bar{t}) \in GGF(P, E)$ iff $[p(\bar{t})] \in [GGF(P, E)]$.

By also establishing equivalence between the fixpoint semantics and the operational semantics based on (P, E)-derivations

Proposition 10. $lfp(T_{(P, E)}) = T_{(P, E)} \uparrow \omega = [SS(P, E)]$

we can easily obtain the soundness and completeness of successful (P, E)-derivations:

Theorem 3. $(P, E) \models p(\bar{t})$ iff $p(\bar{t}) \in SS(P, E)$.

Finally, we present dual results for finitely failed (P, E)-derivations. We define $T_{(P, E)}{\downarrow}n = T^n_{(P, E)}(E\text{-base})$. Thus we obtain a dual to $T_{(P, E)}{\uparrow}\omega$ with $T_{(P, E)}{\downarrow}\omega = \bigcap\limits_{n=0}^{\infty} T_{(P, E)}{\downarrow}n$. There is an intimate connection between $T_{(P, E)}{\uparrow}n$ and $SS_n(P, E)$. The following proposition establishes the same kind of connection.

Proposition 11. $\overline{T_{(P, E)}{\downarrow}\alpha} = [GGF_\alpha(P, E)]$

As in the traditional case, the greatest fixpoint of $T_{(P, E)}$ cannot always be constructed as a simple limit, in the way that the least fixpoint can. Nevertheless, the greatest fixpoint can be used to represent a finite aspect of failure as the following partial dual to Proposition 10 states. It shows that the ground atoms for which every ground (P, E)-derivation is finitely failed are those whose meanings in the canonical domain are elements of the complement of the greatest fixpoint.

Proposition 12. $\overline{gfp(T_{(P, E)})} = [GGF(P, E)]$

This proposition clarifies the relationship between greatest fixpoint semantics and the notion of finite failure, which was first investigated by Apt and van Emden [1]. Finally, a corollary to Proposition 11 gives another partial dual of Proposition 10, i.e. it characterizes those ground atoms for which every (P, E)-derivation is finitely failed.

Theorem 4. $\overline{T_{(P, E)}{\downarrow}\omega} = [FF(P, E)]$

4 COMPLETE LOGIC PROGRAMS

The framework of definite clauses presented so far allows us to obtain only "positive information", i.e. the only literals which are logical consequences are positive. The lack of the ability to obtain "negative information" is a major drawback from both the theoretical and practical points of view. In dealing with models of logic formulas in general, there is duality between both truth values. In practice, this duality can be extremely important, for example in data-

456

base applications.

There are two main approaches to this problem. The first is to extend the language of definite clauses. For example, one familiar extension used in PROLOG systems is that of clauses containing at least one positive literal [6]. Known colloquially as "negation in the body", this extends definite clauses, which are clauses containing exactly one positive literal. Some examples of other extensions are [24] and [31].

The second approach is to adopt special rules or assumptions which tell us, under given circumstances, when information is negative. Amongst the most prominent of these are the closed world assumption [28] and the negation-as-failure rule [6]. The first states that all atoms which are not logical consequences are false. The second is implementation dependent; it states that an atom is false if all attempts to prove it terminate unsuccessfully.

Our approach is a combination of both these approaches. Based on the concept of completed databases and the negation-as-failure rule of [6], our *complete logic programs*, written (P*, E*), allow us to have negative atoms as logical consequences, whereas a definite clause logic program (P, E) cannot. From an operational point of view, we adopt a negation-as-failure rule. We justify our approach by showing that these declarative and operational aspects of negation coincide.

A formal definition of complete logic programs requires the concept of unification completeness of an equality theory.

Recall that we have been dealing with generalized unification over an equality theory E. An important property is that two terms are E-unifiable iff there is a ground substitution over $\tau(\Sigma)$ of the terms such that the ground instances are both in the same class of the finest Σ-congruence over $\tau(\Sigma)$ generated by E. This does not mean, however, that if two terms are equal in another Σ-algebra modelling E then they are E-unifiable. For example the Σ-algebra with a single element models the empty equality theory E, but not all pairs of terms are E-unifiable.

We already have, by definition, an intimate connection between truth in E and E-unification: terms s and t are E-unifiable iff $E \models \exists \bar{x}$ (s = t). With the negation issue at hand, we need a dual property; that is, we need to establish a relationship between non-existence of E-unifiers and falsity in E. We thus require that an equality theory E dictates that equality holds only if E-unification is possible. Formally, we say that an equality theory E is *unification complete* over $\tau(\Sigma)$ if, for every equation s = t,

$$E \models ((s = t) \to \overset{\alpha}{\underset{i=1}{v}} \{\theta_i\}),$$

where $\{\theta_i\}$ is the (possibly empty or infinite) set of E-unifiers of s and t and $\alpha \in \{0, 1, 2, \ldots, \omega\}$. We adopt the convention that an empty disjunction is false. Thus the above expression means that if a valuation of the variables in terms s and t is such that s = t in a model of E, then at least one of the E-unifiers θ_i (looked upon as a set of equations) is also true in the model and valuation. Consequently, when there are no E-unifiers of s and t $(\alpha = 0)$, $E \models s \neq t$. An interesting consequence of this definition is that any unification complete equality theory generates a single Σ-congruence.

The essence of unification completeness is that every possible solution of any given equation can be represented by an E-unifier of the equation. In particular, when there are no E-unifiers, there can be no solution. Whenever all the E-unifiers can be represented by a collection of maximally general E-unifiers (and such a set is called *complete*), it is sufficient to consider only this collection in the definition. For example, the axioms given by [6] which extend the empty theory, can be shown to be unification complete. We will see below another example [16] which extends a theory for rational trees.

An *augmented definite clause logic program* consists of a conjunction of *predicate definitions*, exactly one for each predicate symbol p_i in Π. These definitions take one of two forms:

$$p_i(\bar{x}) \leftrightarrow DB_i, \tag{1}$$

or

$$\neg p_i(\bar{x}) \tag{2}$$

where the $\bar{x}$ are a list of n_i distinct variables, the p_i are n_i-ary predicate symbols, and the DB_i are the *definition bodies* of p_i. These bodies are each a disjunction of formulas of the form

$$\exists \bar{y}(\bar{x} = \bar{t} \wedge e_1 \wedge e_2 \wedge \ldots \wedge e_k \wedge B_1 \wedge B_2 \wedge \ldots \wedge B_m)$$

where the e_j are equations and B_j are atoms and $\bar{y}$ are the variables distinct from $\bar{x}$ appearing in the formula.

Now we can define our complete logic programs: these are of the form (P*, E*) where P* is an augmented definite clause program and E* a unification complete equality theory. This concludes our approach to the negation issue by means of extending definite clause logic programs.

To address the operational semantics of complete logic programs, we return to logic programs. Corresponding to each (P*, E*), we obtain a logic program (P, E) as follows. All that we require of the desired E is that it shares with E* the same finest Σ-congruence. There can be many ways of defining such E, e.g., E = {e: e is a ground equation over $\tau(\Sigma)$ and E* $\models$ e}.

The definite clause logic program P we obtain from P* is defined as follows. For each predicate definition of type (1) in P*, obtain n definite clauses where n is the number of disjunctions in the definition body. Then if

$$\exists \bar{y}(\bar{x} = \bar{t} \wedge e_1 \wedge e_2 \wedge ... \wedge e_k \wedge B_1 \wedge B_2 \wedge ... \wedge B_m) \tag{3}$$

is one such disjunct, obtain the corresponding definite clause

$$p_i(\bar{t}) \leftarrow e_1 \wedge e_2 \wedge ... \wedge e_k \wedge B_1 \wedge B_2 \wedge ... \wedge B_m) \tag{4}$$

Note that we do not construct any definite clauses from predicate definitions of type (2) in P*. Thus we have defined (P, E) corresponding to (P*, E*).

Since E* is unification complete, we say that I is an E*-interpretation to mean, as in section 2, that I has the domain given by $\tau(\Sigma)/E*$, this being the unique Σ-congruence over $\tau(\Sigma)$ generated by E*. Thus I may be regarded as an interpretation of arbitrary formulas in the obvious way, i.e. I defines the domain and functional assignment by virtue of it being an E*-interpretation, and I defines truth values via its elements. We write $p(\bar{s})$ to denote some ground atom. The following proposition generalizes a result of [1]. Let I be an E-interpretation.

Proposition 13. I is a fixpoint of $T_{(P, E)}$ iff I is a model for (P*, E).

We can now give the two main theorems. The first proves the soundness and completeness of successful (P, E)-derivations for positive atoms valid in (P*, E*). We phrase our theorem thus:

459

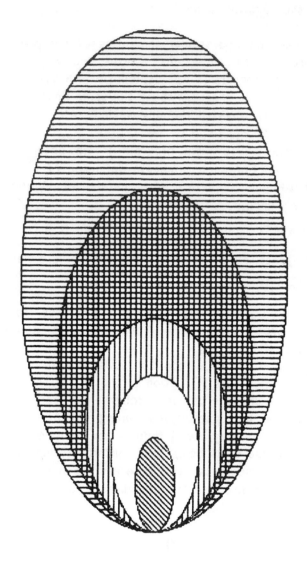

Figure 1: Partition of E-base.

Theorem 5. $(P^*, E^*) \models p(\bar{s})$ iff $p(\bar{s}) \in SS(P, E)$.

The soundness and completeness of generally failed (P, E)-derivations for negative atoms valid in (P^*, E^*) are given by

Theorem 6. $(P^*, E^*) \models \neg p(\bar{s})$ iff $p(\bar{s}) \in GF(P, E)$.

Results from this and the preceding section are conveniently summarised in the diagram of Figure 1. The inclusions E-base $\supseteq$ $T_{(P, E)} \supseteq \overline{GF(P, E)} \supseteq gfp(T_{(P, E)}) \supseteq lfp(T_{(P, E)})$ induce a partition whose components are represented by the shaded areas in the diagram. The (P^*, E^*) model-theoretic properties and the nature of the (P, E)-derivations of a ground atom are given as follows.

The atom has a successful derivation and is true in all models.

The atom has an infinite fair *ground* derivation. It is true in some E-models and false in others.

The atom has an infinite fair derivation, however every fair *ground* derivation is finitely failed. It is false in all E-models, but true in some model.

Every fair derivation of the atom is finitely failed. The length of these derivations is unbounded. The atom is false in all models.

Every fair derivation of the atom is finitely failed. The length of these derivations is bounded. The atom is false in all models.

5 THE SCHEME

The *logic programming language scheme* is denoted CLP(X). The parameter X, when instantiated by a unification complete equality theory E^*, results in a formal basis for a logic programming language whose programs are the complete logic programs (P^*, E^*).

461

This scheme is certainly relevant to various extensions of PRO-LOG that were mentioned in the introduction and presented in this book. In conclusion, we briefly explain how it can be used to provide PROLOG II with a logical foundation which is essentially the same as PROLOG's logical foundation once the equality theory has been abstracted. The full treatment is to be found in [16]. This example is of particular interest since the extension is non-trivial, the implementation efficient and the language well-known. It illustrates the power of the scheme, since all the desirable semantic properties are automatically established as a consequence of a simple analysis of the equality theory.

This example is also representative of some non-trivial applications of the scheme. Indeed the simple equality theory we choose to represent the domain of rational trees is not given in clause form. Consequently, it has to be translated in order to apply the scheme. The resulting operational system is clumsy because of the new functions symbols introduced during the Skolemization process. The system chosen for defining the language is an isomorphic "de-Skolemized" version of the one given by the scheme. The derivations so obtained are essentially those given by [7].

Consider the equality theory given by the axiom schema

$$\forall \bar{y} \ \exists ! \bar{x} \ x_1 = t_1(\bar{x}, \bar{y}) \wedge x_2 = t_2(\bar{x}, \bar{y}) \wedge \ldots \wedge x_n = t_n(\bar{x}, \bar{y})$$

where x_1, x_2, ... , x_n are distinct variables, and t_1, t_2, ... , t_n are terms over the alphabet Σ. These axioms can easily be written in Horn clause form by Skolemizing; call them E. The introduced function symbols extend Σ to $\Sigma+$. There is a least model for E which is essentially the domain of rational trees $R(\Sigma)$ as a consequence of the following theorem.

Theorem 7. $\tau(\Sigma+)/E \cong R(\Sigma)$

By augmenting E with the axioms given by the two simple schemas

$$f(\bar{x}) \neq g(\bar{y}) \qquad \text{for every } f,g \in \Sigma, f \neq g,$$

and

$$f(\bar{x}) = f(\bar{y}) \rightarrow \bar{x} = \bar{y} \qquad \text{for every } f \in \Sigma$$

we obtain an equality theory E* which has the desired property as shown by the following theorem.

Theorem 8. E* is unification complete

Consequently all the results discussed in this paper hold for logic programs over the domain of rational trees. The only remaining problem is one of notation. Rational trees are represented as equations in PROLOG II and in our initial axiomatization. In E they are assigned names due to Skolemization. The (P, E)-derivation sequences and the corresponding E-unification are made awkward, from an implementation point of view, by the presence of Skolem functions. However it can be shown that PROLOG II derivations are equivalent to (P, E)-derivations, as they differ only in the way rational trees are represented.

ACKNOWLEDGEMENTS

This research was supported in part by the Australian Computer Research Board.

463

REFERENCES

1. Apt, K.R., and M.H. van Emden. "Contributions to the Theory of Logic Programming". *J.ACM 29*, 3 (July 1983), pp. 841 - 862.

2. Balbin, I., and K. Lecot. *Logic Programming: A Classified Bibliography*. Wildgrass Books, Melbourne, 1985.

3. Bandes, R.G. Constraining-Unification and the Programming Language Unicorn. Proc. 11th. Symp. on Principles of Programming Languages, Salt Lake City, 1984. Also appears in this volume.

4. Bellia, M., E. Dameri, P. Degano, G. Levi, and M. Martelli. A Formal Model for Lazy Implementations of a Prolog compatible Functional Language. In *Issues in Prolog Implementations*, J.A. Campbell, Ed., Ellis Horwood, 1984, pp. 309 - 328.

5. Chang, C.L., and R. Lee. *Symbolic Logic and Mechanical Theorem Proving*. Academic Press, New York, 1973.

6. Clark, K.L. Negation as Failure. In *Logic and Databases*, H. Gallaire and J. Minker Eds., Plenum Press, New York, 1978, pp. 293 - 322.

7. Colmerauer, A. Prolog and Infinite Trees. In *Logic Programming*, K.L. Clark and S.A. Tarnlund Eds., Academic Press, New York, 1982.

8. van Emden, M.H., and R. Kowalski. "Semantics of Predicate Logic as a Programming Language". *J.ACM 23*, 4 (October 1976), pp. 733 - 742.

9. van Emden, M.H., and J.W. Lloyd. A Logical Reconstruction of Prolog II. Proc. 2nd. International Logic Programming Conference, Uppsala, July 1984, pp. 35 - 40. Also Journal of Logic Programming, to appear.

10. Goguen, J.A., and J. Meseguer. Equality, Types, Modules and Generics for Logic Programming. Proc. 2nd. International Logic Programming Conference, Uppsala, July 1984, pp. 115 - 126.

11. Hansson, A., and A.S. Haridi. Logic programming in a natural deduction framework. Proc. of Workshop on Functional Languages and Computer Architecture, Goteborg, 1981.

12. Huet, G., and D.C. Oppen. Equations and Rewrite Rules: A Survey. In *Formal Languages: Perspectives and Open Problems*, R.V. Book Ed., Academic Press, 1980.

13. Jaffar, J., J-L. Lassez, and J.W. Lloyd. Completeness of the Negation-as-Failure Rule. Proc. 8th. International Joint Conference on Artificial Intelligence, Karlsruhe, August 1983, pp. 500 - 506.

14. Jaffar, J., J-L. Lassez, and M.J. Maher. A Theory of Complete Logic Programs with Equality. Proc. International Conference on Fifth Generation Computer Systems, Tokyo, November 1984. Also Journal of Logic Programming, 1984:3:211-223.

15. Jaffar, J., J-L. Lassez, and M.J. Maher. A Logical Foundation for Prolog II. Technical Report, Department of Computer Science, Monash University, 1984.

16. Kahn, K.M. Uniform – A Language based upon Unification which unifies (much of) Lisp, Prolog and Act 1. This volume.

17. Komorowski, H.J. QLOG – The Programming Environment for Prolog in LISP. in *Logic Programming*, K.L. Clark and S-A. Tarnlund Eds., Academic Press, 1982.

18. Kornfeld, W.A. Equality for Prolog. Proc. 8th. International Joint Conference on Artificial Intelligence, Karlsruhe, August 1983, pp. 514 - 519. Also appears in this volume.

19. Kowalski, R.A. *Logic for Problem Solving.* North-Holland, New York, 1979.

20. Lassez, J-L., and M.J. Maher. "Closures and Fairness in the Semantics of Programming Logic". *Theoretical Computer Science 29* (1984), pp. 167 - 184.

21. Lassez, J-L., and M.J. Maher. Optimal Fixedpoints of Logic Programs. Proc. 3rd. International Conference on Foundations of Software and Theoretical Computer Science, Bangalore, December

1983. Also Theoretical Computer Science, to appear.

22. Lassez, J-L., and M.J. Maher. *The Semantics of Logic Programs.* Oxford University Press, in preparation.

23. Lloyd, J.W. Foundations of Logic Programming, Springer-Verlag, 1984.

24. Lloyd, J.W., and R.W. Topor. "Making Prolog More Expressive". *Journal of Logic Programming* 1984:3:225-240.

25. Loveland, D.W. *Automated Theorem Proving: A Logical Basis.* North-Holland, 1978.

26. Plotkin, G.D. Building in Equational Theories. In *Machine Intelligence 7*, B. Meltzer and D. Michie Eds., Halsted Press, 1972, pp. 73 - 90.

27. Reddy, U.S. On the Relationship between Logic and Functional Languages. This volume.

28. Reiter, R. On Closed World Databases. In *Logic and Databases*, H. Gallaire and J. Minker Eds., Plenum Press, New York, 1978, pp. 55 - 76.

29. Robinson, J.A., and E.E. Sibert. LOGLISP: An Alternative to Prolog. In *Machine Intelligence 10*, Ellis Horwood, 1982.

30. Sakai, K., and T. Matsuda. Universal Unification. in *Several Aspects of Unification*, Technical Memorandum 0046, ICOT - Institute for New Generation Computer Technology, Tokyo, February 1984.

31. Sakai, K., and T. Myachi. Incorporating Naive Negation into Prolog. Technical Report TR-0028, ICOT - Institute for New Generation Computer Technology, Tokyo, 1983.

32. Sato, M. "Theory of Symbolic Expressions I". *Theoretical Computer Science 22* (1983) pp. 19 - 55.

33. Sato, M., and T. Sakurai. Qute: A Prolog/LISP Type Language for Logic Programming. Proc. 8th. International Joint Conference on

Artificial Intelligence, Karlsruhe, August 1983, pp. 507 - 513.

34. Sato, M., and T. Sakurai. Qute: A Functional Language based on Unification. Proc. International Conference on Fifth Generation Computer Systems, Tokyo, November 1984, pp. 157 - 165.

35. Selman, A. "Completeness of Calculi for Axiomatically Defined Classes of Algebras". *Algebra Universalis 2* (1) 1972, pp. 20 - 32.

36. Siekmann, J., and P. Szabo. Universal Unification and a Classification of Equational Theories. Proc. 6th. Conference on Automated Deduction, New York, June 1982, *Lecture Notes in Computer Science 138*, Springer-Verlag, pp. 369 - 389.

37. Subrahmanyam, P.A., and J-H. You. Conceptual Basis and Evaluation Strategies for Integrating Functional and Logic Programming. Proc. International Symposium on Logic Programming, Atlantic City, 1984, pp. 144 - 153.

38. Subrahmanyam, P.A., and J-H. You. "On Embedding Functions in Logic". *Information Processing Letters 19* (1984), pp. 41 - 46.

39. Subrahmanyam, P.A., and J-H. You. FUNLOG: a Computational Model integrating Logic Programming and Functional Programming. This volume.

40. Tamaki, H. Semantics of a Logic Programming Language with a Reducibility Predicate. Proc. International Symposium on Logic Programming, Atlantic City, 1984, pp. 259 - 264.

FRESH:

A HIGHER-ORDER LANGUAGE WITH

UNIFICATION AND MULTIPLE RESULTS

Gert Smolka

Department of Computer Science
Upson Hall
Cornell University
Ithaca, New York 14853

ABSTRACT

This paper presents Fresh, a language that integrates logic programming features into higher-order functional programming. The language incorporates unification, multiple results and a collection construct. Many examples illustrate that these extensions of functional programming are useful. We define an operational semantics along the lines of Plotkin's structural approach. The semantics is of intrinsic interest since it covers backtracking and the collection construct. To illustrate the conceptual similarities and differences between functional and logic programming, we begin with a purely functional core language and add first unification and then backtracking. With each addition we discuss the enhanced eloquence of the language and the concomitant modifications to the semantics.

1 INTRODUCTION

This paper presents Fresh, a language that integrates logic programming features into higher-order functional programming. This language represents an attempt to explore the connections between functional and logic programming, the two major applicative programming styles that have developed over the last twenty years. The presentation of Fresh will focus on two themes: Fresh as a practical programming language and Fresh as a laboratory for exploring the semantic ideas that are needed to describe the combination of reduction, unification and backtracking.

The starting point in our discussion is FM, a higher-order functional language tailored for the extensions to come. FM departs from other functional languages by employing a failure-based evaluation strategy and by incorporating unrestricted pattern matching. In FM, pattern matching serves as the sole computational mechanism for binding variables and for decomposing and comparing objects. The first step from FM to Fresh is the generalization of matching to unification. Variables can now be bound to nonground terms, and unification may refine such incomplete values by binding the variables contained in them. These delayed bindings make it possible to build objects incrementally by imposing constraints as information becomes available. The second extension of FM is the incorporation of multiple results and backtracking. The list of all results of an expression can be computed with a collection construct. The combination of backtracking and collection provides an attractive alternative to recursion. These features give Fresh expressive data base capabilities.

We define an operational semantics for Fresh following Plotkin's structural approach [26]. The semantics is of intrinsic interest because it covers backtracking and the collection construct. The meaning of each construct is defined by a set of proof rules, which justify instances of the reduction relation. A proof for a reduction is a tree whose structure follows closely the structure of the expression being reduced. The result of an expression is computed by constructing the proof tree that justifies the reduction to the result. The semantics is compositional, a property frequently cited for preferring a denotational definition.

Fresh subsumes Horn logic with equality under a depth-first search strategy. Thus a first-order subset of Fresh could be characterized in model theoretic terms. However, full Fresh does not have model-theoretic semantics, since it contains negation as failure [3, 20], collection and higher-order functions. I feel that these features are crucial for a practical programming language. The major difficulties with the logic programming approach are negation and the incorporation of control. So far, logic programming languages do not include a *general form* of negation, and I am not aware of any research in progress that may change this situation. Furthermore, the integration of control constructs necessarily leads to a language that cannot be described in model theoretic terms. Eqlog [9], a recent logic language based on Horn logic with equality, has a clean model theoretic semantics, but includes neither negation nor control constructs. Prolog [3] is no more a logic programming language than Fresh is. In fact, Fresh is an attempt to overcome Prolog's ad hoc features like the cut or the call predicate and to integrate Prolog's useful computational innovations smoothly into a functional framework.

The presentation begins with an informal description of FM, the functional core language of Fresh. To make the comparison between functional programming and Fresh more perspicuous, we then give a formal account of matching and FM's semantics. This also provides a familiar and simple base to introduce our style of semantics. The next two sections discuss the incorporation of unification and backtracking into FM. Many examples illustrate how Fresh relates to Prolog and why the integration of these features is useful. These informal discussions are followed by two technical sections, which give a rigorous account of unification and Fresh's semantics. Finally, we discuss related research and future directions.

2   A FUNCTIONAL LANGUAGE BASED ON MATCHING

In this section we shall discuss a functional language, called FM, based on matching. This language will serve as the starting point in our discussion of the relation between functional and logic programming. The point in presenting FM is to establish a familiar base that can be naturally extended to subsume logic programming. FM contains nearly all constructs of the full language, Fresh. Fresh is obtained by generalizing matching to unification and adding constructs that introduce and eliminate multiple results.

Modern functional languages, like KRC [33], HOPE [2] and Standard ML [22], offer matching constructs as a means to decompose data objects. However, these languages employ matching in a rather restricted form; for instance, patterns cannot contain the same variable twice. Consequently, this stripped down form of matching does not provide for the comparison of data objects. Since decomposition and comparison often interact, these restrictions deprive the programmer of a significant part of matching's expressive power. There are two reasons for these restrictions. First, since general matching is an operation that can fail, a smooth integration into a language whose evaluation strategy does not account for failure is impossible. Second, general matching requires decidable equality on all objects, a property that is not naturally satisfied by higher-order objects.

Since we are aiming at a language that incorporates unification, which is a generalization of matching, FM should overcome these problems. Equality for all objects is obtained by hiding functions behind names, called designators. Abstractions now become reducible expressions. They reduce to a new designator that is bound to the function defined by the abstraction. Although this change is for the most part invisible, it provides the unusual feature that function names can be compared with other objects. The failure problem is addressed by incorporating failure as a general concept. Consequently, the reduction of an expression either *succeeds* with a result or *fails* without a result. This binary character of reduction renders traditional boolean expressions obsolete; the conditional now tests for success or failure. It turns out that the proper integration of matching and failure not only prepares the ground for the addition of unification and multiple results, but also increases the eloquence and compactness of the functional language. Matching now becomes the basic computational construct that binds variables and compares and decomposes data objects. Patterns in FM can contain the same variable more than once and can also contain variables that are bound in an outer context.

Matching and unification are operations that solve equations between terms. Matching is a restricted form of unification and solves equations where one side is a ground term. Consequently, all data objects in FM are ground terms, while patterns are terms that can contain variables.

2.1 Terms and Matching

Terms are tree-structured objects built from atoms, designators and variables. *Atoms* are primitive objects that include identifiers starting with a lower case letter (e.g., maria, apple, x or y), numbers (e.g., 612), or special symbols (e.g., (), %, + or -). *Designators* serve as function names and are written as bold face identifiers or symbols, for instance, **append** or **+**. Functional objects are hidden behind designators since matching and unification are first-order operations, which require equality for terms. *Variables* are identifiers starting with a capital letter, for instance, X, Y or Person. A *term* is either an atom, a designator, a variable, or a *pair* (s, t) that consists of two terms s and t. A term is *ground* if it contains no variables.

472

Matching and unification solve equations between terms with respect to variables and syntactic equality. Matching is a restricted form of unification that solves equations where one side is a ground term. For instance, the equation

(X, (Y, (red, X))) ≡ ((apple, green), (**fun**, (red, (apple, green))))

has the solution X ≡ (apple, green) and Y ≡ **fun**. The equation

(X, (Y, (red, X))) ≡ ((apple, green), (**fun**, (red, (apple, yellow))))

has no solution with matching. Thus an attempt to solve it will *fail*. The left-hand side of a matching equation is called the *pattern* and the right-hand side is called the *argument* of the equation. We say that the pattern is *matched* against the argument. The argument must be ground, whereas the pattern may contain variables. If the match *succeeds* it produces a set of *variable bindings*, which is the unique solution of the equation. If we replace all variables in the pattern by their *values*, that is, by the ground terms the variables are bound to in the solution, we obtain a term that is equal to the argument.

To obtain a palatable syntax for terms, the comma is treated as a right-associative infix operator. Thus (1, 2, 3, 4) is a syntactical variant of (1, (2, (3, 4))). Furthermore, redundant parentheses are possible; for instance, (((1))) is a syntactical variant of the atom 1. These syntactical refinements do not affect matching or other semantic operations, but are just a notational convenience that is invisible at the semantic level.

We call the terms defined above *binary terms* to distinguish them from other terms. Binary terms are simpler than Prolog's first-order terms. However, first-order terms can be expressed as binary terms and their usual syntax can be recovered by a simple abbreviation rule. A *labeled term* is a binary term (%, s, t) where % is the atom % and s is either an atom or a variable. Syntactically, such a term can be written as s(t). Thus

plus(times(X, Y), F(Z, 6))

is a syntactical variant of the term

(%, plus, (%, times, X, Y), %, F, Z, 6) ,

which, when deprived of all syntactical sugar, becomes

(%, (plus, ((%, (times, (X, Y))) , (%, (F, (Z, 6)))))) .

An input processor for FM would translate the first variant into the third variant, which is the unique semantic form. An output processor would retranslate into the refined form. Semantically, labeled terms are just a subset of all terms and do not feature any special properties. The

473

reader may check that matching first-order terms in binary representation is equivalent to matching first-order terms directly, provided that every function symbol is always used with the same number of arguments. This holds as well for unification. One advantage of the binary representation is that we can now solve equations like

$$F(A) \equiv plus(4, 7).$$

where the variable F matches the function symbol and A matches the argument tuple of the coded first-order term plus(4, 7). The solution of this equation is F $\equiv$ plus and A $\equiv$ (4, 7).

Another important subclass of terms are lists. A *list* is either the atom () (the *empty list*) or a term (s, l) where s is a term and l is a list. For instance, (1, 2, 3, ()) is a list with three elements.

Although binary terms are similar to Lisp's S-expressions, we shall now see that their integration into FM is quite different.

2.2 Expressions and Reduction

Figure 1 defines FM's abstract syntax. Note that, for instance, **A** denotes the set of all atoms and that a, b, c are metavariables that range over atoms. Whenever the reader encounters in the following the symbols a, b and c it is understood that they denote an atom. The same holds for the metavariables for designators, variables, terms and expressions. Note that every term is an expression.

The execution of expressions is called *reduction*. The reduction of an expression either *succeeds* or *fails*; if it succeeds it produces a *result*, which is a ground term. A successful reduction also produces a function environment, which binds the designators in the result. Besides the two regular outcomes of reduction, the reduction of certain expressions may not terminate. In contrast to other functional languages, run-time errors cannot occur in FM. Situations that do not allow a successful continuation of a reduction produce a failure. For instance, the application of something that is not a function to an argument will simply fail. Of course, a type discipline for FM would statically enforce that such situations cannot occur.

An expression is *canonical* if it reduces to itself. The canonical expressions of FM are exactly the ground terms. Atoms and designators reduce to themselves. A pair (e, f) reduces to (u, v) if e reduces to u and f reduces to v.

Reduction takes place in the presence of two environments. The *term environment* binds variables to ground terms and is augmented by solving matching equations. The *function environment* binds designators to functions and is augmented by the reduction of abstractions, which creates new functions. Section 4 gives statically verifiable conditions that ensure that all variables and designators are bound when they are reduced.

A variable reduces to its *value*, that is, the ground term to which it is bound in the term environment. Thus a term *t* always reduces to a ground term, which is obtained from *t* by replacing all variables by their values.

As mentioned before, a pair (e, f) reduces to (u, v) if *e* reduces to *u* and *f* reduces to *v*. If one of the components fails the reduction of the entire pair fails.

A *conditional let-clause* has the form $s \equiv e \rightarrow f ; g$ (read "if *s* matches *e* then *f* else *g*") where *s* is the *pattern*, $s \equiv e$ is the *condition part*, *f* is the *then-part* and *g* is the *else-part*. Note that the metavariables indicate that *e*, *f* and *g* can be arbitrary expressions and *s* can be any term. The reduction of a conditional let-clause begins with the reduction of *e*. If *e* *succeeds* with a result *u*, the solution of the equation $s \equiv u$ under the current term environment is attempted. If the equation is solvable its solution yields an augmented term environment, under which the then-

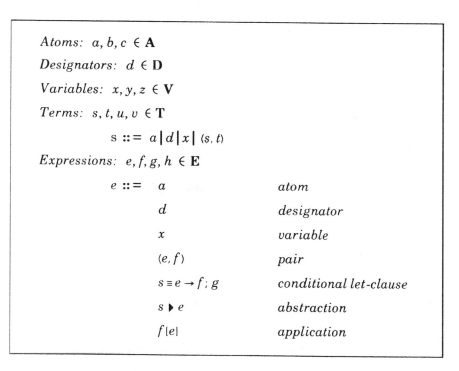

> *Atoms:* $a, b, c \in \mathbf{A}$
>
> *Designators:* $d \in \mathbf{D}$
>
> *Variables:* $x, y, z \in \mathbf{V}$
>
> *Terms:* $s, t, u, v \in \mathbf{T}$
>
> $\qquad s ::= a \mid d \mid x \mid (s, t)$
>
> *Expressions:* $e, f, g, h \in \mathbf{E}$
>
> $\qquad e ::= \quad a \qquad\qquad\qquad atom$
>
> $\qquad\qquad\qquad d \qquad\qquad\qquad designator$
>
> $\qquad\qquad\qquad x \qquad\qquad\qquad variable$
>
> $\qquad\qquad\qquad (e, f) \qquad\qquad pair$
>
> $\qquad\qquad\qquad s \equiv e \rightarrow f ; g \qquad conditional\ let\text{-}clause$
>
> $\qquad\qquad\qquad s \blacktriangleright e \qquad\qquad abstraction$
>
> $\qquad\qquad\qquad f \lfloor e \rfloor \qquad\qquad application$

Figure 1: FM's abstract syntax.

part is reduced. If the then-part fails, the conditional let-clause fails; otherwise its result is the result of the then-part. The else-part is reduced only if the reduction of the condition part fails; that is, either e fails or the match between the pattern and the result of e fails. If the else-part fails the conditional let-clause fails; otherwise, the result of the else-part is the result of the conditional let-clause.

When we discuss functions we will define an expression fail[] that always fails. This expression is helpful for defining other useful extensions. A simple let-clause can now be defined as

$$s \equiv e \to f \qquad \text{is} \qquad s \equiv e \to f \, ; \, \text{fail}[] \, .$$

With that we can express Lisp's car and cdr operation, which yield the head and the tail of a list:

$(H, T) \equiv L \to H$ *car operation*

$(H, T) \equiv L \to T$ *cdr operation*

The variable L is supposed to be bound to a list. If L is bound to the empty list the expression fails. This is in contrast to Lisp, where the application of car or cdr to the empty list results in a run-time error. Note that in FM a cons operation (cons e l) becomes just the pair (e, l).

Another useful syntactic extension is the *wildcard symbol* _ that stands for a variable that occurs only once. With it a *conditional* can be defined as

$$e \to f \, ; \, g \qquad \text{is} \qquad \_ \equiv e \to f \, ; \, g \, .$$

A match with a variable and hence the wildcard symbol always succeeds. The presence of failure makes the conditional independent of distinguished boolean values. If the condition succeeds the then-part determines the result; if the condition fails the else-part is reduced. The boolean connectives are now easily defined. Conjunction becomes pairing, for instance, $(e, f) \to g \, ; \, h$. Conditional disjunction (also called alternation) becomes

$$e \, ; \, f \qquad \text{is} \qquad x \equiv e \to x \, ; \, f$$

where x is a new variable. Negation as failure can be defined as

$$\neg e \qquad \text{is} \qquad e \to \text{fail}[] \, ; \, \text{true}$$

where true is the atom true. Equality could be defined as

$$e = f \qquad \text{is} \qquad x \equiv e \to (x \equiv f \to \text{true})$$

where x is a new variable. Note that the inner pattern is a variable that is bound by the outer pattern.

Let us study reduction in more detail. For now we are not concerned with functions, so reduction operates on configurations $\rho\{e\}$ where ρ is the term environment and e is the expression to be reduced. We start with the configuration

$$\{\, X \equiv 1 \;\rightarrow\; L \equiv (1, 1, 2, ()) \;\rightarrow\; (X, X, R) \equiv L \;\rightarrow\; R \,\}$$

whose term environment is empty. The conditional arrow $\rightarrow$ binds right-associative; thus the expression above is parsed as

$$X \equiv 1 \;\rightarrow\; (\, L \equiv (1, 1, 2, ()) \;\rightarrow\; (\,(X, X, R) \equiv L \;\rightarrow\; R\,)\,)\,.$$

The innermost let-clause checks whether the first two elements of the list L are equal to x and, if so, returns the rest of the list. Thus the entire expression reduces to the list $(2, ())$.

Formally, the expression is reduced by first reducing the condition part $X \equiv 1$ of the outer let-clause. Since 1 reduces to 1, the equation yields the new variable binding $X \equiv 1$. Thus reduction continues with the configuration

$$X \equiv 1 \;\bigl\{\, L \equiv (1, 1, 2, ()) \;\rightarrow\; (X, X, R) \equiv L \;\rightarrow\; R \,\bigr\}\,.$$

By proceeding as before ($(1, 1, 2, ())$ is a ground term and reduces to itself), we obtain the configuration

$$X \equiv 1 \quad L \equiv (1, 1, 2, ()) \;\bigl\{\, (X, X, R) \equiv L \;\rightarrow\; R \,\bigr\}\,.$$

This time the right-hand side of the condition part is the variable L, which reduces to its value $(1, 1, 2, ())$ in the current term environment. Thus the next step is to solve the *matching problem*

$$X \equiv 1 \quad L \equiv (1, 1, 2, ()) \;\bigl\{\, (X, X, R) \equiv (1, 1, 2, ()) \,\bigr\}\,,$$

which consists of the environment and the equation between the pattern and the result of L. First, the equation is split into three equations, yielding

$$X \equiv 1 \quad L \equiv (1, 1, 2, ()) \;\bigl\{\, X \equiv 1 \quad X \equiv 1 \quad R \equiv (2, ()) \,\bigr\}\,.$$

Now the left-hand side of the first equation $X \equiv 1$ is replaced by its value under the environment, yielding

$$X \equiv 1 \quad L \equiv (1, 1, 2, ()) \;\bigl\{\, 1 \equiv 1 \quad X \equiv 1 \quad R \equiv (2, ()) \,\bigr\}\,.$$

Since $1 \equiv 1$ is a tautology it can be discarded. Analogously, the second equation is discarded, yielding

$$X \equiv 1 \quad L \equiv (1, 1, 2, ()) \;\bigl\{\, R \equiv (2, ()) \,\bigr\}\,.$$

Since the left-hand side of the remaining equation is a variable that is not bound in the environment, the equation defines a new binding that is included into the environment, yielding the augmented environment

$$X \equiv 1 \quad L \equiv (1, 1, 2, ()) \quad R \equiv (2, ())$$

as the solution of the matching problem. Thus the reduction of the innermost let-clause continues with the then-part, that is, with the configuration

$$X \equiv 1 \quad L \equiv (1, 1, 2, ()) \quad R \equiv (2, ()) \; \{ R \} \, ,$$

which reduces to the value of R. Thus the entire expression reduces to $(2, ())$.

We complete the informal account of FM's semantics with the description of abstraction and application, which create and apply functions. As in other functional languages, functions have always exactly one argument and their global variables are bound statically, that is, when the function is created rather than when the function is applied. One argument is sufficient since pairs provide implicitly for multiple arguments.

An *abstraction* has form $s \blacktriangleright e$ where the *pattern* s can be any term and the *body* e can be any expression. As a special case we have the form $x \blacktriangleright e$ that is similar to $\lambda x.e$ in the lambda calculus. In contrast to the lambda calculus, however, abstractions are not canonical in FM. Furthermore, variables in the pattern of an abstraction can be bound in the outer context, as, for instance, in $X \blacktriangleright (X \blacktriangleright body)$. An abstraction reduces to a new designator, which is then bound to the closure of the abstraction under the current term environment. The closure represents the created function and consists of the abstraction together with all bindings that exist so far for variables that occur in the abstraction. For instance, the closure of the abstraction $(X,Y) \blacktriangleright Y$ will contain the binding $X \equiv 1$ if the current term environment binds X to 1 and does not bind Y. This closure is equivalent to a closure that contains the abstraction $(1,Y) \blacktriangleright Y$ and no bindings.

An *application* has the form $f \, [e]$ where f and e are expressions. It is reduced by first reducing the pair (f, e). If the pair does not reduce to a pair (d, u) where d is a designator, the application fails. Otherwise, let the designator be bound to the closure $(\rho, s \blacktriangleright g)$. Then the matching equation $s \equiv u$ between the abstraction pattern and the reduced argument is solved under the *closure environment* ρ. If the equation is unsolvable the application fails. Otherwise, the solution of the equation yields an augmented closure environment, under which the abstraction body g is reduced. If the body fails the application fails; otherwise, the application succeeds with the result of the body. As an example, consider the reduction of the application $((X,Y) \blacktriangleright Y)[L]$ under the environment $X \equiv 1$ and $L \equiv (1, 2, ())$. Then the pair $((X,Y \blacktriangleright Y), L)$ reduces to $(d, (1, 2, ()))$ where d is a new designator that is bound to a closure with the environment $X \equiv 1$ and the abstraction $(X,Y) \blacktriangleright Y$. Since the matching problem $X \equiv 1 \{ (X,Y) \equiv (1, 2, ()) \}$ reduces to the environment $X \equiv 1$ and $Y \equiv (2, ())$, the application $((X,Y) \blacktriangleright Y)[L]$ reduces to $(2, ())$.

The expression that always fails can be defined as

fail[]   is $(1 \blacktriangleright 1)[2]$.

Note that without functions failure is not possible since the else-part of the conditional let-clause catches a possible failure of its condition part.

$s(e)$	is	$(\%, s, e)$	*labeled term* $(s \in \mathbf{A} \cup \mathbf{V})$
$\_$	is	a new variable	*wildcard*
fail[]	is	$(1 \blacktriangleright 1)[2]$	*expression that always fails*
$e \to f; g$	is	$\_ \equiv e \to f; g$	*conditional*
$\neg e$	is	$e \to$ **fail**[] ; true	*negation*
$e \to f$	is	$e \to f;$ **fail**[]	*if-clause*
$s \equiv e \to f$	is	$s \equiv e \to f;$ **fail**[]	*let-clause*
$f \leftarrow e$	is	$e \to f;$ **fail**[]	*where-clause*
$f \leftarrow s \equiv e$	is	$s \equiv e \to f;$ **fail**[]	*where-clause with matching*
$e; f$	is	$x = e \to x; f$	*alternation (x is new)*
$s_1 \blacktriangleright e_1 ;;$ $s_2 \blacktriangleright e_2 ;;$ $\vdots$ $s_n \blacktriangleright e_n$	is	$x \blacktriangleright (s_1 \equiv x \to e_1 ;$ $(s_2 \equiv x \to e_2 ;$ $\vdots$ $(s_n \equiv x \to e_n ;$ **fail**[]) ...))	*clausal definition (x is new)*

Operator Precedence: $;;$ ‖ $\blacktriangleright$ ‖ $\to$; $\leftarrow$ ‖ , ‖ $\neg$ ‖ $\equiv$ ‖ $f[e]$ $s(e)$

right-associative: $;;$ $\blacktriangleright$ $\to$; $\neg$ $\equiv$

left-associative: $f[e]$ $\leftarrow$

Figure 2 : Syntactic extensions.

Figure 2 summarizes the syntactic extensions used in this paper. Since FM is a sublanguage of Fresh, all syntax and semantics discussed so far are valid for Fresh as well. As will become clear in the following examples, clausal definition (see Figure 2) is the intended style for function definitions. The conditional let-clause rather than a regular conditional is included as the base construct so that the clausal definition construct can be defined. The reader may convince himself that conditional, abstraction and application are not strong enough to express the clausal definition construct.

As we know from the lambda calculus, abstraction and application alone suffice for the definition of recursive functions. However, to have a convenient facility for the definition of recursive functions, FM supports top-level function declarations. A *function declaration* has the form

$$d \text{ of } s \blacktriangleright e. \qquad (\text{read } "d \text{ of } s \text{ is } e")$$

where d is a designator and $s \blacktriangleright e$ is an abstraction. A *program* is a sequence of function definitions followed by an expression that has to be reduced under this function environment.

2.3 Examples

We begin with some examples of functions acting on lists. Recall that a list is either the atom () (the empty list) or a pair whose right component is a list. The types that appear in the function declarations are comments and have no semantic significance. List concatenation can be defined as

append: *list(T)* × *list(T)* → *list(T)* of
    (), L ▶ L;;
    (H,T), L ▶ H, **append**[T,L].

The comma binds tighter than the abstraction operator (see Figure 2); thus the second clause of **append** is parsed as ((H,T), L) ▶ (H, **append**[T,L]) . Technically, **append** has like any other function just one argument. The type indicates that the argument must be a pair of two lists. A membership function is

member: *T* × *list(T)* → {true} of
    X, (X, T) ▶ true;;
    X, (H, T) ▶ **member**[X, T].

This function takes a term and a list and returns true if the term is in the list and fails otherwise. Note how the test for membership is essentially being carried out by matching with a pattern containing two occurrences of x; the first clause of **member** can succeed only if the first element of the list is equal to the "first argument" of **member**. A typical higher-order function is

> **map**: $(S \to T) \to$ *list(S)* $\to$ *list(T)* of
>   F ▶ (()   ▶ ();;
>   H, T   ▶ F[H], **map**[F][T]).

which maps a list by applying a function to each element. Note that **map** fails if its argument function fails for one element of the list. Thus **map** can also be used to test that all elements of a list have a certain property. The function

> **islist**: *term* $\to$ {true} of
>   () ▶ true;;
>   H,T ▶ **islist**[T].

succeeds with the atom true if its argument is a list. The function

> **succeeds** *term* $\to$ {true} of
>   X ▶ true.

succeeds for every argument with true. The function

> **comp**: $(R \to S) \times (S \to T) \to (R \to T)$ of
>   F, G ▶ X ▶ F[G[X]].

builds the composition of two functions. Thus the expression **comp**[**succeeds**, **map**[**islist**]] reduces to a function that succeeds with the atom true if and only if its argument is a list of lists. The next function

> **powerlist**: *list(T)* $\to$ *list(list(T))* of
>   () ▶ (), ();;
>   H,T ▶ **append**[P, **map**[L ▶ H,L][P]] ← P ≡ **powerlist**[T].

constructs the list of all sublists of a list. We shall see a declarative version of this function when we introduce backtracking. The next function takes a function and a list and returns the result of applying the function to the first member of the list on which the function succeeds.

> **get**: $(S \to T) \to$ *list(S)* $\to T$ of
>   F ▶ H, T ▶ F[H] ; **get**[F][T].

If s is a term the expression **get**[s ▶ s] reduces to a function that, when applied to a list, yields the first element that matches the pattern s. For instance, **get**[(X,2) ▶ (X,2)] yields a function that retrieves the first element that is a pair whose right component is the atom 2.

The function

getvalue: *list(identifier × T) × identifier → T* of
    L, I ▶ **get**[I,V ▶ V] [L].

gets a value from an association list. Note that the pattern of the inner abstraction contains the variable I, which is bound by the pattern of the outer abstraction. The last example is a function for the symbolic differentiation of arithmetic expressions:

d: *unknown → arithmeticExpression → arithmeticExpression* of
    U ▶ (X + Y ▶ **d**[U][X] + **d**[U][Y] ;;
             X – Y ▶ **d**[U][X] – **d**[U][Y] ;;
             X∗Y ▶ **d**[U][X] ∗Y + X∗**d**[U][Y] ;;
             X / Y ▶ (**d**[U][X] ∗Y – X∗**d**[U][Y]) / Y∗Y ;;
             U   ▶ 1 ;;
             C   ▶ 0)

Note that the pattern of the second last clause is the variable U, which is bound by the outer pattern to the unknown with respect to which the derivative is computed. The fancy syntax is obtained by declaring the atoms +, –, ∗, / as infix operators with the appropriate precedence. Then, for instance, X + Y is a syntactical variant of the labeled term + (X, Y), which in turn is an abbreviation for (%, (+, (X, Y))).

As the examples above illustrate, the existence of designators makes no difference to the programming style. Designators were introduced since matching and unification are first-order operations based on syntactical equality. By hiding functions behind designators and treating designators like atoms, matching and unification can cover all objects. Consequently, FM offers the unusual feature that function names can be compared with any term. The suppression of this extra-capability at the computational level would lead to numerous dynamic error conditions. Moreover, the formulation of the algebraic properties of matching and unification would become rather awkward. On the other hand, a type discipline could easily ensure that designators are not compared with other objects.

The next two sections present a formal account of matching and FM's semantics. This prepares the ground for the formal semantics of Fresh and will illustrate the semantic differences between the functional and unification-based language. The reader may first read the informal description of the full language, which appears in sections 5 and 6.

3 MATCHING

This section gives a formal account of substitutions, equations and matching. Substitutions serve as term environments in the formal semantics of FM and Fresh. Equations arise during the reduction of conditional let-clauses and applications. Section 7 will continue this section with the discussion of unification.

Recall the definition of terms given in Figure 1:

$Atoms$: $a, b, c \in \mathbf{A}$

$Designators$: $d \in \mathbf{D}$

$Variables$: $x, y, z \in \mathbf{V}$

$Terms$: $s, t, u, v \in \mathbf{T}$ $s ::= a \mid d \mid x \mid (s, t)$

$\mathbf{V}(s)$ denotes the set of all variables that occur in the term s.

A *substitution* is a function $\theta: \mathbf{T} \to \mathbf{T}$ such that $\theta a = a$ for all atoms a, $\theta d = d$ for all designators d, and $\theta(s, t) = (\theta s, \theta t)$ for all pairs (s, t), where θs denotes the application of θ to the term s. We write $\psi\theta$ for the composition of two substitutions θ and ψ. As always, application and composition are compatible, that is, $(\theta\psi)s = \theta(\psi s)$ holds for all substitutions θ and ψ and all terms s. It is easy to verify that two substitutions are equal if they are equal for all variables. The identity on $\mathbf{T}$ is called the *empty substitution* and is denoted by ε.

An *equation* is an expression $s \equiv t$ whose *left-hand side s* and *right-hand side t* are terms. An *equation system* is a bag of equations. We use bags rather than sets to avoid an implementation having to check for duplicates. A substitution θ is a *solution* for an equation system E if $\theta s = \theta t$ for all equations $s \equiv t$ in E.

The *domain* of a substitution θ is $\mathbf{D}(\theta) := \{ x \in \mathbf{V} \mid \theta x \neq x \}$. A substitution is *finite* if its domain is finite. A finite substitution θ can be *represented* by the finite equation system $\{ x \equiv \theta x \mid x \in \mathbf{D}(\theta) \}$. In the following we will freely switch between viewing a substitution as an equation system and viewing it as a mapping from terms to terms. Furthermore, we will only consider finite substitutions; so in the following, "substitution" always stands for finite substitution. A *ground substitution* is a substitution which maps all variables of its domain to ground terms. Note that a ground substitution is a solved equation system, that is, the solution of θ viewed as an equation system is θ.

A *matching problem* is a pair $\rho\{M\}$ where ρ is a ground substitution and M is a finite equation system whose right-hand sides are ground terms. A *solution* of a matching problem $\rho\{M\}$ is a substitution θ that solves M and ρ (that is, ρ viewed as an equation system) and satisfies

$\mathbf{D}(\theta) = \mathbf{D}(\rho) \cup \mathbf{V}(M)$, where $\mathbf{V}(M)$ is the set of all variables that occur in the equations of M. It is easy to show that a matching problem has at most one solution and that a solution is a ground substitution. If θ solves both M and ρ then θ solves the instantiated equation system ρM. Note that the converse does not hold.

Matching is the process of computing the solution of a matching problem. An indeterministic algorithm for solving matching problems is best specified by *matching rules*, which reduce a matching problem $\rho\{M\}$ by growing the *solved part* ρ and shrinking the *unsolved part* M. Note that ρ already solves ρ. The *failure symbol* $\square$ is the normal form for unsolvable matching problems.

(Taut) $\rho\{s \equiv s, M\} \underset{m}{\rightarrow} \rho\{M\}$ if s is an atom or a designator

(Subst) $\rho\{x \equiv u, M\} \underset{m}{\rightarrow} \rho\{\rho x \equiv u, M\}$ if $x \in \mathbf{D}(\rho)$

(Bind) $\rho\{x \equiv u, M\} \underset{m}{\rightarrow} \{x \equiv u\}\rho\{M\}$ if $x \notin \mathbf{D}(\rho)$

(Split) $\rho\{(s, t) \equiv (u, v), M\} \underset{m}{\rightarrow} \rho\{s \equiv u, t \equiv v, M\}$

(Fail) $\rho\{s \equiv t, M\} \underset{m}{\rightarrow} \square$ if none of the rules above applies

The expression $\rho\{s \equiv u, M\}$ denotes the matching problem $\rho\{M'\}$ where M' is obtained from M by adding the equation $s \equiv u$. Furthermore, $\{x \equiv u\}\rho$ is the composition of the substitutions $\{x \equiv u\}$ and ρ. The following proposition is easy to prove and states that the matching rules are sound.

Proposition 3.1. Let $\rho\{M\} \underset{m}{\rightarrow} \rho'\{M'\}$. Then a substitution θ solves $\rho\{M\}$ if and only if θ solves $\rho'\{M'\}$.

The symbol $\underset{m}{\rightarrow}^{\bullet}$ denotes the reflexive and transitive closure of $\underset{m}{\rightarrow}$ and $\rho\{M\} \underset{m}{\rightarrow}^{\bullet} \rho'$ is an abbreviation for $\rho\{M\} \underset{m}{\rightarrow}^{\bullet} \rho'\{\varnothing\}$. For the the next theorem we need some notations and a theorem from Huet [14]. Let $\rightarrow$ be a binary relation and let $\rightarrow^{\bullet}$ be its reflexive and transitive closure. Then $\rightarrow$ is *locally confluent* if for all x, y, z such that $x \rightarrow y$ and $x \rightarrow z$ there exists a u such that $y \rightarrow^{\bullet} u$ and $z \rightarrow^{\bullet} u$. Furthermore, $\rightarrow$ is *confluent* if for all x, y, z such that $x \rightarrow^{\bullet} y$ and $x \rightarrow^{\bullet} z$ there exists a u such that $y \rightarrow^{\bullet} u$ and $z \rightarrow^{\bullet} u$. Finally, $\rightarrow$ is *noetherian* if there are no infinite sequences $x_1 \rightarrow x_2 \rightarrow x_3 \rightarrow \cdots$. Huet proves that a noetherian relation is confluent if it is locally confluent.

Theorem 3.2. The reduction $\underset{m}{\rightarrow}$ is confluent and noetherian. Furthermore, $\rho\{M\} \underset{m}{\rightarrow}^{\bullet} \rho'$ if an only if ρ' is the solution of $\rho\{M\}$; and $\rho\{M\} \underset{m}{\rightarrow}^{\bullet} \square$ if and only if $\rho\{M\}$ has no solution.

Proof. The matching reduction is noetherian since each rule decreases either the number of variable occurrences or the sum of the depths of the equations in the unsolved part of the matching problem. Since the reduction is noetherian it is confluent if it is locally confluent. The local confluence of $_m\!\to$ is easy to verify. The remaining two claims follow by induction from proposition 3.1. $\square$

Theorem 3.2 tells us that the matching rules in fact specify an algorithm for solving matching problems. Given a matching problem, such an algorithm just applies matching rules as long as they are applicable. Since $_m\!\to$ is noetherian such an algorithm will always terminate. And since $_m\!\to$ is confluent it will always compute the same solution.

4 REDUCTION TREE SEMANTICS OF FM

In this section we shall formalize the informal description of FM and obtain a compact and easy to understand specification of FM's semantics. Recall that the reduction of an expression takes place in the presence of a term environment that binds variables and a function environment that binds designators. Thus reduction starts with a *configuration* $\delta \rho \{e\}$ where δ is the function environment, ρ is the term environment and e is the expression to be reduced. As we already know, the reduction of such a configuration either fails or produces a result together with a function environment that binds the designators occurring in the result. Thus we can write the proposition

$$\delta \rho \{e\} \;\to\; \square$$

to express that the reduction of $\delta \rho \{e\}$ fails; analogously, the proposition

$$\delta \rho \{e\} \;\to\; \delta' \{u\}$$

says that the reduction of $\delta \rho \{e\}$ succeeds with the result u and the function environment δ'. The final function environment δ' is necessary since u can contain designators that are not bound by the initial function environment δ; because the reduction of abstractions creates new designators and functions.

The propositions $\delta \rho \{e\} \to \square$ and $\delta \rho \{e\} \to \delta' \{u\}$ are called *reductions*. To specify the semantics of FM now means to say when a reduction is *valid*, that is, to say when the configuration on the right is indeed the result of executing the configuration on the left. This will be accomplished by proof rules, which allow us to *prove* that a certain reduction is valid. For instance, the proof rule

$$\frac{\delta \rho \{a\} \;\rightarrow\; \delta \{a\}}{}$$

specifies the reduction of atoms by saying that a reduction $\delta \rho \{a\} \rightarrow \delta \{a\}$ is always valid. The proof rule

$$\frac{\delta \rho \{(e, f)\} \;\rightarrow\; \square}{\delta \rho \{e\} \;\rightarrow\; \square}$$
$$\delta \rho \{f\} \;\rightarrow\; F$$

says that a pair reduces to failure if its left component reduces to failure and its right component has a valid reduction. There will be further proof rules for pairs that handle the other cases. The pair rule suggests that proofs for the validity of reductions have a tree structure that follows the structure of the expression being reduced.

The proof rules are called *reduction rules* and the proofs are called *reduction trees*. The *proof theoretic reading* of the rules is complemented by an *operational reading*. Under the operational reading the rules specify an abstract interpreter that starts with a configuration $\delta \rho \{e\}$ and computes a result F such that $\delta \rho \{e\} \rightarrow F$ is a valid reduction. Operationally, a reduction tree is a valid computation. To understand the rules, the proof theoretic or declarative reading is superior since it is less detailed than the operational reading. The operational details are obvious once the declarative meaning of the rules is understood.

Reduction tree semantics is compositional since the tree for a particular reduction is obtained by combining the trees for its components. Lack of compositionality has been the standard reason for preferring a denotational description over an operational description.

We begin with the formalization of environments, configurations and reductions. A *term environment* is a substitution. A *closure* $(\rho, s \blacktriangleright e)$ consists of a term environment ρ and an abstraction $s \blacktriangleright e$. A *function environment* δ is a mapping from a finite set of designators into the set of closures, where $\mathbf{D}(\delta)$ denotes the *domain* of δ. An *initial configuration* $\delta \rho \{e\}$ consists of a function environment δ, a term environment ρ, and an expression e. A *final configuration* is either the *failure configuration* $\square$ or a pair $\delta \{u\}$ where δ is a function environment and and u is a term. A *reduction* has the form $I \rightarrow F$ where I is an initial configuration and F is a final configuration.

A reduction rule consists of a *conclusion* (the reduction above the line), none, one or several *premises* (the reductions beneath the line) and possibly an *application condition* (at the right-hand side of the rule).

The conclusion is valid if all premises are valid and the application condition is satisfied.

Atoms, Designators and Variables

$$\frac{}{\delta\rho\{a\} \;\rightarrow\; \delta\{a\}} \qquad \frac{}{\delta\rho\{d\} \;\rightarrow\; \delta\{d\}} \qquad \frac{}{\delta\rho\{x\} \;\rightarrow\; \delta\{\rho x\}}$$

These rules express the fact that atoms and designators reduce to themselves while variables are replaced by their values. These rules justify leaves of reduction trees.

Pairs

$$\frac{\delta\rho\{(e,f)\} \;\rightarrow\; \delta'\cup\delta''\{(u,v)\}}{\delta\rho\{e\} \;\rightarrow\; \delta'\{u\}} \qquad \text{if } \mathbf{D}(\delta')\cap\mathbf{D}(\delta'') \subset \mathbf{D}(\delta)$$
$$\delta\rho\{f\} \;\rightarrow\; \delta''\{v\}$$

$$\frac{\delta\rho\{(e,f)\} \;\rightarrow\; \square}{\delta\rho\{e\} \;\rightarrow\; \square} \qquad\qquad \frac{\delta\rho\{(e,f)\} \;\rightarrow\; \square}{\delta\rho\{e\} \;\rightarrow\; F}$$
$$\delta\rho\{f\} \;\rightarrow\; F \qquad\qquad\qquad \delta\rho\{f\} \;\rightarrow\; \square$$

The condition $\mathbf{D}(\delta')\cap\mathbf{D}(\delta'') \subset \mathbf{D}(\delta)$ enforces that newly introduced designators are distinct. Note that an existing designator or variable binding is never changed. Thus the condition is sufficient to ensure that the union $\delta'\cup\delta''$ is well-defined. The failure rules require that both components of a pair have valid reductions. Operationally, this means that the reduction of a pair terminates if and only if the reduction of both components terminates.

Conditional Let-Clause

$$\frac{\delta\rho\{s\equiv e \rightarrow f; g\} \;\rightarrow\; F}{\delta\rho\{e\} \;\rightarrow\; \delta'\{u\}} \qquad \text{if } \rho\{s\equiv u\} \;_m\!\rightarrow^* \rho'$$
$$\delta'\rho'\{f\} \;\rightarrow\; F$$

$$\frac{\delta\rho\{s\equiv e \rightarrow f; g\} \;\rightarrow\; F}{\delta\rho\{e\} \;\rightarrow\; \delta'\{u\}} \qquad \text{if } \rho\{s\equiv u\} \;_m\!\rightarrow^* \square$$
$$\delta\rho\{g\} \;\rightarrow\; F$$

$$\frac{\delta\,\rho\{s\equiv e\rightarrow f;g\}\ \rightarrow\ F}{\delta\,\rho\{e\}\ \rightarrow\ \square}$$
$$\delta\,\rho\{g\}\ \rightarrow\ F$$

Abstraction

$$\frac{}{\delta\,\rho\{s\blacktriangleright e\}\ \rightarrow\ \delta[d\leftarrow(\rho',s\blacktriangleright e)]\{d\}}\quad\text{where}\ d\notin D(\delta)\ \text{and}\ \rho'=\rho|_{V(s\blacktriangleright e)}$$

An abstraction reduces to a new designator, which is bound to the closure of the abstraction under the initial term environment. The closure environment ρ' is the restriction of the initial environment to the variables occurring in the abstraction. The updated function environment $\delta[d\leftarrow(\rho',s\blacktriangleright e)]$ is obtained from δ by adding the new binding $d\leftarrow(\rho',s\blacktriangleright e)$.

Application

$$\frac{\delta\,\rho\{f[e]\}\ \rightarrow\ F}{\delta\,\rho\{(f,e)\}\ \rightarrow\ \delta'\{(d,u)\}}\qquad\begin{array}{l}\text{if}\ \ \rho'\{s\equiv u\}\ _{m}\rightarrow^{*}\ \rho''\\[4pt]\quad\text{where}\ (\rho',s\blacktriangleright g)=\delta'(d)\end{array}$$
$$\delta'\,\rho''\{g\}\ \rightarrow\ F$$

$$\frac{\delta\,\rho\{f[e]\}\ \rightarrow\ \square}{\delta\,\rho\{(f,e)\}\ \rightarrow\ \delta'\{(d,u)\}}\qquad\begin{array}{l}\text{if}\ \ \rho'\{s\equiv u\}\ _{m}\rightarrow^{*}\ \square\\[4pt]\quad\text{where}\ (\rho',s\blacktriangleright g)=\delta'(d)\end{array}$$

$$\frac{\delta\,\rho\{f[e]\}\ \rightarrow\ \square}{\delta\,\rho\{(f,e)\}\ \rightarrow\ \delta'\{(v,u)\}}\qquad\text{if}\ \ v\ \text{is not a designator}$$

$$\frac{\delta\,\rho\{f[e]\}\ \rightarrow\ \square}{\delta\,\rho\{(f,e)\}\ \rightarrow\ \square}$$

The third rule covers the case where the first component of an application does not reduce to a function. Other functional languages handle this situation with a run-time error. In FM such an application simply fails. A type discipline for FM would statically enforce conditions that prevent such situations from occurring. Below we shall give statically verifiable conditions that ensure that all designators and variables are bound when they are reduced. For that reason there is no rule that handles unbound designators.

We now complete the semantic account of FM by defining reduction trees. An *instance of a rule* is a tuple $(R, R_1, \ldots, R_n)$ where $n \geq 0$ and R and $R_1, \ldots, R_n$ are instances (under the same interpretation) of the conclusion and the premises (in top-down order) of the rule such that the conditions at the right-hand side of the rule are satisfied. Note that the conclusion R and the premises $R_1, \ldots, R_n$ are reductions.

A *reduction tree for a reduction R* is an expression $(R, T_1, \ldots, T_n)$ such that $T_1, \ldots, T_n$ are reduction trees for $R_1, \ldots, R_n$ where $n \geq 0$ and $(R, R_1, \ldots, R_n)$ is an instance of a rule. A *reduction tree for an initial configuration I* is a reduction tree for some reduction $I \rightarrow F$.

The next theorem formulates the fact that the reduction rules are *deterministic*, that is, a reduction has at most one reduction tree up to designator renaming.

Theorem 4.1. All reduction trees for an initial configuration are equal up to consistent designator renaming.

Proof. By induction on the depth of reduction trees. $\square$

Besides being deterministic, the reduction rules have the additional property that all designators and variables are bound when they are reduced, provided the initial configuration is "closed" under its environments. We begin the formalization of this property by defining free variables of expressions. Variables are bound by patterns of abstractions and conditional let-clauses. The set $\mathbf{FV}(e)$ of variables that are free in the expression e is defined inductively:

$$\mathbf{FV}(a) = \varnothing \qquad\qquad \mathbf{FV}(d) = \varnothing$$

$$\mathbf{FV}(x) = \{x\} \qquad\qquad \mathbf{FV}((e, f)) = \mathbf{FV}(e) \cup \mathbf{FV}(f)$$

$$\mathbf{FV}(s \equiv e \rightarrow f ; g) = \mathbf{FV}(e) \cup (\mathbf{FV}(f) - \mathbf{V}(s)) \cup \mathbf{FV}(g)$$

$$\mathbf{FV}(s \blacktriangleright e) = \mathbf{FV}(e) - \mathbf{V}(s) \qquad\qquad \mathbf{FV}(f[e]) = \mathbf{FV}(f) \cup \mathbf{FV}(e)$$

An expression is *closed* if it has no free variables. This notion of closed expressions is different from the lambda calculus. In the lambda calculus the meaning or reduction of a closed expression is completely independent of the context in which it occurs. This property does not hold for FM since we allowed patterns to contain variables that are bound in an outer context. For instance, although the abstraction $x \blacktriangleright x$ is closed, its meaning depends on the environment as the expression $(x \blacktriangleright (x \blacktriangleright x))[4]$ illustrates.

489

A term environment ρ is *closed under a function environment* δ if for all $x \in \mathbf{D}(\rho)$ all designators occurring in ρx are bound by δ, that is, are in $\mathbf{D}(\delta)$. A function environment δ is *consistent* if for all $d \in \mathbf{D}(\delta)$ where $\delta(d) = (\rho, s \blacktriangleright e)$ the closure environment ρ is a ground substitution closed under δ, all designators that occur in the abstraction $s \blacktriangleright e$ are in $\mathbf{D}(\delta)$, and $\mathbf{FV}(s \blacktriangleright e) \subset \mathbf{D}(\rho) \subset \mathbf{V}(s \blacktriangleright e)$. An initial configuration $\delta \rho \{e\}$ is *consistent* if

- δ is consistent and ρ is a ground substitution closed under δ.

- e is *closed under* δ, that is, e contains only designators bound by δ.

- e is *closed under* ρ, that is, all free variables of e are bound by ρ.

A final configuration $\delta\{u\}$ is *consistent* if δ is consistent and u is a ground term closed under δ. A reduction $\delta \rho \{e\} \to \delta' \{u\}$ is *consistent* if $\delta \rho \{e\}$ and $\delta' \{u\}$ are consistent and the final function environment is an extension of the initial function environment, that is, $\delta = \delta'|_{\mathbf{D}(\delta)}$. Furthermore, a failure reduction $\delta \rho \{e\} \to \square$ is consistent if its initial configuration is consistent. The following theorem is easily proven by structural induction on reduction trees.

Theorem 4.2. Every reduction in every reduction tree for a consistent initial configuration is consistent.

We say that the reduction of a consistent initial configuration I

- *fails* if $I \to \square$ has a reduction tree.

- *succeeds with result u and function environment* δ' if the reduction $I \to \delta' \{u\}$ has a reduction tree.

- *does not terminate* if there exists no final configuration F such that the reduction $I \to F$ has a reduction tree.

We know by theorem 4.1 that every consistent initial configuration has exactly one of these properties. Nonexistence of a reduction tree is equivalent to a nonterminating computation since the rules are *complete* for consistent configurations, that is, an interpreter cannot reach a configuration to which no rule is applicable. The rules are incomplete for inconsistent configurations since there are no rules that handle unbound designators or variables.

The given semantics is essentially proof theoretic rather than denotational or purely operational. As in denotational semantics, all expressions that appear in the initial configurations of a reduction tree are contained in the static program. This is in contrast to the lambda calculus where the β-rule instantiates the bodies of abstractions. Moreover, the rules are "effective" and yield an abstract interpreter.

The tree structure suggests several possibilities for parallelism. The most important one is the parallel execution of the components of a pair. The only communication overhead involved is that the component reductions must introduce distinct designators.

5 GENERALIZING MATCHING TO UNIFICATION

Functional languages are based on a rigid pattern of information flow. Variables become bound when they are introduced and their values cannot be updated or refined. Functions cannot change their argument, and they convey all output through their result. In this section we generalize FM by extending the role of variables. Unbound variables are now treated as first-class objects and can be part of canonical objects. As in FM, variable bindings are created by solving equations between patterns and canonical objects. Since canonical objects can now contain variables, matching is generalized to unification, which solves equations containing variables on both sides. Bindings created for variables in the canonical side are called *delayed bindings*. Since such variables can occur in the values of other variables, a delayed binding may *refine* or *narrow* already existing bindings. The application of a function now not only produces a result, but can also refine the environment by producing delayed bindings. The value of a variable can now be built incrementally by beginning with a skeleton and binding contained variables later as information becomes available.

This model of variables underlies Prolog, the first unification-based language. Such variables are often called "logical variables" since they appeared with logic programming. This paper tries to illustrate that in a functional framework there are virtually no applications of "logical variables" that exhibit significant advantages over a purely functional formulation and that are compatible with the logic programming paradigm. However, if we abandon the logic programming paradigm and use free variables as first-class objects, then in fact many interesting applications become possible.

"Logical variables" and unification do not come free. Delayed variable bindings are side effects and complicate reasoning about programs. We shall discuss *transparency*, a property that, if satisfied, allows a declarative understanding of delayed variable bindings. Roughly, the result of a transparent expression remains unchanged if the produced delayed bindings were supplied a priori. Nontransparency arises because free variables become first-class objects and one can test for properties that are metalinguistic in functional languages.

We shall now discuss FU, a language that is obtained from FM by generalizing matching to unification. FU is a conservative extension of FM, that is, the result of a consistent FM-program remains unchanged under FU's semantics. FU has the same syntax as FM. However, in FU a conditional suffices as a base construct since delayed bindings make the definition of a conditional let-clause possible. Thus the bare syntax of FU is:

$$e ::= a \mid d \mid x \mid (e, f) \mid s \blacktriangleright f \mid f[e] \mid e \rightarrow f; g.$$

The only construct that produces variable bindings is application. All bindings are obtained as solutions of equations between patterns and reduced arguments. The main semantic innovations are:

- Unbound variables reduce to themselves. Thus FU's canonical objects are terms that can contain variables. In particular, functions can be applied to nonground terms and can produce nonground results.

- Equations between patterns and arguments are solved by unification. Thus an application can bind variables contained in the argument. These *delayed bindings* are propagated to the context of an application. Thus a successful reduction not only produces a result but also refines the term environment. Refinement means that new bindings are added, which can apply to variables in the values of existing bindings.

The new features are best illustrated with the example of *open unification*, a function defined by

unif : *term* × *term* → *term* of
    X, X ▶ X.

In FM, **unif** is equality, that is, **unif** $[e, f]$ succeeds with a ground term u if and only if both e and f reduce to u. In FU, the results of e and f can be nonground terms u and v, and **unif** $[e, f]$ succeeds with a most general instance of u and v together with the bindings that form a most general solution of $u \equiv v$. Let us consider the reduction of **unif** $[(1,X), Y]$ under the environment $Y \equiv (Z, U)$ in detail. The argument reduces to the nonground term $((1, X), (Z, U))$. To avoid variable clashes, the reduced argument is applied to a variant of the closure where all variables are renamed to new ones. In general, this renaming is also necessary if the argument and the closure do not share variables, since variables of the closure may become part of the result or the refined environment and are then exported to the outer context. In our example, let the renamed closure be (V,V ▶ V). Then the next step is to solve the equation

$$(V, V) \equiv \langle (1,X), (Z,U) \rangle \ .$$

A most general solution is $\{V \equiv (1,U), X \equiv U, Z \equiv 1\}$. Obviously, infinitely many other solutions can be obtained by binding U to some term. A second most general solution is $\{V \equiv (1,X), U \equiv X, Z \equiv 1\}$. In general, a solvable equation system has always at least one most general solution and there are only finitely many most general solutions. As in the example, most general solutions differ only in the direction they bind variables to variables. Unification is a nondeterministic algorithm that computes one of the most general solutions. This indeterminacy has no significant impact on the language; results are unique up to designator and variable renaming.

To continue the example, we have now to reduce the body V of the renamed closure under an environment that binds V to $(1,U)$. Thus the result of the application is $(1, U)$. But the reduction also refines the term environment by including the delayed bindings produced for variables in the reduced argument. Formally, we have the valid reduction (the function environments are not shown)

$$Y \equiv (Z,U) \ \{ \mathsf{unif}[(1,X), Y] \} \ \to \ Y \equiv (1,U) \quad X \equiv U \quad Z \equiv 1 \ \{(1,U)\} \ .$$

Note that the reduction *refines* or *narrows* the value of Y. It is easy to verify that the application has the same result if we supply the delayed bindings for X and Z a priori, that is, the reduction

$$Y \equiv (1,U) \quad X \equiv U \quad Z \equiv 1 \ \{ \mathsf{unif}[(1,X), Y] \} \ \to \ Y \equiv (1,U) \quad X \equiv U \quad Z \equiv 1 \ \{(1,U)\} \ .$$

is valid as well. In general, an expression is called *transparent* if it reduces to the same result if the refined environment or any further refinement of it is supplied a priori .

A conditional $e \to f \, ; \, g$ is reduced by first reducing e. If e succeeds the then-part f is reduced under the augmented environment produced by the reduction of e. Otherwise, the else-part is reduced under the initial environment. The expression

$$\mathsf{unif}[s, e] \ \to \ f \, ; \, g$$

is a generalization of FM's conditional let-clause. In the following we will abbreviate $\mathsf{unif}[e, f]$ to $e \equiv f$ and use all syntactic extensions defined for FM. If we interpret all conditional let-clauses in a consistent FM-program as above, the resulting FU program is equivalent and produces the same result.

We complete the informal account of FU's semantics by describing the reduction of pairs. As in FM, a pair is reduced by reducing the components independently. If one or both components fail, the pair fails. Otherwise, each component yields a result and a refined term environment. Since the components may have produced delayed bindings for the same variables, a simple union of the two refined environments will not work. Since environments are (solved) equation systems, we build their union and take the solution of this equation system as the refined term environment of the entire pair. If the union of the component environments is unsolvable the reduction of the pair fails. Here are some examples for valid reductions (the function environments are not shown):

$$\{ (X \equiv 1, \ X \equiv 2) \} \ \rightarrow \ \square$$

$$\{ (X \equiv 1, \ Y \equiv 2) \} \ \rightarrow \ X \equiv 1 \ \ Y \equiv 2 \ \{ (1, 2) \}$$

$$\{ (X \equiv (1, Y), \ X \equiv (Z, 4)) \ \} \ \rightarrow \ X \equiv (1,4) \ \ Y \equiv 4 \ \ Z \equiv 1 \ \{ ((1, 4), \ (1, 4)) \}$$

Let us consider the last example in detail. The first component $X \equiv (1, Y)$ produces the result $(1, Y)$ and the refined environment $X \equiv (1, \ Y)$. The second component $X \equiv (Z, 4)$ produces the result $(Z, 4)$ and the refined environment $X \equiv (Z, 4)$. Thus the union of the component environments is $\{ X \equiv (1, Y), \ X \equiv (Z, 4) \}$ and has the solution $\{ X \equiv (1, 4), Y \equiv 4, \ Z \equiv 1 \}$. The new bindings $Y \equiv 4$ and $Z \equiv 1$ are applied to the results of the components and yield $((1, 4), \ (1, 4))$ as the result of the pair.

Pairs offer a clear possibility for parallelism. Sequentialization can be accomplished with an if-clause $e \rightarrow f$.

Once a closure is created, it is separated from the context and is not affected by new variable bindings. For instance, the expression

$$(X \equiv 1, \ Y \equiv (X \blacktriangleright true)) \ \rightarrow \ Y[2]$$

succeeds with the atom true and the bindings $X \equiv 1$ and $Y \equiv d$ where d is a new designator bound to the closure $X \blacktriangleright true$. The closure contains no binding for X since such a binding does not exist in the context where the closure is created. Thus the above expression is nontransparent with respect to X; the expression $(1 \equiv 1, Y \equiv (1 \blacktriangleright true)) \rightarrow Y[2]$ fails.

Free variables are first-class objects in FU. The following function succeeds with the atom true if and only if its argument is a free variable.

var of $\ X \ \blacktriangleright \ \ \neg \neg ((\neg \neg X \equiv 1), \ (\neg \neg X \equiv 2))$.

Recall that negation as failure $\neg e$ is defined as $e \rightarrow$ **fail**[]; true. Since a failure reduction does not propagate delayed bindings, a double negation $\neg \neg e$ succeeds if and only if e succeeds, but discards all bindings that the reduction of e may have produced. A second, quite different possibility to define a variable test is:

var of X ▶ (Y▶true) [(X▶true)[1], (X▶true)[2]].

This works since the variables in a closure become renamed when the closure is applied. We can go further and define equality for free variables:

eqvar of X, Y ▶ (var[X], var[Y]) → ¬(X ≡ 1, Y ≡ 2).

For instance, eqvar[X, Y] reduces to true if the values of X and Y are distinct free variables. The expression X ≡ Y → eqvar[X, Y] fails since before the test X gets bound to Y or vice versa. However, the pair (X ≡ Y, eqvar[X,Y]) succeeds since the components of a pair are reduced independently.

The existence of a variable test allows for nontransparent first-order expressions, for instance, (var[X], X ≡ 1). Furthermore, FU is necessarily nontransparent with respect to variables that become bound to higher-order objects. For instance, the expression X ≡ (Y▶Y) reduces to result *d* and binding X ≡ *d* where *d* is a new designator, but *d* ≡ (Y▶Y) fails since an abstraction always reduces to a new designator.

5.1 The Dictionary Example

This classical example for the use of incomplete data structures appeared first in Warren [36]. The task is to construct a dictionary of pairs (key, value) that is organized as a binary search tree with respect to a linear order on the set of keys. The basic idea is to represent empty subdictionaries as free variables, so that new entries can be inserted by binding an empty subdictionary rather than by constructing a new dictionary. The type of our dictionary is

$$dict(K,V) = ?(\{emptydict\} + K \times V \times dict(K,V) \times dict(K,V))$$

where *K* and *V* are type variables representing the key and the value type. A dictionary is now either a free variable (defined by the ?-operator), the atom emptydict or a tuple consisting of a key, a value, and a left and right subdictionary. As long as the dictionary is not complete all empty subdictionaries are represented as free variables. After all entries are made a dictionary can be *closed* by binding all empty subdictionaries to the atom emptydict. The following predicate defines membership for a closed dictionary:

contains: $(K \times K \to \{true\}) \to dict(K,V) \times K \times ?V \to \{true\}$ of
LT ▶ ((K, V, L, R), K, V   ▶ true ;;
     (K, V, L, R), NK, NV ▶ **contains** [LT] [(LT[NK, K] → L ; R), NK, NV]).

The first argument LT supplies the order according to which the dictionary is organized.

The **contains** predicate can retrieve values from a closed dictionary. The application **contains** [lt] [D, K,V] , where lt is the order, D is bound to a closed dictionary, K is bound to a key and V is a free variable, succeeds if and only if D contains an entry for the key K. In this case the variable V gets bound to the corresponding value. However, the most interesting thing about **contains** is that it can be used to insert a new entry into an open dictionary (that is, all empty subdictionaries are variables). When applied to an open dictionary, **contains** tries to refine (that is, instantiate) the dictionary such that it contains the new entry. The insertion fails if the dictionary already contains an entry for the key in question, but with a different value. Thus **contains** can built a dictionary beginning with a variable. The next predicate refines a dictionary such that it is closed:

> **closed**: *dict(K,V)* → {true} of
>   emptydict   ▸ true ;;
>   (K, V, L, R)   ▸ **closed** [L], **closed** [R] → true.

We can now built a dictionary, close it and retrieve information from it. For instance, the expression

> **contains** [lt] [D, b, 1] → **contains** [lt] [D, a, 2] → **contains** [lt] [D, c, 3] → **closed** [D]
>   → **contains** [lt] [D, a, V] → V

yields the result 2 and binds D to

> (b, 1, (a, 2, emptydict, emptydict), (c, 3, emptydict, emptydict)) .

This expression is transparent; if the binding for D is supplied a priori, the expression reduces to the same result.

What do we do if retrieval is necessary before the dictionary is complete? If we check with **contains** for a key that is not in an open dictionary, a new entry is made, and that is probably not what we want. If we assume that no value in the dictionary is a variable, the following function implements retrieval on open dictionaries:

> **get**: *(K × K → {true})* → *dict(K,V) × K* → V of
>   LT ▸ D, K ▸ **contains** [LT] [D, K, V] → ¬**var**[V] → V.

This function cannot be expressed in a logic programming language since it tests for a metalogical property. Furthermore, **get** and **contains** are higher-order since they take the key order as argument. So far, higher-order logic programming languages have not been developed. In Prolog, a variable test can be defined with the cut, and a predicate parameter for the key order can be simulated with the meta-unification and call constructs.

5.2 Polymorphic Type Inference

Since polymorphic type inference (Milner [7]) employs unification as a basic operation, it should yield a prime example for FU's expressive power. This is in fact the case, but only if we employ some nontransparent features. Let us consider a simple functional language with pairing, abstraction, application and conditional

$$expn ::= identifier \mid (expn, expn) \mid \mathsf{abs}(identifier, expn) \mid$$
$$\mathsf{app}(expn, expn) \mid \mathsf{cond}(expn, expn, expn)$$

and the type structure

$$type ::= identifier \mid variable \mid \mathsf{prod}(type, type) \mid \mathsf{fun}(type, type)$$

where *variable* stands for FU-variables. The nonground term fun(T, T) is an example for a polymorphic type. The function

```
typeof: assignment → base × expression → type  of
   A ▶ ( B,    abs(I,E)   ▶   fun(S, typeof[A][((I,S), B), E]) ;;
        B,    app(F,E)    ▶   T ← typeof[A][B, F] ≡ fun(typeof[A][B, E], T); ;
        B, cond(C,E,F)    ▶   typeof[A][B, E] ≡ typeof[A][B, F]
                                     ← bool ≡ typeof[A][B, C]; ;
        B,     (E,F)      ▶   prod( typeof[A][B, E], typeof[A][B, F] ); ;
        B,      I         ▶   getvalue[B, I] ; A[I] ).
```

infers the type of an expression under a type assignment and a base. The assignment assigns types to defined functions, that is, it is a function from identifiers to types. The base assigns types to identifiers that are introduced by abstractions and is represented as a list of pairs of identifiers and types. The last clause of **typeof** accesses the base and the assignment. The base is given priority since its identifiers correspond to inner scopes. The function **getvalue** is defined in section 2. If the base B contains no binding for the identifier I **getvalue** fails and the assignment is tried. Since the assignment is a function it can be accessed by application. If the assignment contains no binding for the identifier the entire type inference fails.

In the following examples for **typeof** we assume the following type assignment:

$$A \equiv (\text{id} \blacktriangleright \mathsf{fun}(T, T); ;\ \text{eq} \blacktriangleright \mathsf{fun}(\mathsf{prod}(T, T), \mathsf{bool}))$$

The reader may think of id as the identity function and of eq as the equality function. The application

typeof [A] [() , app(id, id)]

yields as expected the result fun(X, X) for the self-application app(id, id). Note that X is a new variable. It will now become clear why we separated the type bindings into the assignment and the base. Since the assignment is a function the variables in its abstraction become renamed upon application. Hence, every access of the assignment yields a type with new type variables. This allows the inference of the correct type for the self-application.

Each clause of **typeof** corresponds directly to a type rule. This succinctness is possible since FU can solve equations that contain function applications. An examples that occurs in **typeof** is

fun(**typeof**[A][B, E], T) ≡ **typeof**[A, B][F] .

This equation is solved for T and for all variables that occur in the base B. Most of the computational work is done by unification; new bindings for type variables are propagated as side effects. For instance, the application

typeof [A] [((x, int), (y, Y), (z, list), (v, V), ()),
        cond(app(eq, (x, y)), z, v)]

yields the result list as the type of the expression and the variable bindings Y ≡ int and V ≡ list for the types of the identifiers y and v in the base. Note that **typeof** is transparent with respect to "type variables" in the base.

The application

typeof [A] [((x, int), (y, real), (z, list), (v, V), ()),
        cond(app(eq, (x, y)), z, v)]

fails since the expression is not well-typed under the given base.

To build a complete type checker we must be able to decide whether a type is an instance of another type. Since types are terms it suffices if we can decide this question for terms. We say that a term *s* *subsumes* a term *t* if there exists a substitution θ such that *s* = θ*t*. A subsumption test can be defined as follows:

subsumes: *term* × *term* → {true} of
    S, T ▶ ¬ ¬(L ≡ **vars**[T] → S ≡ T → **map**[V ▶ **var**[V]] [L]).

vars: *term* → list(term) of
    X ▶ **var**[X] → X, () ;
        X ≡ S, T → **append** [**vars** [S], **vars** [T]] ;
                ().

The function vars computes a list that contains all variables that occur in its argument. If s subsumes ⊤ then s and ⊤ can be unified without binding a variable of ⊤ to anything but a variable. Thus the application of map in subsumes succeeds if no variable in ⊤ was bound to a nonvariable. The double negation makes sure that an application of subsumes has no side effects. It is clear that subsumes is not a transparent function. Since it tests for a metalogical property it cannot be written in a logic programming language. To formulate polymorphic type checking in a logic programming language, we were forced to represent type variables as ground terms and were thus deprived of the advantages of the built-in unification. It is questionable whether a formulation in, say, Horn logic would have any advantages over a functional formulation in FM.

To continue the type checking example, let us assume that programs consist of a sequence of function definitions followed by an expression:

program :: = fundef(*identifier, type,* abs(*identifier, expn*)), *program* | *expn.*

The type checker takes a type assignment and a program and succeeds with the most general type of the result if the program is well-typed. The type assignment specifies the built-in functions and their types.

welltyped: *assignment* × *program* → *type* of
    A, P ▶ welltyped1[fullassignment [A, P], P].

fullassignment: *assignment* × *program* → *assignment* of
    A, (fundef(F, T, E), P) ▶ ¬A[F] → fullassignment [(F▶T;; X▶A[X]), P] ;;
    A, E ▶ A.

welltyped1: *assignment* × *program* → *type* of
    A, (fundef(F, T, E), P) ▶ subsumes [T, typeof [A] [(), E]]
                            → welltyped1[A, P] ;;
    A, E ▶ typeof [A] [(), E].

In the first pass through the program the checker collects all defined functions and their types and makes sure that their names do not conflict with each other or the built-in functions. The second pass checks that all defined functions satisfy their declared types and finally computes the most general type of the expression to be executed. Note that the type checker handles recursive function definitions and that the order of the function definitions is irrelevant.

The goal of this section was to illustrate that unification can be smoothly integrated into a functional language. Two applications were presented that illustrate the use of unification in such a framework and show the advantages over purely functional formulations. Both applications are incompatible with the logic programming paradigm, since they depend crucially on the metalogical test whether a variable is free. There seem to be virtually no applications of practical relevance that employ "logical variables" in an entirely transparent fashion and still show significant advantages over a purely functional formulation.

6 ADDING MULTIPLE RESULTS

Fresh is obtained from FU by adding three constructs for the introduction and elimination of multiple results. Operationally, multiple results lead to a reduction strategy with chronological backtracking. Multiple results and matching yield a language with expressive data base capabilities. Furthermore, the combination of backtracking and collection can often replace recursion and lead to intuitive formulations with a declarative reading. Finally, the incorporation of unification and multiple results yields a language that subsumes Horn logic with equality.

Multiple results are introduced by *disjunctions*. The results of a disjunction $e|f$ are the results of e followed by the results of f. Like Prolog, Fresh employs a left-to-right depth-first search strategy. For instance, the expression $(1|2)|(1|3)$ has the *result sequence* 1, 2, 1, 3. Note that the result 1 occurs twice. The combination of recursion and backtracking allows expressions that have an infinite result sequence. For instance, an application inf[()] where

  inf of () ▶ 1 | inf[()].

has the infinite result sequence 1, 1, 1, ... A useful example for the combination of recursion and backtracking is a list enumerator

  el : *list(T)* → T of
   H, T ▶ H | el[T].

with the declarative reading "an element of a list is either its head or an element of its tail". The application el[1, 2, 3, ()] yields the result sequence 1, 2, 3, □ where the failure result □ stems from the empty list ().

Multiple results extend naturally to pairs and applications. Here are some examples:

((1|2), (3|2))	yields (1, 3), (1, 2), (2, 3), (2, 2)
(X ≡ (1|2), X ≡ (2|3))	yields □, □, (2, 2), □
((1 ▶ (first|second))|(X▶X))[1|2|3]	yields first, second, □, □, 1, 2, 3

The extension of the conditional to multiple results is somewhat more subtle. We introduce a new conditional $e \Rightarrow f; g$ called *soft*

500

conditional. It is reduced by first reducing *e*. If *e* has no success result the reduction proceeds with *g* and the result sequence of *g* is the result sequence of the entire conditional. If the condition part *e* has a success result, the reduction proceeds with *f* under the first environment created by *e*. The result sequence of the entire conditional is then obtained by concatenating the result sequences of the then-part *f* under the refined environments produced by the condition part *e*. In other words, execution can backtrack from the then-part to the condition part. Here are examples:

$X \equiv (1\|2\|3) \Rightarrow X; 5$	yields	1, 2, 3
$X \equiv (1\|2\|3) \Rightarrow ((X \equiv (2\|3)), 4); 5$	yields	$\square$, $\square$, (2, 4), $\square$, $\square$, (3, 4)
$X \equiv 1 \Rightarrow X \equiv 2; 5$	yields	$\square$
$((X \equiv 1), (1 \equiv 2)) \Rightarrow X \equiv 1; (4\|5\|X)$	yields	4, 5, X

The last example shows that bindings produced by the condition part (here $X \equiv 1$) are not propagated to the else-part.

Confinement (written !*e*) discards all but the first success result of an expression. Here are examples:

!(5, X)	yields	(5, X)
!(1|2|3)	yields	1
!(X \equiv (1|2|2) \Rightarrow X = 2, 5)	yields	2
!(X \equiv (1|2|2)) \Rightarrow X \equiv 2; 5	yields	$\square$
!(0 \equiv 1)	yields	$\square$

The last example shows that confinement fails if the expression it is applied to has no success result. Confinement is much weaker than Prolog's cut, which is equivalent to an exit statement for procedures. While the effect of confinement is local (it affects only the expression it is applied to), the effect of cut is global (it affects the entire predicate in whose clauses it appears).

We can now define a *hard conditional*

$$ e \rightarrow f; g \qquad \text{is} \qquad !e \Rightarrow f; g $$

that does not allow backtracking from the then-part to the condition part. In a program without disjunctions the soft and the hard conditional are equivalent since then there are no multiple results that can be cut away.

Collection (written {*e*}) is the second construct for the elimination of multiple results. The expression {*e*} reduces to the *list* of all success results of the expression *e*. If *e* fails, that is, it has only failure results, the collection of *e* reduces to the empty list. Thus collection always has exactly one success result. Here are some examples:

{1}	yields	(1, ())

{1| 2| 3}	yields	$(1, 2, 3, ())$
{ X ≡ (1| 2| 3) | 5 }	yields	$(1, 2, 3, 5, ())$
{0 ≡ 1}	yields	$()$
{el [1, 2, 3, ()]}	yields	$(1, 2, 3, ())$
{ !el [1, 2, 3, ()]}	yields	$(1, ())$

Delayed bindings created during the reduction of a collection are not propagated to the outer context. Furthermore, variables in the elements of the result list are renamed to new ones such that no two elements share variables. For instance, the expression

$$X \equiv (1, Y) \rightarrow \{ X \equiv (Z, (2\| 3\| U\| U)) \}$$

yields the result $(\,(1, 2),\ (1, 3),\ (1, A),\ (1, B),\ ()\,)$ and the delayed binding $X \equiv (1, Y)$ where A and B are new variables. During the reduction of the collection the bindings $Y \equiv 2$, $Y \equiv 3$, $Y \equiv U$, $Y \equiv U$ are created successively. Since these bindings are independent, a propagation of a binding for Y outside of the collection construct is not sensible. This semantics for the collection construct is also supported by an evolving type discipline for Fresh.

A collection of an expression with an infinite result sequence will not terminate. This problem could be resolved if the language employed a lazy reduction strategy for collections. Then confinement could be defined by the collection construct as $(F,S) \equiv \{e\} \Rightarrow F$.

Collection constructs also exist in Prolog [4] and KRC [33]. However, these languages integrate collection somewhat artificially since syntax and semantics inside a collection are different from the rest of the language. In Fresh collection can be applied to any expression.

Fresh's bare syntax is

$$e ::= a \mid d \mid x \mid (e, f) \mid s \blacktriangleright f \mid f[e] \mid e \Rightarrow f; g \mid e \mid f \mid \, !e \mid \{e\} \, .$$

The connection to FM and FU is made by the syntactic extension

$$e \rightarrow f; g \qquad \text{is} \qquad !e \Rightarrow f; g$$

which defines the *hard conditional*. The results of FM or FU programs remain unchanged under Fresh's semantics. Disjunction provides for a second form of the clausal definition construct:

$$
\begin{array}{lll}
s_1 \blacktriangleright e_1 \parallel & \text{is} & X \blacktriangleright (\quad (s_1 \blacktriangleright e_1) \mid \\
s_2 \blacktriangleright e_2 \parallel & & \qquad (s_2 \blacktriangleright e_2) \mid \\
\vdots & & \qquad \vdots \\
s_n \blacktriangleright e_n & & \qquad (s_n \blacktriangleright e_n) \quad) [X] \, .
\end{array}
$$

If the patterns s_i are pairwise nonunifiable (that is, have no common instance) this construct is equivalent to the clausal definition construct based on the conditional. Otherwise, the disjunction-based construct allows more than one clause to contribute to the result sequence.

6.1 Examples

Recall the definition of list enumeration

el : *list(T)* → *T* of
    H, T ▶ H | el[T].

which reads "an element of a list is either its head or an element of its tail". The collection $\{ \langle \text{el}[l_1], \text{el}[l_2] \rangle \}$ yields the cartesian product of the lists l_1 and l_2. Furthermore, the sublist of all elements of a list l that satisfy a predicate p is obtained by $\{ x \Leftarrow p | x \equiv \text{el}[l] | \}$ where the *where-clause* $f \Leftarrow e$ is a syntactical variant of $f \Rightarrow e$; fail[].

In section 2 we defined in FM a function that yields the power list of a list. We can now define a declarative version of this function:

sublist : *list(T)* → *list(T)* of
    () ▶ ();;
    H, T ▶ S | H,S ⇐ S ≡ sublist[T].

This may be read: "The sublist of the empty list is the empty list; and a sublist of a nonempty list is either a sublist of the tail or the head together with a sublist of the tail". The power list of a list l is now simply computed by {sublist [l]}.

The next example illustrates Fresh's data base capabilities. The task is to implement a grade book that contains entries of the form (student, test, grade). A straightforward solution is to represent the grade book as a list of such tuples. In the following we assume that the variable B is bound to such a grade book. The query "all students who received an A in test CS211" is realized by the expression

    { S ⇐ (S, cs211, a) ≡ el [B] } .

The query "all students who ever flunked a test" becomes

    { S ⇐ (S, T, f) ≡ el [B] } .

A list of all students who ever flunked a test together with the list of all tests a student flunked is computed by

    { (S, {T ⇐ (S, T, f) ≡ el [B] }) ⇐ (S, T1, f) ≡ el [B] } .

The query "all students who flunked data bases and received an A in theory" becomes (the where symbol binds left-associative)

    { S ⇐ (S, database, f) ≡ el [B] ⇐ (S, theory, a) ≡ el [B] } .

Finally, the grade book obtained from B by deleting all entries for the test CS211 is computed by

$$\{ E \Leftarrow \neg T \equiv cs211 \Leftarrow E \equiv (S, T, G) \equiv \textbf{el} [B] \} .$$

The next example, a tautology checker for propositional formulas, employs both logical variables and multiple results. Let a truth value be either the atom true or the atom false. The function

truthfunction : *connective* →

$$(\textit{truthvalue} + \textit{truthvalue} \times \textit{truthvalue}) \rightarrow \textit{truthvalue} \text{ of}$$

not	▶ (true ▶ false ;; false ▶ true) ;;
and	▶ (true, true ▶ true ;; __ ▶ false) ;;
or	▶ (false, false ▶ false ;; __ ▶ true) ;;
imp	▶ (true, false ▶ false ;; __ ▶ true) ;;
equiv	▶ (T, T ▶ true ;; __ ▶ false) .

yields the truth function associated with a propositional connective. Let a propositional formula be either a truth value, a variable, or a formula built from a connective and one or two formulas. For instance,

$$imp(and(imp(A, B), imp(B, C)), imp(A,C))$$

is a formula, which is a tautology. The function

truthvalue : *formula* → *truthvalue* of

F ▶	F ≡ (true | false)	⇒ F ;
	F ≡ not(A)	→ **truthfunction** [not] [**truthvalue** [A]] ;
	F ≡ C(A, B)	→ **truthfunction** [C] [**truthvalue**[A], **truthvalue** [B]] .

takes a formula and yields its truth value. If the formula does not contain variables, **truthvalue** has exactly one success result. If the formula contains variables, **truthvalue** binds the variables in the formula to either true or false and returns the truth value of the resulting variable-free formula. In this case, **truthvalue** produces a success result for every possible assignment of truth values to the variables in the formula. Note that the function **truthvalue** is transparent with respect to its argument. The first conditional in **truthvalue** is soft to allow backtracking in case F is a variable.

The expression **truthvalue**[f] ≡ true succeeds if and only if the formula f is satisfiable. If this expression succeeds, the variables in f get bound according to an assignment under which the truth value of the formula f is true. The expression ¬(**truthvalue** [f] ≡ false) succeeds if and only if the formula f is a tautology. Because of the negation this expression has no side effects, that is, no bindings for variables in the formula f are propagated to the outer context.

6.2 Comparison with Prolog

A Prolog program is a set of predicates. Each predicate is defined by a sequence of Horn clauses. Two typical examples are list concatenation and reversal:

```
append( nil, L, L ) ← true
append( cons(H, T), L, cons(H, TL)) ← append(T, L, TL) .

reverse(nil, nil) ← true
reverse( cons(H, T), L) ← reverse(T, R),  append( R, cons(H, nil), L) .
```

The empty list is the atom nil and a list with head *h* and tail *t* is the term cons(*h*, *t*). Horn clauses and predicates can be expressed in Fresh as well:

```
append of
    nil, L, L    ▶ true ‖
    cons(H, T), L, cons(H, TL)  ▶ append [T, L, TL] .

reverse of
    nil, nil ▶ true ‖
    cons(H, T), L ▶ reverse [T, R]  ⇒ append [R, cons(H, nil), L] .
```

Predicates become functions that either fail or yield the atom true as result. Prolog's conjunction is sequential and translates therefore into an if-clause. The two Fresh functions have precisely the same semantics as the corresponding Prolog predicates. In other words, Horn logic with depth-first search is a subset of Fresh. Prolog's cut is easily replaced by confinement and conditional, and Prolog's negation as failure is negation in Fresh.

Horn clauses are not the intended programming style for Fresh. In fact, Fresh is an attempt to offer Prolog's capabilities in a framework that avoids Prolog's drawbacks:

- In Fresh, all constructs can be nested. This avoids the need for auxiliary variables and leads to a compact notation.

- Functions and nesting make information flow explicit. In Prolog, information flow can be accomplished only by side effects (delayed bindings) and is thus difficult to analyze.

- In Fresh, full unification and delayed bindings are the exception. If we consider an open unification $e \equiv f$ where one side reduces to a ground term as matching, only the examples in section 5 and the tautology checker in this section require full unification and employ side effects. In Prolog, every predicate application requires full unification and conveys all output through side effects.

- In Fresh, backtracking is introduced explicitly by disjunction and is localized by confinement and collection. A sufficient condition that implies that a function has at most one result can be easily tested at compile-time. In Prolog, backtracking is the default. Since most applications do not involve backtracking, intellectual effort and numerous cuts are needed to suppress backtracking.

- Higher-order functions and functional abstraction are a structured alternative to Prolog's obscure assert and call constructs. While higher-order functions are easily covered by a static type discipline, this is not the case with Prolog's assert and call constructs.

- Fresh's pair construct offers a clear possibility for parallelism. Since Prolog's conjunction is defined sequentially, the exploitation of and-parallelism requires compile-time analysis or user-provided variable annotations as in Concurrent Prolog [29, 30]. In Fresh, sequentialization is naturally expressed by nesting and conditionals.

7 UNIFICATION

In Fresh, all variable bindings are obtained by solving equations between patterns and reduced arguments. In contrast to FM, both sides of an equation can contain variables. This complicates the situation since such equations can have infinitely many solutions. For instance, the equation

$$(a, X, U, (b, c)) \equiv (a, (Y, c), V, X)$$

is certainly solved by $\{X \equiv (b, c), Y \equiv b, U \equiv V\}$. However, $\{X \equiv (b, c), Y \equiv b, V \equiv U\}$ is a solution as well; and infinitely many further solutions can be obtained by binding the variables V or U to arbitrary terms. Fortunately, solvable unification problems have most general solutions from which all other solutions can be obtained. In our example, the first two solutions are most general. We will prove that most general solutions are unique up to reversal of bindings that bind variables to variables. Thus the task of a unification algorithm is to decide whether an equation system is solvable and, if so, to compute a most general solution.

The purpose of this section is to collect the basic notions and results from unification theory in a framework that is tailored for the semantic account of Fresh. The key results are theorem 7.5 (most general solutions are unique up to binding reversal), theorem 7.9 (the unification rules are noetherian) and theorem 7.12 (the unification rules are confluent up to binding reversal and yield a most general solution).

7.1 Subsumption and Idempotence of Substitutions

In the semantic account of Fresh, idempotent substitutions play the role that ground substitutions play in the semantic account of FM. Idempotent substitutions serve as most general solutions of unification problems and are employed as term environments in the reduction tree semantics for Fresh.

A substitution θ *subsumes* a substitution ψ, written $\theta \leq \psi$, if $\theta = \theta\psi$. A substitution θ is *idempotent* if it subsumes itself, that is, $\theta = \theta\theta$. It is easy to show that $\theta \leq \psi$ is a preorder (that is, reflexive and transitive) on the set of idempotent substitutions. Thus, $\theta \sim \psi \Leftrightarrow \theta \leq \psi \wedge \psi \leq \theta$ defines an equivalence relation $\sim$ on idempotent substitutions. We say that two substitutions θ and ψ are *equivalent* if they are idempotent and subsume each other, that is, $\theta \leq \psi$ and $\psi \leq \theta$. The letter ρ will always range over idempotent substitutions.

Recall that we consider only finite substitutions, and that a finite substitution θ can be identified with its representation, that is, the equation system $\{ x \equiv \theta x \mid x \in \mathbf{D}(\theta) \}$. The following is easy to prove:

Proposition 7.1. θ subsumes ψ if and only if θ solves ψ.

The *variables introduced by a substitution* θ, written $\mathbf{I}(\theta)$, are the variables contained in the right-hand sides of its representation, that is, $\mathbf{I}(\theta) = \{ y \mid \exists x \in \mathbf{D}(\theta). \, y \in \mathbf{V}(\theta x) \}$. Obviously, a substitution is idempotent if and only if its domain and its introduced variables are disjoint. $\mathbf{V}(\theta) := \mathbf{D}(\theta) \cup \mathbf{I}(\theta)$ is the set of all variables occurring in the finite representation of θ. Two substitutions θ and ψ are *independent* if $\mathbf{V}(\theta)$ and $\mathbf{V}(\psi)$ are disjoint. If θ and ψ are independent, then $\theta \cup \psi$ denotes the substitution whose representing equation system is the union of the representing equation systems of θ and ψ.

Proposition 7.2. If θ and ψ are independent then $\theta\psi = \psi\theta = \theta \cup \psi$.

Our next goal is to show that two substitutions are equivalent if and only if they are equal up to binding reversal. The concept of a direct variant makes precise what we mean by binding reversal. A substitution ψ is a *direct variant* of a substitution θ if there exist pairwise distinct variables $x_1, \ldots, x_n, y_1, \ldots, y_n$ such that $\theta x_i = y_i$ for all i and $\psi = \{ y_1 \equiv x_1, \ldots, y_n \equiv x_n \}\theta$. For example, the substitution $\{X \equiv Y, Z \equiv Y\}$

is a direct variant of $\{Y \equiv Z, X \equiv Z\}$ since $\{X \equiv Y, Z \equiv Y\} = \{Z \equiv Y\}\{Y \equiv Z, X \equiv Z\}$. The following proposition is easy to prove:

Proposition 7.3. Direct variants of idempotent substitutions are idempotent.

The following lemma is needed for the proof of the next theorem.

Lemma 7.4. Let θ and ψ be equivalent, but distinct substitutions. Then there exist distinct variables x and y such that $\theta x = y$ and $\psi y = x$.

Proof. Let $|s|$ denote the depth of a term s. First we observe that $|\theta s| = |\psi s| \geq |s|$ since $|\theta s| = |\theta \psi s| \geq |\psi s| = |\psi \theta s| \geq |\theta s| \geq |s|$. Now let s be a term such that $\theta s \neq \psi s$. We prove the claim by induction on $|\theta s|$.

$|\theta s| = 1$. Since substitutions cannot disagree on atoms or designators s must be a variable. Since $\theta s \neq \psi s$ and $\psi s = \psi \theta s$ we have that $y := \theta s$ is a variable. Since $\psi s \neq \theta s$ and $\theta s = \theta \psi s$ we have that $x := \psi s$ is a variable. Thus $\theta x = y$ and $\psi y = x$ and x and y are distinct.

$|\theta s| > 1$. Then $\theta s = (u_1, u_2) = (\theta u_1, \theta u_2)$ and $\psi s = (v_1, v_2) = (\psi v_1, \psi v_2)$ since θ and ψ are idempotent. Since $\theta s \neq \psi s$ we have $\theta u_1 \neq \psi v_1$ without loss of generality. With that the claim follows from the induction hypothesis. $\square$

Theorem 7.5. Let θ and ψ be idempotent substitutions. Then θ and ψ are equivalent if and only if ψ is a direct variant of θ.

Proof. *Right to left.* Let $\psi = \{y_1 \equiv x_1, \ldots, y_n \equiv x_n\}\theta$ and $x_1, \ldots, x_n$, $y_1, \ldots, y_n$ be pairwise distinct variables such that $\theta x_i = y_i$ for all i. Then ψ subsumes θ since θ subsumes θ. On the other hand, θ subsumes ψ (that is, $\theta = \theta\{y_1 \equiv x_1, \ldots, y_n \equiv x_n\}\theta$) since $\theta\{y_1 \equiv x_1, \ldots, y_n \equiv x_n\} = \theta$. Thus θ and ψ are equivalent.

Left to right. We prove that ψ is a direct variant of θ by induction on $n := |\{x \in \mathbf{V} | \theta x \neq \psi x\}|$, that is, the number of variables θ and ψ disagree on.

$n = 0$. Then $\theta = \psi$.

$n > 0$. Then θ and ψ are distinct. Thus by lemma 7.4 there are distinct variables x and y such that $\theta x = y$ and $\psi y = x$. Then $\theta' := \{y \equiv x\}\theta$ is a direct variant of θ. Furthermore, we know by proposition 7.3 that θ' is idempotent. Thus we have by the right to left part of the proof that $\theta \sim \theta'$. Since we assumed that $\theta \sim \psi$ we have $\psi \sim \theta'$. Now the induction hypothesis applies to ψ and θ' and yields that ψ is a direct variant of θ'. Thus there exist pairwise distinct variables $x_1, \ldots, x_n, y_1, \ldots, y_n$ such that $\theta' x_i = y_i$ for all i and $\psi = \{y_1 \equiv x_1, \ldots, y_n \equiv x_n\}\theta'$. Since $\theta' x = x$ we have that x is distinct from all x_i; since $\theta'x=x$ and $\psi x=x$ (ψ is idempotent and $\psi y=x$) we have that x is distinct from all y_i. Since $\theta'y=x$, y and x are distinct and θ' is idempotent we have that y is distinct from all y_i; finally, since $\theta'y=x$ and x is different from all y_i we have that y is different from all x_i. Since $\{y_1 \equiv x_1, \ldots, y_n \equiv x_n\}$ and $\{y \equiv x\}$ are idempotent we have $\psi = \{y_1 \equiv x_1, \ldots, y_n \equiv x_n\}\theta' = \{y_1 \equiv x_1, \ldots, y_n \equiv x_n\}\{y \equiv x\}\theta = \{y_1 \equiv x_1, \ldots, y_n \equiv x_n, y \equiv x\}\theta$. Thus ψ is a direct variant of θ. $\square$

7.2 The Unification Rules

The next lemma justifies a method for the stepwise construction of idempotent substitutions, which is employed by the unification rules.

Lemma 7.6. The composition $\{x \equiv \rho s\}\rho$ is an idempotent substitution if $x \notin D(\rho)\cup V(\rho s)$. Furthermore, $\{x \equiv \rho s\}\rho$ subsumes ρ.

Proof. The second claim is obvious since ρ subsumes ρ. Let y be a variable. To prove that $\{x \equiv \rho s\}\rho$ is idempotent it suffices to show that $\{x \equiv \rho s\}\rho\{x \equiv \rho s\}\rho y = \{x \equiv \rho s\}\rho y$. This equality holds since $D(\{x \equiv \rho s\}\rho) = D(\rho)\cup\{x\}$ and $D(\rho)\cup\{x\}$ and $V(\{x \equiv \rho s\}\rho y)$ are disjoint. $\square$

A *unification problem* is a pair $\rho\{E\}$ where ρ is an idempotent substitution and E is a finite equation system. A *solution* for a unification problem $\rho\{E\}$ is a substitution θ that solves ρ and E. *Unification* is the process of computing the solution of a unification problem. The unification rules reduce a unification problem $\rho\{E\}$ by growing the *solved part* ρ and shrinking the *unsolved part E*. Note that ρ already solves ρ. There are seven unification rules:

(Taut)	$\rho\{s \equiv s,\ E\}$	$\rightarrow\ \rho\{E\}$	if $s \in A\cup D\cup V$
(LSubst)	$\rho\{x \equiv u,\ E\}$	$\rightarrow\ \rho\{\rho x \equiv u,\ E\}$	if $x \in D(\rho)$
(LBind)	$\rho\{x \equiv u,\ E\}$	$\rightarrow\ \{x \equiv \rho u\}\rho\{E\}$	if $x \notin D(\rho)\cup V(\rho u)$
(RSubst)	$\rho\{s \equiv x,\ E\}$	$\rightarrow\ \rho\{s \equiv \rho x,\ E\}$	if $x \in D(\rho)$
(RBind)	$\rho\{s \equiv x,\ E\}$	$\rightarrow\ \{x \equiv \rho s\}\rho\{E\}$	if $x \notin D(\rho)\cup V(\rho s)$
(Split)	$\rho\{(s,\ t) \equiv (u,\ v),\ E\}$	$\rightarrow\ \rho\{s \equiv u, t \equiv v,\ E\}$	
(Fail)	$\rho\{s \equiv u,\ E\}$	$\rightarrow\ \square$	if none of the rules above applies

The unification rules extend the matching rules. Since variables can now occur in the right-hand sides as well, there are symmetric substitution and binding rules for right-hand sides. The significant difference between unification and matching is in the formulation of the binding rules. The augmented environment $\{x \equiv \rho u\}\rho$ is obtained by left-composition with $\{x \equiv \rho u\}$. Since the right-hand sides of the representation of ρ can now contain variables, they may become instantiated under the new binding. A new binding $x \equiv \rho u$ can only be made if it is not cyclic, that is, $x \notin \mathbf{V}(\rho u)$. This is the so-called *occurrence check*. For instance, the equation $x \equiv (x, x)$ has no solution.

Most Prolog systems ignore the occurrence check since it requires a considerable computational overhead. These systems are not only logically inconsistent, but their unification algorithm will also not terminate for certain cyclic equation systems. Colmerauer [5, 6] has developed a consistent theory of cyclic unification and infinite regular trees. However, to guarantee termination, he incorporates a condition that is as expensive as the occurrence check. Van Emden and Lloyd [20] show that Colmerauer's cyclic unification is sound for Horn logic with an augmented equality theory. For Fresh, the occurrence check does not cause problems, since the big majority of unifications can be implemented by matching. In typed Fresh, which is currently under development, compile-time analysis will automatically decide for which equations matching is sufficient. Furthermore, typed Fresh will exploit conditions (like those formulated by Plaisted [25]) that imply that occurrence checks are redundant although both sides contain variables.

In the following $_u\to^*$ denotes the reflexive and transitive closure of $_u\to$ on the set of unification problems. Furthermore, $\rho\{E\}$ $_u\to^*$ ρ' is an abbreviation for $\rho\{E\}$ $_u\to^*$ $\rho'\{\varnothing\}$. The next proposition says that unification generalizes matching.

Proposition 7.7. Let $\rho\{M\}$ be a matching problem. Then $\rho\{M\}$ $_m\to^*$ ρ' if and only if $\rho\{M\}$ $_u\to^*$ ρ'.

Proof. If the right-hand sides of equations are ground terms, the right substitution and binding rules do not apply. Furthermore, the occurrence check in the left binding rule is always satisfied. Thus the applicable unification rules are equivalent to the matching rules. $\square$

Lemma 7.8. Let $\rho\{E\}$ $_u\to^*$ $\rho'\{E'\}$. Then ρ' is an idempotent substitution and subsumes ρ. Furthermore, $\mathbf{V}(\rho') \subseteq \mathbf{V}(\rho) \cup \mathbf{V}(E)$.

Proof. The first claim follows from lemma 7.6 by induction on the length of the reduction sequence. The second claim is obvious since none of the rules introduces new variables. $\square$

The following theorem states that the unification rules do not allow infinite reduction sequences.

Theorem 7.9. The reduction $_u\rightarrow$ is noetherian.

Proof. Suppose there is an infinite reduction sequence starting from $\rho\{E\}$. Since $\rho\{E\}$ contains only finitely many variables, new variables are not introduced, and the binding rules increase the number of variables in the domain of the idempotent substitution ρ, we can assume without loss of generality that the infinite reduction sequence does not employ the binding rules. The remaining rules do not increase the number of occurrences of variables contained in the domain of the idempotent substitution ρ. Since both substitution rules decrease the number of those occurrences at least by one, we can now assume that the infinite reduction sequence employs only the tautology and splitting rule which, is impossible. □

The next lemma states that a solvable unification problem cannot be reduced to the failure configuration □.

Lemma 7.10. If $\rho\{E\}$ has a solution and E is nonempty, then there exist ρ' and E' such that $\rho\{E\}\ _u\rightarrow\ \rho'\{E'\}$.

Proof. Let θ be a solution for $\rho\{E\}$ and E be nonempty. Suppose none of the rules is applicable. Since there is a solution, E does not contain equations of the form $a\equiv b$, $a\equiv\langle s,t\rangle$, or $\langle s,t\rangle\equiv a$ where a is either an atom or a designator. Furthermore, since the tautology and splitting rule are not applicable, all equations in E must have form $x\equiv\langle s,t\rangle$ or $\langle s,t\rangle\equiv x$. Without loss of generality let $x\equiv\langle s,t\rangle$ be in E. Since the substitution rule is not applicable we have $x\notin D(\rho)$. Since the binding rule is not applicable, we have $x\in V(\rho s)$ without loss of generality. Thus we have $\theta x=\theta\langle s,t\rangle=\langle\theta s,\theta t\rangle$. Consequently $|\theta x|>|\theta s|=|\theta\rho s|$ since θ subsumes ρ. Since $x\in V(\rho s)$ we have $|\theta\rho s|\geq|\theta x|$, which is a contradiction. □

The next theorem states that the unification rules are sound, that is, the set of solutions is invariant under reduction with a unification rule.

Theorem 7.11. Let $\rho\{E\}\ _u\rightarrow\ \rho'\{E'\}$. Then θ is a solution of $\rho\{E\}$ if and only if θ is a solution of $\rho'\{E'\}$.

Proof. We have to prove the claim for each except the failure rule. For the tautology and the splitting rule the claim is obvious. Since the left and the right version of the substitution and binding rules are symmetric, it suffices to prove the claim for the left substitution and the left binding rule.

Left substitution rule, left to right. Let θ be a solution of $\rho\{x \equiv s, E\}$. It suffices to prove that $\theta\rho x = \theta s$. This is the case since θ subsumes ρ and θ solves $x \equiv s$.

Left substitution rule, right to left. Let θ be a solution of $\rho\{\rho x \equiv s, E\}$. It suffices to prove that $\theta x = \theta s$. This is the case since θ subsumes ρ and θ solves $\rho x \equiv s$.

Left binding rule, left to right. Let θ solve $\rho\{x \equiv s, E\}$. It suffices to prove that θ subsumes $\{x \equiv \rho s\}\rho$. Since θ subsumes ρ this is the case if θ subsumes $\theta\{x \equiv \rho s\}$. Let y be a variable. If y is different from x, $\theta y = \theta\{x \equiv \rho s\}y$ obviously holds. Otherwise we have $\theta x = \theta s = \theta\rho s = \theta\{x \equiv \rho s\}x$ since θ solves $x \equiv s$ and subsumes ρ.

Left binding rule, right to left. Let θ solve $\{x \equiv \rho s\}\rho \{E\}$ and $x \notin \mathbf{D}(\rho)$. We have to show that θ subsumes ρ and solves $x \equiv s$. We have $\theta = \theta\{x \equiv \rho s\}\rho = \theta\{x \equiv \rho s\}\rho\rho = \theta\rho$ since θ subsumes $\{x \equiv \rho s\}\rho$ and ρ is idempotent. Thus θ subsumes ρ. Furthermore, $\theta x = \theta\{x \equiv \rho s\}\rho x = \theta\{x \equiv \rho s\}x = \theta\rho s = \theta s$ since θ subsumes $\{x \equiv \rho s\}\rho$, $x \notin \mathbf{D}(\rho)$, and θ subsumes ρ. Thus θ solves $x \equiv s$. $\square$

Let Θ be a set of substitutions. Then a substitution $\theta \in \Theta$ is *most general for* Θ if θ is subsumed by every substitution in Θ. It is easy to see that most general substitutions are idempotent and all most general substitutions for Θ are equivalent. The following theorem tells us that if a unification problem can be solved, then the unification rules will solve it and produce a most general solution.

Theorem 7.12. A unification problem $\rho\{E\}$ has a solution if and only if there is a ρ' such that $\rho\{E\} \,_u\to^* \rho'$; and $\rho\{E\} \,_u\to^* \square$ if and only if $\rho\{E\}$ has no solution. Furthermore, if $\rho\{E\} \,_u\to^* \rho'$ then ρ' is a most general solution of $\rho\{E\}$ and satisfies $\mathbf{V}(\rho') \subset \mathbf{V}(\rho) \cup \mathbf{V}(E)$.

Proof. The first and second claim follow by induction on the length of reduction sequences by lemma 7.10 (no dead ends) and theorems 7.9 (no infinite reduction sequences) and 7.11 (solutions are invariant under reductions). Note that a solved problem $\rho\{\varnothing\}$ is solved by ρ. Furthermore, recall that θ is a solution of $\rho\{\varnothing\}$ if and only if θ subsumes ρ. Thus theorem 7.11 yields the third claim by induction on the length of reduction sequences. The last claim is part of lemma 7.8. $\square$

Two substitutions are *compatible* if they are subsumed by a common substitution. Two substitutions θ and ψ are compatible if and only if the equation system $\theta \cup \psi$ has a solution. Recall that we identify a substitution θ with its representing equation system $\{x \equiv \theta x \mid x \in \mathbf{D}(\theta)\}$.

Corollary 7.13. Let θ and ψ be substitutions. Then there exists a substitution that subsumes θ and ψ if and only if there exists ρ such that $\varepsilon\{\theta\cup\psi\}_{n}\to^{*}\rho$; if ρ exists it is a most general substitution that subsumes θ and ψ.

Proof. From proposition 7.1 we know that θ subsumes ψ if and only if θ solves ψ's equation system. Thus the claim follows immediately from theorem 7.12. $\square$

The reader may consult Siekmann [31] for an overview of the current state of first-order unification theory. Unification was first studied by Herbrand [11], who gave the first unification algorithm. But unification only became of real importance with the advent of automatic theorem provers, and unification algorithms were independently rediscovered by Robinson [28], Guard et al. [10] and Knuth and Bendix [16]. Fast unification algorithms exploit a structure sharing representation for terms and were devised by Huet [13], Martelli and Montanari [21], and Patterson and Wegman [24]. Patterson and Wegman's algorithm is linear-time. There is some work on higher-order unification by Huet [12, 13]. Goldfarb [8] shows that second-order unification is undecidable by reducing Hilbert's tenth problem to it. Thus programming languages must use first-order unification.

8 REDUCTION TREE SEMANTICS OF FRESH

In FM, a success reduction has the form

$$\delta\rho\{e\} \to \delta'\{u\}$$

where δ and δ' are function environments, ρ is a term environment, e is the expression to be reduced, and u is the result. An interpreter would begin with the initial configuration $\delta\rho\{e\}$ and compute the final configuration $\delta'\{u\}$. The final function environment is an extension of the initial one and contains the functions that were created during the reduction process. The term environment is a ground substitution, that is, it binds variables to ground terms.

In Fresh, free variables are first-class objects. The term environment can bind variables to nonground terms and the reduction process can produce delayed bindings for variables that occur in the values of other variables. Delayed bindings are propagated to the outer context. For instance, delayed bindings produced for the condition part of a conditional are available during the reduction of the then-part. To propagate delayed bindings, reductions for Fresh employ a final term environment ρ',

$$\delta \rho \{e\} \to \delta' \rho' \{u\}$$

which is obtained from the initial one by including delayed bindings. Thus the final term environment will subsume the initial one, that is, $\rho' = \rho'\rho$. Subsumption captures what we described as refinement or narrowing of the term environment. The fact that the final term environment subsumes the initial one implies $\rho'x = \rho'\rho x$ for all variables x, that is, the final value $\rho'x$ is an instance of the initial value ρx. This means that bindings cannot be arbitrarily changed but can be only refined. Once a variable is bound to a ground term (as is always the case in FM), its value is final and cannot be changed anymore.

Since reduced arguments in Fresh can contain variables, the variables in a closure must be renamed to new ones upon application to avoid variable clashes. New variables can be exported to the context of an application since they may be included in the result or the refined term environment. Thus being a "new variable" is a property that cannot be decided in the local context of an application but must be defined globally. To solve this problem, we will employ reductions of the form

$$\delta \rho \{e\} \to \delta' \rho' \{u\} V$$

where V is the set of all variables that are newly introduced in the reduction tree justifying the reduction and that might occur in δ' or u. The rules that combine reductions will come with conditions that prevent variable clashes.

With these extensions, FU's reduction rules can be easily obtained from the rules for FM. However, to obtain the rules for Fresh, we also have to account for multiple results. Intuitively, when building a reduction tree, we have at every disjunction the choice of proceeding with either the left or the right side. We will make the reduction process deterministic by equipping initial configurations with a choice string that contains the necessary decisions a priori. Thus, the final form of reductions for Fresh is

$$\delta \rho \{e\} \xi \to \delta' \rho' \{u\} V$$

where the choice string ξ is a string over the characters L (left) and R (right). The semantics of disjunctions is then captured by the rules

$$\frac{\delta \rho \{e|f\} \text{L}\xi \to F}{\delta \rho \{e\} \xi \to F} \qquad \frac{\delta \rho \{e|f\} \text{R}\xi \to F}{\delta \rho \{f\} \xi \to F}$$

We now begin the formalization of Fresh's semantics. A *choice string* is a string over the characters L and R. The empty choice string is denoted by ε, and $\xi\xi'$ denotes the concatenation of two choice strings ξ and ξ'. The relation $\xi < \xi'$ (read "ξ is immediately before ξ'") is defined by

$$\xi < \xi' \; :\Leftrightarrow \; \exists\, \zeta. \;\; \xi = \zeta \mathsf{LR} \cdots \mathsf{R} \;\; \wedge \;\; \xi' = \zeta \mathsf{RL} \cdots \mathsf{L}$$

where ζ, $\mathsf{R} \cdots \mathsf{R}$ and $\mathsf{L} \cdots \mathsf{L}$ can be empty strings. This relation is used to formalize chronological backtracking. A sequence $\xi_1, \ldots, \xi_n$ of choice strings is a *chain* if $\xi_1 = \mathsf{L} \cdots \mathsf{L}$ and $\xi_1 < \cdots < \xi_n$. Informally, a chain lists in chronological order choice strings for an expression beginning with the first possible one up to ξ_n. A chain $\xi_1, \ldots, \xi_n$ is *maximal* if $\xi_n = \mathsf{R} \cdots \mathsf{R}$. A maximal chain contains all possible choice strings for an expression in chronological order.

As for FM, we first define a general form of reductions and prove then that every reduction in a reduction tree for a consistent initial configuration is consistent. *Term environments* are substitutions and *function environments* are finite maps from designators to closures. The *domain* of a function environment δ is denoted by $\mathbf{D}(\delta)$. *Closures* consist of a term environment and an abstraction. An *initial configuration* has form $\delta\,\rho\,\{e\}\,\xi$ where δ is a function environment, ρ is a term environment, e is the expression to be reduced, and ξ is a choice string. A *final configuration* is either the *failure configuration* $\square$ or has the form $\delta\,\rho\,\{u\}\,V$ where δ is a function environment, ρ is a term environment, u is a term (the *result*), and V is a set of variables. A *reduction* has the form $I \to F$ where I is an initial and F is a final configuration.

Atoms and Designators

$$\delta\,\rho\,\{a\}\,\varepsilon \;\to\; \delta\,\rho\,\{a\}\,\varnothing \qquad\qquad \delta\,\rho\,\{d\}\,\varepsilon \;\to\; \delta\,\rho\,\{d\}\,\varnothing$$

The symbol ε is the empty choice string and $\varnothing$ is the empty set.

Variables

$$\delta\,\rho\,\{x\}\,\varepsilon \;\to\; \delta\,\rho\,\{\rho x\}\,\varnothing$$

Pairs

$$\frac{\delta \rho \{(e,f)\} \xi_1 \xi_2 \;\rightarrow\; (\delta_1 \cup \delta_2)\, \rho_3 \{\rho_3(u,v)\}\, V_1 \cup V_2}{\delta \rho \{e\} \xi_1 \;\rightarrow\; \delta_1\, \rho_1 \{u\}\, V_1 \qquad \qquad \qquad \qquad} \qquad \text{if } \rho_1\{\rho_2\}_u \rightarrow^* \rho_3$$
$$\delta \rho \{f\} \xi_2 \;\rightarrow\; \delta_2\, \rho_2 \{v\}\, V_2$$

and $\mathbf{D}(\delta_1) \cap \mathbf{D}(\delta_2) \subset \mathbf{D}(\delta)$ and V_1, V_2 and $\mathbf{V}((e,f))$ are pairwise disjoint

$$\frac{\delta \rho \{(e,f)\} \xi_1 \xi_2 \;\rightarrow\; \square}{\delta \rho \{e\} \xi_1 \;\rightarrow\; \delta_1\, \rho_1 \{u\}\, V_1} \qquad \qquad \text{if } \rho_1\{\rho_2\}_u \rightarrow^* \square$$
$$\delta \rho \{f\} \xi_2 \;\rightarrow\; \delta_2\, \rho_2 \{v\}\, V_2 \qquad \qquad \text{and } V_1, V_2 \text{ and } \mathbf{V}((e,f)) \text{ are}$$
pairwise disjoint

$$\frac{\delta \rho \{(e,f)\} \xi_1 \xi_2 \;\rightarrow\; \square}{\delta \rho \{e\} \xi_1 \;\rightarrow\; \square} \qquad\qquad \frac{\delta \rho \{(e,f)\} \xi_1 \xi_2 \;\rightarrow\; \square}{\delta \rho \{e\} \xi_1 \;\rightarrow\; F}$$
$$\delta \rho \{f\} \xi_2 \;\rightarrow\; F \qquad\qquad\qquad \delta \rho \{f\} \xi_2 \;\rightarrow\; \square$$

As in FM, the components of a pair are reduced independently. Then the produced function and term environments are combined. The first failure rule handles the case where the unification of the term environments fails. The expression $(X \equiv 1, X \equiv 4)$ is an example for this case. The condition $\rho_1\{\rho_2\}_u \rightarrow^* \square$ is equivalent to $\rho_2\{\rho_1\}_u \rightarrow^* \square$ and $\varepsilon\{\rho_1 \cup \rho_2\}_u \rightarrow^* \square$ (ε is the empty substitution). The unified term environment must be applied to the result of both components since they can contain variables that are bound by new bindings in the unified term environment. The expression $(X \equiv (1, Y), X \equiv (Z, 4))$ is an example that was discussed in section 5. The conditions for designators and variables ensure that there are no clashes with new designators and variables.

Soft Conditional

$$\frac{\delta \rho \{e \Rightarrow f; g\} \xi_1 \xi_2 \;\rightarrow\; \delta_2\, \rho_2 \{v\}\, V_1 \cup V_2}{\delta \rho \{e\} \xi_1 \;\rightarrow\; \delta_1\, \rho_1 \{u\}\, V_1} \qquad \text{if } V_1, V_2 \text{ and } \mathbf{V}((e,f))$$
$$\delta_1\, \rho_1 \{f\} \xi_2 \;\rightarrow\; \delta_2\, \rho_2 \{v\}\, V_2 \qquad\qquad \text{are pairwise disjoint}$$

$$\delta\,\rho\,\{e \Rightarrow f; g\}\,\xi_1\xi_2 \;\to\; \square \qquad\qquad \text{if } V_1 \text{ and } \mathbf{V}(f) \text{ are disjoint}$$

$$\overline{\delta\,\rho\,\{e\}\,\xi_1 \;\to\; \delta_1\,\rho_1\,\{u\}\,V_1}$$

$$\delta_1\,\rho_1\,\{f\}\,\xi_2 \;\to\; \square$$

$$\delta\,\rho\,\{e \Rightarrow f; g\}\,\xi \;\to\; F$$

$$\overline{\delta\,\rho\,\{e\} \;\to^a\; \square}$$

$$\delta\,\rho\,\{f\}\,\xi \;\to\; F$$

The expression $\delta\,\rho\,\{e\} \to^a \square$ is an abbreviation for a nonempty sequence

$$\delta\,\rho\,\{e\}\,\xi_1 \to \square\,,\,\ldots,\,\delta\,\rho\,\{e\}\,\xi_n \to \square$$

of reductions such that $\xi_1,\ldots,\xi_n$ is a maximal chain. Thus the third rule says that the else-part is reduced only if the condition part has no success result.

Abstraction

$$\delta\,\rho\,\{s \blacktriangleright e\}\,\varepsilon \;\to\; \delta[d \leftarrow (\rho', s \blacktriangleright e)]\,\rho\,\{d\}\,\varnothing \qquad \text{if } d \notin \mathbf{D}(\delta)$$

$$\text{and } \rho' = \rho|_{\mathbf{V}(s \blacktriangleright e)}$$

Once an abstraction is reduced to a closure, the closure is not affected by further variable bindings. For instance, the expression $\mathsf{X} \equiv (1,\mathsf{Y}) \to \mathsf{V} \equiv (\mathsf{Z} \blacktriangleright \mathsf{X}) \to \mathsf{Y} \equiv 5 \to (\mathsf{V}, \mathsf{X})$ reduces to $(d, (1, 5))$ where d is bound to a closure with the term environment $\mathsf{X} \equiv (1,\mathsf{Y})$ and the abstraction $\mathsf{Z} \blacktriangleright \mathsf{X}$. Thus side effects do not apply to closures. Technically, this is easily achieved by keeping closures in a separate environment. This is one reason for having designators.

Application

$$\delta\,\rho\,\{f[e]\}\,\xi_1\xi_2 \;\to\; \delta_2\,\rho_4\,\{v\}\,V_1 \cup V_2 \cup V_3 \qquad \text{if } \rho_1\rho_2\,\{s \equiv u\}\,_u\to^* \rho_3$$

$$\overline{\delta\,\rho\,\{(f, e)\}\,\xi_1 \;\to\; \delta_1\,\rho_1\,\{(d, u)\}\,V_1} \qquad \text{and } (\rho_2, s \blacktriangleright g) \in \mathbf{VAR}(\delta_1(d))$$

$$\delta_1\,\rho_3\,\{g\}\,\xi_2 \;\to\; \delta_2\,\rho_4\,\{v\}\,V_3 \qquad\qquad \text{and } V_2 = \mathbf{V}(\rho_2) \cup \mathbf{V}(s \blacktriangleright g)$$

and V_1, V_2, V_3 are pairwise disjoint
and V_2 and $\mathbf{V}(\rho_1) \cup \mathbf{V}(u)$ are disjoint

$$\frac{\delta\,\rho\,\{f[e]\}\,\xi_1\xi_2 \;\rightarrow\; \square}{\delta\,\rho\,\{(f,e)\}\,\xi_1 \;\rightarrow\; \delta_1\,\rho_1\,\{(d,u)\}\,V_1 \qquad \delta_1\,\rho_3\,\{g\}\,\xi_2 \;\rightarrow\; \square} \qquad \begin{array}{l} \text{if } \rho_1\rho_2\,\{s\equiv u\}\;_u\!\!\rightarrow^*\rho_3 \\[4pt] \text{and } (\rho_2,\,s\blacktriangleright g)\in \mathbf{VAR}(\delta_1(d)) \end{array}$$

and $\mathbf{V}(\rho_2)\cup\mathbf{V}(s\blacktriangleright g)$ and $\mathbf{V}(\rho_1)\cup\mathbf{V}(u)$ are disjoint

$$\frac{\delta\,\rho\,\{f[e]\}\,\xi \;\rightarrow\; \square}{\delta\,\rho\,\{(f,e)\}\,\xi \;\rightarrow\; \delta_1\,\rho_1\,\{(d,u)\}\,V_1} \qquad \begin{array}{l} \text{if } \rho_1\rho_2\,\{s\equiv u\}\;_u\!\!\rightarrow^*\square \\[4pt] \text{and } (\rho_2,\,s\blacktriangleright g)\in \mathbf{VAR}(\delta_1(d)) \end{array}$$

and $\mathbf{V}(\rho_2)\cup\mathbf{V}(s\blacktriangleright g)$ and $\mathbf{V}(\rho_1)\cup\mathbf{V}(u)$ are disjoint

$$\frac{\delta\,\rho\,\{f[e]\}\,\xi \;\rightarrow\; \square}{\delta\,\rho\,\{(f,e)\}\,\xi \;\rightarrow\; \delta_1\,\rho_1\,\{(v,u)\}\,V_1} \qquad \text{if } v \text{ is not a designator}$$

$$\frac{\delta\,\rho\,\{f[e]\}\,\xi \;\rightarrow\; \square}{\delta\,\rho\,\{(f,e)\}\,\xi \;\rightarrow\; \square}$$

$\mathbf{VAR}(\delta_1(d))$ is the set of all *variants* of the closure $\delta_1(d)$. A variant of $\delta_1(d)$ is obtained by renaming the variables in $\delta_1(d)$ consistently.

Disjunction

$$\frac{\delta\,\rho\,\{e\,|\,f\}\,\mathrm{L}\xi \;\rightarrow\; F}{\delta\,\rho\,\{e\}\,\xi \;\rightarrow\; F} \qquad\qquad \frac{\delta\,\rho\,\{e\,|\,f\}\,\mathrm{R}\xi \;\rightarrow\; F}{\delta\,\rho\,\{f\}\,\xi \;\rightarrow\; F}$$

Confinement

$$\frac{\delta\,\rho\,\{!e\}\,\varepsilon \;\rightarrow\; F}{\delta\,\rho\,\{e\} \;\rightarrow^1\; F} \qquad\qquad \frac{\delta\,\rho\,\{!e\}\,\varepsilon \;\rightarrow\; \square}{\delta\,\rho\,\{e\} \;\rightarrow^a\; \square}$$

The abbreviation $\delta\,\rho\,\{e\} \rightarrow^a \square$ was explained with the conditional rules. The expression $\delta\,\rho\,\{e\} \rightarrow^1 F$ abbreviates a nonempty sequence

$$\delta\,\rho\,\{e\}\,\xi_1 \rightarrow \square,\; \ldots,\; \delta\,\rho\,\{e\}\,\xi_{n-1} \rightarrow \square,\; \delta\,\rho\,\{e\}\,\xi_n \rightarrow F$$

of reductions such that $\xi_1,\ldots,\xi_n$ is a chain. Thus F is the first success result under chronological backtracking.

Collection

$$\frac{\delta \rho \{\{e\}\} \varepsilon \rightarrow (\delta_1 \cup \cdots \cup \delta_n) \rho \{(u'_1, \ldots, u'_n)\} \, V((u'_1, \ldots, u'_n))}{\delta \rho \{e \mid () \} \rightarrow^a \delta_1 \{u_1\}, \ldots, \delta_n \{u_n\}}$$

$$\text{if } \forall i,j. \qquad i \neq j \Rightarrow \mathbf{D}(\delta_i) \cap \mathbf{D}(\delta_j) \subset \mathbf{D}(\delta)$$
$$\wedge \quad i \neq j \Rightarrow \mathbf{V}(u'_i) \cap \mathbf{V}(u'_j) = \varnothing$$
$$\wedge \quad u'_i \in \mathbf{VAR}(u_i) \quad \wedge \quad \mathbf{V}(u'_i) \cap \mathbf{V}(\rho) = \varnothing$$

The expression $\delta \rho \{f\} \rightarrow^a \delta_1 \{u_1\}, \ldots, \delta_n \{u_n\}$ abbreviates a sequence of reductions for $\delta \rho \{f\}$ such that their choice strings form a maximal chain and δ_i and u_i are the function environments and results of the success results. $\mathbf{VAR}(u)$ is the set of all variants of u where a *variant* of u is obtained by renaming the variables in u consistently. All elements of the result list are renamed such that they do not share variables with each other or the final term environment. A collection has no side effects since the final configuration inherits the initial term environment.

Reduction trees are defined as for FM. The next proposition says that the existence of a reduction tree does not depend on the choice of designators and variables.

Proposition 8.1. Let R be a reduction. Then R has a reduction tree if and only if every variant of R (under consistent designator and variable renaming) has a reduction tree.

Since initial configurations carry a choice string that determines which side of a disjunction is reduced, Fresh's reduction rules are deterministic. Thus we have:

Theorem 8.2. All reduction trees for an initial configuration are equal up to consistent designator and variable renaming.

We now define consistency of function environments, configurations and reductions. A term environment ρ is *closed* under a function environment δ if for all $x \in \mathbf{D}(\rho)$ all designators in ρx are in $\mathbf{D}(\delta)$. A function environment δ is *consistent* if for all $d \in \mathbf{D}(\delta)$ such that $\delta(d) = (\rho, s \blacktriangleright e)$ the closure environment ρ and the abstraction $s \blacktriangleright e$ are closed under δ and $\mathbf{D}(\rho) \subset \mathbf{V}(s \blacktriangleright e)$. An initial configuration $\delta \rho \{e\} \xi$ is *consistent* if its function environment is consistent, its term environment and its expression are closed under its function environment, and

519

its term environment is idempotent. A final configuration $\delta \rho \{ u \} V$ is *consistent* if its function environment is consistent, its term environment and its result are closed under its function environment, and its term environment is idempotent. A reduction $\delta \rho \{ e \} \xi \rightarrow \delta' \rho' \{ u \} V$ is *consistent* if its initial and final configuration are consistent, the final function environment is an extension of the initial function environment (that is, $\delta = \delta'|_{D(\delta)}$), the final term environment subsumes the initial term environment (that is, $\rho' = \rho' \rho$), and V and $V(\rho) \cup V(e)$ are disjoint. A failure reduction $I \rightarrow \square$ is consistent if its initial configuration is consistent.

Theorem 8.3. Every reduction in every reduction tree for a consistent initial configuration is consistent.

9 CONCLUSION AND RELATED WORK

Fresh is an attempt to reformulate Prolog's computational innovations in the framework of higher-order functional programming. This paper shows that a smooth integration without syntactic or semantic overhead is possible. Since Fresh contains Horn logic with equality, it can be used as a logic programming language. On the other hand, Fresh retains all the advantages of functional programming. Higher-order functions and predicates replace Prolog's obscure assert and call constructs. Information flow can be expressed explicitly by functions and nesting of expressions rather than by delayed bindings and auxiliary variables.

This paper illustrates with examples that in a functional framework there are only very few applications of "logical variables" that exhibit significant advantages over a purely functional formulation and that are compatible with the logic programming paradigm. However, if we abandon the logic programming paradigm and use free variables as first-class objects, then in fact many interesting applications become possible.

I am currently working on a polymorphic type discipline for Fresh. The type system will distinguish between ground and nonground types. Ground types are types whose elements are ground terms, while elements of nonground types can contain variables. Typed Fresh will provide for many compile-time optimizations. For instance, the distinction between ground and nonground types makes it possible to determine at compile-time which instances of unification can be implemented by matching. There has been very little work on type systems for unification-based languages. Mycroft and O'Keefe [23] have adapted ML's type system to a subset of Prolog, but their type discipline does not distinguish between ground and nonground types.

The integration of lazy reduction into Fresh seems promising. This would allow application of collection to expressions with infinite result sequences and would thus interface backtracking more satisfying. Subrahmanyam and You [32] discuss the combination of unification and lazy reduction. Another interesting research topic is the integration of Concurrent Prolog's [29, 30] communication and synchronization mechanisms. Since these mechanisms depend mainly on logical variables and unification, an adaption to Fresh seems straightforward.

Van Emden and Kowalski [34] and Apt and Van Emden [1] provide several precise characterizations of the semantics of Horn clauses. However, these semantics do not apply to Prolog since they do not cover backtracking, the cut or collection. Jones and Mycroft [15] define an operational and a denotational semantics for a subset of Prolog that includes the cut but excludes the collection, assert and call constructs.

There are many recent papers on the integration of functional and logic programming, several of which appear in this volume. One direction was initiated by Kornfeld [17] and is based on Horn logic with equality. In this framework first-order functions can be defined by equality axioms. Goguen and Meseguer's Eqlog [9] extends this approach by employing a many-sorted logic. Eqlog comes with a complete and simple model theoretic semantics and thus is truly a logic programming language. However, this is possible only since Eqlog does not include critical features such as negation, higher-order objects, collection or control constructs.

Work at Utah emphasizes the incorporation of unification into functional programming. Lindstrom [19] shows how to incorporate logical variables into FEL, a functional language featuring lazy evaluation, and gives an implementation technique suitable for reduction architectures. Reddy [27] discusses a first-order functional language, which generalizes reduction to narrowing or resolution. He gives a denotational semantics, examines the extension to lazy narrowing, and discusses a parallel implementation. Reddy's language does not include multiple results.

ACKNOWLEDGEMENTS

I am indebted to Prakash Panangaden for many stimulating discussions and suggestions concerning this paper. The paper also benefited from discussions with Alan Demers and James Hook. Finally, I would like to thank Doug DeGroot and Gary Lindstrom for their encouragement.

REFERENCES

1.   Apt, K. R. and M. H. Van Emden. Contributions to the Theory of Logic Programming. *Journal of the ACM 29,3* (1982), 841-862.

2.   Burstall, R. M., D. B. MacQueen and D. T. Sanella. HOPE: an Experimental Applicative Language. *Lisp Conference*, ACM, 1980, 136-143.

3.   Clark, K. L. Negation as Failure. In *Logic and Data Bases*, H. Gallaire and J. Minker, Eds., Plenum Press, 1978, 293-322.

4.   Clocksin, W. F. and C. S. Mellish. Programming in Prolog. Springer Verlag, 1981.

5.   Colmerauer, A. Prolog and Infinite Trees. In K. L. Clark and S.-A. Tärnlund, Eds., *Logic Programming*, Academic Press, 1982.

6.   Colmerauer, A, H. Kanoui, M. Van Caneghem. Prolog, Theoretical Principles and Current Trends. *Technology and Science of Informatics*, 2, 4 (1983), 255-292.

7.   Damas, L. and R. Milner. Principal Type-Schemes for Functional Programs. *Proc. Principles of Programming Languages*, ACM, 1982, 207-212.

8.   Goldfarb, D. The Undecidability of the Second Order Unification Problem. *Journal of Theoretical Computer Science*, 13 (1981), 225-230.

9.   Goguen, J. A. and J. Meseguer. Eqlog: Equality, Types, and Generic Modules for Logic Programming. *Journal of Logic Programming* 1, 2 (1984), 179-210. Also see this volume.

10.   Guard, J. R., F. C. Oglesby, J. H. Benneth and L. G. Settle. Semi-Automated Mathematics. *Journal of the ACM*, 18, 1 (1969).

11.   Herbrand, J. Recherches sur la Theorie de la Demonstration. In J. Van Heijenoort, Ed., *From Frege to Gödel: a Source Book in Mathematical Logic, 1879-1931*, Harvard University Press, 1967.

12.   Huet, G. Unification in Typed Lambda Calculus. *Proc. Symp. on λ-Calculus and Computer Science*, Springer LNCS 37, 1975, 192-212.

13.   Huet, G. Resolution d'Equations dans les Languages d'Ordre 1, 2, ... , ω. These d'Etat, Specialite Mathematiques, Universite Paris VII, 1976.

14.   Huet, G. Confluent Reductions: Abstract Properties and Applications to Term Rewriting Systems. *Journal of the ACM*, 27, 4 (1980), 797-821.

15.   Jones, N. D. and A. Mycroft. Stepwise Development of Operational and Denotational Semantics for Prolog. *First Int. Symp. on Logic Programming*, IEEE, 1984, 281-288.

16.   Knuth, D. and P. Bendix. Simple Word Problems in Universal Algebras. In J. Leech, Ed., *Computational Problems in Abstract Algebras*, Pergamon Press, 1970, 263-297.

17.   Kornfeld, W. A. Equality for Prolog. *Proc. 7th Int. Joint Conf. on Artificial Intelligence*, 1983, 514-519. Also see this volume.

18.   Kowalski, R. A. Algorithm = Logic + Control. *Communications of the ACM*, 22, 7 (1979), 424-436.

19.   Lindstrom, G. Functional Programming and the Logical Variable. *Proc. Principles of Programming Languages*, ACM, 1985, 266-280.

20.   Lloyd, J. W. Foundations of Logic Programming. Springer Verlag, 1984.

21.   Martelli, A. and U. Montanari. An Efficient Unification Algorithm. *ACM Transactions on Programming Languages and Systems* 4, 2 (1982), 258-282.

22.   Milner, R. A Proposal for Standard ML. *Proc. Symp. on Lisp and Functional Programming*, 1984, 184-197.

23.   Mycroft, A. and R. A. O'Keefe. A Polymorphic Type System for Prolog. *Artificial Intelligence 15* (1984).

24.   Paterson, M. S. and M. N. Wegman. Linear Unification. *Journal of Computer and System Science*, 16 (1978), 158-167.

25. Plaisted, D. A. The Occur-Check Problem in Prolog. *First Int. Symp. on Logic Programming*, IEEE, 1984, 272-280.

26. Plotkin, G.D. A Structural Approach to Operational Semantics. DAIMI FN-19, Comp. Sc. Dept., Aarhus University, Denmark, 1981.

27. Reddy, U. Narrowing as the Operational Semantics of Functional Languages. *Second Int. Symp. on Logic Programming*, IEEE, 1985.

28. Robinson, J. A. A Machine-Oriented Logic based on the Resolution Principle. *Journal of the ACM*, 12, 1 (1965), 23-41.

29. Shapiro, E. Y. and A. Takeuchi. Object-Oriented Programming in Concurrent Prolog. *New Generation Computing*, 1,1 (1983), 25-48.

30. Shapiro, E. Y. Systems Programming in Concurrent Prolog. *Proc. Principles of Programming Languages*, ACM, (1984), 93-105.

31. Siekmann, J. H. Universal Unification. *Proc 7th Int. Conf. on Automated Deduction*, Springer LNCS 170, 1984, 1-42.

32. Subrahmanyam, P. A. and J.-H. You. Pattern Driven Lazy Reduction: a Unifying Evaluation Mechanism for Functional and Logic Programs. *Proc. Principles of Programming Languages*, ACM, 1984, 228-234. Also see this volume.

33. Turner, D. A. Recursion Equations as a Programming Language. In J. Darlington, P. Henderson and D. A. Turner, Eds., *Functional Programming and its Applications*, Cambridge University Press, 1982.

34. Van Emden, M. H. and R. A. Kowalski. The Semantics of Predicate Logic as a Programming Language. *Journal of the ACM*, 23, 4 (1976), 733-742.

35. Van Emden, M. H. and J. W. Lloyd. A Logical Reconstruction of Prolog II. *Second Int. Logic Programming Conference*, 1984, 35-40.

36. Warren, D. Logic Programming and Compiler Writing. *Software — Practice and Experience*, 10 (1980), 97-125.

Index

Abramson, H.   99
Absolute set abstraction   48
Abstract data type   322
Abstraction expression   18
Act 1   411, 421, 422
Actor   422
Acylic moding   15
Adding two polynominals   248
Address translation problem   9
Affirmation   378
Algebraic specification   398
Alpine club puzzle   373
Applicative language   239
Applicative programming   298
Arity   311
Assert   246
Assertion   368, 378
Associative   323
Atom   12
Atom elimination   213
Attribute   323
Augmented unification   411

Backpatch   9
Backtracking   240, 387, 500
Basic function   382
BF-resolution   24
Binary term   473
Breadth first search   45
Built-in function   382
Burge, W.H.   89

Call by reference   256
Canonical form   209
Choice string   515
Church-Rosser property   44, 141
Circularity   420
Clark, K.   98
Clause moding   13
Cofinite set   331
Collection   501, 519
Colmerauer, A.   78
Combination of LISP and PROLOG   240
Combinatory logic   76
Committed-choice nondeterminism   17

Commutative   323
Complete logic program   444, 457, 459, 461
Complete set of T–unifiers   342
Complete solution   317
Completeness   309, 380, 390
Computable abstract data type   347
Computation strategy   212
Concurrent Prolog   414, 422
Conditional let–clause   475, 487
Confinement   501, 518
Confluence property   161
Confusion   316
Conjunction   44
Constraining–unification   397
Constraint language   299
Constructor function   44
Context–free grammar   99
Control   309
Curry, H.B.   89
Cut   240

Data type   99
Database   53
DCG   77
Declarative component   206
Declarative language   299
Deductive tableau   365, 366
Deductive tableau proof system   377
Default view   330
Defined function   382, 383
Definite Clause Grammar   77
Delayed binding   491
Demodulation   76, 280
Dependency preorder   15, 19
Depth first backtracking   44
Derivation   451, 452, 454, 455, 459, 461, 463
Difference list   8
Director   422
Disequality   347
Disjunction   500, 518
Domain of a substitution   342
Domain subsort   306

E–unification   157, 320
E–unifier   320
Eager incremental evaluation   23
Edinburgh C–Prolog   83
Eight queens problem   241

Elementary expression   29
Entry   378
EQLOG   27
Equality   157, 279, 380, 383
Equality rule   380
Equality theory   444, 446, 447, 448, 449, 450, 457, 459, 462
Equation system   483
Equational program   398
Equational specification   397
Equivalence rule   381
Error handler   307
Error value   306
Evaluation   412
Explicit error supersort   307
Explicit error value   306
Expression   135, 367
Expressive power   8
Extensionality   88

Factoring   390
Failure laziness   27
Fair selection rule   452
FEL   4
Fifth generation project   426
Finite failure   444, 451, 452, 453, 454, 455, 456, 461
Finite solution   319
Finite T-unification algorithm   342
First order programming   302
First-order logic   242
First-order logic with equality   159
FIT   421
Fixpoint semantics   219
Flat programming style   244
Formula   367
Forward reference   9
Fraction   333
Free set   67
Free sets   27
FRL   433
Functional language   38
Functional notation   289
Functional programming   157, 298
Functional programming language   132
FUNLOG   30

General failure   452, 455
Generalization   418
Generalized failure   454

Generator   6, 21, 241
Generic module   326
Goal   368, 378
Goal statement   41
Gregory, S.   98
Ground expression   382
Ground solution   317

Hard conditional   501
HArvey's Static Language   73, 74
HASL   79
Head of a clause   311
Herbrand universe   285
Herbrand's theorem   315
Higher order   40
Homomorphism   314
HOPE   4
Hudak, P.   91

IC-Prolog   289
Idempotence of substitutions   507
Imperative programming   300
Implementation   388
Incremental resolution   23
Indefinite mode   7
Inference rule   212
Inference system   10
Infinite data structures   157
Inheritance   412, 418
Initial model   314
Input substitution   45
Input variable   13
Input-output directionality   3
Input-output mode   5
Instantiation   329
Institution   340
Integration interface   226
Iteration function   336

Join-based resolution   10
Junk   316

Kaviar   100
Key-directed search   243
Kranz, D.   91
KRL   433

Labeled term   473

Lambda calculus   242
Lazy evaluation   7, 61, 258, 384
Lazy incremental evaluation   23
LEAF   201
Left crossbow symbol   74
Left-linear abstraction expression   19
Leftmost resolution   16
Lexical relation   83
Lexical specification of HASL   85
Lindstrom, G.   98
Lisp   239, 421
Lisp. vs. TABLOG   376
List decompositions   5
LM-Prolog   422, 428
Local variable   13
Logic and functional language   202
Logic programming   157
Logic programming language   38, 132, 297
Logic programming language scheme   441, 444, 461
Logical variable   8, 43, 491
LOGLISP   30, 100, 240, 251
Loops   421
LUSH resolution   240

MacLisp   421
Mapcar   336
Matched expression   5
Matching   483
Matching rule   484
McDermott, D.   250, 251
Message passing   283, 412
Metamorphosis grammar   78
Missionaries and cannibals problem   348
Mix-fix   323
Mode   42
Mode checking   15
Moded atom   12
Model   313
Model theoretic semantics   218
Modular programming   309
Module   322
Moss, C.D.S.   79
Mosses, P.   100
Most general solution   319
Multiple results   500
Multiple super classes   418
Multiset approximation to a set   20
Mutable array   422

Narrowing   24
Narrowing relation   343
Narrowing substitution   25
Natural language processing   350
Negation and equivalence   372
Negation-as-failure   444, 457
Non-directionality   3
Non-ground outputs   27
Nonclausal resolution   379
Nondeterministic   45
Not   240

Object merging   418
Object-oriented language   282
Occur check   375, 420
Occurrence check   510
One step narrowing   343
One-way unification   74
Operational semantics   219
OR-parallel interpreter   16
OR-sequential interpreter   16
Order of evaluation   383
Output substitution   45
Output variable   13, 382
Overcomputation   7
Overloaded   54

Parallel evaluation   132
Parallelism   391
Parlog   76, 98
Partial algebra   305
Partial data structure   8
Partial evaluator   422, 432
Partial knowledge   430
Partial operator   305
Partial order on modes   12
Partially specified data structure   6
Path in a directed graph   245
Pattern argument   256
Pattern matching   45, 412, 413
Pattern-driven reduction   157
Pereira, F.C.N.   78
Planner-like language   425
Polarity strategy   379
Polymorphic type inference   10, 497
Polymorphically typed   39
POPLOG   30
Primitive operator   382

Procedural and declarative program integration   222
Procedural component   220
Process interpretation   211
Program length   8
Program transformation   38
Programming in logic   250
Programming with equations   397
Prolog   4, 76, 239, 411, 421, 422, 441, 442, 443, 450, 452, 457, 462
Prolog II   428, 443, 444, 462, 463
Prolog vs. TABLOG   371
Prolog-with-Equality   279
Pushout   341

Qlisp   412
QLOG   30
Quantifier   390
Query   368
Queue   8
Quicksort   370, 384
Qute   30, 132, 240, 252

Rank   311
Recovery operator   307
Recursively enumerable complete solution   319
Reduction   4, 41
Reduction relation   84
Reduction rule   486
Reduction to normal form   321
Reduction tree   489
Reduction tree semantics   485, 513
Reduction-by-need   157
Refutation   378
Relational programming   298
Requirements   326
Resolution   41
Retract   307
Rewrite rule   321
Rewrite-rule programming   397
Right crossbow symbol   75
Rightmost resolution   16
Robinson, J.A.   97, 100

SAM   433
SASL   4, 75, 79, 94
Satisfaction   313
Schoenfinkel   88
Second-order unification   419
Semantic relation   84

Semantic specification of HASL   88
Semantic unification   157, 397, 402
Semantics Implementation System   100
Sequential AND   16
Set   331
Set abstraction   6, 20, 48
Side effects   245
Siebert, E.E.   100
Signature   311
Simple expression   383
Simplification   381
Smalltalk   282, 411, 422
Soft conditional   500, 516
Solution   317
Sort   311
Sort constraint   306
Spatial (horizontal) parallelism   19
Special error sort   306
Specialization   418
Specification   47
Specification of HASL reduction   95
Standard ML   4
Standard model   313
Subsort   305, 338
Substitution   342
Subsumption check   76
Subsumption of substitutions   507
Suspension   7
Symbolic evaluation   412
Symbolic expression   133
Symbolic unification   38
Syntactic relation   83
Syntactic specification of HASL   85

T-unifier   342
TABLOG   27
TABLOG syntax   367
Tail of a clause   311
Tautology checker   504
Temporal (lazy) parallelism   23
Term   367
Term rewriting   4, 304, 428
Term rewriting system   161
Theory   326
Theory of directionality   11
Thinglab   433
Time complexity   8
Totally complete solution   319

Transformation constraint   400
Transparency   491, 493
Turner, D.A.   89, 94, 95

Unicorn   397
Unification   5, 45, 97, 137, 375, 389, 412, 444, 449, 450, 457, 506
Unification based conditional binding   75
Unification complete   457, 459, 463
Unification complete equality theory   458, 461
Unification rule   509
Uniform   411
Universal unification   320
Using hierarchy   324

Variable test   494
Variant elimination   210
View   329
Viewpoint   398

Warren, D.H.D.   78, 79, 250
Well-moded clause   13

XPRT   433